International Economics

Recent Economic Thought Series

Warren J. Samuels, Editor
Michigan State University
East Lansing Michigan, U.S.A.

Other titles in the series:

Feiwel, G.R., *Samuelson and Neoclassical Economics*
Wade, L.L., *Political Economy: Modern Views*
Zimbalist, A., *Comparative Economic Systems: Recent Views*
Darity, W., *Labor Economics: Modern Views*
Jarsulic, M., *Money and Macro Policy*
Samuelson, L., *Microeconomic Theory*
Bromley, D., *Natural Resource Economics: Policy Problems and Contemporary Analysis*
Mirowski, P., *The Reconstruction of Economic Theory*
Field, A.J., *The Future of Economic History*
Lowry, S.T., *Pre-Classical Economic Thought*

International Economics

edited by

LAWRENCE H. OFFICER
University of Illinois at Chicago

Kluwer Academic Publishers
Boston/Dordrecht/Lancaster

Distributors

for the United States and Canada: Kluwer Academic Publishers, 101 Philip Drive, Assinippi Park, Norwell, MA 02061

for the UK and Ireland: Kluwer Academic Publishers, MTP Press Limited, Falcon House, Queen Square, Lancaster LA1 1RN, UK

for all other countries: Kluwer Academic Publishers Group, Distribution Centre, P.O. Box 322, 3300 AH Dordrecht. The Netherlands

Library of Congress Cataloging-in-Publication Data

International economics.

(Recent economic thought series)
Includes bibliographies and index.
Contents: Introduction/Lawrence H. Officer —
The theory of international trade/Wilfred J. Ethier —
The issue of protection/H. Peter Gray and Ingo
Walter — [etc.]
1. International economic relations. 2. International
finance. 3. Commerce. I. Officer, Lawrence H.
II. Series: Recent economic thought.
HF1411.I51725 1987 337 86-33776
ISBN 0-89838-196-7

Kluwer Academic Publishers, 101 Philip Drive, Assinippi Park, Norwell, MA 02061

PRINTED IN THE UNITED STATES.

Contents

Contributing Authors

Marianne Baxter, University of Rochester

James H. Cassing, University of Pittsburgh

Michael R. Darby, University of California, Los Angeles

Avinash Dixit, Princeton University

Wilfred J. Ethier, University of Pennsylvania

H. Peter Gray, Rutgers University

Kent P. Kimbrough, Duke University

J. Carter Murphy, Southern Methodist University

Ingo Walter, New York University

Preface

International Economics is unique despite the existence of numerous books of the same title. It is true that no one volume can capture the entire state of the art of the subject, but individuals can apply their own perspectives to identify crucial issues in the development of the field. Therefore, rather than instructions to prepare "surveys" of subfields within international economics, the contributors to this book were informed as follows:

> Your essay should present an affirmative but constructively critical look at your subject. It is not meant to be a survey. Rather, your task is to pinpoint crucial areas of development, to offer a critical evaluation of what's going on in the field and where it might go. Your contribution would be your own personal statement of how you see things. It should be written at the professional level. Beyond these general guidelines, you may develop your essay as you see fit.

How much of "international economics" should be assigned to each author and how many contributions the book should have, required careful consideration. Traditionally, international economics has been divided into pure theory and monetary theory, suggesting a simple division of the field; but this dichotomy has been overturned by the emergence of literature that overlaps both theories. An opposite approach would have been to separate international economics into twelve to fifteen areas, each with a contributor. This procedure divides the field into too many parts and, consequently, overlapping threads of development would be ignored.

I originally divided the book into three parts: (1) the theory of international trade and the issue of protection, (2) exchange rates, the balance of payments, and macroeconomic stability, and (3) international monetary systems, international institutions, and international debt.

It soon became clear that there were two problems. First, part one was too large. The assignment of both trade theory and protection was too burdensome for a single contribution. Therefore the section was bifurcated accordingly. Second, the descriptions of areas two and three were simultaneously too vague and too inclusive, given the instruction to authors that their "personal statement" was requested. Therefore the titles of these sections were changed to conform to the authors' own perspectives of their assigned subfield. The result was a coverage of international economics and a division of this book into four parts: (1) the theory of international trade, (2) the issue of protection, (3) international linkages, exchange-rate regimes, and the international transmission process: perspectives from optimizing models, and (4) national policies and the international monetary system.

Each contribution was then offered to an independent commentator for evaluation, criticism, or extension. The authors were not given the opportunity to respond to these comments, but readers can draw their own inferences and conclusions.

The series editor writes: "This series is devoted to works that present divergent views on the development, prospects, and tensions within some important research areas of international economic thought. . . . The emphasis of the series is on providing a critical, constructive view of each of these fields, as well as a forum through which leading scholars of international reputation may voice their perspectives on important related issues." In my editorial judgment, the authors of the contributions and the commentators have succeeded admirably in fulfilling Professor Samuels' directive.

I should like to thank Sandra Diane Officer for editorial assistance and spousal understanding, Zachary Rolnik for editorial patience, Warren J. Samuels for editorial encouragement, and all the authors and commentators for their contributions.

International Economics

1 THE THEORY OF INTERNATIONAL TRADE

Wilfred J. Ethier*

We have long thought of the pure theory of international trade as pretty much a settled thing—especially by comparison with international monetary economics, which few of us have ever thought we understood. Yet trade theory has now become one of the most active branches of economics and is widely perceived by the profession to be a field "in transition." Why is this so?

The core of trade theory has long consisted of several basic microeconomic ideas embodied in a few "standard" models—most notably the Heckscher-Ohlin-Samuelson model. Most active research in the field, fifteen or twenty years ago, consisted of applications, modifications, or extensions of these models, which also thoroughly conditioned economists' views of the world economy. But we became increasingly aware that what we thought were the principal implications of our theory were dramatically contradicted (quite remarkably almost without exception) by the actual facts of world commerce. This tension between theory and reality has been

* This chapter is based upon a set of lectures delivered at the Katholieke Universiteit Leuven in May of 1985. I am grateful to Avinash Dixit and Lawrence Officer for comments.

for some time now the driving force behind most of the more important work in the field.

The reaction to such a contradiction between theory and fact can take either of two basic forms. The *conservative* reaction is that there really is no contradiction, once the theory is properly understood and properly applied (or once the facts are accurately known). The appropriate research program, therefore, is to continue doing what we were doing but to do it better (and louder). By contrast, the *radical* reaction is that the orthodox theory is intellectually bankrupt and should therefore be replaced by something quite different. Actual responses have included both extremes as well as much of the spectrum between. This paper treats the response to the apparent contradiction between theory and fact. I am, therefore, concerned with the most dynamic part of contemporary trade theory.[1] I start by briefly reviewing, in vague terms, the basic traditional ideas; and the characteristics of trade that these ideas apparently lead us to expect are compared with the stylized facts. I then review and evaluate the response to this and comment upon how I think trade theory ought to proceed from here.

The Fundamental Ideas of Conventional Trade Theory

Comparative advantage

The most fundamental ideas of all is, of course, *comparative advantage*. Consider a world of two economies (home and foreign) and two goods, apples (A) and bearings (B). Denote the *autarkic* price of A in terms of B by P for the home country and by P^* for the foreign. Suppose that $P > P^*$. Then, since relative prices equal marginal rates of substitution, foreign residents could be induced to reduce their consumption of A by the receipt of less B than home residents would be willing to pay for that A. And, since relative prices also equal marginal rates of transformation, the foreign economy could produce more A by reducing B production by less than the home economy could increase it by cutting back A production. Thus gains can be had if the home economy exports bearings abroad in exchange for apples.

The basis for trade here is international *differences* in economic structure reflected in autarky price differences. Thus we would expect the gains from trade to be greatest between countries that are most *dissimilar*, and the temptation to trade should also be greatest for such countries. Since trade is here basically a matter of each country concentrating on producing

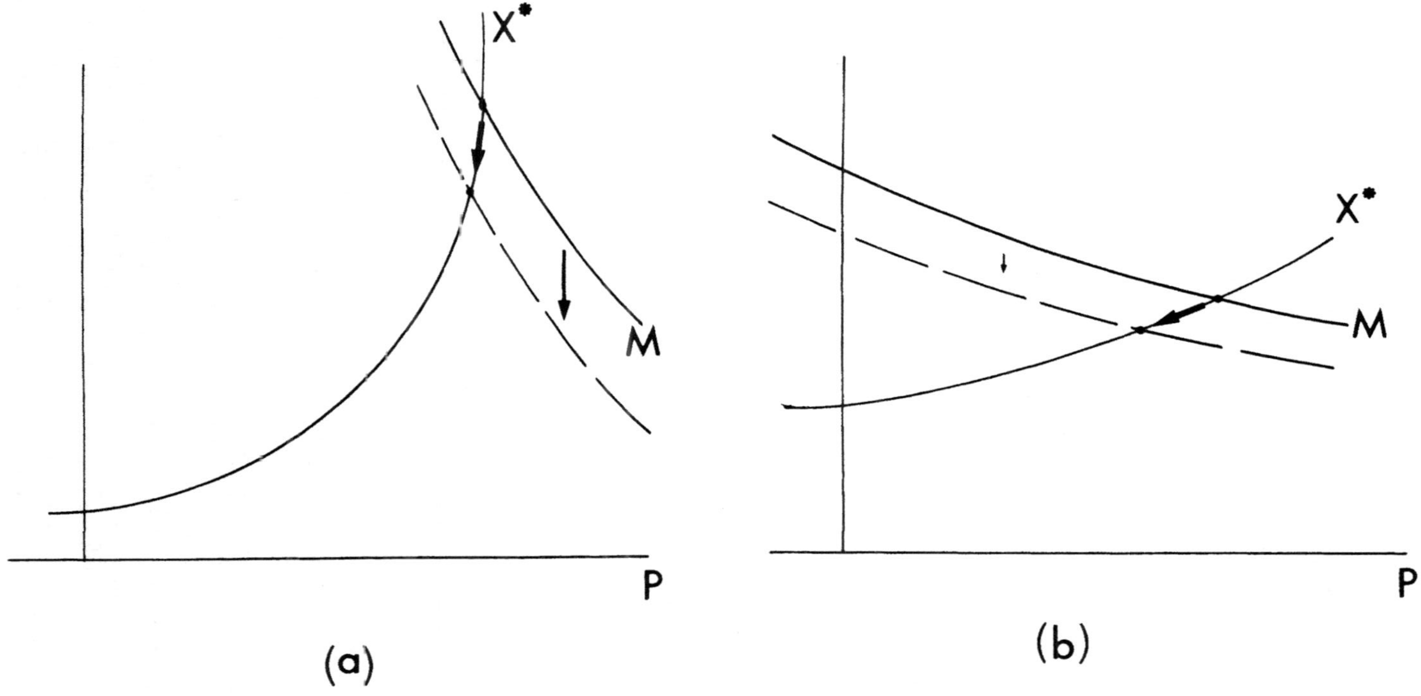

Figure 1–1. The Effect on International Equilibrium of a Restrictive Home Trade Policy

what it "does" relatively well—relative, that is, both to what other countries do and to its own needs—we would expect trade to cause countries to specialize their production structures and to import goods that are quite different from what they produce and export.

Reciprocal Demand

If the home economy were able freely to exchange B for A at some international price p, we would expect the home excess demand for A to be a decreasing function of p: $M(p)$. With the foreign excess supply of A denoted $X^*(p)$, the world market for good A will clear when the international price p satisfies

$$M(p) = X^*(p)$$

This description of how the volume and terms of trade are determined—barely sketched out here—is the *law of reciprocal demand*. Its apparent implications for commercial policy are of interest for our purposes. Such policies can be depicted as shifts of a country's trade curve. The two panels of figure 1–1 show the effect on international equilibrium of a restrictive home trade policy: at each p the home country wants to import less A than before. The new equilibrium in each case has lower values of both M and p than the old equilibrium. This suggests that the welfare of the home country is affected in two countervailing ways by the policy action. The reduction in M below its free-trade level indicates that the country is losing some of the benefits of trade promised by comparative advantage. But the lower p is a national benefit—what the country does import now costs it less. The relative size of these two effects is sensitive to the price elasticities of $M(p)$ and $X^*(p)$. In panel (a) of figure 1–1 the curves are quite elastic and consequently the trade restriction causes a large fall in M but only a minor one in p. The home country is quite likely to be worse off on balance. By contrast, in panel (b), where the curves are inelastic, the price reduction is relatively more dominant, and the home country might well have benefitted from its action.

There are two implications for countries that conduct trade policy so as to maximize national welfare. First, we would expect little conflict between countries whose trade is characterized by large elasticities, since each country individually would have little to gain by restricting trade. It is between countries whose mutual exchange is insensitive to prices that we would expect to see trade warfare. Second, trade policy should take the form of *restricting* trade and not of stimulating it; the latter would merely add a terms-of-trade deterioration to the departure from the free-trade volume, and so necessarily harm the active country.

The Heckscher-Ohlin theory

The predominant explanation of the pattern of comparative advantage is the factor-endowments theory, as expressed in the Heckscher-Ohlin-Samuelson model. Indeed it has been rather common (until recently, at any rate) also to refer to this model, and its predictions, as *the* "modern" theory of international trade. Suppose that apples and bearings can be produced by two factors, capital (K) and labor (L). The home and foreign economies differ only in their endowments of these factors, which are immobile internationally.[2] Call the home country the capital-abundant one and good B the capital-intensive commodity. Then in autarky the wage-rental ratio (w/r) should be greater at home than abroad. This in turn implies that $P > P^*$: the capital-abundant country has a comparative advantage in the capital-intensive good (a result known as the Heckscher-Ohlin theorem).

Trade will cause the home economy to shift resources from apple production to bearing production and to export the latter; the relative price faced by home residents will fall from P to p. The contraction of the labor-intensive sector and expansion of the capital-intensive sector will, at the initial factor prices, cause an excess demand for capital and excess supply of labor. Therefore w/r must fall to induce firms to substitute labor for capital and allow factor markets to clear. Indeed, r must rise relative to both commodity prices and w must fall relative to both, provided the home economy is not driven to specialize completely in B production (the Stolper-Samuelson theorem). If the former did not take place, the price of commodity B would rise relative to both factor prices, thereby producing positive profits, which are inconsistent with equilibrium; without the latter, the price of A would fall relative to both factor prices, thereby producing losses inconsistent with the continued operation of the sector. Thus international trade must raise the real reward of a country's relatively abundant factor and lower the real reward of the relatively scarce factor. Protection induces the opposite effect. There are two important implications: the issue of liberal trade inevitably involves a conflict of interest among domestic groups;[3] the effect on any group is determined by the identity of the factors that generate that group's income, not by the identity of the sectors with which the group is associated.

Since international trade lowers w/r in the capital-abundant home economy, and, by analogy, raises w^*/r^* abroad, relative factor prices in the two countries necessarily become more nearly equal as a result of trade. Indeed, more can be said. As long as bearings remain relatively capital intensive, w/r is necessarily positively related to p, the relative price of A in terms of B, if both goods are produced in equilibrium. This relation is determined by technology and so applies to both countries. With p equalized across countries by trade, w/r is necessarily equalized as well, provided that both countries continue to produce both goods. This must be so if relative factor endowments are not "too" different. Furthermore, equalization of relative factor prices w/r necessarily implies equalization of absolute factor prices as well; otherwise one country would have uniformly higher costs than the other and thus not be able to compete in any sector, a condition inconsistent with equilibrium. In sum, free international trade causes factor prices to become more nearly equal internationally, and necessarily produces complete equality if relative factor endowments are sufficiently similar across countries (a result known as the factor-price-equalization theorem). If countries have identical factor prices, they will use the same production techniques. The apparent implication is that, in a trading equilibrium, countries with roughly similar relative endowments will have similar factor prices and production structures while countries with more divergent relative endowments will not. Another implication is that commodity trade and factor movements are substitutes: by driving factor prices together, commodity trade diminishes the temptation for factor mobility.

Suppose, in a trading equilibrium, the home economy, producing both goods and exporting B, were to become more capital abundant, for some exogenous reason. With commodity prices, and therefore factor prices, restrained by international markets, the additional capital could be utilized only if the capital-intensive sector, the B industry, were to expand. But such an expansion would also require more labor, and that labor can come only from the A sector, which must therefore contract, freeing even more capital for the B sector. Thus, at constant commodity prices, an increase in the capital stock must cause a proportionally even larger increase in the production of the capital-intensive commodity and a lower production of the labor-intensive commodity (a result known as the Rybczynski theorem). This establishes a presumption that growth of a country's relatively abundant factor will generate an excess supply of exportables and an excess demand for importables, at the original terms of trade. That is, growth that makes a country *less* like the rest of the world would cause it to trade more and to experience a deterioration in its terms of trade; growth making the country more like the rest of the world would have the opposite effects.

Since international factor mobility is effectively an example of mutual and opposite growth making two countries more alike, it should cause trade to contract.

Normal Implications of Conventional Trade Theory

It will prove convenient to collect together the various implications of trade theory for what we can expect the broad characteristics of world trade to be.

1. Trade should be greatest between countries with the greatest differences in economic structure.
2. The gains from trade should be greatest between countries with the greatest differences in economic structure.
3. Trade should cause countries to specialize more in production and to export goods distinctly different from their imports.
4. Countries with relatively elastic excess demand and supply curves should be more inclined toward free trade with each other, or indifferent about protection, whereas countries with inelastic excess demand and supply curves should be more prone to tariff wars.
5. Trade policy should take the form of trade restrictions rather than trade stimulants.
6. Countries should export those goods that make relatively intensive use of the countries' relatively abundant factors.
7. Free trade should equalize factor prices between countries with fairly similar relative factor endowments but not between countries with markedly different endowments. The former countries should also employ relatively similar techniques and produce similar goods.
8. Factor prices should be more nearly equal between countries with more liberal mutual trade.
9. Domestic interest groups concerned with protection should be defined on the basis of the identity of the factors providing income rather than on the basis of the identity of the industries where employed.
10. International investment should be stimulated by differences in factor endowments.
11. International trade and international investment should be negatively correlated.

These propositions are *not*—and the point can hardly be emphasized enough—inevitable consequences of the conventional theory of international trade. Each is true only subject to certain conditions. In some cases these conditions are quite severe; and, furthermore, there also exist conditions under which some of the propositions are mutually inconsistent. This lack of inevitability is the basis for the conservative response alluded to above.

But having said all this, I do think that the propositions, as a group, accurately portray that view of the world economy which the conventional theory conditions us to accept as the norm.

Confrontation with Reality

For over thirty years now, the accumulation of knowledge—both quantitative and intuitive—about the world in which we actually live has eroded the picture painted by the eleven propositions of the preceding section. This process was effectively initiated by the Leontief paradox. In an attempt to muscle the actual data of U.S. trade and production into the literal $2 \times 2 \times 2$ Heckscher-Ohlin-Samuelson straightjacket, Leontief found that American exports were significantly less capital intensive (relative to labor) than were American import substitutes. Given the presumption that the United States was capital abundant relative to the rest of the world, this was in dramatic contradiction to proposition 6, the Heckscher-Ohlin theorem.

Other key stylized facts emerged after economists began, in the sixties, to investigate the effects of economic integration in Western Europe. Contrary to proposition 3, this integration was followed, for most countries, by an increase in both imports and exports across most sectors, rather than by an increase in specialization. Subsequently, economists realized that this development was part of a general trend and not confined to the EEC. Furthermore, it became increasingly the case, throughout the postwar period, that the volume of trade among the developed countries—with relatively similar economic structures—dwarfed that between the developed countries as a group and the less-developed countries. This is in sharp contrast to proposition 1. The overall picture of world trade that emerged was of a pattern dominated by the intraindustry exchange of manufactures between roughly similar economies.

How well do the remaining propositions seem to fare? Let's look at them one by one.

4. Countries with relatively elastic excess demand and supply curves

should be more inclined toward free trade with each other, or indifferent about protection, whereas countries with inelastic excess demand and supply curves should be more prone to tariff wars.

This proposition stacks up pretty well in broad, historical terms. Since World War II, trade among the industrial nations has become very liberal by historical standards whereas trade between these states and the less-developed world has remained highly restricted. And one naturally thinks of the relevant elasticities as much higher for the former trade flows than for the latter. But more-recent policy initiatives involve restrictions on trade between developed countries ("the new protectionism"); and the less-developed countries that have been affected are precisely those that are becoming more like the industrial world (the "Newly Industrializing Countries").

5. Trade policy should take the form of trade restrictions rather than trade stimulants.

Import restrictions are, of course, prominent, but so are export promotion measures. It is by no means clear that the latter are, on balance, of a lower order of importance than the former.

7. Free trade should equalize factor prices between countries with fairly similar relative factor endowments but not between countries with markedly different endowments. The former countries should also employ relatively similar techniques and produce similar goods.
8. Factor prices should be more nearly equal between countries with more liberal mutual trade.

Of course, factor prices are not in fact equalized internationally. But trade is not free and costless either. On balance, propositions 7 and 8 accord pretty well with the world in which we live (but note that there is no claim of causality here). Of the major theorems of international trade, it is the factor-price-equalization theorem that coexists most comfortably with reality. That this should be so is a fine irony that would have astounded writers in the fifties. At that time it was common to single out—sometimes with ridicule—the factor-price-equalization theorem as the theorem that was most abstract, most dependent upon unfulfilled assumptions, and least relevant to reality.

9. Domestic interest groups concerned with protection should be de-

fined on the basis of the identity of the factors providing income rather than on the basis of the identity of the industries where employed.

A casual look at public debate strongly suggests that, much more often than not, this is just the reverse of the truth.

10. International investment should be stimulated by differences in factor endowments.
11. International trade and international investment should be negatively correlated.

A large share of international investment takes place among the industrial countries, in defiance of both propositions. This is especially notable with regards to direct investment. About three-fourths of the latter have been between developed countries, and two-way direct investment is increasingly common.[4] There is a striking analogy here with the prominence in world trade of the intraindustry exchange of manufactures between the industrial nations.

What emerges from this cursory review is a truly striking contrast between our picture of reality (admittedly painted in broad strokes) and the apparent implications of our theory. This contrast has come into focus only gradually over the last thirty years or so, in response both to accumulating empirical observation and to the steady evolution of international commerce. The effect on trade theory has been profound. During the fifties, sixties, and early seventies, theorists were primarily concerned with elaborating and tidying up (and rendering more elegant) the received body of theory. For the better part of the last decade, in contrast, the basic task has been to restructure the theory to imply a very different picture of world trade.

The Reaction: Factor Endowments

Responses to this tension between theory and fact have ranged from the purely conservative to the extremely radical. An example of the former would be the hypothesis that the relatively large share of world trade accounted for by the exchange of manufactures between roughly similar (developed) economies can be accounted for by the facts that these economies have a large share of world income and that trade barriers between them are low relative to the barriers they face with the rest of the world. Examples of the latter include Marxist theories.[5] While these two extreme reactions are of inherent interest and importance, they do not attempt to further the evolution of mainstream trade theory. Thus I will confine myself to the broad ground between the extremes. This, of course, still leaves plenty of room for maneuver. In discussing the recent developments, I will start near the conservative end of the spectrum and then gradually work my way toward the radical end.

Specific factors

Pressure groups regarding protectionist issues seem to be determined largely by industry affiliation, in contrast to proposition 9's prediction that factor identity should be the key determinant. This suggests that the Heckscher-Ohlin-Samuelson model's assumption of free internal factor mobility is suspect, at least when that model is used to analyze the consequences of protection. The initial location of the employment of a factor can be of concern to that factor's owner only if that location somehow constrains its subsequent use, that is, if the factor is specific to the sector in some sense. So let's amend the Heckscher-Ohlin-Samuelson model by requiring that both capital and labor be sector-specific, and consider the consequences for real factor rewards of an exogenous rise in p, the relative price of apples in terms of bearings.

With neither factor mobile, the price change cannot bring about an expansion of the A sector and contraction of the B sector, but factor rewards can diverge across sectors. To be concrete, take B as numeraire. With the price of bearings unchanged, wages and rents in the B sector will be unchanged as well. But the price of A has risen. So in real terms those factor rewards have fallen—except in the extreme case where they are spent exclusively on good B. As long as the distribution method in the A sector has not changed, the rise in the price of A must cause wages and rents in that sector to rise by the same proportion.[6] Thus these rewards rise in real terms, except of course for the extreme case where they are spent exclusively on good A.

The real rewards of both factors rise in the A sector and fall in the B sector, regardless of the pattern of factor intensities, and so on. The effect of the price change on any individual's welfare depends only on the sector with which that individual is associated, and not at all on the factor from which his income is derived—just the reverse of the Stolper-Samuelson case.

Such a model is useless for analyzing resource allocation or determi-

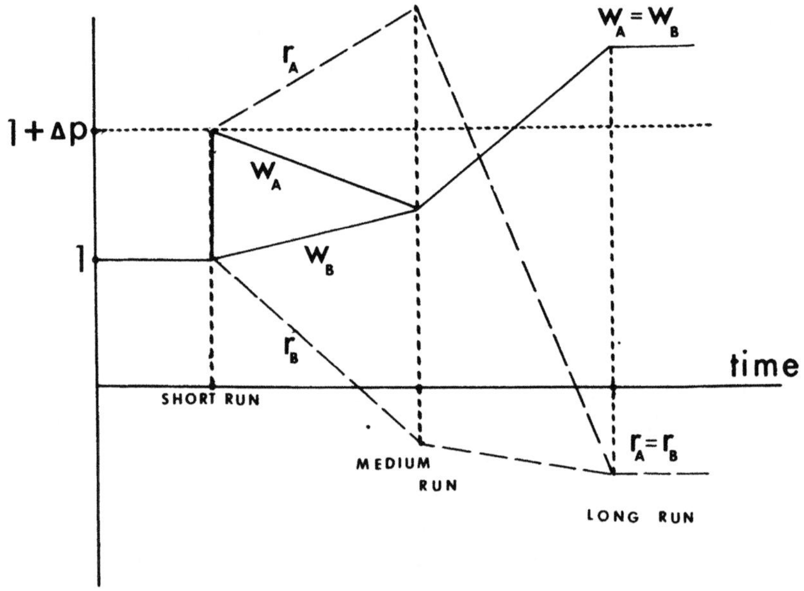

Figure 1–2. Behavior of Wage Rate and Rent of Capital over Time

nants of trade patterns. It is natural, therefore, to regard it as a short-run version of the Heckscher-Ohlin-Samuelson model. Then, since good *A* is labor intensive, in the long run real wages rise and real rents fall, by the Stolper-Samuelson theorem. Thus, labor initially employed in the *A* sector and capital initially employed in the *B* sector are affected by the price change in the same direction in both the short run and the long run, but the long-run effect is the opposite of the short run for initial *A*-capital and initial *B*-labor.

With the sector-specific version of the Heckscher-Ohlin-Samuelson model and the conventional version regarded as complementary short-run and long-run pictures, it is natural to look at the transition between the two. There are many possible ways of doing this. The most common has been to exploit the observation that some factors more readily move between sectors than others, by assuming that one factor is freely mobile while the other is sector specific. This gives a medium-run picture.

Let labor be the mobile factor. Then the increase in the relative price of apples induces a movement of labor from *B* production into *A* production. Since the fixed amount of *A*-sector capital is now combined with an increased quantity of labor, its marginal product must increase. Thus the rent of *A*-capital rises relative to the price of *A*, and therefore relative to the price of *B* as well. The real rental of *A*-capital has accordingly risen. The same argument applied in reverse to the other sector establishes that the real rental of *B*-capital must have fallen. On the other hand, labor's marginal product has risen in the *B* sector and fallen in the *A* sector: the wage rises relative to the price of good *B* but falls relative to the price of good *A*, so the movement in the real wage is ambiguous.

Note that the real rewards of the sector-specific capital stocks are moved in the same direction (but by larger amounts) in the medium run as in the short run. Thus the reversal in the fortunes of *A* capital occurs between the medium run and the long run. But the behavior of the wage is now different from that in the extremes, neither of which admits of any ambiguity regarding factor rewards. Labor initially employed in the *B* sector loses in the short run and gains in the long run; so the ambiguous medium-run position looks like a natural step in its transition. But the fate of labor initially in the *A* sector is the most curious: it necessarily gains in both the short run and the long, but might lose for a while in between! Figure 1–2 shows the behavior of the four groups over time in response to a rise in the price of good *A*. Note that for both factors initially in the *A* sector, the medium-run behavior cannot be described as intermediate between the short-run and long-run responses.

The above medium-run model has been the subject of a great amount of work during the last fifteen years or so.[7] The reason for this is really not. I think, that the *specific-factors model*, as it has come to be known, tells us a lot about protection and income distribution.[8] The short-run model with all factors specific makes the basic point much more clearly and directly. And as a snapshot of the midpoint in the transition from short run to long run, the specific-factors model is too arbitrary to be instructive. Rather, the great virtue of the model is just that it is so very useful. It has a very simple and transparent structure and yet is complex enough to serve as the vehicle for investigating a host of issues. The application of simple general-equilibrium models is, after all, still the predominant method in international trade theory.

I have described the specific-factors model as a relatively conservative development in trade theory. Perhaps it should rather be thought of as reactionary. Before Stolper and Samuelson it was a major component of the tool kits of all trade theorists, so the current interest is best viewed as a revival.[9] Indeed, much of the recent literature simply expresses in contemporary jargon results clearly described many decades ago.

Higher Dimensions

The appearance of the Leontief paradox was identified above as a key initial point in the development of skepticism about the consistency of trade theory with trade reality. Subsequent investigations confirmed the paradox as a basic feature of U.S. trade patterns and discovered similar apparent anomalies for other countries. Empirical and theoretical work were both strongly stimulated.

Early theoretical developments included the elucidation of factor-intensity reversals and of demand reversals as possible explanations of the paradox. A reduction in the wage-rental ratio in a country will induce all firms to substitute labor for capital. If this substitution is easier in the bearing sector than in the apple sector, a sufficient fall in w/r might turn bearings from the relatively capital-intensive commodity into the labor-intensive one. This is known as a factor-intensity reversal. If the factor endowments of the two countries differ sufficiently so that, when they trade, the wage-rental ratio at home significantly exceeds that abroad, the two could be on opposite sides of such a reversal. That is, commodity B could be capital intensive in the capital-abundant home country and labor intensive in the labor-abundant foreign country, according to each country's *own technology in use*. Since one of the two countries must be importing good B, the prediction of the Heckscher-Ohlin theorem must be violated for that country. Thus this is a potential explanation of the paradox.

A demand reversal could result from international taste differences. Suppose home residents have a significantly smaller relative preference for apples than do foreign residents. Then the autarky w/r might be geater abroad than at home, with the foreign labor abundance overwhelmed by the foreign demand for labor-intensive goods. If so, we would have $P < P^*$, and comparative advantage would imply that the home country would export A in exchange for B.[10] Thus such a demand reversal can also potentially account for the Leontief paradox.

These two developments, involving as they do tinkering with the Heckscher-Ohlin-Samuelson model, are quite conservative in spirit. But as explanations of the Leontief paradox they are either not amenable to, or unsupported by, empirical investigations. The large and accumulating body of empirical evidence concerned with determinants of international trade has gradually established an awareness that actual trade flows are quite consistent with the hypothesis that they have a factor-endowments basis, but that the $2 \times 2 \times 2$ model is far too restrictive to provide a vehicle for expressing that basis.[11] Unfortunately, it is just that model that has been the major workhorse of trade theory for about four decades. In particular, the four basic results of the modern theory are based upon the $2 \times 2 \times 2$ assumption. Thus the sensitivity of these theorems to dimensionality—on the face of it an unexciting technical issue—is in fact the key question for the practical relevance of the larger part of contemporary international-trade theory.

Indeed, early work in higher dimensions had strongly indicated that the basic trade theorems were in fact essentially dependent upon the $2 \times 2 \times 2$ assumption, and therefore presumably of little practical relevance after all. This work began with research into the circumstances under which the factor-price-equalization theorem holds in the presence of n goods and n factors. The problem was formalized as that of whether the relation between factor prices and commodity prices was *globally univalent*, that is, as whether there is a one-to-one relation between the (n-dimensional) vector w of factor prices and the (n-dimensional) vector p of commodity prices that is globally valid. In equilibrium, the price of any good must equal its unit cost if that good is to be produced. With all goods produced, univalence thus becomes a property of the cost functions. Free international trade of all goods will equalize commodity prices across countries; it will therefore also equalize unit costs, if all countries produce all goods. Global univalence then implies factor-price equalization as well.

In the 2×2 case, global univalence must hold if the technology has no factor-intensity reversals. The natural higher-dimensional analog of this condition might be that, for *all* vectors of factor prices, the techniques used by the n sectors all be linearly independent of each other. However, this condition is not in fact sufficient for global univalence once n exceeds 2. The very large literature devoted to the hunt for such conditions treated us to arcane relationships with slender economic content. The effect was to reinforce powerfully the view, held by the balance of the profession, that factor-price equalization was of little practical relevance.

Like results followed subsequent attempts to extend the Stolper-Samuelson and Rybczynski theorems to the $n \times n$ context. Attention was directed toward the discovery of those circumstances under which an increase in the price of one commodity, with all other commodity prices held constant, would cause a more than proportional rise in the reward of one factor and an absolute decline in the rewards of all other factors. The higher-dimensional formulation of the Rybczynski theorem was analogous. Again, conditions implying these properties turned out to be complicated and to have little intuitive economic content.

The general impression conveyed by this large body of formidable work was that the basic theorems of the Heckscher-Ohlin-Samuelson model are, for all practical purposes, consequences of the 2×2 assumptions rather than reflections of general properties implied by a factor-endowments basis of trade. This appeared to be fatal for the relevance of the larger part of modern trade theory, in the light of the apparent empirical conclusion that, although actual trade flows seemed to have a quite significant factor-endowments basis, the 2×2 model is totally inadequate to capture it.

We began to crawl out of this conundrum in the mid 70s.[12] The chosen route was the (cowardly) one of redefining the question until we could answer it. This was done in two distinct ways. The first was to focus on propositions that were not, in some sense, fully comprehensive. That is, propositions that said something concrete about *some* goods and/or factors, but not about *all*.

Consider, for example, the Stolper-Samuelson theorem. Suppose the price of some produced good, say the first, rises. If this good is to continue to be produced in equilibrium after the price rise, its unit cost must increase by the same amount as its price. This requires that at least one factor reward rise by at least the same proportion as the price of good one. Suppose that the reward of factor one does so. Now, if factor one is also used by some other commodity, call it the second, whose price has not changed and which continues to be produced after the rise in the price of the first good, there must be an absolute fall in the reward of some other factor (call it the second) used in the production of good two. Otherwise the unit cost of the latter would necessarily rise above its unchanged price, thereby forcing production to cease. Thus an increase in the price of any commodity causes an at-least-as-large (proportionally) rise in the reward of some factor and an absolute decline in the reward of some other factor.

Since the reward of factor one has risen in terms of all goods except the first, and not fallen in terms of that, its real value must have risen, as long as its recipients do not spend all their income on good one alone.[13] Also, the fact that the reward of factor two has fallen absolutely while no commodity price has declined implies that the real reward of this factor has deteriorated. Thus we can be sure that, in general, a rise in the price of any good will benefit *some* factor in real terms and harm *some* other factor. An analogous logic can be applied to Rybczynski questions: at constant factor prices, an increase in the endowment of one factor must result in a more-than-proportional rise in the output of some good and an absolute fall in the output of some other good. If the number of goods equals the number of factors, the "reciprocity" relations of Samuelson can be invoked to use the Rybczynski results to derive further Stolper-Samuelson results, and vice versa. For example, in this $n \times n$ case, for each factor there must be some good a rise in whose price will produce a fall in the real reward of the factor.

The general conclusion is that each good is a "friend" to *some* factor and an "enemy" to *some* other factor (to use the terminology of Jones and Scheinkman), and furthermore, if there are an equal number of goods and factors, each factor has some good as an "enemy." None of this requires the technology to possess a special mathematical structure. What is lost relative to the earlier literature, which dwelled on such structures, is that (if n exceeds two) our conclusions apply only to *some* factors, leaving open the possibility that a rise in some commodity price could cause some factor reward to rise in terms of one good while falling in terms of another.[14] On the other hand, the present results are stronger than the earlier in the crucial sense that they can easily be applied to *any* relative price change, whereas the earlier results apply only to two-dimensional price changes, where the prices of one group of commodities all rise in a common proportion relative to the prices of all others. Much more important, though, is that the essential Stolper-Samuelson message—that commodity price changes are inevitably conflict-generating by shifting real income from one factor to another, independently of how that income is spent—is an essential property of factor-endowments models rather than an artifact of the unrealistic 2×2 assumption.

This is a good example of the rewards that sometimes follow a willingness to ask slightly different questions. In this case we altered our quest from one for a particular good-by-good (and factor-by-factor) result to the apparently more modest one for the basic spirit of the Stolper-Samuelson property. As a result, we were able to free ourselves from a mass of arcane technical detail and to see in clear relief the basic nature of that property. And in the end we were left with a result even more powerful, for practical purposes, than the earlier higher-dimensional one.

A similar situation exists with regard to factor-price equalization. In the 2×2 case, factor-price equalization occurs if the two economies have sufficiently similar relative factor endowments; disparate endowments preclude equalization regardless of the global properties of the technology. A factor-intensity reversal opens up the possibility that both countries will produce both goods, but factor prices will not be equalized in any event. The same holds true in higher dimensions. Global univalence is a stronger property than needed to get to the heart of the factor-price-equalization property.

A particular vector w of factor prices determines, for each sector i, the least-cost vector $k_i(w)$ of unit-level inputs. The cone $K(w)$, formed from all nonnegative combinations of the $k_i(w)$, determines those endowments for which a country might be in productive equilibrium with the factor prices w. These factor prices also determine the vector $c(w)$ of least-cost techniques of production. If international commodity prices $p = c(w)$, any country with endowments in the cone $K(w)$ can be in equilibrium with factor prices equal to w. This shows directly that free trade, establishing the international price vector p, must feature factor-price equalization between countries with sufficiently similar relative endowments [i.e., those with endowments in the cone $K(w)$], *if* it is also true that any country with endowments in $K(w)$ can be in equilibrium *only* with factor prices equal to w. That this must be so is revealed by a simple argument originally due to McKenzie (1955).

Suppose some endowment vector v is contained in both $K(w)$ and $K(w')$, for $w \neq w'$, and let s and s' denote output vectors when $p = c(w)$ and $p' = c(w')$ are the respective commodity price vectors. Now $c(w) < w'[dc(w)]$ and $c(w') < w[dc(w')]$ by properties of cost functions (I ignore "ties"). Then $wv = ps < w'[dc(w)]x = w'v$, since the term in brackets equals the technique used at factor prices w. Thus $wv < w'v$. Reversing the roles of the two factor-price vectors yields $w'v < wv$. Thus the supposed v cannot exist.

For the conclusion that countries with endowments in $K(w)$ must experience factor-price equalization whenever trading freely at prices p to be meaningful, the cone $K(w)$ must also be of full dimensionality, that is, there must be at least as many goods as factors. Actually, this requirement is weakened if a factor is mobile internationally, for then its reward will be equalized directly by the process of international competition. Thus the more general requirement is that there be a sufficiently large number of international markets (whether of goods or factors). The point is that the complicated properties of the technology, emphasized by the global univalence literature, have nothing to do with factor-price equalization: it is all a matter of (1) the similarity of different countries' factor endowments, and (2) the number of international markets.[15] These are easy to understand.

The second sort of result is that which applies to all factors or to all goods "on average," but does not attempt to assert anything about any single good or factor. A good example is the higher-dimensional fate of the principle of comparative advantage, that most holy (and most useful) result of our field.

The proposition that a country will export that commodity which has the lower relative autarky price, compared to the rest of the world, completely describes the pattern of commodity trade if there are but two goods. But with higher dimensions, problems arise. Suppose, for example, that we rank the n goods in descending order according to the ratio P_i/P_i^* of home to foreign autarky prices. One would expect the home country to import the goods earlier in the list and export those later in the list. With a simple-enough technology, such as a Ricardian model (one factor and n goods), such an idea can be made precise. But still there are problems: the line between imports and exports must be drawn somewhere, and where it is drawn depends, if there are more than two goods, on country sizes and on the nature of demand. Thus a change in either can potentially change a good from an import to an export or vice versa. Further ambiguity can arise with a more general technology. For example, suppose that a country exports good *1*, which had a relatively low autarky price, and accordingly produces much more of the good when trading than it would in autarky. It could be that another commodity, good *2*, is so complementary to good *1* in production that the expansion of the latter greatly reduces the cost of the former: good *2* could be exported even if it had a quite high relative autarky price.

What needs to be sacrificed are commodity-by-commodity predictions. What we can predict is that, *on average*, goods with relatively low autarky prices will be exported and those with relatively high autarky prices will be imported; we no longer attempt to identify just which goods fall into each camp.[16]

Let P and p denote, respectively, the vectors of home autarky prices and international prices, D and d the home autarky and free-trade consumption vectors, and S and s the home autarky and free-trade production vectors. Then, if free trade is at least as good as autarky for the home country, it must be the case that $Pd \geq PD$. But $PD = PS$, since in autarky $D = S$, and $PS \geq Ps$, since firms were maximizing profit in autarky. Putting these together, we have $Pd \geq Ps$, or

$$PM \geq 0$$

where $M = d - s$, the vector of imports. For trade to balance, we require that $pM = 0$, so that

$$(P - p)M \geq 0$$

This inequality says that the elements of the vector $P - p$ are *correlated* with the elements of M. For example, in the two-dimensional case we can choose our method of normalizing prices so that one component of $P - p$ is positive and one is negative. Then the above inequality requires M to have the same sign pattern: the country must export the good with the lower autarky price (relative to the free-trade price) and import the other: the standard 2×2 result. But with more than two goods the inequality implies nothing about the trade status of any particular good: relatively cheap goods are exported on average.

Similar logic applied to the rest-of-the-world yields $(P^* - p)M^* \geq 0$, where P^* and M^* denote the foreign autarky price vector and net import vector, respectively. Noting that $M = -M^*$ and subtracting the foreign equation from the home one gives us

$$(P - P^*)M \geq 0$$

The trade vector is positively correlated with autarky price differences: each country *on average* exports those goods that are relatively cheap in autarky, compared with the other country.

Thus, just as in the 2×2 model, gainful trade implies a pattern of trade as predicted by comparative advantage. However, the latter is no longer a commodity-by-commodity description of the direction of trade, but instead a correlation, or an assertion about average behavior. This is the price we have to pay for general results.

A similar change in objectives allows higher-dimensional versions of the Heckscher-Ohlin theorem. One possibility emerges if we make the assumption that free trade is characterized by factor-price equalization. As we have seen, a sufficiently large number of traded goods (and/or factors) and sufficiently similar relative endowments across countries will indeed produce such a free-trade equilibrium. This implies that each commodity is produced by a single technique, irrespective of the location of production. Assume further, as is done in the 2×2 quantity version, that all countries have identical homothetic tastes. Then, with commodity prices equalized by free trade, each country must consume the various goods in the same proportion as each other country, that is, each country consumes a fraction of the world production of each good just equal to that country's share of world income. This in turn implies that the goods consumed by any country embody in their production a fraction of the world endowment of each factor that is also just equal to that country's share of world income. This enables us to describe precisely the *factor content* of each country's trade. Let M_j denote the home country's net imports of factor j, that is, the total amount of factor j used in the production of the home-commodity import vector minus the total amount of factor j used in the production of the home export vector. Then

$$M_j = (\mu - \delta_j)V_j$$

where μ denotes home income as a fraction of world income, δ_j denotes the home endowment of factor j as a fraction of the world endowment, and V_j denotes that world endowment. The home country therefore "imports" each factor for which $\delta_j < \mu$ and "exports" each factor for which $\delta_j > \mu$. We have said nothing about the commodity composition of trade, but its factor content can be described precisely. We can in fact say something about commodity composition, but the statement is only a correlation, as in the general principle of comparative advantage. Because factor prices are equalized internationally,

$$v = AX \quad \text{and} \quad v^* = AX^*$$

where v and v^* denote the home and the rest-of-the-world endowment vectors, X and X^* the respective output vectors, and A the matrix of techniques actually employed (in both countries). Multiplying the first equation by $1-\mu$, the second by μ, and subtracting the first from the second gives

$$[\mu(v+v^*)-v] = A[\mu(X+X^*)-X] = AM$$

where M denotes the home import vector. Multiplying both sides of this equation by the vector $[\mu(v+v^*)-v]$ then implies

$$[\mu(v+v^*)-v]AM > 0$$

Thus the vector AM is positively correlated with $[\mu(v+v^*)-v]$: on average, the economy tends to import those goods that make relatively intensive use of relatively scarce factors.

The price version also generalizes in the form of a correlation. This is closely related to another generalization of the Stolper-Samuelson theorem. In two dimensions this latter proposition makes two assertions about the effect of commodity price changes upon factor rewards: that relative factor intensities predict the direction of the latter, and that the changes in factor rewards will *magnify* those in commodity prices. We have already discussed generalization of the latter. Consider the former. Suppose we have two equilibria with $p' = c(w')$ and $p'' = c(w'')$ for those goods actually produced in *both* equilibria, where $c(w)$ denotes the unit cost function. Define the scalar-valued function $b(w) = c(w)(p''-p')$. Then, by the mean-value theorem,

$$b(w'') = b(w') + (w''-w')\,db(\tilde{w}) \tag{1.1}$$

where $db(\tilde{w})$ denotes the differential of $b(w)$ at some intermediate vector $b(\tilde{w})$. Thus $db(\tilde{w}) = c_w(\tilde{w})(p''-p') = A(\tilde{w})(p''-p')$, so that equation (1.1) becomes

$$b(w'') - b(w') = (p''-p')(p''-p') = (w''-w')A(\tilde{w})(p''-p'). \tag{1.2}$$

Thus we have

$$(w''-w')A(\tilde{w})(p''-p') > 0$$

That is, positive values of $p_i''-p_i'$ tend, on average, to be associated with positive values of $w_j'' - w_j'$ when a_{ij} is large and with negative values when a_{ij} is low. The directional aspect of the Stolper-Samuelson theorem extends to higher dimensions as a correlation.

This result can be used to assert a generalization of the price version of the Heckscher-Ohlin theorem. Let (p',w') denote the home autarky equilibrium and (p'',w'') the foreign autarky equilibrium. Then our result states that the home country tends to have a comparative advantage in goods making relatively intensive use of the country's relatively abundant (in a price sense) factors.

The same method can be used to obtain a price version expressed in terms of the commodity-trade pattern (rather than in terms of autarky relative-price differences). Define the scaler-valued function $g(w) = c(w)M$, where M denotes the actual free-trade home import vector. Then applying to $g(w)$ the same technique we applied earlier to $b(w)$ yields the following correlation:

$$(w'' - w')A(\hat{w})M > 0$$

where $\hat{w}$ is some intermediate price vector. The home economy tends, on average, to import those goods making relatively intensive use of relatively scarce factors.

Each of the four basic propositions of the Heckscher-Ohlin-Samuelson model thus generalizes in some simple way (or ways) to higher dimensions. Early attempts to do so were unsuccessful in the sense that they generated the impression that such extensions would necessarily be arcane affairs of little practical relevance. It was not until we learned to formulate our questions in useful ways that we became aware of the higher-dimensional nature of these propositions. The conclusion that now seems inescapable is that, although a nontrivial part of the standard 2×2 results can not survive generalization, a central core of those propositions does indeed reflect the essential factor-endowments view of trade and thus is not simply a reflection of low dimensionality.[17] It is this conclusion that rescues the modern theory of international trade from practical irrelevance.

The Reaction: Scale Economies

The fact that the preponderant share of world trade consists of the intraindustry exchange of manufactures between similar economies simply does not sit well with comparative advantage. There is no *logical* inconsistency here: the larger incomes and lower trade barriers of the industrial world could in principle explain the relative trade volumes consistently with comparative advantage. And the fact that a large part of the trade between the industrial economies is intraindustry *is* consistent with a factor-endowments (and therefore comparative-advantage) explanation. For, suppose that a pair of countries trade in order to exchange factors, by the proxy of commodity trade. If the goods produced by the two countries use relatively similar factor intensities (a reasonable interpretation of intraindustry trade), a given volume of commodity trade will serve to exchange, by proxy, only a small quantity of factors: the goods exported by each country will differ only slightly in terms of factor content from those imported. Thus, the more similar the factor intensities of the goods produced in the two countries, the greater the volume of commodity trade necessary to effect a given volume of implicit factor trade.[18]

But the fact that actual trade is not logically inconsistent with comparative advantage is of little comfort if the latter in fact addresses concerns that are only tangential to the former.[19] This certainly seems to be the case. But what difference does it make if this trade is in fact due to something quite different from comparative advantage? Why should we care?

The reason is that the principle of comparative advantage has normative implications. These must be taken into account if actual trade is due significantly to comparative advantage, but they may be misleading otherwise. For example, DC-LDC trade, between countries with significant differences in economic structure, would appear to promise large gains, and DC-DC trade would likewise seem to offer modest gains, if comparative advantage explains trade. This would seem to imply that we ought to try hard to integrate the LDCs into the world economy and not worry overmuch about new marginal barriers to trade among the DCs. But this policy prescription could easily be disastrously wide of the mark if trade is in fact driven by considerations quite different from comparative advantage.

But what other candidates are there? There is in fact a very old one: increasing returns to scale.[20] The fundamental idea behind comparative advantage is that countries trade in order to exploit their *differences*. Another possibility is that they might trade in order to *specialize*, that is, to become more productive by doing less but doing it better.[21] Of course, the exploitation of differences quite likely involves some specialization; so it is not completely clear that the two bases for trade are in fact distinct. Formal models help here.[22]

National External Economies of Scale

Until this most recent decade, trade theory—when it was explicit on the point—almost universally assumed that increasing returns to scale were internal to the national industry but external to the firm. There were two reasons for this. First, scale economies internal to the firm do not sit well with competitive equilibrium, and analysis of the latter has been the basic method of trade theory.[23] Second, the most common motivating policy concern was that of the benefits of industrialization of the national economy, and such possible benefits were most naturally modeled as external economies. Not present at all, to my knowledge, was any conviction that scale economies external to the firm exhausted the interesting or relevant possibilities.

Consider now a simple two-country, two-commodity, one-factor model in which one of the goods possesses increasing returns to scale external to the firm but internal to the national industry.[24] Let apples (A) denote the good produced subject to constant returns, and measure each country's factor, called labor (with endowment denoted L), so that in each country one unit of labor can produce one apple. Scale economies are relevant to production of the second good, bearings (B). Suppose that, in each country, the quantity B of bearings that can be produced from M units of labor is given by $B = kM$. Each firm takes the parameter k as given independently of its own actions, and so behaves as if subject to constant returns to scale. However, k depends in fact on the size of the national industry: $k = (M)^{\alpha}$. If $\alpha > 1$, there are increasing returns to scale that are external to the firm and internal to the national industry.

Figure 1–3 shows the production-possibility frontier of such a country. Production at any point on that frontier, such as X in the figure, can be sustained by a relative price P of apples in terms of bearings indicated by a line joining that point with the A-intercept of the frontier. Thus $P = CX/LC$ in the figure. The difference of the relative price from the marginal rate of transformation reflects the distortion because scale economies are external to the firm.

Suppose first that the two countries have identical relative prices in autarky. This would be true if they had identical tastes and were the same size (and so completely identical). Then there is no basis for trade in a comparative-advantage sense. And it is clear that the no-trade case, with each country continuing to do what it had done in autarky even after all trade barriers are gone, is indeed a free-trade equilibrium. But with scale economies this cannot be Pareto-optimal: the two countries are equally productive in apple production and there are economies of scale in bearing production, so any pattern of production with both countries producing both goods is inefficient. Thus scale economies provide a basis for trade logically independent of comparative advantage. This is our first major conclusion.

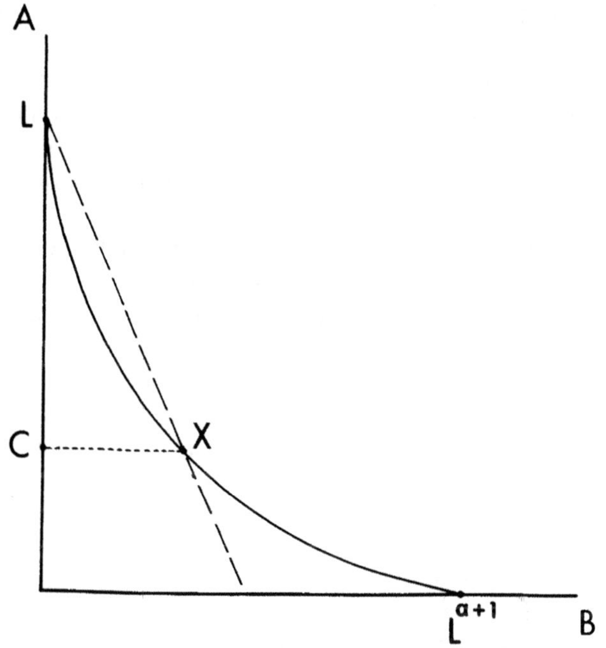

Figure 1–3. Production-Possibility Frontier under Increasing Returns to Scale.

Though the no-trade situation is clearly an equilibrium, one soon suspects that it may not be a very stable one. Suppose the home economy produces a few more bearings, and the foreign economy fewer, than in the no-trade equilibrium. Then the home k is greater than k^*, the foreign analog, so home bearing firms can undersell their foreign rivals; while the two countries can still produce apples on equal terms. Thus the new situation is not an equilibrium. Furthermore, one would expect home bearing producers to increase their market share at the expense of their foreign competitors, so that foreign resources move into the apple sector. If so, this development causes k to rise further and k^* to fall, increasing the home bearing advantage still more. This process must continue until a new equilibrium is reached with the home economy producing only bearings and/or the foreign economy producing only apples. Thus there is a second equilibrium. Indeed there is more than that: since the two countries are identical, we can find a third equilibrium by simply reversing the home and foreign roles in the second. Thus we have two mirror-image equilibria with at least one country completely specialized, separated by an equilibrium where both countries produce both goods. Our dynamic argument suggests that the latter is unstable and the former stable, though of course such dynamics reflect an arbitrary description of disequilibrium behavior. The basic idea behind comparative advantage is that countries should do what they can do relatively well; this implies some particular role in the world economy. Scale economies, on the other hand, require countries to concentrate on a small number of tasks; who does what is secondary. Thus scale economies introduce a bias toward a multiplicity of equilibria. This is our second major result.[25]

I have assumed the two countries to be completely identical, because that is the most dramatic way to demonstrate that scale economies provide a basis for trade independently of comparative advantage. But even if tastes and sizes differ, it will be possible to find a separating equilibrium with both countries producing both goods, provided that it is possible to divide evenly an equilibrium quantity of world bearing production between the two countries. Only if they differ sufficiently in size and if equilibrium world demand for bearings is sufficiently great will this not be possible.

The other equilibria might involve one country completely specialized in bearings and/or one completely specialized in apples. It makes a great deal of difference which occurs. Suppose that the dynamic adjustment process described above comes to an end when the home country specializes in bearing production, with the foreign economy still producing both goods. Since $k > k^*$, foreign wages must be lower than home wages for this to be an equilibrium. As the home economy adjusted to this equilibrium, it moved down and to the right along its production-possibility frontier in figure 1–3, so that its budget line, pivoting on point L, swung out. Thus the home economy was made better off. As the foreign economy adjusted to its new equilibrium, its budget line swung inward, so its real income must have declined. Thus trade has benefitted the home economy, relative to autarky, but has made the foreign economy worse off. There is quite likely a mirror-image equilibrium in which the roles of the two countries reverse (this is obviously true if they are identical). Thus potential international conflict is inherent. This is our third major result.

Suppose now that, instead, the dynamic adjustment ends with the foreign economy specialized in apples and the home economy producing both goods. Since both countries produce apples, wages must be the same internationally, in sharp contrast to the previous case. Thus residents of both countries fare the same. Home residents must be better off than in autarky, for the same reason as in the previous case; and foreign residents will also be better off if and only if the home bearing industry is larger with free trade than the foreign bearing industry was in autarky, since in that case the foreign budget line must pivot out. There will again be another mirror-image equilibrium, as long as the foreign economy is larger than is necessary to produce the world output of bearings. But, unlike the previous case, this is of no consequence, because everyone fares the same regardless of country of residence.

The final possibility is that both countries specialize. If the specialization outputs are consistent with an international equilibrium, it matters not that scale economies are involved in bearing production. (For example, the model will be identical to a Ricardian model with k fixed at the equilibrium level.) In this sense scale economies do not matter. Note that in this case the international equilibrium is Pareto-optimal, unlike both of the other cases, where too few bearings are produced.

To summarize, with scale economies there are four potential types of equilibria:

1. Equilibria in which both countries produce both goods. We might call this the *knife-edge* case, since there is some reason to regard such equilibria as unstable. In this case world production is inefficient, residents of both countries have identical free-trade consumption possibilities, and either country may be better or worse off than in autarky.
2. Equilibria in which one country specializes in bearing production and the other produces both goods. In this case one country gains from trade and the other loses; and there can easily be mirror-image equilibria in which the countries reverse roles. We might call this the *Graham* case, since it corresponds to Frank Graham's (1923) argument for protection.
3. Equilibria in which one country specializes in apple production and the other produces both goods. We might call this the *factor-price-equalization* case, since wages must be equal in the two countries. In this case the possibility of multiple equilibria is of no real interest.
4. Equilibria in which both countries specialize. We might call this the *Ricardian* case, because scale economies really make no difference.

These types of equilibria are not mutually exclusive. That is, if tastes, technology, and size imply multiple equilibria, the equilibria could be (and usually will be) of different types.

Knife-edge equilibria are perhaps of little practical relevance. Ricardian and factor-price-equalization equilibria are simple to analyze but add little of real importance to the understanding of the world economy beyond what can be derived from models without scale economies at all. It is the possibility of Graham equilibria that produces the real value-added that can come from consideration of increasing returns to scale. These equilibria produce positive and normative implications in sharp contrast to those of comparative advantage and can therefore be used in support of quite different policy recommendations. They are of direct relevance to the "grand old debates" over the wisdom of participating in the international trading system.

But this analysis of national external economies of scale is less than fully satisfying, for several reasons, and has accordingly had to play a role very much subservient to that of comparative advantage. For one thing, the indeterminacy of results due to the likelihood of multiple equilibria renders the theory cumbersome to use. Also, the "grand old debates" may be important, but they are not all-important; and our investigation of scale economies was motivated in large part by a desire to address more directly a world in which the lion's share of trade consists of the exchange of similar commodities between similar economies. But the influence of scale economies, enhancing the possibility of specialization, is to move us in just the opposite direction! Finally, it is unsatisfying to confine our analysis of scale economies to those that are external to the firm but internal to the national industry. Additional methods of modelling scale economies are needed.

Intraindustry Trade

As is so often the case, it will prove convenient to proceed a step at a time. Continue to assume that increasing returns are external to the firm and internal to the national industry. But, to try to come to grips with intraindustry trade, disaggregate the bearing sector. That is, suppose that there are n distinct bearing subindustries, each producing a differentiated product. Each subindustry possesses the technology described earlier, with one exception. Instead of requiring the scale parameter α to be a constant, as before, I now suppose that it decreases, at a constant rate, with the size of the subindustry. That is, for subindustry i, $\alpha = (M_i)^{\epsilon}$, where $\epsilon < 0$, except that α converges to $\alpha' > 1$ as subindustry size M_i becomes indefinitely large, and $\alpha = \alpha'' > \alpha'$ when the subindustry size falls short of some critical level c. The number n of bearing varieties will be determined endogenously. Each firm produces each existing variety and takes each k as given, though the total output in a subindustry, from all firms, determines the value of k in that subindustry.[26]

Suppose, for simplicity, that all existing varieties of bearings enter consumers' utility functions in symmetric ways. Given the symmetry in production, this implies that in equilibrium all varieties produced in a country are produced and consumed in equal amounts. Let b denote the consumption of each produced variety, equal to the output in autarky. Suppose that national tastes can be represented by a utility function of the form $u = A^{\delta}(nb^{\theta})^{1-\delta}$, where $1 \geq \theta > 0$ and $1 > \delta > 0$. If $\theta = 1$, the different varieties are perfect substitutes and only the total number of bearings consumed matters for utility. If $\theta < 1$, the varieties are imperfect substitutes and consumers prefer more variety to less; an increase in n and reduction in b leaving nb unaltered will improve welfare. The parameter θ can therefore be interpreted as an index of the "taste for variety," with lower values of θ indicating stronger preferences for variety.

For maximum utility, a closed economy must devote the fraction δ of its labor force to the apple sector. As n increases, the effect on welfare is given by $du/dn = [1 - \theta\epsilon \log c - \theta\alpha]u/n$. This term is decreasing in n. If the taste for diversity is sufficiently strong, and/or the returns to scale sufficiently weak, so that $1 > \theta\alpha''$, then du/dn will always be positive, so there should be an indefinitely large number of indefinitely small subindustries.

Sufficiently strong scale economies, on the other hand, imply that n should equal unity. In this case there is only one subindustry, and the model reduces to that of the preceding subsection. The most interesting possibility, therefore, arises when $du/dn = 0$ possesses an interior solution. This condition then determines the optimal value of M/n, the size of each subindustry. Changes in the size of the bearing sector (resulting from changes in country size L, say, or in the parameter δ) would change the number of bearing varieties and not the scale of each subindustry. Thus the industry as a whole would behave as if it had constant returns to scale.

Now allow international trade between two such countries, identical in every way except that foreign labor is more productive than home labor in apple production. Then the home economy will export bearings to the rest of the world for apples. If the foreign economy produces only apples, this interindustry trade is all that will happen. But the foreign economy, though exporting apples, might also produce some bearings. In the previous section this gave rise to Graham equilibria, with all their complications. Here it generates *intraindustry* trade: the varieties of bearings produced at home should differ from those produced abroad, so each country exports a fraction of the output of each of its bearing subindustries. As the home economy has more subindustries, it runs an intraindustry trade surplus to exchange (*interindustry* trade) for foreign apples.

There is a sense in which intraindustry trade depends upon similarities across countries, while interindustry trade depends upon differences. Suppose, for example, that both countries' labor is equally productive in the apple industry, so that the two countries are completely alike. Then there is no basis at all for interindustry trade, and each country will be self-sufficient in apples. But they should still trade: if they produce different assortments of bearing varieties, they can both gain by exchanging these. All trade will then be intraindustry.

This picture can be generalized somewhat with little difficulty from the one-factor model. Consider the following separable production structure. Several factors determine a frontier of possible combinations of apple production A and bearing resources M, and the latter are used, as described above, to produce bearings. The factors might be two, with a Heckscher-Ohlin model essentially giving a production-possibility frontier of A and M. In this case, relatively distinct factor endowments at home and abroad would produce mainly interindustry trade, whereas endowment similarities would cause trade to be largely intraindustry. An international factor movement making the endowments more similar would shrink interindustry trade and expand intraindustry trade. That is, the former is a substitute for international factor mobility whereas the latter is complementary to it. This *complementarity theorem* expresses the essence of recent theories of intraindustry trade.

Like the earlier Graham case, there is a good deal of indeterminacy here. The actual assortment of bearings produced by each country is indeterminate; so there are multiple equilibria in this sense. But this indeterminacy is of little consequence, and the model has been built to focus on other things. There is another sort of indeterminacy as well. The above analysis proceeded in terms of the optimal degree of product differentiation, n. This was indeed an equilibrium, but no argument was presented to the effect that this n would actually be realized. In fact, other equilibria, with many different values of n, are possible. This indeterminacy is not inconsequential, but it is not surprising either, given what we already know about external economies.

This model is unattractive for reasons beyond its indeterminacy. With scale economies internal to the individual subindustry, rather than only to manufacturing as a whole, the model is no longer really a natural one for addressing the "grand old debates" dealing with industrialization and so on. But the fact that the economies are still external to individual firms severely limits the real-life situations to which they could correspond. The real value of this model is the basic theoretical point that it makes quite clear: basic features of intraindustry trade, and its relation to interindustry trade, emerge directly simply from the *disaggregation* of scale economies; details about the nature of scale economies or about market structure are quite extraneous. The latter matter because they exist, not because they are central to intraindustry trade.

The development of a theory of intraindustry trade like that summarized above has been one of the major accomplishments of the international-trade theory of the preceding decade. This theory was in fact developed in more complex models than that just discussed, no doubt because of the latter's tenuous relation to reality. But the most remarkable aspect of the development of this theory was that it was reached, almost simultaneously, by two independent lines of inquiry proceeding from two quite different starting points. I discuss each in turn.

International Economies of Scale

The first starting point was an attempt to reformulate the theory of external economies described earlier. Recall that that theory had a tendency for multiple equilibria, complete specialization, and uncertain welfare properties. These features, and the general inconvenience of Graham equilibria, caused scale economies to be incorporated into trade models much less frequently than most economists probably thought their inherent importance warranted.

External economies have generally been identified in the literature with an increased division of labor made possible by a larger market: Adam Smith's pin factory and the Swiss watch industry are the prominent hoary examples. Less common are examples having to do with a larger volume of public information generated by a larger industry. In principle, none of these requires an industry to be physically located in one place. A dispersed industry can realize a great division of labor if intermediate components can be shipped from place to place; public information can be dispersed within the industry if communication is efficient. What matters, under these conditions, is the global size of the industry, not its geographical concentration.

This suggests that the returns to scale depend upon the size of the *world* industry, not the national industry. This is what is meant by *international* returns to scale.[27] To uncover the implications, return to a simple formal model. Suppose, as above, that capital and labor are combined, in a Heckscher-Ohlin framework, to produce apples, A, and M. M is an index of the scale of operations of the national bearing industry, subject to increasing returns to scale. With *national* returns to scale, national bearing production B has been related to M by

$$B = kM \qquad \text{where } k = k(M),\ k' > 0$$

With *international* returns to scale, on the other hand, we have instead

$$B + B^* = k(M + M^*) \qquad \text{where } k = k(M + M^*),\ k' > 0$$

Here an asterisk refers to the foreign country. Of course, one might argue that, even in the modern-world economy, some determinants of external economies require geographical concentration, so the appropriate general formulation would have $k = k(M,M^*)$ and $k^* = k^*(M,M^*)$, with perhaps the additional requirement that k be relatively more sensitive to M and k^* to M^*. But this exposition can make its points more effectively if I stick to the case of pure international scale effects.

At first glance, it might seem that we have complicated matters enormously. National production-possibility frontiers between final goods are not even defined, because productivity in each country's bearing industry depends upon the size of the other country's bearing industry. But the situation becomes almost transparent as soon as we focus on patterns of resource allocation rather than on goods.

To see why this is so, consider the world production-possibility frontier between apples and bearings. This is certainly well defined. A point on it can be found by maximizing world bearing production for a given feasible volume of world apple production, that is, by

$$\text{maximizing:} \quad B + B^* = k(M + M^*)[M + M^*]$$
$$\text{subject to:} \quad T(M) + T^*(M^*) = \text{some specified value}$$

Here T and T^* denote the home and foreign production-possibility frontiers between apple and bearing resources. It is immediately clear that $B + B^*$ will be maximized by maximizing $M + M^*$. That is, efficient patterns of world activity in apples and bearings correspond to efficient patterns in apple and bearing resources, ignoring the scale economies.

Productive efficiency is as in the constant-returns model, and firms behave competitively because the economies are external to them. The result is that the complex tendencies associated with Graham equilibria when scale economies are national disappear when they become international.[28]

The second major implication of international economies of scale is that they imply a theory of the intraindustry exchange of intermediate goods between relatively similar economies. The essential idea behind international returns is that a dispersed industry can realize the benefits of a large division of labor if intermediate goods can be shipped within the industry. Thus the more nearly equal in size M and M^* are, the greater the volume of intraindustry trade in bearing components.

The picture of intraindustry trade, and of its relation to interindustry trade, is very much like that of the previous subsection. With identical homothetic demands across countries, the pattern of interindustry trade and specialization is determined in the familiar Heckscher-Ohlin fashion. If apples are relatively labor intensive, the relatively labor-abundant country will export apples for bearings. This interindustry trade will comprise all trade if the endowment disparity causes the labor-abundant country to specialize completely in apples. Small endowment differences reduce the incentive for interindustry trade but cause the integrated bearing industry to be divided relatively evenly between countries, thereby inducing intraindustry trade. In the limiting case where the countries have identical capital-labor endowment ratios, they will both be self-sufficient in apples. But they can gain from trade by establishing a single, rationalized bearing industry; all trade will be intraindustry. It should be clear that the prototypical complementarity theorem holds in this context.[29]

The reformulation of external economies as international returns to scale has, in sum, had two accomplishments. First, the inconveniences of Graham equilibria have been swept away, firmly establishing the relevance of traditional trade theory for increasing returns to scale. (For example, the "grand old debates" now appear in a completely different light.) Second, it provides a basis for a theory of the intraindustry exchange of intermediate goods between similar economies.

International economies have not really eliminated the tendency for indeterminacy of the sort introduced by external economies. Instead it has been buried by reformulating the model to focus on the allocation of resources rather than on individual firms. If "the division of labor is limited by the extent of the market," there must be indivisibilities of some sort; otherwise the division of labor could be made indefinitely fine for any market size by making each activity infinitesimal. This means that there must be scale economies of some sort *within* the bearing industry, so that there could well be a good deal of lurking indeterminacy about the allocation of the stages of bearing production and therefore about the details of intraindustry trade.[30] The point of view behind the present model is that these micro details are of secondary importance and are, therefore, not modeled explicitly.

They could, of course, be made explicit in various ways.[31] Indivisibilites associated with individual stages of production suggest scale economies internal to the firm. This in turn motivates us to think about the relation between internal and external (and national and international) economies, as well as about market structures other than perfect competition. Such considerations lead us to the second, independent, route of development of theories of intraindustry trade.

Product Differentiation

Several general-equilibrium theories of monopolistic competition were developed during the seventies.[32] It was natural to apply these theories to intraindustry trade, and that application constituted the second independent approach.[33]

To fix ideas, consider a model of the sort discussed in the preceding two subsections. Capital and labor combine to produce apples (A) and M, with the latter transformed into bearings. There are now no scale economies for the bearing industry overall (so $k = k^* = 1$); but, as in intraindustry trade, that industry is now disaggregated into an endogenously determined number, n, of subindustries, producing different varieties of finished bearings. Each subindustry operates under increasing returns to scale. But—this is the distinction made earlier and the source of the added complications to come—the scale economies are now internalized by individual firms. The bearing industry is modelled as one of monopolistic competition, with each variety produced by a single firm operating under increasing returns to scale. The firm acts as a minimonopolist, maximizing its profit by equating marginal cost to marginal revenue, given the prices charged by its many fellow bearing producers. Profits are driven to zero by the entry and exit of new firms (with new varieties), that is, by adjustment of n.

The substantial number of papers on product differentiation can be classified according to how they model the taste for variety. In all cases, greater variety increases social welfare in some sense; so it is best to have a given number of bearings divided into as many varieties as possible. (The countervailing influence is, of course, the increasing returns to scale in the production of individual varieties: a given amount of M can produce more bearings the fewer the number of bearing varieties there are.) One group of papers considers *vertical* product differentiation, in which the varieties of bearings can be ranked so that, if all varieties were priced equally, all consumers would choose to purchase only the first variety. That is, some measure of quality is the basis for product differentiation. With lower-quality bearings selling for less than higher-quality ones, consumers with different incomes can more easily accommodate themselves. Models with vertical product differentiation have generally dealt with cases in which the number of varieties is small, and so have not typically considered monopolistic competition. For this reason I shall not discuss them further.[34]

In the second group of papers, all consumers are identical and each buys all varieties of a *horizontally* differentiated good.[35] If two bundles contain the same number of apples and bearings, the consumer always prefers the bundle with a greater number of bearing varieties. (Since it is almost always assumed that all varieties have the same technology and are regarded symmetrically by consumers, they all sell for the same price and are consumed in the same amount in equilibrium.) The utility function described in the discussion of intraindustry trade is a typical example. Some economists regard the assumption that all people consume all varieties as unacceptably unrealistic and prefer instead to regard the utility function reflecting these preferences as a social-welfare function expressing the idea that society is, somehow, better off with more variety.

The final class of contributions supposes that each consumer buys only one variety, but that different consumers have different tastes.[36] Thus, if more varieties are made available, more consumers can each purchase a type of bearing closer to his most-preferred variety. This assumption is usually described as one of horizontal product differentiation with each individual consuming a single variety, but it could just as well be referred to as vertical differentiation with each individual having a different ranking. So let's call it *individualized* product differentiation.

It should be apparent, after a little thought, that the model of this section, with either of the latter two assumptions about preferences, generates the same picture of intraindustry trade that emerged in the previous subsection. That is, comparative advantage determines the interindustry exchange of apples for bearings, similarities between countries induces the intraindustry exchange of bearing varieties, and the complementarity theorem holds. But for some purposes the precise nature of preferences does matter. The general impression is that individualized product differentiation is more realistic than horizontal differentiation, but more cumbersome to use. The latter generates demand curves for individual varieties with constant price elasticity, whereas the demands generated by the former type of preferences have variable elasticity. With constant elasticity, an expansion of the bearing sector increases the number of varieties, with the output of each variety remaining constant, as we have seen. But with individualized preferences, an increase in bearing production increases both the number of varieties and the scale of production of each variety (so that its average cost falls), thereby introducing an additional effect.[37]

Nevertheless, the dominant impression is that the details of preferences really do not matter for the important aspects. Even more striking, in view of the radical difference in starting points, is the fact that international returns to scale and product differentiation generate essentially the same theory of intraindustry trade even though one applies to producer goods and one to consumer goods. A formal model of either can be reinterpreted as a formal model of the other (see Ethier 1982c). It is worth pointing out, however, that if the preference structures described in this subsection are reinterpreted as descriptions of a technology transforming a collection of differentiated intermediate goods into a single final output, horizontal product differentiation seems more "realistic" than individualized differentiation, just the reverse of the common belief. And trade in producer goods is more prominent in fact than is trade in consumer goods.[38]

Thus far we have encountered various combinations of internal and external economies and of national and international economies. Perhaps the most notable case not yet addressed is that of international returns to scale that are nevertheless internal to the firm. This would introduce the multinational firm; but we are not yet ready for that. So let me postpone for a while introduction of internal international returns to scale.

The Reaction: International Oligopoly

The discussion of scale economies in the previous section brought us to a consideration of imperfect competition. It is natural to continue in this direction and to consider even more imperfect market structures than monopolistic competition. In this section I suppose that the number of firms in an industry is small, so that each firm is aware that others may respond to its own actions, and fixed (or at least less than completely contestable), so that profits need not be bid down to zero.

This general area of industrial organization has been perhaps the most active branch of economic theory for some years now. The spillover into international trade theory has thus far been quite limited in terms of content, but important in terms of spirit and perspective.

By its very nature, oligopoly theory is treacherous as regards long-term significance. The ad hoc is the all hoc. But it can identify general problems even if it can not give a general analysis.

Oligopoly as a Basis for Trade

Consider the same production model as above (in each country capital and labor produce apples and several varieties of bearings), except that the number, n, of bearing producers is small and fixed, and all varieties of bearings are regarded by consumers as perfect substitutes. There may be increasing returns in bearing production, but they are internalized by firms.

Suppose that the home and foreign economies are identical, and that initially they do not trade and have identical autarky equilibria. Then there is no comparative-advantage basis for trade, and both product differentiation and international returns to scale have also been assumed away. Scale economies are a reason to trade, and there will in general be free-trade equilibria in which some bearing producers close down. But we are not interested in this, so confine attention to cases where the number of active bearing producers remains at n in each country.

In spite of all this, the removal of trade barriers will not be without its effects.[39] Each bearing producer will experience an increase in the number of its competitors from $n - 1$ to $2n - 1$. Exactly what effects this will have will depend, as is so often the case with oligopoly theory, on what the firms' strategy variables are and on what equilibrium concept is used to analyze the situation.

Suppose equilibrium is Cournot-Nash, and that each firm decides how many bearings to supply to the single world bearing market.[40] It should not be surprising that, under fairly reasonable conditions, the price of bearings will be lower and the supply greater without trade barriers than with them, because of the greater competition faced by each firm in the former case. Thus oligopoly provides an independent basis for trade. Indeed, no actual trade need take place! In the symmetric equilibrium of the present model, for example, both countries remain self-sufficient in both goods.[41] The two countries in effect trade competition rather than goods.

It is easy now to illustrate how sensitive the analysis is to arbitrary behavioral assumptions. Suppose that the strategy variable of each firm is not the number of bearings to supply to the world market but rather the number of bearings to sell in each country. (Suppose also that there is no second-hand market in bearings, so that firms sell directly only to consumers.) Equilibrium will clearly be as before, except that each firm will sell half its output in each market.[42] There will thus be two-way trade in identical products, that is, intraindustry trade that cannot be made statistically to disappear by defining an industry narrowly enough.

This seems quite innocuous, if a bit odd; but suppose now that we alter the model by introducing a modest transport cost of shipping bearings between national markets. Continue to assume that the countries are identical and that firms' strategies consist of the number of bearings to sell in each market. Foreign firms will now be at a disadvantage, relative to domestic ones, in each market; since their goods bear the transport cost. Under reasonable assumptions the equilibrium will be one in which each firm sells part, but less than half, of its output in the other country. Each firm will charge a lower export price (by the amount of the per-unit transportation cost) than domestic price.[43]

Thus there will still be two-way trade; but now it is costly, since resources are used up in shipping bearings both ways. Trade is now a two-edged sword, with the wasteful transportation expenses the price paid for the better allocative efficiency that comes from the increased competition. Of course, it would be even better to have the competition without the transportation. This is what happens if the strategy variable is total supply rather than supply to each market.[44]

Oligopoly Profits

The bearing producers need not earn zero profits in equilibrium. This distinguishes oligopoly from the market structures we dealt with earlier. These profits are part of national income and therefore must be considered in an analysis of the welfare implications of trade or of trade policy.[45]

It will prove convenient to alter our model slightly to isolate the profit aspect. To do this, suppose that the home and foreign countries do not trade at all with each other but rather with a third country which itself produces only apples, and that only apples are consumed in the home and foreign countries. This makes bearings pure exports in both countries, and therefore frees us from the need of considering the effect of a distorted bearing market on home and foreign consumers. An increase in the profits of a country's bearing producers thus constitutes an increase in national income.

Suppose initially that $n = n^* = 1$, so that the home and foreign firms constitute a duopoly in the third country. In figure 1–4, X denotes the number of bearings supplied by the home firm and Y the number supplied by the foreign firm. The parabolic-type curves are isoprofit contours for the home firm: for given X, increases in Y reduce home profit; if Y is held fixed, increases in X will first raise and then lower home profit. The line marked R is the home firm's Cournot-Nash equilibrium curve (or reaction function); it shows for each value of Y that value of X consistent with the home firm being in Cournot-Nash equilibrium, that is, the value of X that maximizes home profit. Thus R is the locus of maximum points of home isoprofit contours. Analogously, R^* is the foreign Cournot-Nash equilibrium line. (Foreign isoprofit contours are not shown.) Under not-unreasonable assumptions the two lines will look as shown in the figure.

The intersection N gives Cournot-Nash equilibrium. S shows the point on the foreign equilibrium line where home profit is maximized. This would be a Stackelberg equilibrium with the home firm as leader and the foreign firm as follower. But the home firm cannot achieve S if the two firms are treated symmetrically. For, suppose the home firm attempts to

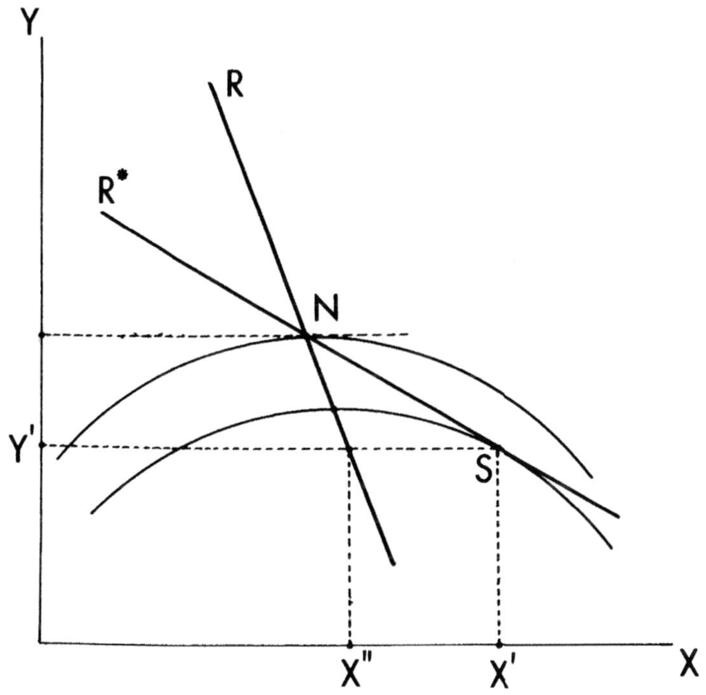

Figure 1–4. Cournot-Nash Equilibrium

get there by announcing that it will supply X' no matter what. If this announcement were to be believed, the best the foreign firm could do would be to supply Y', thereby achieving S. But the announcement would not be believed. The foreign firm is aware that if it did supply Y', the home firm would wish to supply X'' and would have no reason not to do so. Thus the announcement of X' is not credible. The only pair of credible announcements are, of course, those corresponding to N.

The home government enters the analysis at this point. The government can tax (or subsidize) bearing exports—equivalent to a production tax, since all bearings are exported. The government wishes to maximize national income. Because of the special assumptions made, this is equivalent to maximizing the profits of the home bearing firm. Of course, this is just what that firm wants to do; so there is a role for government action only if the government has some power the firm does not.

The power that has been discussed in this context is that of credible commitment. The government can announce a tax rate on home bearing exports, and both firms believe that that rate will in fact be implemented.

A per-unit export tax in effect shifts the home firm's marginal-cost curve up by that amount. The marginal-revenue curve corresponding to any given volume of Y is not affected; so the level of X that maximizes home profit given Y will fall. That is, an export tax shifts the firm's isoprofit curves to the left, and an export subsidy shifts them to the right. (Of course, the *national* isoprofit lines, about which the government cares, do not shift.) This implies that a tax shifts the equilibrium curve R to the left, and a subsidy shifts it to the right.

It is now evident what government policy should be. The government should *subsidize* exports just enough so that R passes through point S, which then becomes the Cournot-Nash equilibrium. The subsidy, in effect, makes credible a home-firm threat to sell X' no matter what. Both firms realize that, if the foreign firm makes its best response of Y', the home firm will find it in its own interest actually to supply X', because of the subsidy. The analysis gives us a possible explanation why trade policy might take the form of trade promotion rather than trade restriction.[46]

There are really three important ideas here, sensitive in varying degree to the special assumptions that have been made. The first is simply that oligopoly profit constitutes a new element of national income and thus a new concern of trade policy. This point is clearly quite general.

The second is that, with oligopoly, a new potential for trade policy comes from the fact that the government can make credible promises which individuals cannot. This is more problematic. In the present model, the assumption that the government can credibly commit itself to a tax rate but that a firm cannot credibly commit itself to any export level is completely arbitrary. Both firms know that, should the government announce the subsidy rate that, in figure 1–4, shifts R through S, and should the foreign firm sell the quantity Y', it would not be in the government's interest actually to pay the subsidy. Note that the assumption that such a promise is nevertheless credible runs counter to recent developments in macroeconomics, which increasingly stress the role of credibility constraints on the government. But the general notion that the domain of credibility of the government might be different from that of private agents is a valuable insight, even if we must become arbitrary in order to utilize it.

The final important idea is that oligopoly might well render it in the national interest to subsidize trade rather than restrict it. This conclusion, however, is quite fragile.[47] One reason, of course, is that it depends upon the arbitrary credibility assumption just discussed. But there are other reasons as well. For example, the conclusion that a subsidy is optimal depends on the assumption that there is just one home bearing firm. In this case, we want the home firm to become more competitive with its foreign rival and expand its share of the market and so its share of bearing profits. But if there are two or more home firms, they compete against each other as well as against the foreign firm. We would like to *restrict* this competition, to improve the terms of trade. If n becomes large enough, the bearing industry will become competitive and the familiar optimum-tariff argument will imply an export tax. Thus we would expect that, as n rises above one, the optimal export subsidy falls and then becomes a tax.

Another reason is that the conclusion is sensitive to the equilibrium concept employed. For example, suppose we replace the Cournot-Nash assumption with the requirement that, in equilibrium, each firm sells the amount that maximizes its own profit, given the *price* charged by the other firm.[48] The line labelled P^* in figure 1–5 shows combinations of X and Y resulting in a particular price for foreign bearings. Given this price, the best the home firm can do is determined by the point of tangency between P^* and a home isoprofit curve. The locus of all such tangency points, for different values of the foreign price, is the home equilibrium curve, depicted by E in the figure. E^* is the analogous foreign equilibrium curve. Not-unreasonable assumptions imply that the relations between the P^*, E, and E^* curves are as shown in the figure.[49]

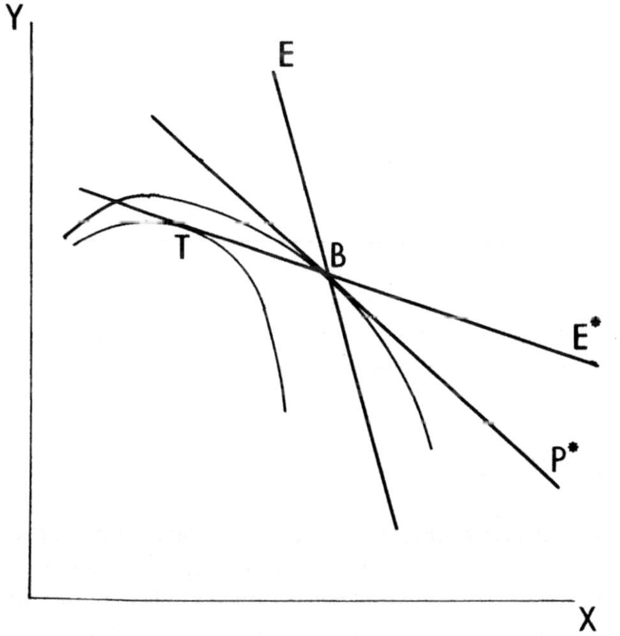

Figure 1–5. Bertrand-Nash Equilibrium

Equilibrium is at point B. Point T, on the other hand, maximizes the home firm's profit (and home national income), given that the foreign firm is in equilibrium. Since T must now lie to the left of B along the foreign equilibrium curve, an argument similar to the earlier Cournot-Nash one now implies that the optimal policy is an export *tax*. Evidently, the conclusion that trade should be subsidized rather than taxed is very sensitive to the equilibrium concept.[50]

The Reaction: Direct Investment

Now that we have begun to analyze international trade with oligopolistic firms, it is natural to relax the assumption that the firm produces in just one country. That is, we turn next to the multinational firm. This is doubly appropriate in view of the failure of traditional trade theory to explain direct investment.

Although traditional general-equilibrium trade theory has indeed had little to say about the multinational firm, a huge, less formal, theoretical literature on the subject has existed for a long time. (The situation has been much like that in the literature on intraindustry trade, but even more so.)

This literature is concerned in part with why multinational firms should exist at all in the face of presumed costs of operating across national frontiers.[51] The theory has three components. First, the firm should possess an *ownership* advantage, such as a patent or some managerial or organizational ability, that it wishes to exploit in several national markets. Second, *locational* considerations should be such that the firm does not find it attractive to concentrate all operations in one country and export to others. Finally, the *internalization* of international transactions must be preferable to the arm's-length use of markets. The firm, for example, should find it advantageous to conduct foreign manufacturing itself rather than to license a foreign firm to do it.

Multinational Oligopoly

To see how our theory might try to deal with such considerations, consider the following model.[52] I assume, as in the earlier discussion of oligopoly profits, that two identical countries produce apples and bearings, that each exports bearings to a third country for apples, that there are but two bearing-producing firms (one in each exporting country), and that the third country produces only apples. But now elaborate the story as follows. Apples are produced by labor and land, whereas bearings are produced by labor and capital. The capital stock in each bearing-producing country is owned by its bearing firm, and the third country has no capital. The third country is relatively labor abundant in the sense that, in the trading equilibrium, its wage is lower than wages in the home and foreign countries.

It should be clear that if trade takes place, and no international factor mobility is allowed, the discussion of oligopoly profits applies completely. If capital were to become internationally mobile, each bearing producer would move at least some of its capital stock to the third country and produce bearings there, displacing exports. If costs are equalized before the entire capital stock has been moved, the two bearing producers will each produce in two countries: they will have become multinational firms.

This is, of course, just the standard factor-endowments story of factor movements substituting for commodity trade.[53] It is interesting, and useful, to see that it can be used in a straightforward way to explain direct investment. But there are two important reasons not to stop here. First, this theory does not incorporate some of the features described above as of concern to the literature on the multinational, and it does not distinguish between direct investment and real factor movements.[54] Second, it does not address the prominent phenomena discussed under *Confrontation with Reality*: the preponderant share of direct investment, much of it two-way, between countries with relatively similar endowments.

So take a different tack. Distinguish real factor movements from direct investment by assuming that all factors, including capital, are internationally immobile, but that bearing firms can operate in either country. Interpret capital not as physical capital, but as the input to an intermediate activity, such as research or management, that can be conducted at a distance from the productive units that utilize it. That is, assume that each firm can produce bearings by combining its capital with labor located in any country. Some examples of such activities, such as research, have at least a partial public-good aspect. It's natural to try to capture this by supposing that bearing production entails increasing returns to scale. Thus I now consider international economies of scale that are internal to the firm.

Suppose now that we allow home and foreign bearing producers to transact with the third country (and no one else). With wages lowest in the third country, each bearing producer will establish production there and become multinational. To simplify the exposition, suppose that third-country wages are never driven up to the level in the home and foreign countries. Then each bearing firm is a multinational employing capital in the source country and labor in the host country. Trade in bearings ceases, with the home and foreign countries importing apples as payment for their repatriated profits. Clearly, direct investment has substituted for trade in the same way that real capital movements did in the previous example.

Note also that the discussion of trade policy in *Oligopoly Profits* holds here exactly. That is, an increase in the profits of the home-based multinational will raise home national income. If the government can precommit itself while the firm cannot, there is scope for a direct-investment policy; and if equilibrium is Cournot-Nash, the optimal policy will call for a subsidy on direct investment abroad. Of course, all of the qualifications discussed under *Oligopoly Profits* apply here as well. But even so, the analysis gives a valuable new perspective on policy toward foreign direct investment.

Now drop the third country and suppose that the home and foreign economies consume both goods and deal directly with each other. (This will complicate the welfare implications, but we are through with them.) Suppose, as before, that equilibrium is Cournot-Nash and that each country determines strategy variables for each market, rather than for the world as a whole. Then each bearing firm will supply half of each market, as we saw above. There will be two-way trade in identical products and no reason to undertake direct investment.

Next, add a transportation cost for bearings, as we did in *Oligopoly as a Basis for Trade*. Now there is an incentive to go multinational. Each firm will continue to supply one half of each market, but it will do so by means of local production and the exchange of bearings will cease.[55] We at last have an example of two-way direct investment between similar economies. This cross-penetration is not pointless: it allows the countries to experience the benefits of increased competition without incurring the costs of shipping bearings back and forth.

This is another case of direct investment substituting for trade. We obtained two-way direct investment simply because the initial trade model featured two-way trade.

Multinational Monopolistic Competition

Our multinationals have thus far been oligopolists. This has had the effect of making the consequences of direct investment depend upon the choice of arbitrary assumptions used to analyze what trade would be like without direct investment. It is tempting, therefore, to try to purge our analysis of this by examining alternative market structures. The natural candidate is monopolistic competition, since it gives the individual firm a role to play.[56]

So let us tamper with our model once more. The bearing sector in each country is again composed of an endogenous number (*n* and n^*, respectively) of firms producing differentiated products. Each firm employs capital at home together with labor, in either country, to produce its unique variety, subject to increasing returns to scale. Consumers have a preference for variety that allows the existence of many bearing firms in equilibrium.

Suppose that the two countries are identical, and open them up to trade and direct investment with each other. With identical endowments and homothetic preferences, there is no basis for the interindustry exchange of apples and bearings, and factor price equalization ensures that there is no motive for direct investment. As in the section on *Product Differentiation*, international exchange will consist of the intraindustry trade of bearing varieties.

Now let endowments differ slightly, with the home country the relatively capital-abundant one. Then the home country will export the capital-intensive commodity, bearings, for apples; with world bearing production somewhat more concentrated at home, there are fewer varieties to import. Thus interindustry trade displaces intraindustry trade, as before. As modest endowment differences still allow trade to produce factor-price equalization, direct investment still does not take place.

Larger endowment differences would prevent trade from itself establishing factor-price equalization. Foreign wages would tend to fall below home wages, and at least one country would tend to specialize. The lower foreign wage would induce home bearing producers to hire foreign labor and thereby become multinational firms. Foreign bearing producers remain national, if some foreign capital remains in the bearing sector. If home firms employ labor in both countries, wages must be equal; the direct investment will have prevented factor-price disparities from emerging. But if the endowment difference is sufficiently pronounced, home bearing producers will employ only capital at home and factor prices will diverge.

Thus endowment differences generate direct investment, which cannot occur in cases where trade alone would equalize factor prices. The formation of multinationals is associated, in this model, with a decline in intraindustry trade relative to interindustry trade. Two-way direct investment can never take place, but the introduction of barriers to intraindustry trade could induce it, just as in the preceding section. In this model, direct investment is in effect a proxy for real international capital mobility.

Internalization

In the models discussed thus far, direct investment has basically functioned the way real capital movements would. This has given us a rich variety of behavior, although it has been basically due to the rich variety of trade models, without direct investment, into which we could introduce the multinational firm. But despite their richness, these multiplant scale-economy models of the multinational firm are unsatisfying in two ways.

First, they do not address the phenomenon of the larger part of direct investment, much of it two-way, taking place between similar economies. We did come upon such behavior earlier, but only because we started with a trade model featuring the mutual exchange of identical goods. It is as though such a model were our only tool for studying intraindustry trade between similar economies. The multiplant economy approach has left us in a position analogous to that we were in when we found that the addition of national external scale economies had not helped us understand intra-industry trade (and had actually moved us in the other direction).

The second point is conceptual. The dominant paradigm of direct investment views it as determined by a coincidence of ownership, locational, and internalization considerations. The above models were concerned in detail with the first two of these, but they simply took it for granted that internalization was advantageous. This is arbitrary, because there is no reason in principle why the activities considered above as those of a multinational firm could not instead be performed on a contractural basis between independent national firms. Ownership and locational considerations have always been basic to trade and imperfect competition without direct investment; the internalization issue is the new element introduced by consideration of the multinational firm. Of course, it is worthwhile to study new and interesting combinations of old considerations, as we have done; but it is with internalization that the conceptual value-added of studying direct investment lies.

So let us consider the internalization question.[57] The issue of whether a transaction should be internalized is basically a matter of the exchange of information between agents, and the latter becomes substantive only when some agents face uncertainty. Start with the product-differentiation model just discussed. Suppose, though, that finished bearings are nontraded in the sense that the labor employed to produce them must reside in the country where they are consumed. This means that each variety of bearing will involve labor in both countries. This assumes away locational considerations and allows us to focus on the internalization question of whether the labor used in the two countries will be employed by a single firm or by two firms. To introduce uncertainty and complete our description of the bearing industry, suppose that each variety involves an upstream activity, which uses only capital and so is located in the source country, and a downstream activity, which uses only labor and so must locate in both countries. The upstream activity involves undertaking research and, after the results of the research are known, producing the sensitive innards of the bearings. These parts are then shipped to the downstream firms, which use labor to produce finished bearings for consumers. The cost of the innards produced upstream might be either high or low, and is unknown until the outcome of the research project. The more research that is done, the greater the chance that the cost will turn out to be low. The upstream firm must commit itself to research, and the downstream firms to labor, before the outcome of the research project is known. The choice of whether to produce innards can be made ex post.

The basic problem is to distinguish those cases in which the upstream and downstream units can, without cost, deal with each other at arm's length from the cases in which they cannot, and therefore must internalize their transactions and become a single firm. Presumably there is some ex ante contract—calling for the upstream firm to conduct a certain amount of research and to produce a certain quantity of innards for each possible outcome of the research project, and calling for the downstream firms to employ certain quantities of labor and to make certain payments to the upstream firm—that will maximize joint profit.

There are various possible assumptions that might be made about when such an optimal contract can be implemented at arm's length. For example, the upstream firm might be unwilling to let independent downstream firms observe its research effort or the outcome of that effort: this is, after all, the source of its ownership advantage. This could then give rise to an incentive-compatibility problem; and we could require that any arm's-length contract be incentive compatible, whereas an integrated firm would not be subject to such a constraint. This constraint would not, in fact, be binding if the independent firms were risk neutral and if it were feasible to write contracts covering all conceivable states. Otherwise, there would be circumstances under which the constraint would bind, and when we would therefore expect multinational firms to emerge.

Another possibility would be to require that a contract must be "simple" in order to be implementable. For example, in industries where research is important or where tastes and techniques are subject to significant change, the number of conceivable states of nature might be so vast that any conceivable contract would necessarily be incomplete or insensitive to some contingencies. It is relatively simple to pursue this in the present framework; so let us do so. Since there are only two possible states, we can call a contract that calls for behavior to differ across states "complex" and one that does not "simple." That is, the upstream and downstream firms are constrained to implement a state-invariant contract if they remain at arm's length, but can free themselves of the constraint by integrating.

When will the constraint be binding, that is, when will the optimal contract vary across states? Production of each variety entails fixed costs (research and employment) that must be met whether any innards are actually produced or not, and variable cost (innard production) that can be avoided by not producing. Bearings are capital intensive; so we would expect, other things equal, that if rents are sufficiently low, the optimal contract will call for innards to be produced in both possible outcomes. (If rents are low enough, variable costs can be covered in either case.) But if rents are high, it is likely that the contract would call for production to occur with a favorable outcome, producing a positive profit, but not with an unfavorable outcome. Thus we would expect the optimal contract to be simple when rents, in the source country, are low and to be complex when they are high.

But bearings are capital intensive, and the relatively capital-abundant country will be operating (upstream) bearing firms. Thus we would expect rents in the source country to be relatively high when endowment differences are modest and relatively low when they are great. That is, direct investment will be induced by *similarities* in endowments rather than by differences, as in the previous subsections.[58] Sufficient endowment similarity could induce two-way direct investment.

Internalization, when modeled in this general way, produces results quite different from those of multiplant-economies models of direct investment that abstract from internalization. They also come to grips with the phenomenon of two-way direct investment between similar economies. It remains to be seen, however, what happens when internalization is modeled differently.

Concluding Remarks

The response of trade theory to the extensive contradictions between apparent theory and apparent fact has transformed the subject during the last fifteen years. Each of the contradictions has had its response, but with varying success. Specific-factor models have demonstrated their usefulness. The higher-dimensional literature has given traditional trade theory a robustness that few would have expected to find a dozen years ago. And the international-economies, product-differentiation development has both altered the fundamental perspective of our theory and added to our tool kit of basic models. But the oligopoly literature, though contributing important original insights, now seems to be developing via a succession of virtuoso exercises the long-term significance of which remains in doubt. This, of course, is an honest reflection of the nature of the phenomena being studied. As regards the multinational firm, it is still too early to say. The "easy" application of existing models to direct investment has been done. Now it is time to investigate the complex of issues associated with "internalization," and to commence a welfare and policy analysis.

This chapter has necessarily had to ignore many important topics in trade theory. Some were excluded because they were straightforward extensions of traditional theory and seem to have run their creative courses, even though they have given us valuable insights. Examples are effective protection and the theory of trade policy with domestic distortions. Note that scale economies and imperfect competition could have made their appearance as special cases of the latter, but in fact their contributions came from the use of a quite different perspective.

Two omitted areas deserve special mention because they are large, important, and currently vigorous. The first is that of real international factor mobility. Capital movements, labor migration, and the relation between the two are being investigated with the tools of traditional trade theory, a testimonial to the latter's continued power and usefulness. Migration—a vital topic that has not yet received the attention it deserves—is also bringing new concepts into the field: the economics of crime, contract theory, informational asymmetries, and so on.

The second omitted topic is, in contrast, very much in the spirit of the present chapter: endogenous theories of protection. Actual policies appear not to coincide with what theory suggests national welfare demands. Oligopoly theory has responded to this by constructing models in which the optimal national policy differs from those of traditional theory. Another active approach is to attempt to explain actual policies directly. These explanations have involved "rent-seeking" models, in which real resources are devoted to obtaining protection, applications of formal models of the political process, and attempts to reveal empirically the determinants of tariffs. This formidable area of inquiry has not yet really "scored," but its vigor and importance promise interesting results to come.

A final important literature has been left out simply because it does not yet exist. This is the analysis of protection as a set of explicit and implicit rules for responding to change (the "new protectionism"), rather than as a set of barriers in place. This is something else to which we have to look forward.

Notes

1. One testimonial to the renewed vigor of the theory of international trade is the appearance, after a long hiatus, of surveys of the subject, or of its more dynamic aspects. See Deardorff (1985), Dixit (1985), Grossman and Richardson (1985), Kierzkowski (1985), Krugman (1985), Venables (1985) and, of course, the very valuable *Handbook* edited by Jones and Kenen (1984).

2. In particular, production functions are identical across countries and have constant returns to scale, and tastes are identical across countries and homothetic.

3. Inevitably, that is, if different groups do not draw incomes from the respective factors in about equal proportions, and if there is no other policy intended to counter the distributional effect of trade policy.

4. One might rightfully object that propositions 10 and 11 cannot be required to apply to direct investment, since the latter need not correspond to a movement of real capital. But this is just another way of phrasing the point: conventional trade theory does not appear to be able to explain reality.

5. There are also theories that claim to be radical but which in fact are not. Much of the Neo-Ricardian literature is of this sort. See Ethier (1979b) and the exchange between Metcalfe and Steedman (1981) and Ethier (1981).

6. For example, this will be the competitive solution if both factors are freely mobile among firms in the apple industry, even if completely immobile between industries.

7. The major contributions include Jones (1971), Samuelson (1971), Mayer (1974), Mussa (1974), and Neary (1978). The model has now become standard fare in undergraduate textbooks; see, for example, Caves and Jones (1985, ch. 6) and Ethier (1983, ch. 6).

8. This is an unfortunate name, since the presence of a mobile factor is as important as that of the specific one.

9. Samuelson (1971) refers to the model as the *Ricardo-Viner* model. The concept of noncompeting groups is identified with Cairnes (1874). Especially clear expositions of the model can be found in Pigou (1906) and Haberler (1936).

10. Such a free-trade equilibrium would necessarily be characterized by factor-price equalization.

11. For a good appreciation of these conclusions, see Leamer (1984).

12. See Ethier (1974), Jones and Scheinkman (1977), and Jones (1977). A detailed survey is Jones and Kenen (1984, ch. 3).

13. Even this extreme case can be eliminated if we assume that good one also uses factor two in its production. For then the absolute fall in the reward of the latter factor requires that some factor reward rise proportionally *more* than the price of good one, if the unit cost of the latter is not to exceed its price.

14. The present results are are also sometimes said to be weaker than the earlier results in that they do not predict *which* good is a friend and which is an enemy of each factor. But this distinction is spurious, since in either case the entire technology must be "solved" to determine this.

15. Of course, all this presumes that the basis of trade is in fact differences in international factor endowments. In particular, the technology must be freely available to all countries.

16. For more about "on average" results, see Deardorff (1980, 1982), Dixit and Norman (1980), and Ethier (1982b).

17. It is really remarkable, to me, how robust the 2×2 factor-endowments story has turned out to be. That part of the basic propositions that is independent of dimension has also been shown to survive, to a great extent, other relaxations of the basic Heckscher-Ohlin-

Samuelson model. See Ethier (1982b). For a consideration of joint production, see Chang, Ethier, and Kemp (1980); for intermediate goods and time-phased production, see Ethier (1979b); for factor mobility, see Ethier and Svensson (1986).

18. This logic is the basis of the numerical examples presented in Chipman (1985) and Rodgers (1985), good examples of the "conservative" response.

19. Although the traditional theory of international trade had little to say about intra-industry trade before the late seventies, a less formal but vigorous literature did exist. See Balassa (1961, 1967), Grubel and Lloyd (1975), and Gray (1976).

20. See Melvin (1969) for an early development of this point along contemporary lines.

21. The distinction between these two bases for trade was made by Cairnes (1874).

22. See Krugman (1985) for a perceptive overview, from which the present treatment of economies of scale has profited considerably.

23. In recent years, though, investigation of other market structures has been one of the most active topics in trade theory, and it will concern much of the rest of this chapter. The indispensable reference for this recent work is Helpman and Krugman (1985).

24. See Matthews (1950) and Ethier (1982a).

25. Of course, circumstances might allow multiple equilibria even when the technology exhibits constant returns to scale, and they might imply a unique equilibrium even with increasing returns. The point is only that the latter, by themselves, render multiple equilibria "more likely."

26. It does not matter whether a firm is active in all subindustries or just one or a few, but it is critical that, within each subindustry, the firm takes k as parametric.

27. See Ethier (1979a, 1982c) and Helpman (1984a).

28. Of course, scale economies increase the tendency for multiple equilibria even in a closed economy, and this should be no different in an open economy with international returns. But the added indeterminacy of the roles played by respective countries is not present in the latter case. See Helpman (1984a).

29. Indeed, this is the context in which the complementarity theorem was originally developed. See Ethier (1979a, p. 19). Markusen (1983) makes the general argument that trade and factor mobility can be expected to be complementary when the basis for trade is something other than factor-endowment differences. See also Svensson (1984) and Ethier and Svensson (1986).

30. Note, however, that these remarks apply equally well to the traditional models of national external economies discussed earlier.

31. Alternatives are discussed in Ethier (1979a), and Ethier (1982c) performs the exercise of modelling one of the suggestions in detail.

32. See Spence (1976), Dixit and Stiglitz (1977), Lancaster (1979) and, more recently, Hart (1985).

33. The early contributions—independent of each other as well as of the international scale-economies development—were Dixit and Norman (1980), Krugman (1979), and Lancaster (1980). See also Helpman (1981), Krugman (1981), and Helpman and Krugman (1985). There have been a large number of subsequent papers on the subject.

34. See Shaked and Sutton (1983, 1984). For an application to monopolistic competition, see Falvey and Kierzkowski (1984).

35. See Dixit and Norman (1980, ch. 9) and Krugman (1979, 1981).

36. See Lancaster (1980) and Helpman (1981).

37. I should point out, simply because it is seldom done, that the difference in behavior in the two types of models is *not* really a reflection of the implications of whether each individual consumes all varieties or just one. Rather, it is due to the special functional forms that are in practice used to illustrate the two types of preferences.

38. This has been known for many years. Related empirical studies are found in Marvel and Ray (1986) and Ray (1986).

39. For more on the subject of this subsection, see Brander (1981), Brander and Krugman (1983), and Helpman and Krugman (1985, ch. 5).

40. For Cournot-Nash equilibrium, the strategy variable is quantity, and each firm's equilibrium quantity is optimal given the other firm's equilibrium quantity.

41. So perhaps we should speak of oligopoly as "a basis for the removal of trade barriers" rather than as a basis for trade.

42. Strictly speaking, this was a possible outcome before, since the point of sale of each firm's bearings was really indeterminate in the equilibrium described. Note also that in the present case it is not really necessary to assume away the reselling of bearings, since it is consistent with the Nash concept where each agent behaves optimally given the behavior of other agents, to describe the symmetric equilibrium obtained as one in which bearing arbitragers choose not to trade. But once the countries cease to be identical, arbitrage will matter.

43. Brander and Krugman (1983) refer to such a situation as "reciprocal dumping."

44. Total supply would have to be the variable if there were bearing arbitragers (or potential arbitragers) who could buy at the export price (either from the firms or from the firms' foreign customers before they took delivery) and sell at the domestic price instead of exporting.

45. This was the topic of a series of papers by Brander and Spencer (1984, 1985).

46. One could take the analysis the final step and allow both governments to conduct trade policy and then examine the conflict between them. I shall not consider this. See Cooper and Riezman (1986).

47. This is the basic theme of Eaton and Grossman (1986). See also Cooper and Riezman (1986).

48. This is equivalent to Bertrand-Nash equilibrium (price is the strategy variable) if home and foreign bearings are imperfect substitutes.

49. For example, if home and foreign bearings are perfect substitutes, P^* will have a slope of minus one. If also the two countries are identical, their equilibrium curves will be symmetric about the 45° line, and therefore they will both be steeper, or both flatter, than P^*. E and E^* may have positive or negative slopes, depending upon details of the cost and demand functions.

50. Eaton and Grossman (1986) also show that consistent conjectures about rivals' responses to a firm's change in strategy imply an optimal export tax of zero.

51. This approach derives from Coase (1937). See, for example: Hymer (1960), Kindleberger (1970), Caves (1971, 1974), Buckley and Casson (1976), Dunning (1977, 1981), Casson (1979), and Rugman (1980).

52. The basic reference for the multiplant economies model of the multinational firm, which I am about to discuss, is Markusen (1984). However, my discussion will use a somewhat different (and simpler) formal model and will address different points.

53. See Caves (1971) and Jones, Neary, and Ruane (1983).

54. The fact that the former need not coincide with the latter has been very important in practice. A related empirical investigation is Ruffin and Rassekh (1986).

55. This recalls Mundell (1957).

56. Product differentiation was introduced into the multiplant economies model of direct investment by Helpman (1984b). See also Helpman (1985) and Helpman and Krugman (1985, chs. 12, 13).

57. See Ethier (1986). Williamson (1975) contains a general discussion of relevant transactions-cost issues.

58. See Ethier (1986) for details.

References

Balassa, B. 1961. *The Theory of Economic Integration*. Homewood, Ill.: Irwin.

Balassa, B. 1967. *Trade Liberalization Among Industrial Countries*. New York: McGraw-Hill.

Brander, J. A. 1981. "Intra-Industry Trade in Identical Commodities." *Journal of International Economics* 11 (February), pp. 1–14.

Brander, J. A., and P. Krugman. 1983. "A 'Reciprocal Dumping' Model of International Trade." *Journal of International Economics* 15 (November), pp. 313–321.

Brander, J. A., and B. J. Spencer. 1984. "Tariff Protection and Imperfect Competition." In H. Kierzkowski, ed., *Monopolistic Competition in International Trade*, pp. 194–206. Oxford: Oxford University Press, 1984.

Brander, J. A., and B. J. Spencer. 1985. '"Export Subsidies and International Market Share Rivalry." *Journal of International Economics* 18 (February), pp. 83–100.

Buckely, P. J., and M. Casson. 1976. *The Future of the Multinational Enterprise*. London: Macmillan.

Cairnes, J. E. 1974. *Some Leading Principles of Political Economy*. London: Macmillan.

Casson, M. 1979. *Alternatives to the Multinational Enterprise*. London: Macmillan.

Caves, R. E. 1971. "International Corporations: The Industrial Economics of Foreign Investment." *Economica* 38 (February), pp. 1–27.

Caves, R. E. 1974. "Multinational Firms, Competition, and Productivity in Host-Country Markets." *Economica* 41 (May), pp. 176–193.

Caves, R. E. 1982. *Multinational Enterprise and Economic Analysis*. Cambridge: Cambridge University Press.

Caves, R. E., and R. W. Jones. 1985. *World Trade and Payments*. 4th ed. Boston: Little, Brown.

Chang, W. W., W. J. Ethier, and M. C. Kemp. 1980. "The Theorems of International Trade with Joint Production." *Journal of International Economics* 10 (August), pp. 377–394.

Chipman, J. 1985. "Intra-Industry Trade, Factor Proportions and Aggregation." Processed, 1985.

Coase, R. H. 1937. "The Nature of the Firm." *Economica* 4 (November), pp. 386–405.

Cooper, R., and R. Riezman. 1986. "Optimal Trade Policy with Oligopoly." Processed, 1986.

Deardorff, A. V. 1980. "The General Validity of the Law of Comparative Advantage." *Journal of Political Economy* 88 (October), pp. 941–957.

Deardorff, A. V. 1982. "The General Validity of the Heckscher-Ohlin Theorem." *American Economic Review* 72 (September), pp. 683–694.

Deardorff, A. V. 1985. "Major Recent Developments in International Trade Theory." In T. Peeters, P. Praet, and P. Reding, eds., *International Trade and Exchange Rates*, pp. 3–27. Amsterdam: North-Holland, 1985.

Dixit, A. K. 1985. "Strategic Trade Policy." Processed, 1985.

Dixit, A. K., and V. Norman. 1980. *Theory of International Trade*. Cambridge: Nisbet and Cambridge University Press.

Dixit, A. K., and J. E. Stiglitz. 1977. "Monopolistic Competition and Optimum Product Diversity." *American Economic Review* 67 (June), pp. 297–308.

Dunning, J. H. 1977. "Trade, Location of Economic Activity and the MNE: A Search for an Eclectic Approach." In B. Ohlin, P.-O. Hesselborn, and P. M. Wijkman, eds., *The International Allocation of Economic Activity*, pp. 395–418. London: Macmillan, 1977.

Dunning, J. H. 1981. "Explaining the International Direct Investment Position of Countries: Towards a Dynamic or Developmental Approach." *Weltwirtschaftliches Archiv* 117(1), pp. 30–64.

Eaton, J., and G. M. Grossman, 1986. "Optimal Trade and Industrial Policy under Oligopoly." *Quarterly Journal of Economics* 101 (May), pp. 383–406.

Ethier W. J. 1983. *Modern International Economics*. New York: Norton.

Ethier W. J. 1974. "Some of the Theorems of International Trade with Many Goods and Factors." *Journal of International Economics* 4 (May), pp. 199–206.

Ethier, W. J. 1979a. "Internationally Decreasing Costs and World Trade." *Journal of International Economics* 9 (February), pp. 1–24.

Ethier, W. J. 1979b. "The Theorems of International Trade in Time-Phased Economies." *Journal of International Economics* 9 (May), pp. 225–238.

Ethier, W. J. 1981. "A Reply to Professors Metcalfe and Steedman." *Journal of International Economics* 11 (May), pp. 273–277.

Ethier, W. J. 1982a. "Decreasing Costs in International Trade and Frank Graham's Argument for Protection." *Econometrica* 50 (September), pp. 243–268.

Ethier, W. J. 1982b. "The General Role of Factor Intensity in the Theorems of International Trade." *Economics Letters* 10, pp. 337–342.

Ethier, W. J. 1982c. "National and International Returns to Scale in the Modern Theory of International Trade." *American Economic Review* 72 (June), pp. 389–405.

Ethier, W. J. 1986. "The Multinational Firm." *Quarterly Journal of Economics* 101 (November), pp. 805–833.

Ethier, W. J., and L. E. O. Svensson. 1986. "The Theorems of International Trade with Factor Mobility." *Journal of International Economics* 20 (February), pp. 21–42.

Falvey, R., and H. Kierzkowski. 1984. "Product Quality, Intra-Industry Trade and (Im)perfect Competition." Processed, 1984.

Graham, F. A. 1923. "Some Aspects of Protection Further Considered." *Quarterly Journal of Economics* 37 (February), pp. 199–227.

Gray, H. P. 1976. *A Generalized Theory of International Trade*. New York: Holmes and Meier.

Grossman, G. M., and J. D. Richardson. 1985. *Strategic Trade Policy: A Survey of Issues and Early Analysis*. Special Papers in International Economics, No. 15, April 1985. Princeton, NJ: International Finance Section, Princeton University.

Grubel, H. G., and P. J. Lloyd. 1975. *Intra-Industry Trade: The Theory and Measurement of International Trade in Differentiated Products*. London: Macmillan.

Haberler, G. 1936. *The Theory of International Trade with its Applications to Commercial Policy*. London: William Hodge.

Hart, O. D. 1985. "Monopolistic Competition in the Spirit of Chamberlin: A General Model." *Review of Economic Studies* 52 (October), pp. 529–546.

Helpman, E. 1981. "International Trade in the Presence of Product Differentiation, Economies of Scale and Monopolistic Competition." *Journal of International Economics* 11 (August), pp. 305–340.

Helpman, E. 1984a. "Increasing Returns, Imperfect Markets, and Trade Theory." In R. W. Jones and P. B. Kenen, eds., *Handbook of International Economics*, vol. 1, pp. 325–365. Amsterdam: North Holland, 1984.

Helpman, E. 1984b. "A Simple Theory of International Trade with Multinational Corporations." *Journal of Political Economy* 92 (June), pp. 451–471.

Helpman, E. 1985. "Multinational Corporations and Trade Structure." *Review of Economic Studies* 52 (July), pp. 443–457.

Helpman, E., and P. R. Krugman. 1985. *Market Structure and Foreign Trade*. Cambridge: MIT Press.

Hymer, S. 1960. *The International Operations of National Firms*. Ph.D. dissertation, Massachusetts Institute of Technology.

Jones, R. W. 1971. "A Three-Factor Model in Theory, Trade, and History." In J. N. Bhagwati et al., eds., *Trade, Balance of Payments and Growth*, pp. 3–21. Amsterdam: North-Holland, 1971.

Jones, R. W. 1977. *"Two-ness" in Trade Theory: Costs and Benefits*. Special Papers in International Economics, No. 12, April 1977, Princeton, NJ: International Finance Section, Princeton University.

Jones, R. W., and P. B. Kenen, eds. 1984. *Handbook of International Economics*, vol. 1. Amsterdam: North-Holland.

Jones, R. W., J. P. Neary, and F. P. Ruane. 1983. "Two-Way Capital Flows: Cross Hauling in a Model of Foreign Investment." *Journal of International Economics* 14 (May), pp. 357–366.

Jones, R. W., and J. Scheinkman. 1977. "The Relevance of the Two-Sector Production Model in Trade Theory." *Journal of Political Economy* 85 (October), pp. 909–935.

Kierzkowski, H. 1985. "Models of International Trade in Differentiated Goods." In D. Greenaway, ed., *Current Issues in International Trade*, pp. 7–24. London: Macmillan, 1985.

Kindleberger, C. P., ed. 1970. *The International Corporation*. Cambridge: MIT Press.

Krugman, P. R. 1979. "Increasing Returns, Monopolistic Competition, and International Trade." *Journal of International Economics* 9 (November), pp. 469–480.

Krugman, P. R. 1981. "Intraindustry Specialization and the Gains from Trade." *Journal of Political Economy* 89 (October), pp. 959–973.

Krugman, P. R. 1985. "Increasing Returns and the Theory of International Trade." Processed, 1985.

Lancaster, K. 1979. *Variety, Equity, and Efficiency*. New York: Columbia University Press.

Lancaster, K. 1980. "Intra-Industry Trade under Perfect Monopolistic Competition." *Journal of International Economics* 10 (May), pp. 151–176.

Leamer, E. E. 1984. *Sources of International Comparative Advantage*. Cambridge: MIT Press.

Markusen, J. R. 1983. "Factor Movements and Commodity Trade as Complements." *Journal of International Economics* 14 (May), pp. 341–356.

Markusen, J. R. 1984. "Multinationals, Multi-Plant Economies, and the Gains from Trade." *Journal of International Economics* 16 (May), pp. 205–226.

Markusen, J. R., and J. R. Melvin. 1981. "Trade, Factor Prices and Gains from Trade with Increasing Returns to Scale." *Canadian Journal of Economics* 14 (August), pp. 450–469.

Marvel, H. P., and E. J. Ray. 1986. "Intraindustry Trade: Sources and Effects on Protection." Processed, 1986.

Matthews, R. C. O. 1950. "Reciprocal Demand and Increasing Returns." *Review of Economic Studies* 17(2), pp. 149–158.

Mayer, W. 1974. "Short-Run and Long-Run Equilibrium for a Small Open Economy." *Journal of Political Economy* 82 (September/October), pp. 955–968.

McKenzie, L. W. 1955. "Equality of Factor Prices in World Trade." *Econometrica* 23 (July 1955), pp. 239–257.

Melvin, J. R. 1969. "Increasing Returns to Scale as a Determinant of Trade." *Canadian Journal of Economics* 2 (August), pp. 389–402.

Metcalfe, J. S., and I. Steedman. 1981. "On the Transformation of Theorems." *Journal of International Economics* 11 (May), pp. 267–271.

Mundell, R. A. 1957. "International Trade and Factor Mobility." *American Economic Review* 47 (June), pp. 321–335.

Mussa, M. 1974. "Tariffs and Distribution of Income: The Importance of Factor Specificity, Substitutability, and Intensity in the Short and Long Run." *Journal of Political Economy* 82 (November/December), pp. 1192–1204.

Neary, J. P. 1978. "Short-Run Capital Specificity and the Pure Theory of International Trade." *Economic Journal* 88 (September), pp. 488–510.

Pigou, A. 1906. *Protective and Preferential Import Duties*. London: Macmillan.

Ray, E. J. 1986. "An Empirical Analysis of U.S. Intra-Industry Trade." Processed, 1986.

Rodgers, J. R. 1985. "Examples of Intra-Industry Trade in a Heckscher-Ohlin-Samuelson Model." Processed, 1985.

Ruffin, R. J., and F. Rassekh. 1986. "The Role of Foreign Direct Investment in U.S. Capital Outflows." *American Economic Review* 76 (December), pp. 1126–1130.

Rugman, A. M. 1980. "Internalization as a General Theory of Foreign Direct Investment: A Re-Appraisal of the Literature." *Weltwirtschaftliches Archiv* 116(2), pp. 365–379.

Samuelson, P. A. 1971. "Ohlin Was Right," *Swedish Journal of Economics* 73 (December), pp. 365–384.

Shaked, A., and J. Sutton, 1983. "Natural Oligopolies." *Econometrica* 51 (September), pp. 1469–1484.

Shaked, A., and J. Sutton. 1984. "Natural Oligopolies and International Trade." In H. Kierzkowski, ed., *Monopolistic Competition and International Trade*, pp. 334–350. Oxford: Oxford University Press.

Spence, M. 1976. "Product Selection, Fixed Costs, and Monopolistic Competition." *Review of Economic Studies* 43 (June), pp. 217–235.

Svensson, L. E. O. 1984. "Factor Trade and Goods Trade." *Journal of International Economics* 16 (May), pp. 365–378.

Venables, A. 1985. "International Trade, Trade and Industrial Policy and Imperfect Competition: A Survey." Processed, 1985.

Williamson, O. 1975. *Markets and Hierarchies*. New York: Norton.

Woodland, A. D. 1982. *International Trade and Resource Allocation*. Amsterdam: North-Holland.

COMMENT

Avinash Dixit

Ethier has given us an excellent account of the state of the art in international-trade theory. The exposition of conventional theory is clear, succinct, and constructively critical. The new views are nicely classified by their degree of departure from the orthodoxy, their success to date is evaluated, and their prospects are assessed. In short, the essay is a discussant's nightmare; it forces me to search desperately hard for something interesting and nonrepetitive to say.

My first such point supplements Ethier's discussion of factor-price equalization. I shall offer an analogy that may help some readers better to understand the significance of his cone $K(w)$. The basis of orthodox trade theory is that countries have different factor endowments. If factor services were directly tradable, the world would achieve all possible gains from the efficient allocation of resources. The standard model rules out factor trade. However, goods can be regarded as embodied bundles of factors; so trade in goods is, indirectly, trade in factor services. This can be just as good as their direct trade, if the bundles allow us to reconstruct the amounts of factors we would have wished to trade. This whole story is formally just like the theory of spanning in securities markets. Consumers can best respond to uncertainty if they can trade in claims to goods and services contingent upon the state of nature; for example, umbrellas in the event of rain, or income replacement in the event of illness. But they have access only to securities that are specified vectors, or fixed-proportion bundles, of such claims. This is just as good, provided that in equilibrium the available securities can be used to reconstruct the desired vector of state-contingent claims. When short sales are allowed, the set of all linear combinations of securities, that is, the subspace spanned by them, gives us the set of attainable state-contingent consumption vectors. In trade theory, there are no short sales of goods. Therefore we must confine ourselves to nonnegative linear combinations of the vectors $k_i(w)$ of factor services embodied in goods i, or the cone $K(w)$ formed by them. Once again, this is a property that should hold in equilibrium; hence the dependence of the whole construct on the equilibrium factor-price vector w.[1]

My second remark is intended to lend support to Ethier's view (note 17) that the orthodox theory is more robust and relevant than it is often given credit for. I shall do this by applying it to the issue of international lending and borrowing, a subject that is usually treated in a macroeconomic context. In the process, I hope to shed some light on the recent history of exchange rates and trade deficits. I also give a more prominent place to demand reversals, which are usually a very minor part of the conventional theory, as we see from the one brief paragraph that Ethier awards them.

General-equilibrium theory has taught us to distinguish goods according to their dates of availability. Relative prices across time of physically identical goods measure intertemporal marginal rates of substitution and transformation, that is, interest rates. Now think of a two-good, two-country model of the standard kind with one twist: the goods are not apples and bearings, but present apples and future apples. If the United States has a higher autarkic price of present apples than does Japan, then in free trade the United States will be an importer of present apples and an exporter of future ones. U.S. consumption of present apples will exceed production. In more common terminology, the United States will be a borrower country, or will have a trade deficit in the present period.

Such a state can arise for either of two reasons. (1) The United States has a high marginal product of investment; so the Japanese find it an attractive place to locate their capital. (2) The United States has a high degree of impatience; so it is willing to offer high rates of return to attract Japanese saving. The former corresponds to the production-side explanation of trade that is usual in orthodox trade theory. However, in this instance the latter, or demand-based explanation better accords with the experience of the early 1980s (Branson 1986).

The high U.S. demand for present goods is in this instance attributable mainly to the public sector. The political process has a propensity to spend now, postponing any sacrifices to the future. Of course, perfectly foresighted consumers will calculate their future tax obligations and cut back present consumption accordingly. But this effect is less than complete, mainly because of the generational structure of consumers: many of the current beneficiaries of public spending will not be around when the time comes to pay the taxes, and many of the future taxpayers are not yet born.

The above model says nothing about exchange rates; but a small step into higher dimensions allows us to discuss them. Divide time into the present and the future as above, and also distinguish physical goods according to the country of origin. Thus there are four economically distinct commodities; call them "today's Chevy," "tomorrow's Chevy," "today's Honda," and "tomorrow's Honda." In each country, the price of its present good relative to its future good is (one plus) that country's real interest rate. In each period, the price of the U.S. good relative to the Japanese good is the real dollar/yen exchange rate.

Now suppose a shift of U.S. government expenditures toward the present raises the demand for today's Chevy and lowers that for tomorrow's Chevy. In the first instance, the excess demand for today's Chevy raises its price, and the excess supply of tomorrow's Chevy lowers its price. These price changes induce substitutions and therefore further price changes. The normal presumption is that the closest substitutes to today's Chevy are today's Honda and tomorrow's Chevy. Their relative strength depends on the distance between today and tomorrow. In this instance we have in mind the time horizon of a few years, and cross-country substitution is likely to be stronger than the intertemporal kind. Therefore some of the initial excess demand for today's Chevies spills over to today's Hondas, and some of the excess supply of tomorrow's Chevies spills over into tomorrow's Hondas. Then in the new equilibrium the commodities will be ranked in descending order of their price increases as follows: today's Chevy, today's Honda, tomorrow's Honda, and tomorrow's Chevy. Of course, only relative prices matter; so any one of these prices can be normalized to stay constant. Then the others earlier in the order will increase and those later will fall. No matter how this is done, the U.S. real interest rate will rise, the Japanese real interest rate will rise but by less, and the dollar will undergo a real appreciation in the present and a real depreciation in the future. The last will show up today in forward markets if they are of sufficient duration; otherwise it is only a rational expectation concerning tomorrow's spot market. Once again, this simple theory has a lot of explanatory power with respect to the events of the early 1980s.

This viewpoint tells us something that the usual macroeconomic approach conceals. As usual, the general equilibrium described above is Pareto efficient given the preferences implicit in the demands. One may complain that the pattern of U.S. public consumption is shortsighted and harmful to other countries and to the U.S. private sector; but that is a political issue, not an economic one. In particular, attempts to intervene in the exchange market, or in current trade in goods, or in borrowing and lending, will only make matters worse by making the economic allocation of resources inefficient.

Let me turn to a proposition that arises from orthodox theory but takes us into the realm of strategic policy issues.

> Countries with relatively elastic excess demand and supply curves should be more inclined toward free trade with each other, or indifferent about protection, whereas countries with inelastic excess demand and supply curves should be more prone to tariff wars.

This is stated for a pair of countries that are alike in that the elasticities for the two are both high or both low. If we allowed asymmetry, we would find that country B's inelastic excess supply or demand gives country A monopsony or monopoly power in trade, and therefore the temptation to restrict trade.

When countries differ in their economic size, the normal presumption is that the smaller countries will have the more inelastic demands and supplies. Therefore the larger countries will stand to gain more from tariff wars. This intuition is formalized by Kennan and Riezman (1984). In reality, it is only partly borne out. The tendency empirically is for very small countries to have relatively liberal trade regimes (Katzenstein 1985). Middle-sized countries are often relatively more protectionist. The largest country in world trade, instead of being the most protectionist, is usually the staunchest proponent of free trade; for example, Britain in the 19th century and the United States in the three decades following World War II.

This phenomenon is best understood from the viewpoint of strategic trade policy. A liberal trade regime is a public good for the group of countries. Each would like the others to supply it (that is, to adhere to the policy of free trade) while itself becoming a free rider (that is, while pursuing its own optimal trade restriction). Small countries do not gain by doing so, but medium-size ones do. Only a country dominant in world trade can have the incentive to provide the public good even when it knows that the other countries will take advantage of it. However, if the dominance erodes with time, the leader starts to lapse into protectionist actions and the regime is threatened, as has happened in the case of the United States over the last decade.[2]

Finally, I shall take up the only point where I differ from Ethier in interpretation and judgment. This concerns the status and the role of oligopoly theory. Ethier's characterization is that in oligopoly "the ad hoc is the all hoc," and that it "seems to be developing via a succession of virtuoso exercises." This reminds me of Shubik's complaint (1970, p. 415) that "There is no oligopoly theory. There are bits and pieces of models." I regard this as a strength, not a weakness. There are hundreds of industries, and they differ from one another in dozens of dimensions: the rate of technical change, the extent of economies of scale and scope, the degree to which costs are sunk, the risk-adjusted cost of capital, the trends and fluctuations in demand, asymmetry of information across firms, and the impact of tax and trade policies, to mention just a few. Attempts to build a general theory of this will be futile, leading to confusion rather than comprehension. Bits and pieces of models, or "virtuoso exercises," each of which examines the operation of one of these forces, constitute a better approach. This gives us a dozen central insights: the roles of commitment, reputation, signaling, etc. When we apply the theory to an actual industry, we should examine its characteristics, identify the relevant forces, and pick out the appropriate insights. Of course, like any research program, this can be well or badly executed; but in my judgment it is more promising than the chimera of an all-embracing general theory of oligopoly.

Notes

1. For more details of this, see Dixit and Norman (1980, ch. 4) and Helpman and Krugman (1985, ch. 1).

2. Formal analyses of this issue can be found in Schelling (1978, ch. 7) and Olson and Zeckhauser (1966). In political theory, such a system is called a hegemony; a recent interesting discussion from an economist's point of view is Kindleberger (1986).

References

Branson, W. H. 1986. "Causes of Appreciation and Volatility of the Dollar." In *The U.S. Dollar—Recent Developments, Outlook, and Policy Options*, pp. 33–52. Kansas City, MO: Federal Reserve Bank of Kansas City, 1986.

Dixit, A., and V. Norman. 1980. *Theory of International Trade*. Cambridge: Nisbets and Cambridge University Press.

Helpman, E., and P. Krugman. 1985. *Market Structure and Foreign Trade*. Cambridge, MA: MIT Press.

Katzenstein, P 1985. *Small States in World Markets*. Ithaca, NY: Cornell University Press.

Kennan, J., and R., Riezman. 1984. *Do Big Countries Win Tariff Wars?* Working Paper No. 84–33, University of Iowa.

Kindleberger, C. P. 1986. "International Public Goods without Interntional Government." *American Economic Review* 76 (March), pp. 1–13.

Olson, M., and R. Zeckhauser. 1966. "An Economic Theory of Alliances." *Review of Economics and Statistics* 48 (August), pp. 266–279.

Schelling, T. C. 1978. *Micromotives and Macrobehavior.* New York: Norton.

Shubik, M. 1970. "A Curmudgeon's Guide to Microeconomics." *Journal of Economic Literature* 8 (June), pp. 405–434.

2 THE ISSUE OF PROTECTION

H. Peter Gray
Ingo Walter

Protection may be defined as intervention by government in markets for internationally traded goods and services in order to provide an artificial competitive advantage to a domestic industry vis-à-vis foreign competition. This type of governmental intervention is part of what is generally known as *commercial policy*. It generates price discrimination between goods and services of domestic origin and those produced abroad. This definition can be applied equally to protection of home industries against competition from imports, and to measures that enable domestically produced goods to be sold more favorably abroad in competition with foreign goods or services. The usual means of aiding the sale of home-produced goods in foreign markets is to subsidize their production or export.

The pure theory of protection, like the pure theory of international trade from which it is derived, is set in partial- or general-equilibrium static analysis. General-equilibrium analysis of protection indicates a loss of global efficiency in resource allocation in the presence of trade discrimination. This underlies the doctrine that protection, with rare exceptions, is a social bad undertaken to institute or preserve a gain for a small subset of players in the global economy at the expense of nearly all others.[1]

Explorations in the pure theory of commercial policy have fallen into relative quiescence after a burst of energy in the 1960s, when the concepts of effective rates of protection and optimum intervention were developed, and when the importance of nontariff barriers to trade was recognized. Since that time, the main center of interest has been the political economy of protection. Topics of current concern sit uncomfortably within a body of theory grounded in static, political analysis. They focus on: (a) the problem of preventing a retrogression of the existing system of world trade from the relatively open, nondiscriminatory conditions achieved under the auspices of the General Agreement of Tariffs and Trade (GATT); (b) how to deal with problem industries damaged by foreign competition—especially by industrial "targeting" or import surges; (c) the deteriorating state of economic relations between the industrialized and the developing countries; and (d) an understanding of the political mechanism by which some consensus on commercial policy is reached within the context of the national state.

This chapter comprises six sections. The first section provides a brief summary of traditional analysis of commercial policy. The second section considers the problems that confront the existing trading system. It raises the possibility of dynamic instability, and a possible retrogression toward a more protectionist, discriminatory era. The next section confronts the dynamics of adjustment and negotiation with particular reference to North-South trade. The fourth section addresses the mechanisms that underlie the political economy of protection in industrialized democracies. We then develop a view of protection in the context of economic growth and structural change of national economies. The concluding section draws some implications for policy analysis.

Traditional Analysis

The traditional analysis of protection has emphasized the role of the tariff and the quota as the chief techniques used to discriminate against foreign-made goods in domestic markets. The analysis has been framed in both partial- and general-equilibrium terms, and the argument for liberal trade (that is, the costs of protection) relies on both roots. As in all analyses with welfare connotations, the main emphasis is placed on world and national resource allocation, respectively, and on income distribution.

Figure 2–1 shows a partial-equilibrium diagram of the effects of a tariff or quota on the domestic market for a single good, including the redistribution effects.

A perfectly elastic foreign supply schedule (S_F) and a less-than-perfect-

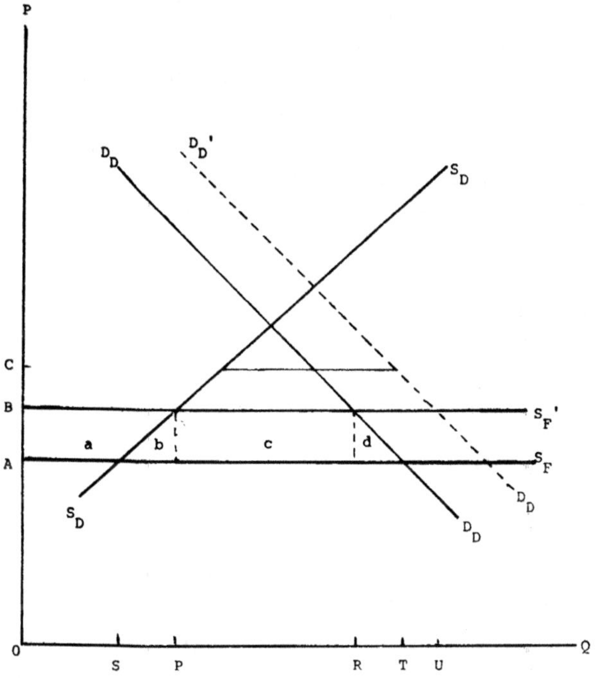

Figure 2–1. Effect of Tariff or Quota on Domestic Market

ly-elastic domestic supply schedule (S_D) combine with a domestic demand curve (D_D) to give a market-clearing price of *A* and consumption of *T* (comprising *S* units of home-produced goods and *ST* units of imports). This is the partial-equilibrium free-trade position.

The imposition of an import duty (tariff) of 20 percent shifts the foreign supply schedule upward to a price of *B* (= 1.2*A*). The market-clearing price is now *B* and the market-clearing quantity has been cut to *R*. Home production has increased to *P* units and imports have declined from *ST* to *PR* units.

The loss in consumer welfare (measured in terms of consumer surplus) has declined by the sum of the four areas *a*, *b*, *c*, and *d*. The triangle *b* represents the increase in per-unit costs of production associated with the additional home production, and constitutes a deadweight loss without any redistributive countereffects. The triangle *d* is also a deadweight loss, of consumer surplus caused by the higher price of imports. These two triangles represent the loss in global allocative efficiency within the context of static partial-equilibrium analysis. The rectangle *c* is the tariff revenue and, if the revenue results in an offsetting reduction in other taxes, will have a redistributive effect of relatively minor proportions. The area *a* is the increase in revenues of the home industry *net of any increase in costs*—the increase in producer surplus. This effect of protection is purely redistributive, reducing the welfare of consumers and benefiting people with a production stake in the industry.

The partial-equilibrium diagram gives no information on the distribution of *a* among the groups (stockholders, labor) connected with the protected industry. This will depend upon the conditions that prevail in the nation's factor markets.

The same diagram can also be used to analyze the effects of a quota limiting imports to *PR* units. Except for the problem of area *c*, the analysis is identical to that of a tariff of *AB*/*A* percent. The area *c* is now a potential quasi rent for importers in the home country or foreign producers, depending on which group has the greater market power.

The foregoing discussion can be made more realistic by changing the assumptions slightly. The analysis implicit in figure 2–1 is that protection is afforded an industry for no other reason than that it has the political power to capture the resulting redistributive effects (rent-seeking). This is undoubtedly true for some industries, and it is particularly likely to be true for "infant" or "growth" industries in developing nations. However, in the industrialized countries protection tends to be granted largely to industries in danger of bankruptcy or severe distress because of an increase in the pressure on the home industry from abroad. For example, in the United States industries may apply to the International Trade Commission for protection on four specific grounds: (a) injurious import competition; (b) market disruption; (c) national security; and (d) unfair trade practices.[2]

Figure 2–1 can be used to illustrate such conditions by having the original free-trade equilibrium represented by a market-clearing combination of *R* units at price *B*. If now the competitor industry abroad achieves a reduction in costs (for any reason) in the amount of *AB*/*B* percent, imports would increase to *ST* units and domestic production would decrease by *SP* units. Under such circumstances, the industry might seek to preserve the *status quo ante* by appealing for protection to retain the existing rate of profit and level of employment—thus ensuring the support of labor organizations. Protection will prevent consumers from enjoying the cost reductions achieved by the foreign competitor but, because they have never enjoyed these gains in the first place, consumers may be expected to assume a fairly passive role in any public debate on the matter. The industry is no better or worse off, except in the sense that it could indeed have been worse off in the absence of protection.

In either case, figure 2–1 clearly illustrates that the "degree of protection" generated by a tariff or quota depends upon the arc elasticities of domestic supply and demand in the importing country. This has important implications for the analysis of protection in a general-equilibrium context.

The Structure of Protection

There is, however, a major problem of aggregation. In a multiproduct setting, a common tariff would involve an equivalent degree of protection for each unit of import-competing output, implying for each individual good a diffferent tariff rate that is computed with the full knowledge of the applicable domestic supply and demand elasticities. Concepts such as the optimum tariff, however analytically interesting, would under such circumstances be nonoperational.

A second factor that severely limits the validity of basic tariff analysis is the question of the effective rate of protection.[3] Implicitly, traditional analysis assumes that the good is produced entirely from domestic inputs or is imported in its finished state. This assumption is in direct conflict with the large volume of international trade that takes place in raw materials and semifinished goods. When a good is produced in several stages, different stages of production can be undertaken in different countries. Different rates of protection on goods at different stages of production will thus be capable of causing major variations in the degree of protection afforded domestic firms performing a particular stage of production. This is a problem of tariff structure—as in so-called cascading tariffs, where the rate of protection increases as the imported product approaches final form. The nominal rate of protection, AB/A in traditional analysis (figure 2–1), is no longer a valid measure of the *rate* of protection. Instead, the effective rate of protection (equivalent to the nominal tariff in traditional analysis) must be computed from the production costs at home and abroad, and from the nominal protection rates applicable to the inputs used in traded goods.

Another problem of tariff structure is the granting of an exemption from duty of the value of domestically produced components contained in imports that have received further processing abroad by a foreign firm. Sections 806.3 and 807 of the U.S. Tariff Code—the so-called offshore-assembly provisions—limit the base for computation of duty to the actual value-added abroad. This provision affects the attractiveness of combining a multistage production process among production units located in different countries according to the relative costs of production, and therefore affects the shares of national income likely to be earned by internationally mobile and internationally immobile factors of production.[4]

Activities of this type (foreign sourcing) are carried out predominantly by multinational corporations (MNCs) that, in addition to achieving potential cost reductions by distributing the stages of production among different countries, can also realize economies of internalization of production derived from the combination of different stages of production under the aegis of a single firm (Casson 1982). The offshore-assembly provisions thus encourage production-sharing to the detriment of the interests of the immobile factors of production in a high-cost country, while cascading tariffs discourage foreign production-sharing between a single foreign source or among multiple foreign units and a marketing-and-distribution organization in the home country. Because the offshore-assembly provisions reduce the base on which import duties are levied, they also negate any cascading effect on domestically produced inputs.

The creation of "export zones" in developing countries in order to attract production subsidiaries of foreign-based MNCs by offering more favorable treatment in terms of regulation, taxation, and tariffs (Moxon 1984) works counter to the effects of a cascading tariff structure by effectively subsidizing operations within these zones. Some countries offer "net-incentive packages of inducements" to MNC affiliates that are export-oriented and can be attracted to such development zones (Gray and Walter 1983).

Protection and X-Efficiency

Traditional partial-equilibrium analysis (as represented by figure 2–1) implicitly assumes that the domestic industry successfully achieves input minimization and minimum costs of production. It therefore neglects the impact of market structure on the industry's cost of production—its domestic supply schedule. The possibility that domestic industries collude informally was one of the stronger facets of Adam Smith's advocacy of free trade. The neoclassical emphasis on allocative efficiency derives from David Ricardo and John Stuart Mill.

Harvey Leibenstein (1978) has developed the concept of X-efficiency to portray the possibility that firms do not in fact minimize inputs in the production process, so that existing costs could be reduced by more efficient managerial practices. Leibenstein identifies the cause of X-inefficiency as the failure of individuals to perform up to their potential, singly and collectively, and asserts that individuals raise their level of effort only when pressures (external or self-imposed) force them to achieve that potential. External motivations derive from competition (and concern for job security), from discipline imposed by management, and from peer-group pressures. They will be positively related to the "tightness of the environmental cost-containing forces." Self-imposed motivations derive from the inherent satisfaction and pride gained from the quality of individual performance and from any direct link between effort and reward.

While Leibenstein's emphasis on the failure to achieve the appropriate quantity and mix of inputs is important, other factors can also affect the price-competitiveness of an industry and make it vulnerable to foreign competition. These include inflated profit rates (or mark-ups) attributable to a previous combination of comparative advantage and market power, inflated wage rates, and unequally restrictive government regulations on an industry at home or abroad, as well as impediments to the importation of inputs.

The possibility that an industry is not achieving minimal *cost* of production can be incorporated into the traditional partial-equilibrium diagram (figure 2–1) by allowing for the domestic supply schedule to shift downward in the face of foreign competition, or to shift upward in the aftermath of protection so that output does not increase as a result of the imposition of a tariff.

To the extent that international competition enhances the X-efficiency of the domestic industry, the argument against a tariff is strengthened. Recognition of the fact that the position of the supply schedule is a function of wage rates actually paid suggests that an industry can combat foreign competition by reducing any wage premia enjoyed by workers (and management) as a result of earlier and union-bargaining successes and by reducing any return paid to industry-specific skills acquired by workers.[5]

Tariffs vs. Quotas

While traditional analysis presupposes a static equivalence between a tariff and a quota, there are two important exceptions to this rule, which can be considered in terms of the partial-equilibrium analysis of trade restrictions. These are the differential effects of a change in demand or supply and the social costs of the rent-seeking inducement of a quota.

Kreinin (1970) and Walter (1971) have shown that the difference between a tariff and a quota is important when one of the curves shifts. The results can be illustrated by considering a simple increase in domestic demand. In figure 2–1, the dashed line represents an increase in domestic demand. If a tariff is in place, the market-clearing price remains constant at *B* and the quantity of imports increases to *PU*. If instead a quota is in force, imports necessarily remain restricted to *PR*, so that the price increases to *C*. Under such circumstances, a tariff is preferable to a quota because it avoids further allocative inefficiency triggered by the increase in demand.

An important variation exists when the foreign supply schedule shifts downward because of cost reductions by foreign production units. A tariff under such circumstances will reduce domestic production and increase imports, while a quota will retain the existing volume of domestic production and retain the price (*B*). If the purpose of the commercial-policy measure is to preserve a given volume of domestic production (*P* units), then a quota is preferred to a tariff and automatically brings about the needed increase in the degree of protection.

Krueger (1974), in an analysis pertaining to developing economies, argues that quotas have greater social costs than tariffs because quotas create a quasi rent—area *c* in figure 2–1. The existence of a quasi rent leads to resources being devoted to the attempt to acquire a share of that rent. If the quota is effected through the issuance of licenses, then the quasi rents become embodied in the acquisition of a license. On the presumption that the resources devoted to the search for licenses are, in fact, scarce and have a positive opportunity cost, Krueger presents a neoclassical model to illustrate the mechanism by which the search for licenses generates a social cost. Certainly quasi rents are quantitatively important in the two countries (Turkey and India) for which Krueger has provided estimates.[6] The analysis is quite compatible with Leibestein's X-inefficiency in that Krueger argues that quotas contribute to X-inefficiency by the employment of more resources than the minimum amount needed for the prescribed rate of domestic production.

The efficiency implications of smuggling resemble those of rent-seeking in that smugglers use resources to seek the rents that reward the evasion of either a tariff or a quota. In addition to the X-inefficiency that is inherent in any clandestine operation such as bribery and smuggling, the practice also incurs additional social costs of preventive action. A pessimist would recognize the mutually reinforcing interaction between the X-inefficiency of smuggling and the efficiency of the preventive activities.

General Equilibrium

The general-equilibrium analysis of the effects of protection is traditionally cast in the form of a single diagram showing two sets of offer curves—see

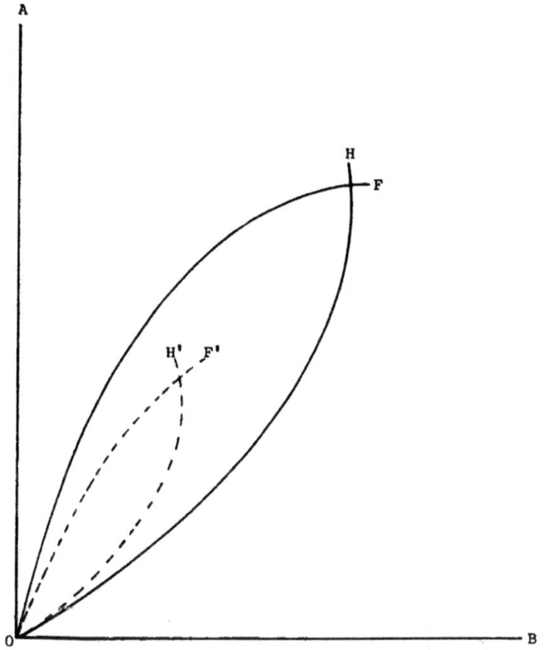

Figure 2–2. Free-Trade and Protection-Ridden Offer Curves

figure 2–2. The pair of free-trade offer curves (OH and OF) indicates the free-trade equilibrium, while the two protection-ridden offer curves (OH' and OF') establish the alternative equilibrium. As in the partial-equilibrium approach, the main matters of interest are the redistributive effects of protection (in the general-equilibrium version these are international effects), and the loss of gains from trade brought about by the reduction in the volume of trade (allocative efficiency). General-equilibrium analyses of this type encounter the insuperable problems of aggregation of goods with different sensitivities to a given level of nominal tariff protection or a given quota level.

Meade's (1955) classic analysis of the welfare implications of international trade recognized the possibility that conditions within a country might not automatically lead to an equilibrium that is optimal, and therefore imposed the condition of "modified laissez faire" on the trading countries. He also recognized that international markets might turn out to be imperfect for reasons other than man-made impediments to trade. Meade's call was, then, for "modified free trade."

The possibility of interaction between the two sets of imperfections led to the identification of the possible need for analysis of the "second-best" solution, and free-trade loses the inevitability of optimality thrust on it by Mill. Consideration of the possibility of the need for second-best solutions allowed for analysis of "optimum intervention" (Corden 1974). In all cases, the general-equilibrium analysis is set in a world of two countries and homogeneous factors of production, and the concern is with static or comparative-static solutions.

This analytic framework is forced to exclude from consideration all concerns with the process of adaptation from one set of global conditions to another. Meade acknowledges this limitation of his analysis by explicitly confining its domain to marginl changes in conditions and by assuming that "there are no real costs of movements of factors when they turn from one industry to another" (Meade 1955, p. 52). In this, Meade follows the practice of both Smith and Mill. This assumption, as well as the presumed essential homogeneity of factors of production, is the key to the incompatibility between the static, orthodox theory and many current problems confronting international trade and protectionism. The problems that face the international trading system involve ongoing, rapid change, and resistance to change, rather than classic forms of rent-seeking behavior.

Maintaining an Open Trading System

The growth in world trade since World War II has been impressive, with the volume of trade expanding at a rate well over twice the rate of growth of world output. The benefits that this growth has brought must be attributed in large measure to the existence of the General Agreement on Tariffs and Trade (GATT), and to the success of multilateral trade negotiations carried out under its auspices. The major focus has been on reductions in the rate of tariff protection affecting manufactured goods. But even as the most successful of all GATT bargaining sessions was being launched during 1962–1967, the Kennedy administration was preparing a special program of sectoral protection for the textile and apparel industries (Wolf 1983, p. 457). The 1974–1979 Tokyo Round lowered tariffs on industrial goods still further; so that the average tariff on finished manufactured goods in 1987 was 6.5 percent.[7]

The crux of the system of international-trade rules established under the GATT comprises: (a) a general willingness to obey the rules of the agreement and to abide by its dispute-resolution process, (b) a willingness to extend trade concessions to all signatories so that the system is nondiscriminatory with respect to the origins of traded goods, and (c) a willingness to reallocate factors of production from declining to expanding sectors of the national economy (adjustment). This system, which comprises "the spirit of the GATT," has been increasingly threatened as nations seem to weaken in their political resolve to support the GATT principles and are increasingly willing to sacrifice the principles of liberal trade and of nondiscrimination to special interests and short-run political convenience.

It is arguable that the international trading system is dynamically unstable so that, in the absence of any collective commitment and initiative to promote further trade liberalization, domestic pressures for protection from industries under competitive threat from abroad will force governments to encroach on those aspects of the existing system that contribute most to its success.

Once new protective measures are put in place, the practice of discriminatory trade treatment and the search for appropriate retaliation will feed upon itself. Just as the principle of nondiscrimination and the unconditional most-favored-nation treatment has provided a fundamental degree of integrity to the international trading system, so too will selective protection (discrimination among suppliers) tend to contribute to its gradual erosion and inflict permanent damage to the gains from trade.

Sources of Instability

If, as many foresee, the world faces major structural adjustments over the next decade, it may not be possible either to launch new trade-liberalization initiatives or to prevent governments from further undermining the system by responding to political pressures from industries in distress. Under such conditions, the task of policymakers must be defensive—to contain dynamic instability and minimize further systemic deterioration. The participating countries, in short, must seek to prevent continued erosion of "the spirit of the GATT." The danger can be attributed to three separate sources.

First, the GATT is not a body of international law, but rather an agreement by sovereign nations to observe a code of behavior and rules of dispute settlement that are perceived to be fair to all parties. Under stress (severe problems of economic adjustment), agreements can be broken more easily than can laws.

Second, the global recession of the early 1980s appears to have reduced the ability of economies to adjust to new conditions. Efficient adjustment requires high levels of aggregate demand (OECD 1979, pp. 1–4), and the recession compounded measures which, by introducing rigidities into the system and blocking the operation of market forces, may have reduced the resilience of the market mechanism in these economies (Michalski 1983).[8] Political pressures from threatened industries increase as their perception of existing alternatives becomes less optimistic. Rather than accepting structural adjustment as an efficiency-promoting phenomenon, industries strive to have the burden shifted to other groups or other nations, or to abort the need for adjustment altogether by suppressing the level of foreign competition.

Third, the Japanese economy has run a large surplus on trade in manufactured goods. This surplus, reinforced by the growth of capacity on the part of the newly industrializing countries to export acceptable manufactured goods, augments the strain of adjustment on certain sectors in the major trading economies of Western Europe and North America.

Because the two articles of the GATT that allow nations to rescind previous tariff concessions (Articles XXIII and XXVIII) are clumsy and can involve compensatory reductions in other tariff barriers, most of the devices used to protect threatened idustries have taken the form of nontariff barriers (NTBs). These include a wide range of explicit and implicit commercial-policy measures. Many of them can be used to reduce materially the transparency of protection—making a negotiated settlement of trade disputes more difficult.

Application of Nontariff Barriers and Sectoral Protection

NTBs range from measures as straightforward as import quotas and a series of variations on quotas intended to concentrate the impact of the protectionism, to export duties imposed on goods in which a country holds a monopoly position, to direct or indirect subsidies afforded selected industries (Walter 1969, pp. 21–22). The rapid spread of measures of this kind may be attributed in part to the unwillingness of countries to depart from commitments made on tariffs under the GATT and to the decline in the degree of protection afforded by tariffs following successive cuts in rates of duties. Indeed, there is some suggestion that NTBs actually have increased in importance in absolute terms, as distinct from merely assuming greater relative importance as a consequence of the decline in tariffs.

The importance of NTBs resulted in their becoming a primary focus during the 1974–1979 Tokyo Round of trade negotiations. Agreement was reached to institute codes of conduct governing the use of certain NTBs, such as subsidies, government-procurement rules, technical standards, licensing, and customs practices. Unfortunately, the codes that were negotiated have not been agreed to by all of the GATT signatories, and many countries consider that they are obliged to honor the code only insofar as other signatories are concerned. This attempted solution to the problem of NTBs may thus have contributed to the decline in the principle of nondiscrimination.

The dangers that beset the existing system of international trade are serious.[9] Under the pressures emanating from persistent global recession and misalignment of exchange rates, industrialized nations have developed policies of *sectoral protection*. Sectoral protection is usually based on a compromise between industry demands for shielding from imports and governmental perceptions of the national interest. Both domestic consumers and foreign suppliers (and sometimes even downstream industries) are excluded from the arrangement, and little or no restraint is imposed on the form that the protection will take. Unless this kind of protection also has built-in features that can be relied on to phase out the protection over time, sectoral protection can result in the complete alteration of global trading conditions in the affected products. That burden of protection will then be shifted to actual or potential foreign suppliers, the domestic consumer, a downstream industry, or the same industry in a third country in cases where the frustrated exporter focuses his sales efforts on that market. Such trade diversion could bring waves of protectionism in its wake, as other countries react to pressure on their industries and as the precepts of intervention at the sectoral level are more readily accepted.

The less transparent the means of protection, the more difficult it is to achieve liberalization. When NTBs are particularly difficult to identify, negotiations leading to suitable redress become less easily achieved. Those NTBs that do not have protectionist effects as their main purpose (that are imposed primarily for domestic reasons) can still have substantial indirect repercussions in international markets.

Subsidies

The difficulties of creating a satisfactory means of dispute settlement and redress for NTBs can best be illustrated by referring to the problem of subsidies.[10] In a review of the problems of countering the possible encroachment of subsidies on an open, liberal trading system, Hufbauer (1983) distinguishes three major difficulties that must be solved before the problems of liberalization and dispute settlement can be usefully attacked. Negotiators must be able to define subsidies, to determine the criteria to identify which subsidies merit counteraction, and to conceptualize what counteractions are appropriate. A subsidy can make itself felt in the home market of the complaining country, in a third-country market, and in the home market of the country instituting the subsidy. The first two represent *export subsidies* and the third can be considered a *domestic subsidy*.

Export subsidies can take the form of concessionary export credits; exemption, remission, or deferral of direct taxes; and export performance requirements coupled to some sort of domestic incentive. Domestic subsidies can be instituted by regional-location incentives, subsidization of the production of goods and services used by an industry, subsidized loans, and subsidies paid on research-and-development activities.

Export subsidies, by definition, inflict "material injury" on foreign industries. However, even in such clear-cut cases, the level and type of subsidy can be important in the determination of whether or not counteraction is warranted. Developing nations have traditionally been less severely treated on this issue. Indeed, in many instances subsidization by developing countries in heavy industries benefiting from significant economies of scale is difficult to distinguish from dumping. Domestic subsidies may have international effects and still not be considered to merit counteraction, particularly if they exist in a setting in which flexible exchange rates produce balanced international trade (or payments).

Per contra, some subsidies do allow a nation to develop a potential growth industry, so that it may eventually establish a viable position in that industry in world markets. Such a subsidy is particularly likely to engender matching subsidies by other nations, and raises the possibility of excess global capacity.

A domestic subsidy can also be used to protect an industry that should be allowed to decline, so that the subsidizing nation reduces its own costs of adjustment. This kind of subsidy is also likely to generate offsetting measures in other countries, as nations with a comparative advantage in the affected industry increase their sales efforts in other (third) countries that do not protect the industry. The usual criterion for counteraction is material injury to a domestic industry by a foreign domestic subsidy. *Material injury* in its simplest meaning can be established by a substantial increase in imports, increased unemployment, and low rates of capacity utilization and profits in the home industry. When the concept of material injury is defined as a "threat" of material injury or the likelihood of decreased growth, this criterion becomes much less objective.

Because the effect of a domestic subsidy could in theory be felt in three separate markets, forms of redress necessarily vary according to circumstance. For material injury in the home market of the complaining country, a simple counterailing duty will offset the foreign subsidy and provide a potentially effective remedy. Because foreign domestic subsidies are difficult to measure, there is a danger that countervailing duties will exceed the amount of subsidy and contain a residual degree of net protection.

A countervailing duty is of no value in a third-country market; and even if some appropriate remedy is developed, it will take time to evolve. In the interim, the subsidized industry may have established a commanding market share in that market. A potentially effective counteraction is a matching subsidy.

A domestic subsidy used to protect an industry against low-cost foreign competition will require an ad hoc response unless such measures can be incorporated into the existing framework of dispute settlement under Article XXIII of the GATT, which covers the reduction or withdrawal of previous concessions. Countermeasures may be imposed under these circumstances.

Complexities such as these are intrinsic to most, if not all, NTBs. The greater reliance on NTBs in current trade relations suggests that the liberalism imbedded in the existing system is in considerable danger, simply because these measures do not lend themselves as easily as tariffs to fair and effective means of dispute settlement.

Problems of Structural Adjustment

The nondiscriminatory aspects of the postwar trading system have been endangered by particular emphasis on "bilateral fairness" and concern with safeguards against the rapid erosion of a domestic industry under pressure from imports. The question of bilateral fairness can be attributed largely to the very large bilateral trade surpluses in manufactured goods run by Japan. While the logic for this position is weak (Hadley 1982), concern with bilateral balances can easily lead to discriminatory protection.[11] Surges of imports of a particular good have caused the rapid decline of industries in North America and Europe, so that measures have been taken to discriminate against the source of disruptive imports. These measures usually take the form of discriminatory quotas which have come to be known as *orderly marketing arrangements* (OMAs) and *voluntary export restraints* (VERs).

The arguments for trade discrimination point to unequal access to markets. One possible cause of discrimination is that certain industries have been targeted as a national policy by export-oriented governments. Targeting can involve collusion on export strategy on an industry-wide basis as well as governmental subsidization of research and development (with a particular emphasis on product innovation). It is also possible that the temptation to indulge in industrial targeting is the existence of a sector that suffers from inflated costs (X-inefficiency and related factors) and in which product development has lagged.

The increased reliance on discriminatory and nondiscriminatory NTBs and emphasis on bilateral issues can be attributed to a fundamental change in global economic conditions that began with the inflation of the late 1960s and was reinforced by the breakdown of Bretton Woods, the oil-price shocks of 1974 and 1979/80, and the different rates of adaptation to the new conditions by various economies. These changes in global conditions required industrialized (and other) nations to undergo substantial adjustments—to reallocate resources and to accept changes in international and domestic income distribution. As countries fell into recession in the early 1980s, large established industries fell prey to severe competition from imports.

Michalski (1983) suggests that the difficulty of dealing with these problems in Europe and North America was substantially increased by the adoption—in earlier, more benign years—of measures that reduced the effectiveness of market forces. The choice between adjusting to new competitive conditions and trying to suppress the sources of change through the use of commercial policy was profoundly influenced by the political pressures for potection from the old, large industries which were suffering obvious material injury. The three forces of prolonged recession, greater economic rigidity in resource markets, and dynamic changes in global conditions have proven to be mutually reinforcing. They increased the amount of adjustment needed; at the same time they made the adjustment process more difficult. It is this change in global trading conditions that underlies a policy orientation of damage control as opposed to a broader set of policies founded on basic principles of liberal trade.

If the gains from an open international trading system are to be preserved, it is necessary for countries to focus on the need for adjustment, and to countenance the process of structural change. It is useful to distinguish among four categories of policies required:

1. Suppressive policies seek to preserve the *status quo ante* by negating the forces for change.
2. Retarding policies attempt to slow down the process of change so that change is spread out over a longer period and total social costs are reduced.
3. Adjustment-assistance policies may be implemented, whereby the institutional arrangements in the economy are tailored to facilitate

change—particularly change in labor skills.

4. Accelerating policies recognize the existence of industries with excess capacity and take positive measures to reduce that capacity.

The first of these policy categories is negative. Such policies seek to prevent change and to maintain the *status quo*. Both the economic and political benefits are short run in nature. The dislocations of economic adjustment are avoided or postponed, so that underutilization of plant capacity is prevented and workers are not displaced from industries in which they have acquired industry-specific skills. Politically, the incumbent office holders are more likely to be reelected by constituents employed in declining industries whose standards of living have been preserved. The opportunity costs of such policies are long run in nature, and are likely to grow with time. The protected industries are likely to be old and inefficient with low rates of innovation and capital formation, and their preservation will rob the economy of some of its growth potential. If the costs of adjustment to new international competitive conditions grow with time, the difficulties of adjustment will naturally become greater with time as well. The economy may become rigid and resist change, so that the potential gains from international trade are increasingly sacrificed and opposition to adjustment becomes more deeply entrenched.

Retardation policies attempt to slow, but not stop, the process of change. These policies leave the discipline of change to be exerted by market forces and leave for government the seemingly positive role of helping in the *process* of adjustment. This may require slowing down the impact of change by the application of protective policies that have a finite life and have built-in phase-out conditions. It is clearly important that these conditions be enforced, or retardation becomes suppression.

Retardation policies will probably be more effective if they incorporate *conditional protection*, whereby the adjustment-retarding measures require the protected industry to improve its own efficiency by lowering managerial salaries and wage rates, eliminating productivity-impeding work rules, and accepting restrictions on dividends (if any), and by requiring that all profits be ploughed back into the industry to upgrade equipment and finance research-and-development. It is possible that measures such as these will reduce the overall extent of adjustment needed by the economy.

Adjustment-facilitating policies, like adjustment-accelerating policies, are positive in the sense that they promote change. The difference is that facilitating policies are likely to be politically acceptable, while accelerating policies will give rise to active political opposition. The essence of adjustment is the transfer of resources among sectors or industries. Government's role, even in a purely laissez-faire economy, is to perform those services that have a *public-goods component*.

The provision of retraining facilities for displaced workers, financial aid for relocation (particularly for low-skilled workers), and information services on job vacancies by geographic region and skill, are all activities with a public-goods dimension. They are affirmative actions, but probably need to be in place for some time before they can hope to reduce resistance to change and economic restructuring; and they are activities in which governments have not had a sustained record of success in peacetime. It is important that any financial aid given to displaced workers to assist in adjustment be tied closely to retraining and relocation, given an inevitable tendency for workers to want to remain in their "old" industry in which they will have acquired industry-specific skills.

Adjustment-accelerating policies require a great deal of political courage, because they expedite the destruction of industries that have lost their international competitiveness. It is possible to combine decisions to eliminate high-cost production units with the offer of phase-out protection, but such initiatives are likely to engender considerable political strain.

Recently the concept of *industrial policy* has become widespread. Industrial policy is not a term that has yet arrived at a precise definition. However, it generally involves direct and indirect government intervention in the adjustment process.[12] Schultze (1983) argues that government does not have the knowledge to "pick the winners" and certainly does not want to "protect the losers" (suppressive policies). Another view of industrial policy involves the creation of forums in which government, business, and management can address the problem of adjustment strategies (Weil 1983). It is difficult to see how such forums will manage to impose decisions without reliance on the forces generated by the market mechanism, but some intervention by government may ultimately prove necessary when the amount of change needed exceeds that of which the economy is politically capable.

Protection in North-South Trade and Problems of Structural Adjustment

In addition to disturbances that have required adjustment in traditional international-trade patterns, growth in the capacity of developing countries to produce reliable, high-quality manufactured goods as well as basic labor-intensive goods has imposed additional adjustment strains on developed economies. This greater capacity to produce goods of the quality acceptable in industrialized economies derives in part from the success of export-led growth, the upgrading of skills, and the increased manufacturing capacity of the newly industrializig nations, and in part from the transfer of technology through MNCs and licensing.

The problems of adjustment in the industrialized countries are enhanced by the rapid growth of developing-country exports—the social costs of adjustment are cumulative. The response to these costs is political pressure for protection.

North-South trade and protection merit separate treatment from the adjustment associated with North-North trade for four reasons:

1. Developing countries, because of their inherent disadvantage in international trade in manufactures, are acknowledged to be entitled to "special and differential treatment." The most concrete result of such treatment has been the *generalized system of preferences* (GSP), which accorded to developing-country exports preferential tariff reductions in relation to the exports of countries enjoying most-favored-nation (MFN) status (Murray 1977). Since the inception of the GSP in 1971, the privileges afforded to developing countries have been gradually eroded. An interesting but unresolved issue has been whether preferential tariffs are more beneficial than generally lower tariffs that are nondiscriminatory. Because most exports of manufactures by developing countries fall into the category of "sensitive goods," the burden of NTBs has fallen more heavily on LDC exports. This fact and the general erosion of the GSP benefits, suggest strongly that freer trade is more desirable than the system of weak trade preferences for LDCs that has evolved.
2. Adjustment costs among industrialized countries derive from the disruptions of the global economy in response to the oil-price shocks of the 1970s and the widespread recession of the early 1980s. If these conditions have finite duration and the degree of damage to the liberal system of international trade can be contained, it is likely that North-North trade will resume a substantial degree of openness after a period of time. In contrast, North-South trade will present the industrialized economies with problems of severe structural adjustment on a much more permanent basis.
3. The kinds of adjustment costs that derive from increases in imports of manufactures from LDCs may well be qualitatively different from the effects of increased competition among the industrialized countries.
4. The political milieu is different. Developing countries have only recently acceded to GATT membership in any numbers, and that body

> remains dominated by industrialized nations. The principal forum for interbloc discussion of North-South economic problems has been the United Nations Conference on Trade and Development UNCTAD), which held its sixth session in the summer of 1983. The strain between the two blocs at that time was sufficiently great that the sixth session of UNCTAD achieved little except the avoidance of a serious rupture in the North-South dialogue. This is amply documented by the outright negative or half-hearted "reflections" of the delegates.[13]

Such a breakdown in the North-South dialogue would constitute the equivalent of dynamic instability in trading relations between the developed and developing countries. It would lead to less concern with the effects of the enactment of NTBs on the economies of supplier nations in the South. This, in turn, would frustrate policies of export-led growth and would probably lead to a reversion to policies of import substitution. Export-led growth, which had proven so successful for the newly industrializing countries, depends directly on the willingness of developed economies to accept increasing amounts of imports of manufactures from developing nations. While South-South trade may grow over time, the role of the industrialized nations as export markets will continue to be vital. If the social costs of adjustment in the developed countries lead to stifling protective measures against exports of LDC manufactures, so that their growth is held below some critical rate, export-led growth may prove to have been a short-lived phenomenon that is dependent upon a latent but exhaustible capacity to adjust with tolerable social cost on the part of the industrialized nations. An alternative LDC strategy of import substitution, on the other hand, will reduce industrial-country exports of high-technology goods to the LDCs and will certainly erode their rate of economic growth as well.

This section addresses two aspects of the problem: (1) the greater severity of adjustment costs associated with imports from the LDCs and (2) the greater expected duration of the need for adjustment to growth in LDC exports if the North-South dialogue is not to end in failure. Both concepts are important, because they are the causes of increased reliance by industrial countries on discriminatory trade measures (voluntary export restraints and orderly marketing arrangements) as well as of the erosion of benefits granted under the generalized system of preferences.

Adjustment Costs

The greater severity of adjustment to LDC imports derives from: (a) their tendency to erode aggregate demand in the importing (industrialized) countries, particularly the derived demand for labor; (b) the effects of imports on the demand for labor by skill-level and the need for upgrading of skills; and (c) the reinforcing effects of new technologies such as robotics and microchips.

Increased LDC exports of high-quality, sophisticated manufactured goods in addition to increased sales of labor-intensive goods generate additional demand for exports from the industrialized countries. But these additional exports are likely to take the form of capital-intensive goods, which utilize less labor than the imports displaced. In addition, the increased volume of hard-currency earnings by the LDCs may not be spent entirely on increased imports from the industrialized countries, so that the developed countries may experience a leakage from the expenditure stream.

It is possible that any growth in LDC hard-currency receipts would be spent entirely in the developed countries on additional exports. But the short-run impact is likely to be a leakage from the developed-countries' expenditure stream, caused by a net increase in expenditures on goods produced within the LDCs. This cause of unemployment of labor will not be easily offset, either by aggregate-demand policies within the industrialized countries (especially with required interindustry adjustments) or if individual nations find their aggregate-demand policies inhibited by balance-of-payments constraints.

The traditional Heckscher-Ohlin-Samuelson adjustment mechanism in response to a decrease in the demand for labor—caused by increased exports of capital-intensive goods and increased imports of labor-intensive goods—is for the wage rate to fall relative to the return on capital and for substitution of labor for capital to take place. While the change in relative factor prices may well take place, there can be less assurance that production units will respond to changed factor prices to the degree needed to eliminate unemployment. As Hager has noted:

> The implicit assumption by adjustment optimists that there is equilibrium in a free exchange between high-cost and low-cost areas of production which maintains something like full employment in the high-cost area is implausible to the point of being disingenuous. (Hager 1982, p. 123)

The change in the mix of traded goods induced by the increased LDC capability to sell manufactures in major markets will also involve a change in the required mix of skill levels on the part of the employed labor force in industrialized countries. Expanding export industries will tend to use relatively more highly skilled workers than the declining import-substitute industries. Skill-upgrading will therefore be required. Displaced workers face the prospect of possible protracted unemployment and a choice between upgrading their skill levels or downgrading themselves to lower employment levels for which they remain qualified but which will involve a reduction in their income. Displaced workers from import-competing industries will lose income in three ways: (1) The increase in LDC exports will reduce the wage rate relative to the return on capital, and in particular reduce wages for low-skilled workers relative to those of highly skilled workers. (2) Any income that derives from industry-specific, nontransferable skills acquired in the declining industry will be lost, as will any wage premia negotiated by unions in earlier times. (3) There will be a possible reduction in total employment.

The decision as to whether to try and upgrade to some of the vacancies available at new, higher levels of labor skills or to downgrade depends upon several factors. The first is the question of expected returns and costs. The expected returns depend on the expected wage differential, while costs are determined by the degree of support provided by government, the real costs of training, and the time taken to acquire the necessary skills. Only if the present value of the job with the higher skill level exceeds the present value of the costs of obtaining the required additional skills (net of any income in a lower-stratum job), will the worker seek to upgrade himself or herself.

Second, there is the degree of confidence that the requisite skills can be acquired. Older workers may feel that their abilities to acquire "new tricks" are diminished; workers with low levels of formal education and few transferable skills will certainly be constrained in their ability to acquire new, higher-level skills. Such workers will probably choose to seek employment at the same or lower skill requirements by "bumping" another, less-qualified worker. The phenomenon of bumping will tend to ensure that the unemployed workers consist primarily of those with the lowest skills and the least capacity for skill acquisition.

The capacity of a country's workforce to upgrade its skill levels will depend in part upon the latent capacity of individuals to acquire skills and on the willingness to acquire them. The greater the difference between the skill levels of displaced workers and the labor requirements prevailing in the expanding industries, the more severe will be the social costs of adjustment and the possibility of a prolonged disequilibrium.

Over time, the capacity of a country's workforce to upgrade its skill levels by any substantial degree will diminish, as workers with individual capacity for acquiring higher skills will have used up much of their latent capacity, and those continuing to be displaced will be workers with ever-smaller chances of upgrading. Thus, the capacity for adjustment to increased inflows of imports from the LDCs will decrease with time, and the corresponding social costs will increase—except for some general improvements in education and technical training, and some improvement in the facilities in which workers can upgrade themselves through trade adjustment assistance.[14]

It is possible for governments to aid the process of adjustment by providing more efficient adjustment-assistance facilities, more generous support conditions for displaced workers, and better quality of education and training. Such improvements will not be accomplished in the short run, and need to be in place at the time the adjustment strain is imposed. Given that the condition in the labor market is one of a potential mismatch of skills, policies cannot be limited to tradable-goods industries but must apply across-the-board. Measures must be taken that will encourage all industries to utilize more low-skilled workers in accordance with the traditional mechanism of factor substitution. Any measures to reduce the cost of employing low-skilled labor should apply to both tradable and nontradable goods industries. Finally, it would seem sensible to suggest that the more severe the disruption of the labor market by the changes in skill mixes demanded and supplied, the more likely are in-house training programs to be the most cost-effective means of upgrading workers. In addition to direct knowledge of in-firm needs and personnel, it is possible for a firm to conceive of sequential multiple level "upward-bumping" as workers are upgraded.

The problems of skill-upgrading may be aggravated by the concurrent technological innovations that afflict the labor markets in the industrialized countries. New technologies associated with robotics and microchips seem likely to reinforce the aforementioned effects of manufactured imports from LDCs. The new technologies will tend to displace workers on balance, and to displace in particular low-skilled workers at the same time that they raise the demand for higher-skilled labor.

Duration of Adjustment

The duration of the pressures exerted by developing nations seeking to achieve higher standards of living and economic growth by the promotion of export industries can continue for long periods. LDCs that have already imposed substantial strains on the import-competing industries of industrialized countries may be expected to want their exports to continue growing steadily, if less spectacularly, and to attain successively higher degrees of product sophistication as their own workers become more skilled. This process can be augmented by an increasing flow of proprietary technology to these countries via MNCs. And there always exist successor nations ready to compete in the markets for manufactured goods in the industrialized countries—Malaysia, Indonesia, the Philippines, India, Sri Lanka, Mexico, Brazil, the Peoples Republic of China, to name a few.

Firms in developing countries lack the experience needed to create their own marketing-and-distribution networks in the industrialized countries. Organizations that service consumer durables and other "experience goods" are the essence of sophisticated marketing, and domestic conditions will impede the development of experience in this type of activity. Additionally, such activities are very sensitive to the culture and character of the importing nation. Consequently, it might be expected that the rate of growth of imports from the more advanced LDCs, even without impediments to trade, will slow once they have become the dominant suppliers of standardized products and "experience goods" become of increasing importance.

However, this barrier cannot be relied upon to mitigate the flow of manufactured imports into the industrialized countries. MNCs are fully capable of combining existing marketing-and-distribution organizations in the industrialized countries with production in the LDCs, benefiting from any economies of internalization in the process. Given the population base in many LDCs, the high rates of population growth, and the possibility for the easy transfer of proprietary product and process technology by MNCs, the limiting factor on LDC exports of manufactures is likely to involve problems in the training of workers up to semiskilled and skilled status, and possibly the limits of full employment. Nevertheless, the adjustment strains and the accompanying costs in the industrialized countries will be long lasting.

Under these circumstances, intense pressure on politicians to discriminate against low-cost, labor-intensive imports from the LDCs is inevitable. To the extent that recessions create further strains in intra-developed-country trade and the industrialized economies show signs of "economic sclerosis," the difficulties of preventing a breakdown in North-South trading relations will grow further.

Elements of the Political Economy of Protection

The kinds of problems associated with structural adjustment discussed in the previous section suggest the basis for political action aimed at creating distortions of international trade. Three more-or-less distinct motivations can be discussed: (1) distortions that are thought to be in the national interest, (2) distortions that are clearly rent-seeking in character within a static framework of analysis, and (3) distortions that arise from dynamic adjustment problems in the context of the comparative evolution of national economies.

Political Arguments Based on Concepts of the National Interest

Traditional views of international trade presuppose that the national interest is perceived largely in terms of economic efficiency in the allocation of resources. The fact that there are positive and negative externalities associated with the operation of market forces is not generally recognized in the received doctrine of international trade. The classic case is national defense, whereby liberal trade may well result in a supply level on the part of key industries that is deemed inadequate to provide for required defense capabilities. Environmental externalities may represent another case, where free markets reduce the quality of the environment to the point that it is no longer considered politically acceptable. And there are social issues involving income distribution, problems of regional development, and racial and ethnic tensions that may have a political bearing on matters of trade policy—for example, the argument that the low-skill-labor content of imports prevents the lowest stratum of the population from achieving a basic work ethic, and thus locking it into a permanent cycle of economic deprivation and dependence with associated increases in the crime rate and other social ills.

Many such arguments can be dismissed out of hand by economists as special-pleading, or because they are seen as being better attacked by means of targeted subsidies at much lower economic cost. However, the political reality needs to be recognized and the case against the use of these arguments as a pretext for pure rent-seeking political activity needs to be made. Further, the application of socioeconomic cost-benefit analysis needs to be institutionalized in order to focus on the least costly tools for achieving objectives related to those externalities that are, according to the political consensus, deserving of attention. In trade policy, as in many other areas of economic policy, arguments relating to externalities can be extremely dangerous.

Another application of protection in the national interest—one that has been well developed in a general-equilibrium context—relates to the terms of trade. It is clear that, depending on domestic and foreign demand and supply elasticities for traded goods, countries may improve their terms of trade by engaging in action that disrupts the free interplay of market forces. As long as a country is a price maker rather than a price taker with respect to import or export goods, it has the power to achieve a terms-of-trade improvement at the expense of its trading partners. In effect, its share of the gains from international trade expands while that of its trading partners contracts, while at the same time the gains from trade as a whole are eroded. If the improvement in its share exceeds its proportionate part of the overall erosion of the gains from trade, it will be better off. There exists an extensive literature on the determinants of an optimum degree of market distortion in the search for maximum national gain. Of course, the country's trading partners will suffer an unambiguous loss—due both to the adverse terms-of-trade shift and to the erosion of the gains from trade—and the probability of retaliation always exists. In the event of retaliation, the global gains from trade will be further eroded and the terms of trade will shift against the initiating country, possibly provoking counter-retaliation.

An additional national-interest consideration involves countervailing duties and antidumping measures.

The matter of subsidies is exceedingly complex, in terms of their forms and their welfare effects and the impact on trade and economic structure. As noted earlier, subsidies to production or exports can occur in the form of cash grants, concessionary credits, tax abatements, labor training underwritten by the state, and various other ways, including public ownership of firms in international competition that operate at a loss. Measuring the effective degree of subsidization is a task that assumes close familiarity with cost structures and free-market benchmarks that often does not exist.

Subsidies bearing on exports tend to worsen the terms of trade of the subsidizing country, and to improve the terms of trade of countries that import subsidized products. There is a clear transfer of income from the former to the latter. But the focus of public policy is not on the transfer of purchasing power, but on the associated distortions in production and trade flows. The playing field is no longer level, and countervailing barriers may be imposed to neutralize the distortive effect of the subsidies.

Similarly, dumping transfers wealth from the seller to the buyer but also has effects on economic structure even if the motivation reflects nothing more than straightforward business practices—such as price discrimination between markets characterized by different demand elasticities where resale is impossible. It is predatory dumping—involving a recapture of economic rents once the import-competing players have been driven from the market, followed by permanent excess returns based on monopoly power—that is generally seen as unequivocally demanding of countervailing trade-policy action. Both in the subsidies and dumping areas, practical difficulties involved in ascertaining de facto market distortions raise the probability that countervailing measures will be used as a national-interest pretext for purely protectionist purposes.

Finally, there are macroeconomic arguments related to aggregate policy targets. There is no question, in the absence of retaliation, that beggar-thy-neighbor policies may improve the output and employment picture for a given country. The fact is, however, that any number can play this game; and this has often been sufficiently clear to discourage such policies in recent years.

All of these national-interest arguments for trade distortions are essentially static in nature. There are also dynamic arguments that focus on what kind of economic evolution is in the national interest. These range from the traditional infant-industry arguments raised by developing countries to industrial-structure arguments raised in developed countries at the frontiers of technology. At the other end of the economic spectrum are dynamic arguments concerning senile-industry protection and the terms and conditions underlying the disengagement of economic resources. Both are captured in the concepts of "industrial policy" that have evolved in both developing and developed countries. Both involve some sort of political or administrative mechanism for picking winners and losers and distinguishing between the two. Whether the eventual outcomes are superior to those determined entirely by market forces remains in doubt.

Rent-Seeking Distortions

Trade distortions clearly involve the transfer of economic rents, and quasi rents: this fundamental incentive underlies much protectionist behavior. In the kind of static partial-equilibrium framework presented in figure 2–1, this is captured in the increased producer surplus involved and capitalized in the value of the protected firm. However, protection may not be guaranteed, since it is the product of a political decision process that has a variety of probabilistic outcomes. The value of protection thus has to be adjusted for political risk, and it is this risk-adjusted cash flow that is in fact capitalized in the value of the firm to its shareholders.

The discussion of effective protection indicated that positive rents accruing to one industry can be accompanied by negative rents in another, if the protected product is an intermediate good such as carbon steel or petrochemical feedstocks. This can have the consequence of further de-

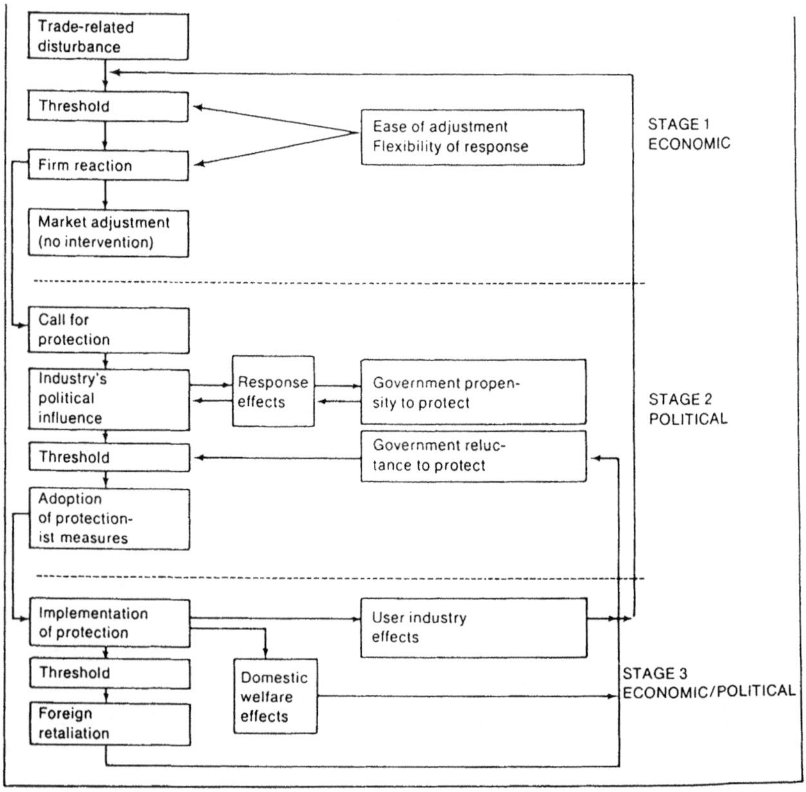

Figure 2–3. Political and Economic Elements in Sectoral Protection

mands for protection by downstream industries whose capitalized values have been eroded by protection-induced increases in production costs, or of political agitation against protection by these same industries.

Dynamic Adjustment Problems

Of particular interest in the analysis of the political economy of protection is the interaction between economic and political variables in the determination of final outcomes. Figure 2–3 presents a pathology of protection in which a trade-related disturbance, such as an improvement of production technology abroad, leads to an increase in market penetration on the part of imports. Pressure on market shares and prices reduce returns in the import-competing industry with respect to both labor and capital. Those under pressure must then decide whether to seek protection. This decision is based in part on the probability of success in the political arena and in part on the perceived costs of not seeking protection; the latter is a function of the ease of adjustment to market-driven competitive shifts. This threshold produces one of two responses, to seek protection or to adjust with the pressures of market forces. The entire process is largely driven by economic criteria, and can occur at the industry level—if there are sufficient commonalities among firms—or only at the level of the individual firm.

Once the call for protection has gone out, the process enters the political phase. Again a threshold is reached, which will decide whether or not protection will be accorded. This will depend on the political influence the firm or industry can command (regional concentration, employment level, upstream and downstream linkages, positive externalities, etc.) set against the propensity of the government to protect in the light of ideological considerations, effects on consumers, other industries, and the like. This is also influenced by the likelihood of foreign retaliation against the country's export industries. It is at this point that other sources of political influence enter the equation, including logrolling and financial contributions that can easily be supported by protection-induced gains in (preservation of) rents.

At this point the threshold again has two possible outcomes—protection and no protection. In the latter case, the firm or industry goes back to market-driven adjustment, possibly under less favorable circumstances because of the time and effort devoted to protection-seeking that has proved to be futile. In the former case, the protection-seeking activity may turn out to have extraordinarily high returns for the firm in terms of the returns invested, although, by increasing its dependence on protectionist policies, these must be discounted by the political risks (of reversal) involved.

Firms or industries that call for protection but do not have much chance of succeeding (for example, due to small size) within the context of the standard (*high-road*) trade-policy machinery may also have access to administrative (*low-road*) protection by means of nontariff barriers such as technical standards, customs practices, licensing procedures, and the like.

Once the decision has been made to protect, the vehicle for protection has to be selected, and at this point the process reenters the economic realm. Tariffs may be used, but they are in all likelihood bound under the GATT and thus incur a high probability of retaliation. Quotas may be used, but they too are covered under GATT, Article XIX. Subsidies may be used, but they involve a fiscal cost and in any case tend to be highly visible. Such constraints tend to bias the techniques of protection toward

NTBs, particularly, in recent years, toward VERs and OMAs. Economists do not have a hard time showing that the adverse welfare effects of VER/OMAs exceed those of quotas, which exceed those of tariffs, which in turn exceed those of subsidies. Yet in fact the political selection process seems consistently to produce exactly the opposite hierarchy, with seriously adverse welfare effects on the implementing country and on the international trading system.

There are, finally, a number of feedback effects identified in figure 2–3. The effects of protection on downstream industries may, as noted, lead to further calls for protection. The effects on domestic welfare, once recognized politically, will influence government attitides toward protection in the next period, as will the event of foreign retaliation against the home-country's export industries.

The system of political-economic interactions just described is obviously highly country specific in terms of the institutional overlay as well as the various parameters that determine the outcomes. The same trade-related disturbance may result in quite different outcomes in one country than in another, so that it is impossible to generalize. However, some sort of conceptual model such as the one presented here is quite helpful in analyzing the protection process as well as in developing prognoses as to its probable outcomes.

Protection, Structural Change, and Economic Growth

All of the discussion presented up to this point can be rather neatly summarized in terms of a diagram such as that presented in figure 2–4. The S-shaped curve represents a stylized development of an industry life cycle within the context of a national economy through time. An industry develops (phase 1), runs through a high-growth period (phase 2) and matures and ultimately may decline (phase 3) in terms of domestic value-added. The national economy can be represented as hundreds of such profiles (the number depending on the level of aggregation in industry definitions) superimposed upon one-another, with some profiles extending over decades or even centuries and others over a matter of months. At any given point in time, an industry can be envisaged as operating at a particular point on its unique life-cycle profile. Whereas static allocative efficiency in resource use can be evaluated using conventional general-equilibrium tools of analysis, a maximum *rate* of growth depends in this analysis on the proportion of labor, capital, and other resources that are lodged in the second phase of a country's industry profiles.

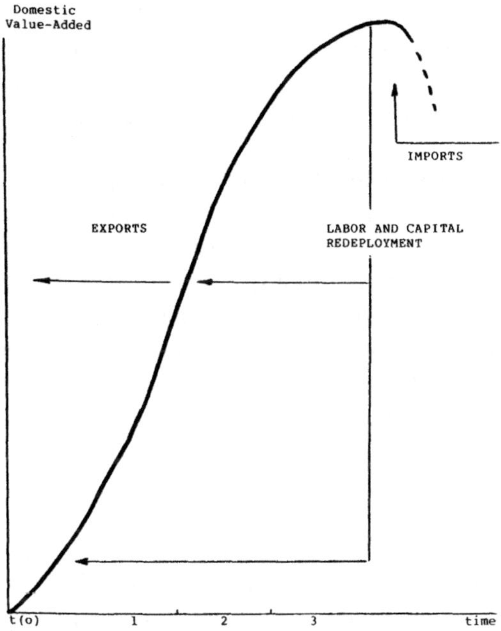

Figure 2–4. International Trade and Structural Adjustment

In an advanced country, industries lodged in phase 1 depend heavily on research-and-development spending, venture-capital availability, etc., and are most often based on breakthroughs in product technology. Firms engaged in these activities are often poorly capitalized, with a high failure rate, high costs, and short production runs. In less-advanced countries, they are based on product and process technologies brought in from outside, to be combined with locally available factors of production, particularly labor. In either case, they are the future economic powerhouses of their respective countries.

Phase 2 industries benefit from economics of scale, expanding markets, good cash flows, access to debt and equity capital, and production dividends associated with scale economies and management riding the "experience curve." They are highly profitable, based in advanced countries on the continued application of proprietary technology in products or processes, and in less-advanced countries on Heckscher-Ohlin benefits of factor availability and cost. Particularly toward the end of this phase, high-growth industries are attractive targets for organized labor. Since they are both profitable and often oligopolistically organized, management is frequently receptive to demands for improved wages, benefits, and working conditions, based on its ability to pass these costs on to customers. Once conferred, however, such labor gains may not be easy to reverse and may in fact give labor increased bargaining leverage once the industry goes into decline.

In phase 3 the industry has lost its competitive edge. Product and process technologies are no longer proprietary. Market structure has become increasingly competitive. Cost sensitivity becomes more of a problem, and management often has lost its cutting-edge as a result of its comfortable experience during the latter part of the golden age of high growth. Markets usually have matured and become saturated, showing increasing price sensitivity with respect to goods or services that have essentially become commodities. Organized labor is likely to have acquired a determining position driving the economics of the industry, with compensation levels well in excess of those prevailing in other parts of the national economy. This further erodes returns to capital and impedes management's ability to acquire labor-saving capital equipment and state-of-the art product and process technologies, as well as its ability to diversify into other, more-viable lines of business. Labor's power during the phase of an industry's decline may thus actually increase, and wage settlements may well exceed anything that is competitively tolerable, thereby accelerating the industry's erosion. Labor is in a position to resist fiercely a movement in the opposite direction ("give-backs") and to demand a say in the management of the firm. The two sides, however, may well become allies in the political battle to draw resources from the rest of the economy through subsidies or to retain the *status quo* through protection.

Even in a closed economy, growth in this framework depends in significant part on the reallocation of productive resources from industries that are in phase 3 to industries that are in phase 2 and, to a much smaller extent, phase 1. This "churning" of labor and capital is a necessary part of the economic-development process in both advanced and less-advanced economies. Like a tree, an economy grows in size, but it also changes shape. Technology changes as well as differential rates of growth in factor availabilities drive this continuous restructuring process which, as we have seen, is hardly free of adjustment costs for those most immediately concerned.

Enter international trade! Exports tend to be highly, though not exclusively, concentrated in industries that are in phase 2 of their respective evolutionary profiles, and these industries therefore have high stakes in obtaining access to foreign markets. Imports, meanwhile, tend to drive in and compete with industries that are in phase 3, accelerating the expulsion of labor and capital—with the weakest, high-cost players feeling the pressure first. The structural adjustment process accelerates, and so does the rate of economic growth. If adjustment costs are in part a function of the pace of market-driven economic restructuring, these burdens will be proportionately higher in more-open economies than in more-closed ones.

The owners of labor and capital subject to restructuring correctly perceive the associated costs to be largely private and to exceed their respective shares of the resulting efficiency and dynamic gains. Absent public policies to the contrary, they will have the incentive to take their case out of the Darwinian world of market-driven economics and into the political world of special-pleading driven by equity concerns, coalitions, and power relationships. If they are successful in obtaining protection, they will have succeeded in wounding the "killers" (imports), eroding allocative efficiency, and slowing economic growth. The results make no sense from a national economic standpoint if the objective is economic performance and growth in a competitive world economy, but it makes a great deal of sense if equity considerations are paramount—and it certainly makes sense from the standpoint of the affected interest groups.

The real question is how a maximum of efficiency and growth gains can be retained within a politically defensible definition of equity. The trade-offs are as clear-cut as they are difficult to measure. One option noted earlier is trade adjustment assistance (TAA), wherein society bears some or most of the costs of adjustment that otherwise would have to be carried by individuals. This could logically be expected to defuse protectionist pressure, and (unless the social discount rate is extraordinarily low) the net present value of the future stream of economic gains is likely to far exceed the once-and-for-all costs of TAA.

The most serious problem comes in designing TAA systems that will in fact ensure "adjustment out" rather than "adjustment in," whereby the benefits of TAA are captured by factor owners who have no intention of engaging in affirmative restructuring. And there is the moral-hazard issue that factor owners who know that TAA is available will have far less incentive to prepare themselves (possibly preemptively) for affirmative restructuring than those who see the handwriting on the wall, who know they will eventually have to suffer the costs on their own, and who are convinced that these costs will increase with time. Actual experience with TAA has not been promising, and it is not clear that modern democratically based political institutions are capable of coming to grips with this problem.

The problem is no less serious for technology-follower countries, except that the possibility of infant-industry protection enters the picture at phase

1 and involves the problem of picking winners alongside the ubiquitous problems of disengagement and restructuring. Industrial policy may have a more important role to play here, given the likelihood that less reliance may be placed on free markets both in this respect and in culling losers. The fundamental question is how to integrate market signals in a manner that is economically defensible and politically acceptable.

Conclusion

The theoretical model that underlies the argument for free trade and a liberal open-trading system fails to countenance many of the new complexities of the real world. Analyses of protection must, therefore, be more intricate and subtle than a straightforward emphasis on free trade as the first-best policy at all times and in all places. The existence of shocks and the rapid evolution of comparative advantage that mark dynamic reality, contradict the theory's static assumptions (Gordon 1976). Similarly, neglect of the existence of political pressures in industrialized democracies restricts the ability of the system to diagnose dynamic instability in national commercial policies.

The fact that dynamic change can provide valid reason for temporary protection (retardation but not suppression) does not mean that policymakers should lose sights of the long-run efficiencies of an open trading system. Nor should policymakers react to every instance of shock or change by instituting retardation policies. The problems of identifying the correct policy, the assessment of its costs and benefits, and the difficulties in instituting such policies with the appropriate safeguards all argue that protection in its adjustment-through-time dimension must be instituted cautiously and in times of substantial and identifiable turbulence only. Recognition that political factors can generate dynamic instability requires that the approach to international cooperation needs to pay greater attention to the political mechanisms and that analysts concentrate on the development of mechanisms whereby temporary, phase-out protection can be incorporated within the frameworks of the GATT.

Notes

1. This view finds its most authoritative expression in the opening sentence of a chapter in John Stuart Mill's *Principles of Political Economy* entitled "Of Interferences of Governments Grounded on Erroneous Theories." Mill opens the topic with "Of these false theories, the

most notable is the doctrine of Protection to Native Industry" (1909, p. 917).

2. For a description of U.S. regulations, see Gray, Pugel, and Walter (1982, sect. II).

3. The mechanics are described in detail in Grubel (1971).

4. This method of distributing production geographically according to relative national costs is called *production sharing* (Drucker 1977).

5. Relinquishing the wage premia or the returns to industry-specific skills will engender great opposition within the industry to the free-trade ideal and will contribute importantly to political pressures for protection—see the section *Elements of the Political Economy of Protection* below.

6. More interesting than the highly simplified model adduced to support the argument are Krueger's insights into the way in which rent-seeking—by virtue of the arbitrary quality of the distribution of rents (possibly through bribery, favoritism, or nepotism)—makes the market suspect in the eyes of the general population and encourages further intervention to control the allocative mechanism. Given the greater faith in planning that exists in many developing countries, Krueger's insights could prove valuable in offering one reason for what appears to be a relatively general preference for a "command system" in developing countries.

7. Cascading is still a feature of the modern tariff system. At the end of the implementation of all tariff reductions negotiated in the Tokyo Round, the average duty on raw materials was 0.3 percent and on semimanufactures 4.0 percent.

8. Some nations show an unwillingness to adjust at all, and the term "economic sclerosis" is used to describe this refusal to allow industries to decline.

9. Because membership in the GATT is heavily made up of industrialized nations, this section will emphasize North-North conflicts.

10. Subsidies did generate a code of conduct under the Tokyo Round: the Agreement on Interpretation and Application of Articles VI, XVI and XXIII of the GATT.

11. The U.S., bilateral deficit with Japan has, of course, also been attributable to the strength of the U.S. dollar in the 1980s.

12. Industrial policy extends beyond matters of international concern and protectionism.

13. Gray (1985) argues that much of the disillusionment on the part of LDC delegates derives from a lack of awareness of the political and economic problems of adjustment imposed by rapidly increasing exports of LDC manufactures.

14. These are the "adjustment-facilitating" measures discussed in the previous section.

References

Baldwin, R. E. 1976. *The Political Economy of U.S. Trade Policy*. The Bulletin, Bulletin 1976–4. Center for the Study of Financial Institutions, Graduate School of Business Administration, New York University.

Baldwin, R. E. 1978. "The Economics of the Gatt." In P. Oppenheimer, ed., *Issues in International Economics*, pp. 82–93. Stocksfield: Oriel Press.

Barry, J. R. J. 1981. "International Political Economy: Problems and Issues—Part I." *Review of International Studies* 7 (March), pp. 245–260.

Bergsten, C. F., O. Keohane, and J. S. Nye, Jr. 1975. "International Economics and International Politics: A Framework for Analysis." In C. F. Bergsten and L. B. Krause, eds., *World Politics and International Economics*, pp. 3–36. Washington, DC: Brookings Institution.

Bhagwati, J. N., ed. 1974. *Illegal Transactions in International Trade*. Amsterdam: North-Holland.

Bhagwati, J. N., and B. Hansen. 1973. "A Theoretical Analysis of Smuggling." *Quarterly Journal of Economics* 87 (May), pp. 172–187.

Brock, W. A., and S. P. Magee, 1978. "The Economics of Special Interest Politics: The Case of the Tariff." *American Economic Review* 68 (May), pp. 246–250.

Brock, W. A., and S. P. Magee. 1980. "Tariff Formation in a Democracy." In J. Black and B. Hindley, eds., *Current Issues in Commercial Policy and Diplomacy*, pp. 1–9. New York: St. Martin's Press, 1980.

Brock, W. A., and S. P. Magee. 1980. "A Model of Politics, Tariffs and Rent-Seeking in General Equilibrium." Paper presented at the International Economic Association, Sixth World Congress of Economists, Mexico City, August 7, 1980.

Casson, M. C. 1982. "Transaction Costs and the Theory of Multinational Enterprise." In A. M. Rugman, ed., *New Theories of Multinational Enterprise*, pp. 24–43. London: Croom Helm, 1982.

Caves, R. E. 1976. "Economic Models of Political Choice: Canada's Tariff Structure." *Canadian Journal of Economics* 9 (May), pp. 278–300.

Connolly, M. 1970. "Public Goods, Externalities, and International Relations." *Journal of Political Economy* 78 (March/April), pp. 279–290.

Corden, M. W. 1974. *Trade Policy and Economic Welfare*. London: Oxford University Press.

Drucker, P. F. 1977. "The Rise of Production Sharing." *Wall Street Journal*, March 15, p. 22.

Findley, R., and S. Wellisz. 1982. "Endogenous Tariffs, The Political Economy of Trade Restrictions and Welfare." In J. N. Bhagwati, ed., *Import Competition and Response*, pp. 223–243. Chicago: University of Chicago Press, 1982.

Finger, J. M., H. K. Hall, and D. R. Nelson. 1982. "The Political Economy of Administered Protection." *American Economic Review* 72 (June), pp. 452–466.

Glismann, H. H., and F. D. Weiss. 1980. *On the Political Economy of Protection in Germany*. World Bank Staff Working Paper 427. Washington, DC: World Bank.

Gordon, R. A. 1976. "Rigor and Relevance in a Changing International Setting." *American Economic Review* 66 (March), pp. 1–14.

Gray, H. P. 1985. "North-South Trade: An Impasse in Policy Formulation." *European Journal of Political Economy* 1(3), pp. 325–341.

Gray, H. P., T. A. Pugel, and I. Walter. 1982. *Employment, Trade and North-South Cooperation: United States Country Study*. WEB Working Paper. Geneva: International Labor Office.

Gray, H. P., and I. Walter. 1983. "Investment-Related Trade Distortions in Petrochemicals." *Journal of World Trade Law* 17 (July/August), pp. 283–307.

Grubel, H. G. 1971. "Effective Tariff Protection: A Non-Specialist Introduction to the Theory, Policy Implications and Controversies." In H. G. Grubel and H. G. Johnson, eds., *Effective Tariff Protection*, pp. 1–15. Geneva: General Agreement on Tariffs and Trade and Graduate Institute of International Studies, 1971.

Hadley, E. M. 1982. "Is the US-Japan Trade Imbalance a Problem?" *Journal of Northeast Asian Studies* 1 (March), pp. 35–36.

Hager, Wolfgang. 1982. "North-South Trade and Socio-Economic Autonomy: A Peace Formula." *Trade and Development UNCTAD Review* (Winter), pp. 119–128.

Helleiner, G. K. 1977. "The Political Economy of Canada's Tariff Structure: An Alternative Model." *Canadian Journal of Economics* 10 (May), pp. 318–326.

Hufbauer, G. C. 1983. "Subsidy Issues after the Tokyo Round." In W. R. Cline, ed., *Trade Policy in the 1980s*, pp. 327–361. Washington, DC: Institute for International Economics, 1983.

Johnson, H. G. 1960. "The Cost of Protection and the Scientific Tariff." *Journal of Political Economy* 68 (August), pp. 327–345.

Johnson, H. G. 1965. "An Economic Theory of Protectionism, Tariff Bargaining, and the Formation of Customs Unions." *Journal of Political Economy* 73 (June), pp. 256–283.

Kemp, M. C. 1976. "Smuggling and Optimal Commercial Policy." *Journal of Public Economics* 5 (April–May), pp. 381–384.

Keohane, R. O., and J. S. Nye. 1973. "World Politics and the International System." In C. F. Bergsten, ed., *The Future of the International Economic Order: An Agenda for Research*, pp. 115–179. Lexington, MA: Heath, 1973.

Kindleberger, C. P. 1951. "Group Behavior and International Trade." *Journal of Political Economy* 59 (February), pp. 30–47. Reprinted in C. P. Kindleberger, *Economic Response: Comparative Studies in Trade, Finance, and Growth*, pp. 19–38. Cambridge, MA: Harvard University Press, 1978.

Kreinin, M. E. 1970. "On the Equivalence of Tariffs and Quotas." *Kyklos* 23, pp. 75–79.

Krueger, A. O. 1974. "The Political Economy of the Rent-Seeking Society." *American Economic Review* 64 (June), pp. 291–303.

Leibenstein, H. 1978. "On the Basic Proposition of X-Efficiency Theory." *American Economic Review* 68 (May), pp. 328–332.

Meade, J. E. 1955. *Trade and Welfare*. Oxford: Oxford University Press.

Messerlin, P. A. 1981. "The Political Economy of Protectionism: The Bureaucratic Case." *Weltwirtschaftliches Archiv* 117, pp. 469–496.

Michalski, W. 1983. "The Need for Positive Adjustment Policies in the 1980s." *Intereconomics* 8 (January/February), pp. 42–48.

Mill, J. S. 1909. *Principles of Political Economy*. London: Longmans, Green.

Moxon, R. W. 1984. "Export Platform Foreign Investments in the Asia-Pacific Region." In R. W. Moxon, T. W. Roehl, and J. F. Truitt, eds., *International Business Strategies in the Asia-Pacific Region*. Greenwich, CT: JAI Press, 1984.

Murray, T. 1977. *Trade Preferences for Developing Countries*. London: Macmillan Press.

OECD. 1979. *The Impact of the Newly Industrializing Countries*. Paris: OECD.

Pincus, J. J. 1962. *Sharing the Costs of Military Alliance and International Econo-*

mic Aid. Santa Monica, CA: Rand Corporation.

Pugel, T. A., and I. Walter. 1985. "U.S. Corporate Interests and the Political Economy of Trade Policy." *Review of Economics and Statistics* 67 (August), pp. 465–473.

Riedel, J. 1977. "Tariff Concession in the Kennedy Round and the Structure of Protection in West Germany, An Econometric Assessment." *Journal of International Economics* 7 (May), pp. 133–143.

Russett, B. M., ed. 1968. *Economic Theories of International Politics*. Chicago: Markham.

Schultze, C. L. 1983. "Industrial Policy: A Solution in Search of a Problem." *California Management Review* 25 (Summer), pp. 5–15.

Tullock, G. 1967. "The Welfare Costs of Tariffs, Monopolies and Theft." *Western Economic Journal* 5 (June), pp. 224–232.

Walter, I. 1969. "Nontariff Barriers and the Free-Trade Area Option." *Banca Nazionale del Lavoro Quarterly Review* 88 (March), pp. 16–45.

Walter, I. 1971. "On the Equivalence of Tariffs and Quotas: Comment." *Kyklos* 24, pp. 111–112.

Weil, F. A. 1983. "U.S. Industrial Policy: A Process in Need of a Federal Industrial Coordination Board." *Law and Policy in International Business* 14(4), pp. 981–1039.

Wolf, Martin. 1983. "Managed Trade in Practice: Implications of the Textile Arrangements." In William R. Cline, ed., *Trade Policy in the 1980s*, pp. 455–482. Washington, DC: Institute for International Economics, 1983.

COMMENT

James H. Cassing

Professors Gray and Walter (G-W) present a very timely and critical evaluation of recent developments in the area of "protection." Traditionally, they take protection to mean intervention or regulation of foreign commerce and, while "industry assistance" might be a more apt description, the real hallmark of a protective policy is, as they say, discrimination in favor of domestic industry over foreign producers. The following comments also take this definition and largely aim to complement and extend what G-W have to say about such policy intervention, albeit from a slightly different perspective.

The central paradox posed by protection is that while under certain competitive conditions such intervention is not Pareto efficient, it nonetheless seems to persist. Thus society apparently adopts a commercial policy which by unanimous consent is inferior to an alternative policy. Popular examples from U.S. trade policy include costs of \$74,000 per year to protect one job in the television-receiver industry, where the average wage is \$22,900; \$110,000 to protect one job in the steel industry; and an astonishing \$300,000 per job annually in the automobile industry. A vast literature—really the heart of normative trade theory—has attempted to clarify the sense in which such protection harms society and to reconcile this with the apparent ubiquity of protectionism.

The reconciliation between theory and fact has itself followed one of two tacks. First, it can be argued that there are circumstances under which protection is on balance in the national interest and so the paradox of nationally harmful intervention disappears. For example, nations may use trade taxes or export quotas to exploit monopoly power in international trade, as with coffee or oil. Second, one can focus instead upon the income redistributional consequences of protection within a nation and argue that the politically expedient response to special-interest-group demands can logically result in policies that are in sum nationally harmful. Thus, for example, concentrating the obvious "benefits" of protection on a few producers and spreading the costs widely over consumers at large may bias self-interested politicians toward advocating some protectionist policies.

The "national interest" reconciliation, as G-W report, was the focus of considerable past research which typically dismissed first- and second-best arguments for protection as practically nonimplementable—for example, the "optimum tariff"—or as inferior to some purely domestic policy—for example, the superiority of a production subsidy over a trade tax in order to underwrite some import-competing industry's output for national defense purposes. In many ways, it was the success of this literature that sharpened the paradox and led to a more intense investigation of pressure-group politics as protection's root cause.

While research aimed at an understanding of the political economy of protection continues to evolve, however, the national-interest explanation is itself enjoying a bit of a resurgence. And this suggests a framework for comments on G-W. The next section reviews recent developments in what G-W term the "traditional analysis" of protection and suggests that protection in the national interest remains an active research area. Nonetheless, the G-W thesis of a "dynamically unstable" international trading system owing more to a lack of cooperation and political will than to any "national interest" argument seems to ring true. So, the subsequent sections attempt to corroborate the G-W thesis in fact and then turn to recent research which attempts to explain trade controls in terms of the political economy of protection.

Traditional Analysis and the National-Interest Explanation of Protection

G-W clearly elucidate the traditional analysis of protection. As they indicate, the emphasis has always been on investigating and measuring the allocative effects of various commercial policies. Thus there is a blizzard of theoretical and empirical research which identifies and measures the effects of tariffs, quotas, voluntary export restraints, subsidies, discriminatory procurement, import surveillance, product safety requirements, and so on, within both partial- and general-equilibrium contexts. While subtle differences are introduced by each new protectionist device—and this is why the analysis of new policy tools is always an important area for new research—the qualitative conclusions are inevitably the same. In the absence of terms-of-trade effects, protection drives a wedge between foreign and domestic prices and so confers the usual net deadweight cost of an equivalent distortionary tax or subsidy. While the introduction of various market imperfections and uncertainty admits the possibility of a net welfare improvement, trade restrictions in these cases are dominated by superior policies and more typically protection is more, not less, costly in the presence of market imperfections. (This explains why the bulk of disinterested economists favor free trade as a policy which promotes economic efficiency.)

The national-interest case for protection then turns on the efficacy of trade policy as an instrument for terms-of-trade improvement. But such government-orchestrated policies as the "optimum tariff" are usually dismissed, especially in the presence of retaliation. Thus, as G-W comment, interest has been drawn away from coherent intervention in the national interest as an explantion of protection and research has been directed increasingly toward the political economy of protection.

Recently, however, attention has again focused on the possibility of a national-welfare-improving activist trade policy under the rubric of "strategic trade policy."[1] The possibility of beneficial intervention rests on the perception that governments and firms do not operate in a passive world. Rather, government policy makers and domestic firms find themselves in a strategic game-like environment in which other governments and foreign competitors react to new trade policies or business decisions. Thus there is some latitude through national policy to shape favorably the range of choices perceived as optimal from the foreign standpoint.

At the national level, strategic trade policy has as its genesis Harry Johnson's (1954) study of the optimum tariff with retaliation wherein two countries play a Cournot game with tariff policy. That study admits of two possible Nash equilibria outcomes: (1) both countries enact tariffs and are worse off than with free trade or (2) both countries enact tariffs and one country is better off than with free trade. The first outcome is the standard "prisoner's dilemma" result and would never occur if countries cooperated. This is undoubtedly what G-W have in mind as the case for nations supporting "rules of the game" such as the GATT. In this view, international cooperation underwrites the mutually beneficial open-trading system and the erosion of its principles are justifiably viewed with dismay. Recent and continuing research has reinforced this view by deriving the mutually destructive noncooperative equilibrium in more realistic environments.[2] (Similarly, some "rules" or policies often characterized as protectionist in spirit—antidumping laws and countervailing duties—can be argued to be unilaterally optimal tactics to encourage free trade in a strategic trade environment.)

In the second possible equilibrium outcome, one country actually wins the tariff war. This outcome has also generated some recent interest and stands as a theoretically legitimate explanation of tariffs or, more generally, protection.[3] In this view, free trade is predictably not observed, since it is not in everyone's national interest, and policies that sidestep the GATT are inevitable. Moreover, those nations that lose tariff wars must nonetheless strategically enact some protection in order at least to mitigate their losses, and so protection becomes pervasive. An important line of research might attempt to discriminate between these two competing hypotheses of protection and, for example, investigate the system-wide terms-of-trade effects of existing trade policies, appealing perhaps to some computable general-equilibrium model.

At the industry level, strategic trade policy in the national interest becomes credible if the market environment is imperfectly competitive and, in particular, if positive economic profits are being reaped. This may in fact come very close to the world described by G-W, since the source of extranormal profits typically resides in an environment of rapid change, high tech, R&D, special proprietary knowledge, and economies of scale. Also, the stylized facts are consistent with the timely topic of trade and protection in services such as transport, insurance, and banking. In such a world, firms establish market shares as in a game—for example, Cournot oligopoly—and profits accrue in proportion.

The thrust of the new literature is that governments can alter the way in which firms play the "quest for rents" game. Thus, a government can potentially intervene to raise domestic firms' profits not at the expense of still lower domestic consumer welfare, as in the traditional static analysis, but at the expense of lower foreign-firm profits—a net domestic welfare gain. And the tools of intervention run the gamut of protectionist devices.

The practical implications of the new strategic trade policy research are muddled, however. Much of the analysis is highly stylized and draws heavily on specific numerical examples. And, while the models are suggestive, they really provide little specific guidance as to how governments should or whether governments do, or could, shape trade policy in the national interest. In fact, there is some professional agreement that, all matters of implementation considered, herein lies no case for government intervention after all.[4]

Nonetheless, G-W probably go too far in asserting that "explorations in the pure theory of commercial policy have fallen into relative quiescence." I suspect that the theory of commercial policy, recast in a strategic environment and using the tools of modern game theory, will continue to be an area of active research interest in the traditional spirit of analyzing the allocative effects of protection. One might also suspect, however, that the new national-interest arguments will be rejected as a valid case for protection and that generally such first-best arguments have little to do with the observed pattern of protection in the world. But this is an empirical issue which needs research.

In any case, if the national-interest arguments, old or new, are dismissed, then the paradox of ubiquitous protection is thrown open and the explanation must be sought either in political economy or, more boldly, in the claim that there is little actual government intervention in international competition.

The World Trading System: Is There a Resurgence of Protection?

G-W argue that the post-World War II liberal trading system represents an important institution that is currently threatened with piecemeal abandonment of its principles by constituent governments themselves confronted by domestic pressures for protection. The problem then arises that, once governments begin to desert the rules of the game, the breakdown in the international trading system may snowball with increasing resort to bilateralism and the imposition of subtle, difficult-to-negotiate, nontariff barriers.

There is certainly concern currently over the perceived resurgence of a "new protectionism" characterized by trade barriers far less transparent than traditional tariffs. The actual facts, however, are impressionistic and there is considerable need here for empirical research. Since World War II, the series of multilateral trade negotiations conducted under the auspices of the General Agreement on Tariffs and Trade (GATT) have virtually eliminated tariffs. The Tokyo Round (1979) guaranteed that average tariffs on industrial-country dutiable imports fell to about 6 percent by 1988; and, since the variance of tariffs has been reduced, it is generally conceded that tariff protection in major trading countries is negligible. However, as if to fill the vacuum, nontariff barriers (NTBs) to trade have emerged. In the 1950s the European Economic Community forged its protectionist Common Agricultural Policy. In the 1950s and 1960s clothing and textiles began to come under quota restraints. In 1961, the United States pioneered voluntary export restraints (VERs) with the Short Term Cotton Textile Arrangement which eventually grew into the highly protectionist Arrangement Regarding International Trade in Textiles or Multifibre Arrangement (MFA). Originally an informal, temporary agreement between the United States and Japan, the restraints on trade grew in depth and coverage. By 1986 there were 42 signatories to the MFA, covering four-fifths of the world trade in textiles and clothing. The footwear industry in industrial countries also came under quota protection early. And by the mid-1970s, VERs affected bicycles, electronic components, television sets, and cutlery. From the mid-1970s, this and other forms of managed trade proliferated.

Many NTBs, such as seasonal restrictions on agricultural imports, have the explicit intent of frustrating the international division of labor by protecting certain domestic industries from foreign competition. Such measures work to restrict artificially imports or to promote exports. Other NTBs, such as health and sanitary restrictions, purport to raise real national income but introduce trade-distorting barriers when applied (intentionally?) overzealously. Since appearances can so deceive, any list of NTBs is necessarily fuzzy, and some studies list as many as 200 such distortions.

Such a wide range of NTBs which often lack transparency makes it difficult to assess the extent to which NTBs actually affect international trade, however. Unlike tariffs, for which schedules are published in detail by government and international agencies, nontariff barriers are very difficult to evaluate. Essentially, three problems arise. First, data are not uniformly or accurately collected. For example, in 1981 temporary protection under safeguard measures reported to the GATT covered $2 billion worth of trade, while $60 billion worth of trade was so restricted without reference to the GATT.[5] Second, many nontariff barriers overlap in the sense that a given product is subject to several impediments, and so it is difficult to isolate the impact of any given NTB. Finally, it is difficult to assess potential trade that would have occurred in the absence of NTBs and the uncertainty created by their presence. Nonetheless, some recent research has yielded insights into the extent of the new protectionism and it tends to corroborate the G-W hypothesis of a dynamically unstable system.[6]

Most countries appear now to employ some form of nontariff trade barriers, and the usage is growing. About two-thirds of the world's nations use export controls, and nearly half of the nations employ licensing. The

EEC and the United States use most standard types of trade restriction. Japan appears to use a somewhat narrower range of barriers. The disparity in usage by country, however, is large: Nigeria controls all of its imports, while Saudi Arabia has virtually no import controls.

The actual degree to which various countries incorporate particular NTBs in commercial policy is very difficult to measure. The UNCTAD (1981a), however, offers a first approximation by calculating a *coverage measure* that shows the proportion of total imports subject to certain nontariff measures. These data indicate that United States commercial policy incorporates a number of NTBs, of which quotas are the most prevalent, that cover about 2.6 percent of trade by value. Minimum prices tend to affect primarily developed-countries' exports, while export restraints fall especially on developing-countries' exports. Japan employs such NTBs as quotas and licensing, especially in the case of developed-countries' exports, and subjects over 25 percent of its developed-country imports to health and sanitary regulations. (This compares with 2.4 and 4.4 percent for the United States and the EEC, respectively.) The EEC uses every NTB listed, to some extent. In terms of the coverage index, quotas and licensing affect the most imports and variable levies apply to 6.6 percent of developed-countries' exports to the EEC.

The G-W concern is that the use of NTBs is growing, which appears to be the case for "managed trade" based on data from 1974 to 1980.[7] Worldwide, the proportion of managed trade for all goods increased about 13 percent—from 40.3 to 45.7 percent. Both the EEC and the United States recorded higher than the average increases but remained absolutely below the world average. Japan's proportion of managed trade remained above the average, but grew by only 6 percent—from 51.4 to 54.7 percent. Oil exporters accounted for the largest increase in managed trade, from 54.0 to 63.4 percent, while non-oil-developing countries actually decreased their managed-trade proportions for all goods.

Consistent with the G-W scenario, the trend toward managed trade in manufactures for industrial countries is considerably more pronounced. The worldwide proportion of managed manufacturing trade nearly doubled, from 12.9 to 21.3 percent. Almost all of this increase can be attributed to OECD countries, with a jump from 4.0 to 14.6 percent. The most dramatic increase in managed manufacturing trade was the EEC rise from only 0.1 to 13.7 percent. This increase was typical of each individual-member's experience. The United States' increase from 5.6 to 18.3 percent was proportionately lower, but the levels remain absolutely higher than for the EEC. The increase for Japan was from zero to 4.1 percent.

Of course, these trends indicate an increase only in the use of *potential* nontariff barriers. There is little direct evidence that exposes the extent to which most NTBs actually retard or divert trade, and this remains an important subject for the empirical investigation of protection.

One of the research difficulties is that, as G-W emphasize, static trade theory is less suited to evaluating the new protection than the "old." Trade barriers associated with the "old protection" focus on preserving capital values in particular sectors by artificially raising the domestic-output prices. Such measures as tariffs, if successful, entail net welfare losses to the extent that resources are lured out of more profitable (at world prices) sectors into the protected sectors and consumer demand is diverted away from the otherwise first-choice quantity of the protected commodity toward other goods. In addition to these deadweight costs, income distribution is affected as inputs tied more closely to protected sectors gain relative to other inputs and, in the case of trade taxes, the government collects some tax revenue. Naturally, foreign exporters lose markets.

The new protection differs in spirit and method from the old, and this introduces some new costs. In particular, the current rise in the use of nontariff barriers has been accompanied by an erosion in the post-World War II liberal-trading principles such as nondiscrimination and an emphasis on "order" and "equity" at the expense of allocational efficiency. Nontariff barriers, in the name of "order," now have become a part of many nations' commercial policies.

Undoubtedly the greatest long-run cost of the new protection is the one identified by G-W: the cost associated with destroying the system of rules that prevailed in the post-World War II era. The highly protectionist, and in welfare terms very costly, Multifibre Arrangement illustrates the trend. The MFA conflicts with the GATT principles in that the MFA replaces the nondiscriminatory with discriminatory treatment of trading partners, uses quotas rather than tariffs to restrict trade, and contravenes security of market access. Now the rules are being circumvented by a series of bilaterally negotiated export-restraint agreements in automobiles, steel, and other important sectors. The evenhandedness and transparency of the industrial countries' commercial policies are disappearing.

As the GATT rules are gradually ignored and replaced with arbitrary—and often nonsensical—conditions or agreements between governments, the amount of uncertainty in the trading community must increase, and this further reduces trade. Least-cost production is no longer a guarantee of sales in the presence of arbitrary health and safety standards, preferential government procurement policies, or the threat of quantitative restrictions imposed if some economically meaningless import-penetration ratio is exceeded. The threat of countervailing duties or antidumping investigations has a similar trade-retarding effect which, the new strategic-trade-policy research notwithstanding, is probably quite harmful.

Also greatly enhanced by the new protection with its dependence on NTBs is the cost associated with negotiating, monitoring, and enforcing a complex system of agreements. For example, the MFA has been negotiated periodically over nearly two decades and now has 42 signatories, counting the EEC as one, covering four-fifths ($80 billion) of the world trade in textiles and clothing. Attempts to bypass restrictions illegally have flourished, and the response has been to erect still more controls.

Finally, NTBs entail the usual static costs of protection and some difficult-to-measure dynamic costs as well. To the extent that competition is diminished, efficiency—or X-efficiency in G-W—incentives may be lessened or more monopolistic market structures may be underwritten. Here one's attitude toward the new strategic-trade-policy research assumes importance. Is the change in the competitive environment a cost? In any case, the possibility of additional protection from foreign competition undoubtedly ushers energy and resources into rent-seeking activity and encourages a reluctance to adjust to shifting patterns of comparative advantage.

The G-W discussion of political economy now becomes pertinent. While economists and policymakers increasingly agree that there has been a resurgence of protection in industrial countries in the 1980s and that the new protection is characterized by a heavy reliance on nontariff barriers, there is no agreement on the source of the current mood of protectionism. Explanations range from the decline of hegemonic stability to overvalued or undervalued currencies. G-W take the view that the erosion of the international trading system stems initially from recession and government-policy response to domestic-industry pressure ignited by unanticipated shifts in comparative advantage.

New Strains on the System and the Adjustment Issue

In their political-economy discussion of the source of protectionist pressure, G-W distinguish between rent-seeking and dynamic-adjustment problems or resistance to unanticipated losses necessitated by change, especially increased import penetration by developing countries. While the former explanation has received the most recent attention, I agree with G-W that something along their "adjustment problem" lines is closer to the mark on both theoretical and empirical grounds.

Rent-Seeking

Much theoretical, and almost all empirical, research on the observed pattern of protection rests on the existence of industry-specific factors and the characterization of the industry as the beneficiary of protection.[8] (Alternatively, one could look at the functional distribution of income along Stolper-Samuelson lines.) Thus, the gain from securing protection is identified with the increased rents—area a in figure 2–1—associated with protection. The quest for such rents then creates the demand for protection and the rent-seeking model is closed along lines of the regulated-industry literature by assuming the existence of a protection-granting authority that balances the marginal favor gleaned from protecting an industry against the marginal disfavor incurred from raising prices to consumers. The empirical literature furthermore specifies industry characteristics that are more or less amenable to forming cohesive rent-seeking coalitions, following Downs (1957) or Olson (1965), while controlling for the regulatory and opposition environment.

The problem is that while everyone identifies the rents, no one ever identifies the seekers. Presumably the rents accrue to owners of industry-specific assets—roughly, the physical capital—and so to the shareholders. But stock markets allow individuals to diversify their ownership portfolios across industries and the prudent investor should have little interest in augmenting the profits of one industry at the expense of more than offsetting profit losses in other industries. It is difficult to find a protectionist mutual fund.

Nonetheless, protectionist coalitions do exist and there is some evidence that their spokespeople follow industry cleavages (Magee 1978). This suggests two lines of potential research. First, one might identify corporate interests beyond those of the mere shareholder. One possibility is that when shareholders, in order to overcome the principle-agent problem, tie management to the firm's prosperity—for example, by loading managers' portfolios with a disproportionately high amount of own-firm shares—they inadvertently confer on management an interest in industry protection counter to that of the diversified shareholder. The explosion of employee stock-ownership plans since the tax-law change in 1974 may also tie workers more closely to physical capital. Similarly, to the extent that union bargaining provides a mechanism for sharing in capital's rents, more-unionized sectors might represent the rent-seekers. (The existence of undiversified owners of human capital is discussed below.)

A second line of useful research would identify undiversified owners of assets the values of which are tied to industry output levels but are not specific to the industry per se. For example, for various reasons individuals tend to hold a disproportionately large share of their asset portfolios in place-specific assets such as homes or small businesses. These individuals are naturally interested in the prosperity of important local industries, since the level of employment translates into higher regional income and so into higher values for place-specific assets. To the extent that protection leads to output expansion, this group represents a strong community-based rent-seeking coalition. Such coalitions probably play a crucial role in what G-W refer to as "dynamic adjustment problems."[9]

Dynamic-Adjustment Problems

G-W take the view that much protection is rooted in industries' reluctance to adjust to trade-related disturbances in prospect of an appeal to the political process which, depending on the industry and the political climate, may result in protection. While this seems to explain the observed pattern of protection in advanced industrial countries at least, in order to understand the ultimate source of the protectionist appeal it is necessary to clarify what is meant by adjustment.

When terms of trade change, productivity gains may be secured with a proper reallocation of the domestic resource base. Over time, the relatively favored (higher-return) industries should expand and absorb resources from the relatively unfavored (lower-return) industries, which must contract and release resources. The speed at which this process unfolds depends upon the atomistic decision making of resource owners who respond to newly structured incentives. Optimally, the factor reallocation would proceed at a pace that maximizes the discounted present value of real national income. (This does not ordinarily entail maximizing real national income at each point in time.) Since national income is just the sum of individuals' incomes, we would expect individual-income-maximizing behavior to ensure that the optimal rate of resource redeployment obtains.

Thus, factors of production must physically adjust. But the adjustment costs that motivate protectionist demands are not the physical adjustment costs. Rather, the relevant costs are the written-down capital values associated with the restructured market incentives attendant to an unanticipated deterioration in an industry's terms of trade. These costs fall on the owners of factors tied to the industry and in proportion to the extent of industry specificity.[10] Therefore owners of mobile factors such as unskilled labor incur relatively low adjustment costs while owners of very industry-specific skills or physical capital incur large capital losses. Since mobile factors by definition can change jobs to minimize their loss and marginal firms can avoid some losses through shut-down, it is paradoxically the owners of physically nonadjusting factors who incur the largest capital losses and so are the most vocal constituency for protection. This has implications for both the source of protectionist pressure and any positive policies aimed to underwrite or encourage adjustment for trade.

In regard to the source of protectionist demands, there is motivation for undiversified specific-factor owners in increasingly import-competitive industries to oppose the restructured market incentives that must accompany structural change. To the extent that changing patterns of comparative advantage can inflict adjustment costs and capital loss, there is ample opportunity to protect values through commercial policy. But the paradox remains that such protection is Pareto inefficient. That is, simply accepting terms-of-trade shifts and adjusting to exploit true comparative advantage increases real national income. The gains accrue to consumers, owners of productive factors specific to the favored industries, and owners of relatively mobile factors. In principle, the gains from adjusting to comparative-advantage shifts can many times offset the losses inflicted on a few.[11] But since protection is Pareto inefficient, a natural question arises: how can protectionism persist if by unanimous agreement an alternative resource allocation dominates? In other words, why have market institutions not arisen that will effect compensating transfers in order to secure Pareto-efficient resource allocation? Why do factor owners not diversify? At the heart of the answer is the source of protectionism.

A significant source of factor-owners' resistance to adjustment apparently resides in the failure of "insurance" markets, broadly defined, to operate. In a world of fluctuating prices, individuals may avoid risk or capital loss through portfolio diversification and preserve capital values by diversifying their ownership portfolios. If a landowner, for example, would rather not bear the entire risk of owning land, then he may sell some portion of the land and acquire ownership of an asset for which the price moves countercyclically with land prices. In general, the existence of stock (equity) markets allows owners of nonhuman wealth to spread the risk of capital loss through portfolio diversification. Many firms even spread risk internally by diversifying product lines. The principal asset of most individuals, however, resides in their human-labor potential and in skills acquired over time. But diversification or divestiture in human capital across humans is not legal. And, for an individual, diversification of skills is not practical. Consequently, the burden of structural change is apt to fall more heavily on a group that really has little opportunity to spread risk. Demands for protection seem inevitable, and it may therefore be entirely fitting that government policy socialize the risk of human-capital loss even at the expense of lower national income. To some extent, the same argument applies to trade-impacted communities as a whole. Policy intervention, however, is justifiable only if private insurance markets have indeed failed and if government policy can succeed where private actions cannot.[12]

Private programs to spread the trade-related risk of capital loss may fail for reasons other than legal constraints regarding human capital. Private insurance companies may themselves be unable to spread the risk of a general depression during which they would go bankrupt. Hence, private enterprise does not sell income insurance. Also, sufficient actuarial data are difficult to collect. Furthermore, the moral hazard and adverse selection involved in underwriting a worker's or firm's income stream might be significant.

In sum, structural change, although net beneficial, inflicts adjustment costs and capital losses for which market institutions do not compensate. The incentive for protection remains and the G-W discussion surrounding their figure 2–3 portrays fairly accurately how this incentive for a suboptimal resource allocation is translated into policy.

An important direction future research might pursue in the G-W framework is to explore the implications of incomplete markets for the structure of protectionist coalitions. All current research simply posits implicitly the inability of individuals to participate in the general growth of an open economy because asset ownership cannot be diversified across industries. The suggestion is to specify explicitly the source of the inability to diversify and then to couch positive adjustment policies in terms of providing the missing markets or, at least, exposing why they cannot be provided.

Finally, the G-W political-economy discussion emphasizes that the economics profession has concentrated on the analytics of protectionist tools and the source of protectionist demands. The response to such demands—the supply of protection—has long been the purview of political scientists and is only now, through the public-choice literature, being integrated into the economist's model of protection. For example, Baldwin (1986) studies trade policy decisions in the Congress, International Trade Commission, and Executive Branch, and finds that both pressure-group and government self-interest models are needed to explain trade policy.[13] I wholly agree with G-W that greater attention paid to the political mechanisms at both the national and international level is likely to occupy profitably an increasing proportion of the research effort expended on protection.

Notes

1. See Grossman and Richardson (1985) and Richardson (1986).
2. For example, Jensen and Thursby (1983).
3. See Riezman (1982) or Riezman and Kennan (1984).
4. For a discussion, see Dixit (1985), Dixit and Kyle (1984), and Krugman (1984).
5. *The Economist* (1982).
6. Studies include *GATT Activities*, annual; UNCTAD (1981a, 1981b); Page (1980), and Curzon (1981).
7. "Managed trade" includes any trade flow that is subject to some nontariff barrier by an exporter, importer, or both.
8. See the surveys in Colander (1984) and Lavergne (1983).
9. See Cassing, McKeown, and Ochs (1986).
10. On the possibility of "congested" labor or capital markets, wherein the private costs of adjustment to any one factor owner depend upon the *total* volume of adjusting factors, see Cassing and Ochs (1978).
11. For example, see Magee (1972).
12. For a discussion, see Cassing, Hillman; and Long (1986).
13. For a discussion of theoretical models of the government decision-making process and its implications for trade policy or adjustment, see, for example, Bhagwati and Srinivasan (1980), and Cassing and Hillman (1985, 1986).

References

Baldwin, R. E. 1986. *The Political Economy of U.S. Import Policy*. Cambridge, MA: MIT Press.

Bhagwati, J. N., and T. N. Srinivasan. 1980. "Revenue Seeking: A Generalization of the Theory of Tariffs." *Journal of Political Economy* 88 (December), pp. 1069–1087.

Cassing, J., and J. Ochs. 1978. "International Trade, Factor Market Distortions and the Optimal Dynamic Subsidy: Comment." *American Economic Review* 68 (December), pp. 950–955.

Cassing, J., and A. L. Hillman. 1985. "Political Influence Motives and the Choice Between Tariffs and Quotas." *Journal of International Economics* 19 (November), pp. 279–290.

Cassing, J., and A. L. Hillman. 1986. "Shifting Comparative Advantage and Senescent Industry Collapse." *American Economic Review* 76 (June), pp. 516–523.

Cassing, J., A. L. Hillman, and N. V. Long. 1986. "Risk Aversion, Terms of Trade Uncertainty, and Social-Consensus Trade Policy." *Oxford Economic Papers* 38 (July), pp. 234–242.

Cassing, J., T. McKeown, and J. Ochs. 1986. "The Political Economy of the Tariff Cycle." *American Political Science Review* 80 (September), pp. 843–862.

Colander, D., ed. 1984. *Neoclassical Political Economy*. Cambridge, MA: Ballinger.

Curzon, G. 1981. "Neo-protectionism, the MFA and the European Community." *The World Economy* 4 (September), pp. 251–262.

Dixit, A. K. 1985. "Strategic Aspects of Trade Policy." Paper presented at the Fifth World Congress of the Econometrics Society, 1985.

Dixit, A. K., and A. S. Kyle. 1984. "On the Use of Trade Restrictions for Entry Promotion and Deterrence." Discussion Papers in Economics No. 56, Woodrow Wilson School of Public and International Affairs, Princeton University.

Downs, A. 1957. *An Economic Theory of Democracy*. New York: Harper & Row.

The Economist, April 24, 1982, p. 92.

GATT. 1981. *GATT Activities*. (Annual.) Geneva.

Grossman, G. M., and J. D. Richardson. 1985. *Strategic Trade Policy: A Survey of Issues and Early Analysis*. Princeton Special Papers in International Economics No. 15, April 1985. Princeton, NJ: International Finance Section, Princeton University.

Jensen, R., and M. Thursby. 1983. "Free Trade: Two Non-cooperative Equilibrium Approaches." Ohio State University, processed, 1983.

Johnson, H. G. 1954. "Optimum Tariffs and Retaliation." *Review of Economic Studies*, 21(2), pp. 142–153.

Krugman, P. R. 1984. "The U.S. Response to Foreign Industrial Targeting." *Brookings Papers on Economic Activity* (No. 1, 1984), pp. 77–131.

Lavergne, R. P. 1983. *The Political Economy of U.S. Tariffs*. New York: Academic Press.

Magee, S. P. 1972. "The Welfare Effects of Restrictions on U.S. Trade." *Brookings Papers on Economic Activity* (No. 3, 1972), pp. 645–701.

Magee, S. P. 1978. "Three Simple Tests of the Stolper-Samuelson Theorem." In P. Oppenheimer, ed., *Issues in International Economics*, pp. 138–153. Stocksfield: Oriel Press, 1978.

Olson, M. 1965. *The Logic of Collective Action*. Cambridge, MA: Harvard University Press.

Page, S. A. B. 1980. "The Increased Use of Trade Controls by the Industrial Countries." *Intereconomics* 3 (May/June), pp. 144–151.

Richardson, J. D. 1986. "Trade-Policy Implications of Strategic Economic Models." National Bureau of Economic Research, processed, 1986.

Riezman, R. 1982. "Tariff Retaliation from a Strategic Viewpoint." *Southern Economic Journal* 48 (January), pp. 583–593.

Riezman, R., and J. Kennan. 1984. "Do Big Countries Win Tariff Wars?" Discussion paper, University of Iowa, November 1984.

UNCTAD. 1981a. *Non-Tariff Measures Facing Developing Countries Exports of Primary and Processed Commodities*. Report by the UNCTAD secretariat.

UNCTAD. 1981b. *Protectionism and Structural Adjustment*. Report by the UNCTAD secretariat.

3 INTERNATIONAL LINKAGES, EXCHANGE-RATE REGIMES, AND THE INTERNATIONAL TRANSMISSION PROCESS: PERSPECTIVES FROM OPTIMIZING MODELS

Kent P. Kimbrough*

Much progress has been made in recent years toward a better understanding of the behavior of prices and quantities in international goods and financial markets. The work during the seventies on the monetary, or asset-market, approach to the balance of payments and the exchange rate (see, e.g., Frenkel and Johnson 1976, 1978) has gone from being an alternative to the conventional wisdom to being the benchmark against which further progress is measured. Work on current-account behavior grounded in the permanent-income hypothesis (such as Sachs 1981 and Greenwood 1983) has gained widespread acceptance and replaced or supplemented the traditional elasticities approach. The portfolio-balance model has been elaborated and refined by incorporating advances from the field of finance (see Branson and Henderson 1985).

Recently, the advances made possible by this work have been extended and additional insights gained by integrating various aspects of international monetary theory into an explicit optimizing framework. The advan-

* I should like to thank Phil Brock, Grant Gardner, and Jeremy Greenwood for their comments.

tage of this approach is that, rather than being asserted as a useful theory, the monetary approach to the balance of payments and the exchange rate, or even more fundamental relationships such as goods-market arbitrage and interest-rate parity, are derived as equilibrium outcomes. The gain from this is that it lays bare the underlying assumptions about tastes, technology, institutional arrangements, and the behavior of economic actors such as consumers and the government. Therefore, when an open economy is subjected to various shocks and alternative policies, the comparative-statics results are assured of being consistent with such an environment rather than being based on assumptions that might or might not be compatible with any coherent underlying economic structure.

This chapter is an attempt to examine the insights optimizing models have provided into the nature of international linkages in goods and asset markets, the functioning of alternative exchange-rate regimes, and the characteristics of the international-transmission process. The first section of the chapter outlines a benchmark cash-in-advance model based on the work of Helpman (1981), which serves as a reference point for the discussion that follows. The next two sections explore international goods and asset-market linkages from the perspective of the benchmark model. Issues relating to goods-market arbitrage and purchasing power parity are dealt with first. The emphasis is on the role of alternative monetary payments mechanisms for goods-market arbitrage relationships and on the significance of these factors and of relative-price movements for the viability of purchasing-power parity. International asset-market linkages are then discussed, the focus being on covered interest parity, the relationship between spot and forward exchange rates, and the comovement and possible equality of real interest rates across countries. Alternative exchange-rate regimes are explored in the fourth section. The impact of monetary and exchange-rate policies under fixed exchange rates, flexible exchange rates, dual exchange rates, and foreign-exchange controls are outlined. The economic effects of capital controls are also covered. The final section deals with fiscal policies and the international transmission process. The effects of changes in government spending and the role of government financing decisions in the international transmission process are both examined.

A Benchmark World Economy

Consider a world economy comprised of two countries, home and foreign. The two countries engage in unrestricted international trade in goods and assets. Each country is inhabited by an infinitely lived representative consumer and a government that enacts monetary and fiscal policies. For expositional purposes it will be convenient to divide artificially each government into a monetary authority and a fiscal authority.

Output streams at home and abroad are exogenously given and consist of both traded and nontraded goods. The domestic outputs of traded and nontraded goods at time t are y_{Tt} and y_{Nt} and the corresponding outputs abroad are y^*_{Tt} and y^*_{Nt}.[1] The two countries produce identical traded goods, so that from the consumption standpoint they are perfect substitutes. Domestic consumption of traded and nontraded goods at time t is given by c_{Tt} and c_{Nt}. Domestic consumption of traded goods can be satisfied by purchases from home or foreign firms. These purchases are denoted c_{HTt} and c_{FTt} where, of course $c_{Tt} = c_{HTt} + c_{FTt}$. Foreign consumption of traded and nontraded goods is given by $c^*_{Tt} = c^*_{HTt} + c^*_{FTt}$ and c^*_{Nt}.

The monetary authorities in each country issue and, depending on the exchange-rate regime that is in place, are charged with controlling either the stock of noninterest bearing, fiat currency or the value of their nation's currency in the foreign-exchange market (i.e., the exchange rate). The two currencies are held because the exchange mechanism dictates that domestic money be used to purchase domestically produced goods and foreign money be used to purchase foreign-produced goods. That is, money holdings are motivated by cash-in-advance constraints and the convention is adopted that goods must be paid for using the seller's currency. The implications of alternative monetary mechanisms, such as those introduced by Helpman and Razin (1984, 1985a), will be discussed later. It should also be noted at this point that money can be held from one period to the next, so that the framework potentially allows for money to be held as a store-of-value as well as for transactions purposes.

One of the appealing features of the cash-in-advance approach to modeling money is that it allows for money to enter the economy in a very precise, well-specified fashion. The exact sequencing of monetary transactions is important for the behavior of the world economy; so a brief sketch of the transactions carried out in a typical period will now be given.

At the start of period t, consumers receive payment of principle and interest on the bonds they purchased in period $t-1$ and they pay off all debts. For simplicity, it is assumed that in the benchmark economy all bonds are one-period bonds denominated in terms of traded goods. As will be seen in a later section, where interest-rate parity and other asset-market arbitrage conditions are discussed, this involves no loss of generality in the benchmark environment without uncertainty, but needs to be relaxed when uncertainty is introduced in order to obtain standard international asset-pricing relationships. Bond holdings of domestic and foreign consumers at the start of period t are given by b_{t-1} and b^*_{t-1}, so, in real terms, domestic and foreign consumers receive principle and interest payments of $(1+r_{t-1})b_{t-1}$ and $(1+r_{t-1})b^*_{t-1}$ at the beginning of period t, where r_{t-1} is the real interest rate, in terms of traded goods, on bonds issued in period $t-1$ and maturing in period t. Since world capital markets are fully integrated, the real interest rate in terms of traded goods is equalized across countries.

In addition to settling their outstanding debts at the start of each period, domestic and foreign consumers also receive monetary transfers from their country's monetary authorities in the amounts $P_{Tt}\mu_t$ and $P^*_{Tt}\mu^*_t$, and pay lump-sum taxes to the fiscal authorities, in the amounts $P_{Tt}\tau_t$ and $P^*_{Tt}\tau^*_t$, where $P_{Tt}(P^*_{Tt})$ is the domestic-currency (foreign-currency) price of the traded good.

While these transactions are taking place, consumers are also free to issue new bonds on the international bond market and to buy and sell domestic and foreign currencies. Currency transactions are carried out in the foreign exchange market, where a unit of foreign currency exchanges for e_t units of domestic currency, under both fixed and flexible exchange-rate systems. However, under fixed rates, accommodating transactions by the monetary authorities will typically be required to peg the exchange rate at the desired level. This issue will be examined further in the section on alternative exchange-rate regimes.

After these transactions have been completed, the asset markets shut down and consumers use their holdings of the domestic and foreign currencies to buy goods. These transactions are subject to the cash-in-advance constraints described earlier. Hence if the home consumers' holdings of domestic and foreign currency are M_{Ht} and M_{Ft}, their goods purchases must satisfy

$$P_{Tt}c_{HTt} + P_{Nt}c_{Nt} \leq M_{Ht} \qquad P^*_{Tt}c_{FTt} \leq M_{Ft} \tag{3.1a}$$

for $t=1, 2, \ldots$, where P_{Nt} is the period-t domestic currency price of nontraded goods. Similarly, with foreign consumers holding currency stocks of M^*_{Ht} and M^*_{Ft}, their period-t goods purchases must satisfy

$$P_{Tt}c^*_{HTt} \leq M^*_{Ht} \qquad P^*_{Tt}c^*_{FTt} + P^*_{Nt}c^*_{Nt} \leq M^*_{Ft} \tag{3.1b}$$

for $t=1, 2, \ldots$.

Any cash not spent on goods during period t is carried over by consumers to period $t+1$ and is available to be spent on goods or assets then. Additionally, during period t firms are selling goods and accumulating their country's currency. At the end of the period, firms use the cash they have on hand to pay dividends to their owners. Firms are assumed to be owned entirely by the representative consumer located in their country.[2] Domestic and foreign consumers thus enter period $t+1$ with cash on hand from their dividend receipts of $P_{Tt}y_{Tt} + P_{Nt}y_{Nt}$ and $P^*_{Tt}y^*_{Tt} + P^*_{Nt}y^*_{Nt}$ and cash left over from their goods-market transactions worth

$$M_{Ht} - P_{Tt}c_{HTt} - P_{Nt}c_{Nt} + e_t(M_{Ft} - P^*_{Tt}c_{FTt})$$

and

$$(1/e_t)(M^*_{Ht} - P_{Tt}c^*_{HTt}) + M^*_{Ft} - P^*_{Tt}c^*_{FTt} - P^*_{Nt}c^*_{Nt}$$

The entire process then repeats itself.

In light of the sequencing of asset-market transactions and dividend disbursements just described, it should be apparent that the cash holdings available to domestic and foreign consumers when they enter the goods market must satisfy the following budget constraints for $t = 1, 2, \ldots$:

$$\begin{aligned} M_{Ht} + e_tM_{Ft} = {} & P_{Tt-1}y_{Tt-1} + P_{Nt-1}y_{Nt-1} \\ & + (M_{Ht-1} - P_{Tt-1}c_{HTt-1} - P_{Nt-1}c_{Nt-1}) \\ & + e_t(M_{Ft-1} - P^*_{Tt-1}c_{FTt-1}) \\ & + (1 + r_{t-1})P_{Tt}b_{t-1} - P_{Tt}b_t + P_{Tt}(\mu_t - \tau_t) \end{aligned} \tag{3.2a}$$

$$\begin{aligned} (1/e_t)M^*_{Ht} + M^*_{Ft} = {} & P^*_{Tt-1}y^*_{Tt-1} + P^*_{Nt-1}y^*_{Nt-1} \\ & + (1/e_t)(M^*_{Ht-1} - P_{Tt-1}c^*_{HTt-1}) \\ & + (M^*_{Ft-1} - P^*_{Tt-1}c^*_{FTt-1} - P^*_{Nt-1}c^*_{Nt-1}) \\ & + (1 + r_{t-1})P^*_{Tt}b^*_{t-1} - P^*_{Tt}b^*_t + P^*_{Tt}(\mu^*_t - \tau^*_t) \end{aligned} \tag{3.2b}$$

The goal in life of both domestic and foreign consumers is to maximize their lifetime utility, which depends directly on their consumption profiles according to the utility functions

$$\bar{U} = \sum_{t=1}^{\infty} \beta^{t-1}U(c_{HTt} + c_{FTt}, c_{Nt}) \tag{3.3a}$$

and

$$\bar{U}^* = \sum_{t=1}^{\infty} \beta^{*t-1}U^*(c^*_{HTt} + c^*_{FTt}, c^*_{Nt}) \tag{3.3b}$$

where $\bar{U}$ and $\bar{U}^*$ are the lifetime utilities of domestic and foreign consumers, $0 < \beta, \beta^* < 1$ are their subjective discount factors, and the within-period utility functions $U(\cdot)$ and $U^*(\cdot)$ satisfy standard properties. The home consumer thus chooses $\{c_{HTt}, c_{FTt}, c_{Nt}, M_{Ht}, M_{Ft}, b_t\}_{t=1}^{\infty}$ so as to maximize (3.3a) subject to (3.1a) and (3.2a). Abroad, the foreign consumer chooses $\{c^*_{HTt}, c^*_{FTt}, c^*_{Nt}, M^*_{Ht}, M^*_{Ft}, b^*_t\}_{t=1}^{\infty}$ so as to maximize (3.3b) subject to (3.1b) and (3.2b). More will be said in the following sections about the maximization problem confronting domestic and foreign consumers and the demand functions to which they give rise.

Besides the home and foreign consumers, the other actors in the world economy are the monetary and fiscal authorities at home and abroad. Like consumers, these actors also face budget constraints. The fiscal authorities at home and abroad are assumed to issue debt and levy lump-sum taxes in order to finance purchases of traded and nontraded goods. Domestic and foreign government bonds are perfect substitutes for private bonds and hence must pay the same rate of interest. Since the monetary mechanism of exchange dictates that cash be used to carry out all transactions, the fiscal authorities in the world economy collect their net revenues from taxes and debt-management operations in cash, M_{gt} and M^*_{gt}, and then use their resulting cash holdings to purchase traded and nontraded goods. Therefore, the home and foreign fiscal authorities budget constraints for $t = 1, 2, \ldots$ are

$$M_{gt} = P_{Tt}[\tau_t + (1 + r_{t-1})b_{gt-1} - b_{gt}] \tag{3.4a}$$

and

$$M^*_{gt} = P^*_{Tt}[\tau^*_t + (1 + r_{t-1})b^*_{gt-1} - b^*_{gt}] \tag{3.4b}$$

where b_{gt} and b^*_{gt} are the period t bond purchases (sales if negative) of the home and foreign fiscal authorities ($b_{gt} - b_{gt-1} < 0$ thus corresponds to a domestic fiscal budget deficit in period t). The fiscal authorities then enter the goods markets and use their cash holdings to purchase traded and nontraded goods in accord with the cash-in-advance constraints for $t = 1, 2, \ldots$ given by

$$P_{Tt}g_{Tt} + P_{Nt}g_{Nt} = M_{gt} \tag{3.5a}$$

and

$$P^*_{Tt}g^*_{Tt} + P^*_{Nt}g^*_{Nt} = M^*_{gt} \tag{3.5b}$$

where g_{Tt} and g_{Nt} are the home fiscal-authorities' purchases of traded and nontraded goods, and g^*_{Tt} and g^*_{Nt} the foreign fiscal-authorities' purchases. In order to economize on notation, it has been assumed, without any substantive loss of generality, that each fiscal authority purchases traded goods only from its own country's firms. It should also be noted at this point that (3.4a) and (3.5a), and similarly (3.4b) and (3.5b), can be combined to yield a more standard-looking budget constraint for the fiscal authorities. However, the presentation here is more useful for highlighting the use of money by the fiscal authorities to carry out their transactions.

The other branch of the home and foreign governments, the monetary authorities, control the money supply or peg the exchange rate via manipulation of monetary transfers and their holdings of interest-bearing international reserves, b_{Rt} and b^*_{Rt}. The budget constaints that home and foreign monetary policies must satisfy for $t = 1, 2, \ldots$ are

$$M_t - M_{t-1} = P_{Tt}[\mu_t + b_{Rt} - (1 + r_{t-1})b_{Rt-1}] \tag{3.6a}$$

and

$$M^*_t - M^*_{t-1} = P^*_{Tt}[\mu^*_t + b^*_{Rt} - (1 + r_{t-1})b^*_{Rt-1}] \tag{3.6b}$$

where M_t and M^*_t are the home and foreign money supplies at time t. The monetary authorities must resort to money creation in order to finance any excess of transfers and reserve accumulation over interest earnings on their initial reserve holdings.

Equilibrium in the world economy requires that the markets for home and foreign traded goods, home and foreign nontraded goods, home and foreign monies, and international bonds clear in all periods. Therefore, in equilibrium, the following conditions must be satisfied for $t = 1, 2, \ldots$:

$$c_{HTt} + c^*_{HTt} + g_{Tt} = y_{Tt} \tag{3.7a}$$
$$c_{FTt} + c^*_{FTt} + g^*_{Tt} = y^*_{Tt} \tag{3.7b}$$
$$c_{Nt} + g_{Nt} = y_{Nt} \tag{3.8a}$$
$$c^*_{Nt} + g^*_{Nt} = y^*_{Nt} \tag{3.8b}$$
$$M_{Ht} + M^*_{Ht} + M_{gt} = M_t \tag{3.9a}$$
$$M_{Ft} + M^*_{Ft} + M^*_{gt} = M^*_t \tag{3.9b}$$
$$b_t + b^*_t + b_{gt} + b^*_{gt} + b_{Rt} + b^*_{Rt} = 0 \tag{3.10}$$

International Goods-Market Linkages

From the perspective of a progressive research program, one of the advantages of the benchmark model and other choice-theoretic models of international macroeconomic equilibrium is that goods-market arbitrage conditions and international asset pricing equations are derived from the model rather than merely postulated in an ad hoc fashion. As a consequence, international goods- and asset-market linkages in choice-theoretic macroeconomic models reflect the underlying economic environment, including its central institutional features (such as the role played by money in the economy). The advantage of this approach is that such models generate structural implications pertaining to international goods- and asset-market linkages and suggest specific empirical tests that can potentially discriminate between the predicted linkages and certain various alternatives. Additionally, once empirical tests are carried out, the structural features of the benchmark theoretical model can be modified to generate a new set of predictions regarding international linkages that are consistent with the stylized facts emerging from the empirical studies. That is, theoretical work can be directed toward providing alternative economic structures that yield revised international linkages to replace any of the initially proposed linkages that are not borne out by empirical testing. The scope for feedback between theory and measurement is thus immense and natural.

Much of the recent work directed toward improving the profession's understanding of international goods- and asset-market linkages has been in this spirit.[3] This section deals with theory and evidence relating to international goods-market linkages. Issues concerning goods-market arbitrage are discussed first, and then the broader concept of purchasing power parity is examined. The following section of the chapter deals briefly with topics pertaining to international asset-market linkages.

Goods-Market Arbitrage

From the benchmark model of the world economy outlined above, the standard goods-market arbitrage condition

$$P_{Tt} = e_t P^*_{Tt} \qquad t = 1, 2, \ldots \tag{3.11}$$

emerges. The result follows from the fact that the solutions to the home and foreign consumer's problems are not consistent with the market-clearing conditions for traded goods, (3.7a) and (3.7b), unless the arbitrage condition (3.11) is satisfied. To see this, suppose that $P_{Tt} < e_t P^*_{Tt}$. Confronted with such prices, and in light of the fact that domestic and foreign traded goods are perfect substitutes from the consumption standpoint, it follows that utility-maximizing consumers will not demand any traded goods from foreign firms. Hence $0 = c_{FTt} + c^*_{FTt} < y^*_{Tt} - g^*_{Tt}$, in violation of the market-clearing condition (3.7b).[4] A similar argument demonstrates that the market-clearing condition (3.7a) would be violated if $P_{Tt} > e_t P^*_{Tt}$. Therefore, equilibrium in the market for traded goods in the presence of utility-maximizing consumers implies that (3.11) must hold. Of course, this means that there is truly an integrated international market for traded goods, and hence for some purposes it will be useful to exploit the fact that (3.7a) and (3.7b) can be combined to yield

$$c_{Tt} + c^*_{Tt} + g_{Tt} + g^*_{Tt} = y_{Tt} + y^*_{Tt}, \tag{3.12}$$

where use has been made of the fact that $c_{Tt} = c_{HTt} + c_{FTt}$ and $c^*_{Tt} = c^*_{HTt} + c^*_{FTt}$.

A large body of empirical evidence has been compiled in an attempt to test the validity of the arbitrage condition shown in equation (3.11). A number of recent empirical studies, for example Isard (1977) and Kravis and Lipsey (1978), report findings that seem to indicate that the arbitrage condition (3.11) does not hold. These studies do not adjust the raw data for transport costs, tariffs, and other barriers to international trade. Perhaps in part for that reason, they generally tend to conclude that "the products of different countries exhibit relative price behavior which marks them as differentiated products rather than near-perfect substitutes" (Isard 1977, p. 942).[5] The claim, however, is that the arbitrage condition (3.11) fails to hold because noncompetitive market structures are an essential feature of the economic environment. Recent empirical and theoretical work by Dornbusch (1984), Aizenman (1985), and Giovannini (1985) has picked up on this theme and examined international goods-market linkages in the presence of monopolistic competition. However, there are available several alternative modifications to the benchmark model which preserve the competitive-markets paradigm and yet are potentially consistent with the empirical evidence presented by these and other studies. These modifications will be briefly sketched and then their implications for the empirical analysis of international goods-market linkages will be considered.

First, suppose that the monetary mechanism of exchange in the benchmark model is modified along the lines of Helpman and Razin (1984), so that the buyer's rather than the seller's currency serves as the medium of exchange in all goods-market transactions. Suppose further that all other features of the economy are the same as in the benchmark setup. In this case the goods-market arbitrage condition (3.11) is replaced by

$$P_{Tt} = e_{t+1}P^*_{Tt} \qquad t = 1, 2, \ldots \tag{3.13}$$

To understand this result, consider the problem confronting a domestic firm selling traded goods. They are offered P_{Tt} for their goods by domestic residents and P^*_{Tt} by foreign residents, since transactions are carried out in the buyer's currency. These cash proceeds will then be handed over to the owners of the firm at the end of the period. Therefore, at the start of period $t+1$, the owners of domestic firms will have on hand cash worth P_{Tt} for each unit of traded goods sold to domestic consumers in period t and $e_{t+1}P^*_{Tt}$ for each unit of traded goods sold to foreign consumers in period t. If, for example, $P_{Tt} > e_{t+1}P^*_{Tt}$, the value of the firm will be maximized by selling all output to domestic residents in period t and none to foreigners. A similar argument shows that when $P_{Tt} > e_{t+1}P^*_{Tt}$, foreign firms will also prefer to sell only to domestic residents. Therefore, when $P_{Tt} > e_{t+1}P^*_{Tt}$, foreign consumers will be unable to purchase traded goods; a condition that will generally be inconsistent with goods-market equilibrium. Similarly, when $P_{Tt} < e_{t+1}P^*_{Tt}$, domestic consumers will be unable to purchase traded goods; a result that is also inconsistent with goods-market equilibrium. Therefore, equilibrium in the goods market requires that the arbitrage condition (3.13) hold when the buyer's currency is used to facilitate goods purchases.

To see the implications of the arbitrage condition (3.13) for the "traditional" arbitrage condition (3.11), multiply and divide the right-hand side of (3.13) by the period-t exchange rate, e_t, to obtain

$$P_{Tt} = (1 + \varepsilon_t)e_t P^*_{Tt} \qquad t = 1, 2, \ldots \tag{3.14}$$

where $\varepsilon_t \equiv (e_{t+1} - e_t)/e_t$ is the rate of depreciation of the domestic currency. Condition (3.14) is the arbitrage condition one would expect to hold in the traded-goods market when the buyer's currency is used for goods-market transactions. More generally, in an economy with many traded goods, (3.14) is the relevant arbitrage condition for those traded goods that are invoiced in the buyer's currency. Work by Grassman (1973) indicates that trade in manufactured goods between developed countries is typically conducted using the seller's currency as the invoicing currency. However, to the extent that some traded goods are invoiced in the buyer's currency, the arbitrage condition (3.14) has a number of general implications for tests of the traditional arbitrage condition (3.11).

The most obvious implication of (3.14) for tests of the traditional arbitrage condition (3.11) is that when the buyer's currency is used for transactions purposes there is no reason, generally speaking, for the traditional arbitrage condition to hold. That condition can be systematically violated, but such a result would not by itself be indicative of unexploited profit opportunities or a noncompetitive market structure. Additionally, the wedge driven between the domestic-currency price of traded goods and the exchange-rate-adjusted foreign-currency price of traded goods is directly related to the behavior of the exchange rate over time as captured by the rate of depreciation, ε_t. Therefore, to the extent that monetary and institutional factors governing the evolution of the exchange rate are volatile, the link between domestic and foreign prices may appear to be highly variable. For example, under fixed exchange rates when the buyer's currency is used to carry out transactions, the arbitrage condition (3.14) would be well approximated by the traditional condition, (3.11), since $e_{t+1} = e_t = \bar{e}$, where $\bar{e}$ is the fixed exchange rate. However, if the world economy were to switch from fixed to floating rates, a researcher viewing things from the perspective of the traditional arbitrage condition, $P_{Tt} = e_t P^*_{Tt}$, would be (incorrectly) tempted to conclude that goods markets (arbitrage) had been disrupted by the switch to floating rates, since international price linkages would have appeared to weaken due to the emergence of the wedge $1 + \varepsilon_t$ between domestic currency and exchange-rate-adjusted foreign-currency prices. In principle, then, to the extent that some traded goods are bought and sold using the buyer's currency, one would expect a breakdown of the traditional arbitrage condition when the world economy moves from fixed to floating exchange rates. A one-good version of the model with the buyer's currency used for transactions purposes is thus entirely consistent with the findings of Cumby and Obstfeld (1984, p. 141) that "the floating rate period has been a period of much higher real exchange rate variability vis-à-vis the United States than was the Bretton Woods era."

A second modification of the benchmark model that has a similar sort of impact on the traditional goods-market arbitrage condition (3.11) is to assume, following Benninga and Protopapadakis (1984), that importing takes time. To illustrate the importance of this for international goods-market linkages, define a period as the length of time it takes to ship goods from one country to another. No real resources are used up in shipping goods, but nonetheless there are transactions costs associated with importing activities. These costs are reflected in the time a consumer must wait between ordering goods and receiving them. If the home country imports (i.e., purchases) traded goods from abroad in period t at a foreign-currency price of P^*_{Tt}, they will have these goods available for consumption purposes in period $t + 1$. Alternatively, the same quantity of goods could be purchased from domestic firms in period $t + 1$ at the price P_{Tt+1}. These goods would be available for immediate consumption in period $t + 1$. Arbitrage requires that the two methods of obtaining a unit of traded goods in period $t + 1$, importing and waiting a period or buying domestically for immediate consumption, have the same price in present-value terms, or that

$$\frac{P_{Tt+1}}{1 + i_t} = e_t P^*_{Tt}$$

where i_t is the domestic nominal interest rate. Similarly, in periods where foreigners import domestic goods, the arbitrage condition for traded goods when importing takes time is

$$\frac{P^*_{Tt+1}}{1 + i^*_t} = \frac{P_{Tt}}{e_t}$$

where i^*_t is the foreign nominal interest rate. Using the facts that $1 + i_t \equiv (P_{Tt+1}/P_{Tt})(1 + r_t)$ and $1 + i^*_t \equiv (P^*_{Tt+1}/P^*_{Tt})(1 + r_t)$, it can be shown that when importing takes time, the appropriate goods-market arbitrage conditions are

$$P_{Tt} = (1 + r_t)e_t P^*_{Tt} \qquad (3.15a)$$

when the home country imports traded goods (i.e., when $c_{Tt} + g_{Tt} - y_{Tt} > 0$) and

$$(1 + r_t)P_{Tt} = e_t P^*_{Tt} \qquad (3.15b)$$

when foreigners import traded goods. More generally, when there are several traded goods and importing takes time, a condition like (3.15a) will characterize the markets for those goods imported by the home country and conditions similar to (3.15b) will characterize the markets for those goods imported by the foreign country. In both markets, however, a wedge is driven between domestic-currency prices and exchange-rate-adjusted foreign-currency prices, thus invalidating the traditional goods-market arbitrage condition. This wedge, which can fluctuate over time, reflects the cost to importers of doing business which, given the time it takes to import goods, is accurately measured by the real interest rate (in terms of the good being traded).

With these potential modifications of the benchmark model in mind, it is time to consider their implications for some recent empirical studies purporting to provide evidence indicating the central role of noncompetitive elements, such as monopolistic competition, in international market structures. One well-known and often cited study in this vein is that of Isard (1977). He essentially presents two pieces of evidence to support his view that such elements are an important feature of the international economic environment. First, he presents diagrams and tables showing that for several traded commodities the domestic-to-foreign price ratio, $P_{Tt}/e_t P^*_{Tt}$, is strongly and directly influenced by movements of the exchange rate.[6] Second, he regresses the domestic-to-foreign price ratio on the exchange rate and notes that the coefficient on the latter is typically significantly different from zero at standard significance levels.

Since the traditional arbitrage condition (3.11) predicts that $P_{Tt}/e_t P^*_{Tt} = 1$, Isard takes these results as an indication that elements such as differentiated products and monopolistic competition must be introduced to explain the data. This may be so, but Isard's results are not necessarily indicative of this. To see this, suppose that the economy's underlying economic structure was characterized by the benchmark model modified so that the buyer's currency is used to carry out goods-market transactions. If an econometrician were to test the traditional arbitrage condition $P_{Tt} = e_t P^*_{Tt}$ by running the regression

$$\frac{P_{Tt}}{e_t P^*_{Tt}} = b_0 + b_1 e_t + u_t$$

then, given the underlying economic structure, it is to be expected that the econometrician would find

$$b_1 = \frac{\text{cov}\,(1+\varepsilon_t, e_t)}{\text{var}\,(e_t)}$$

where use has been made of the economy's true goods-market arbitrage condition, (3.14). Therefore, if there is any correlation between the level of the exchange rate and the rate of depreciation, the econometrician would be expected to find $b_1 \neq 0$ and, if viewing the world from the perspective of (3.11), could mistakenly conclude that markets were not being effectively arbitraged in a manner consistent with a competitive market structure when in fact they were.[7]

Another study that presents evidence concerning the importance of noncompetitive market structures for international goods trade is Giovannini (1985). He outlines a theoretical model, similar in some respects to that of Aizenman (1985), characterized by price discrimination and preset prices. The model's key empirical implication is that in the absence of price discrimination the price ratio $e_t P^*_{Tt}/P_{Tt}$ should be uncorrelated with information dated $t-1$ and earlier, whereas with price discrimination such a correlation could arise. Any correlation between $e_t P^*_{Tt}/P_{Tt}$ and past events is taken to be evidence in favor of price discrimination. The empirical test conducted by Giovannini consists of running the regression

$$\ln\left(\frac{e_t P^*_{Tt}}{P_{Tt}}\right) = b_0 + b_1\pi^*_{t-2} + b_2\pi_{t-2} + b_3\lambda^*_{t-2} + b_4\lambda_{t-2} + u_t$$

where π_{t-2} (π^*_{t-2}) is the United States (Japanese) inflation rate at time $t-2$ and λ_{t-2} (λ^*_{t-2}) is the United States (Japanese) output growth rate, and testing for the joint significance of b_1, b_2, b_3, and b_4. The test is carried out for three goods (ball bearings, screws, and nuts and bolts) exported by the Japanese and invoiced in U.S. dollars.

In two of the three cases, the null hypotheses $b_1 = b_2 = b_3 = b_4 = 0$ is strongly rejected, and this is taken as evidence of price discrimination and preset prices. However, this conclusion may not be warranted. All of the goods Giovannini looks at are invoiced in the buyer's currency and hence the appropriate arbitrage condition is given by (3.13) or (3.14). These conditions imply that

$$\ln\left(\frac{e_t P^*_{Tt}}{P_{Tt}}\right) = \ln\left(\frac{1}{1+\varepsilon_t}\right) = \ln\left(\frac{P^*_{Tt}/P^*_{Tt-1}}{P_{Tt}/P_{Tt-1}}\right)$$

Assuming for purposes of illustration that there are no nontraded goods, this implies that $\ln(e_t P^*_{Tt}/P_{Tt}) \approx \pi^*_{t-1} - \pi_{t-1}$ so that Giovannini's regression in this case would reduce to

$$\pi^*_{t-1} - \pi_{t-1} = b_0 + b_1\pi^*_{t-2} + b_2\pi_{t-2} + b_3\lambda^*_{t-2} + b_4\lambda_{t-2} + \tilde{u}_t$$

where $\tilde{u}_t$ incorporates the approximation error involved in replacing $\ln(e_t P^*_{Tt}/P_{Tt})$ with the inflation differential. The regression coefficients b_1 and b_2 would not be expected to be zero in this case if, for example, a vector autoregressive process characterized the time-series properties of national inflation rates. In a multigood world with nontraded goods, real factors reflecting relative price movements would appear in the dependent variable and, along the lines of Balassa (1964), could lead to nonzero values for the regression coefficients b_3 and b_4. Therefore, Giovannini's results are not entirely inconsistent with a world economy characterized by a competitive market structure and flexible prices.

The preceding discussion illustrates how, by admitting alternative structural features, the benchmark model with its competitive market structure can, in principle, be reconciled with empirical evidence claiming to show the fundamental importance of noncompetitive market structures in the world economy and the need to modify our notions of international goods-market linkages accordingly. The modification used here for illustrative purposes entailed altering the monetary mechanism of exchange from one where the seller's currency is used for transactions purposes to one where the buyer's currency is used. While this enables the model to explain some empirical regularities, it also underscores the need for future research on the choice of invoicing arrangements and monetary mechanisms of exchange. In particular, research directed toward ultimately providing a general-equilibrium framework for which (a) the currency-invoicing decision is endogenous and, (b) in equilibrium invoicing practices can differ across commodities, would be extremely valuable to the profession.[8]

Purchasing Power Parity

A concept closely associated with goods-market arbitrage yet considerably broader in scope is purchasing power parity. As the survey sections of Frenkel (1976, 1978) and Officer (1976) clearly document, purchasing power parity has a long history in economics. One of the most influential versions of purchasing power parity has been the quantity-theory-of-money-based view of Cassel (1916), which has recently been outlined by Frenkel (1976, 1978) and Dornbusch (1985) and used as a cornerstone in many recent asset-based models of exchange-rate determination. This view argues that the equilibrium exchange rate is essentially determined by money-market equilibrium and that national price levels, P_t at home and P_t^* abroad, adequately summarize money-market conditions. Therefore, since the exchange rate is the relative price of two monies and the ratio of national price levels, P_t/P_t^*, is the ratio of purchasing powers of these two monies, the existing stocks will be willingly held only if $e_t = P_t/P_t^*$ or if

$$\frac{e_t P_t^*}{P_t} = 1 \tag{3.16}$$

This version of purchasing power parity has come to be known as the *absolute* version. A somewhat weaker version of purchasing power parity, in the sense of permitting time-invariant deviations from (3.16), is the *relative* version, which postulates that national inflation rates are linked to the rate of change of the exchange rate by

$$1 + \pi_t = (1 + \varepsilon_t)(1 + \pi_t^*) \Rightarrow \pi_t^* + \varepsilon_t - \pi_t \approx 0 \tag{3.17}$$

for low rates of inflation and currency depreciation.

Although the quantity theory of money and purchasing power parity have traditionally been tied with one another, in a multigood economy the theoretical connection between the two concepts is fairly tenuous. This can be seen by, for illustrative purposes, letting the within-period utility functions appearing in (3.3a) and (3.3b) be given by

$$U(c_{Tt}, c_{Nt}) = (1 - \theta) \ln c_{Tt} + \theta \ln c_{Nt} \tag{3.18a}$$

and

$$U^*(c_{Tt}^*, c_{Nt}^*) = (1 - \theta^*) \ln c_{Tt}^* + \theta^* \ln c_{Nt}^* \tag{3.18b}$$

where $0 < \theta,\ \theta^* < 1$ are the equilibrium shares of period-t expenditure falling on nontraded goods at home and abroad. It is well known (see, e.g., Helpman and Razin 1982) that, for this preference structure, the appropriate (consumer) price levels are

$$P_t = P_{Tt}^{1-\theta} P_{Nt}^{\theta} \tag{3.19a}$$

and

$$P_t^* = (P_{Tt}^*)^{1-\theta^*} (P_{Nt}^*)^{\theta^*} \tag{3.19b}$$

By combining (3.19a) and (3.19b) with the goods-market arbitrage condition (3.11) from the benchmark model, it can be seen that

$$\frac{e_t P_t^*}{P_t} = p_t^{-\theta} (p_t^*)^{\theta^*} \tag{3.20}$$

where $p_t \equiv P_{Nt}/P_{Tt}$ and $p_t^* \equiv P_{Nt}^*/P_{Tt}^*$ are the relative prices of nontraded goods at home and abroad. Generally speaking, (3.20) indicates that the benchmark model predicts that the absolute version of purchasing power parity given by (3.16) will be systematically violated. It can also be seen by manipulating (3.20) that the benchmark model predicts that

$$(1+\pi_t)(p_{t+1}/p_t)^{-\theta} = (1+\varepsilon_t)(1+\pi_t^*)(p_{t+1}^*/p_t^*)^{-\theta}$$
$$\Rightarrow \pi_t^* + \varepsilon_t - \pi_t \approx -\theta\rho_t + \theta^*\rho_t^* \qquad (3.21)$$

where $\rho_t \equiv (p_{t+1} - p_t)/p_t$ and $\rho_t^* \equiv (p_{t+1}^* - p_t^*)/p_t^*$. This implies that, unless the time profiles for the relative prices of nontraded goods at home and abroad are flat, relative purchasing power parity, (3.17), will also be violated according to the benchmark model.

As illustrated by (3.20) and (3.21), the predictions of the benchmark model are generally inconsistent with the concept of purchasing power parity in either its absolute or relative form. This is true despite the fact that the benchmark model is consistent with the quantity theory of money. To see this, note that when domestic and foreign nominal interest rates are positive, bonds dominate money as a store of value, since holding money entails foregone interest earnings. Therefore, the cash-in-advance constraints (3.1a) and (3.1b), along with (3.5a) and (3.5b), will hold with equality. Combining this result with the goods and money-market equilibrium conditions (3.7a)–(3.9a) and (3.7b)–(3.9b), it follows that money-market equilibrium in the benchmark model is characterized by the quantity-theory conditions

$$M_t = P_{Tt}y_{Tt} + P_{Nt}y_{Nt} \qquad (3.22a)$$

and

$$M_t^* = P_{Tt}^*y_{Tt}^* + P_{Nt}^*y_{Nt}^* \qquad (3.22b)$$

where the velocity of money at home and abroad is constant at unity. The fact that a fully articulated general-equilibrium model produces results consistent with the quantity theory of money, yet predicts violations of purchasing power parity associated with international differences in expenditure shares and nontraded-goods market conditions, highlights the fact that, while linked by early researchers, the two theories are conceptually distinct approaches to organizing thinking about international monetary conditions.[9]

The preceding discussion of purchasing power parity and its relationship to the benchmark model provides a convenient vantage point for a somewhat selective overview of the recent empirical work on purchasing power parity. The studies selected for discussion are intended to be representative of both the econometric methodology that has been used to study purchasing power parity and the empirical regularities that have been uncovered. Officer (1976) provides a detailed survey of earlier empirical work and Mussa (1979) contains a succinct statement of many stylized facts regarding purchasing power parity.

Frenkel (1978, 1981a, 1981b) has undertaken a series of empirical studies dealing with purchasing power parity. He tests the absolute version of purchasing power parity by running the regression

$$\ln e_t = a + b \ln (P_t/P_t^*) + u_t$$

and checking for $b = 1$, and he tests the relative version of purchasing power parity by running the regression

$$\Delta \ln e_t = a' + b' \Delta \ln (P_t/P_t^*) + u_t'$$

and checking for $b' = 1$. Since exchange rates and national price levels are endogenous variables, these regressions are potentially subject to simultaneous-equations bias. To avoid this problem, Frenkel (1981a, 1981b) uses an instrumental-variables approach to estimate the coefficients in the purchasing-power-parity regressions. Additionally, in most of the empirical work the error term u_t in the regression testing the absolute version of purchasing power parity is allowed to follow a first-order autoregressive process so that $u_t = cu_{t-1} + v_t$. Under the null hypothesis that $b = 1$, the error term u_t represents the deviation from purchasing power parity during period t. Hence the estimates of c provide evidence on the persistence of deviations from purchasing power parity.

The basic empirical results emerging from Frenkel's inquiries are the following: First, deviations from purchasing-power parity come close to following a random walk. The point estimates of the autoregressive parameter, c, are typically slightly below one, but the null hypothesis of a random walk, $c = 1$, usually cannot be rejected. Adler and Lehmann (1983) and Hakkio (1984) also report results consistent with this finding. These results highlight the fact that, at best, purchasing power parity may be a guide to long-run movements in exchange rates and national price levels. Second, Frenkel finds that purchasing power parity is a much more reliable guide for evaluating long-run trend movements in exchange rates and price levels when shocks are predominantly of a monetary nature; it is much less useful when shocks are predominantly real in nature. Evidence favoring this view arises from Frenkel's (1981a) finding that purchasing power parity held during the 1920s when monetary shocks such as the German hyperinflation were prevalent, but seems to have broken down (in the sense that $b = 1$ or $b' = 1$ can be rejected) during the 1970s. Since the decade of the 1970s is typically thought of as being characterized by a number of large real shocks, the oil-price shocks being the most obvious, they are viewed as the proximate cause of the collapse of purchasing power parity.[10] In fact, Frenkel explains the collapse of purchasing power parity during the 1970s in terms of movements in the relative price of nontraded goods that were triggered by real shocks. The finding that purchasing power parity works well when monetary shocks are dominant but fails when real shocks are dominant is consistent with the predictions of the benchmark model found in equations (3.20) and (3.21).

Hakkio (1984) has recently reexamined Frenkel's (1981a) empirical results. Using the same methodology, he too concludes that purchasing power parity held up better in the 1920s than in the 1970s. However, Hakkio notes that the failure of purchasing power parity in the 1970s is not due so much to the fact that $b = 1$ is rejected as it is to the fact that the regression coefficient b is so imprecisely estimated (in most cases $b = 0$ cannot be rejected). Standard tests of purchasing power parity, such as Frenkel's, usually consist of running regressions like those outlined earlier for several currencies against some "base" currency such as the U.S. dollar. However, for a number of reasons the error terms in such regressions, the u's, may be contemporaneously correlated. This possibility crops up because of world business-cycle effects arising either from world shocks or the international transmission of domestic shocks and because of the base-country element in all such regressions. Hakkio's fundamental insight is to realize that, by exploiting such information, more-precise estimates of the slope coefficients in the purchasing-power-parity regressions can be obtained. Generally speaking, after accounting for the contemporaneous correlation of deviations from purchasing power parity, Hakkio is unable to reject purchasing power parity as a reasonable description of the data for the 1970s as well as the 1920s.

A modified version of the benchmark model, along the lines of Lucas (1982) for instance, is potentially able to account for some of the key stylized facts emerging from these and other empirical studies of purchasing power parity. A world economy characterized by a predominance of permanent real shocks would produce deviations from purchasing power parity that follow a random walk, but yet the concept would still be useful for describing expected exchange-rate movements over time, since fluctuations in the magnitude of deviations from purchasing power parity would be completely unpredictable.[11] A useful next step would be to specify a structural macroeconomic model along the lines of, say, Cantor and Mark (1985), and identify the types of real shocks (such as fiscal policies) that might give rise to movements in relative prices of a permanent nature.

Then the model could be estimated or calibrated to macroeconomic time-series data, as in Kydland and Prescott (1982), in order to capture the comovements of deviations from purchasing power parity, the underlying real shocks, and other macroeconomic aggregates.

International Asset-Market Linkages

Besides goods markets, the other fundamental channel through which domestic and world shocks are transmitted to different national economies is the asset market. In fact, it is fair to say that the recent literature on the international transmission process has come to view the asset market as the key channel of influence, especially in the short run (see, e.g., Dornbusch 1976b, whose influential model is based on the view that "exchange rates and asset markets adjust fast relative to goods markets"). Three of the most carefully studied and crucial asset-market linkages concern those between nominal interest rates, spot and forward exchange rates, and real interest rates. This section examines each of these international asset-market linkages.[12]

The benchmark model that was outlined earlier easily yields predictions concerning international linkages of nominal interest rates. To see this, combine the goods-market arbitrage condition (3.11) with the Fisher-type equations $1 + i_t \equiv (P_{Tt+1}/P_{Tt})(1 + r_t)$ and $1 + i_t^* \equiv (P_{Tt+1}^*/P_{Tt}^*)(1 + r_t)$ to obtain the uncovered-interest-parity condition

$$1 + i_t = \frac{e_{t+1}}{e_t}(1 + i_t^*) \qquad t = 1, 2, \ldots \tag{3.23}$$

Since there is no uncertainty in the benchmark model, it is readily apparent that if a forward market for foreign exchange were introduced, the forward exchange rate at time t for a contract to be consummated at time $t + 1$, f_t, would satisfy the equilibium condition

$$f_t = e_{t+1} \qquad t = 1, 2, \ldots \tag{3.24}$$

Combining (3.23) and (3.24) produces the covered-interest-parity condition

$$1 + i_t = \frac{f_t}{e_t}(1 + i_t^*) \qquad t = 1, 2, \ldots \tag{3.25}$$

Covered Interest Parity

In the benchmark model, the covered- and uncovered-interest-parity conditions, (3.25) and (3.23), are equivalent equilibrium conditions linking nominal interest rates.[13] However, as is apparent from (3.24), the two conditions are not necessarily equivalent if the underlying economic environment is such that forward rates and expected future spot rates diverge because of risk premia in the foreign-exchange market. This possibility arises when the benchmark model is extended to incorporate uncertainty along the lines of Lucas (1982), Svensson (1985), or Frenkel and Razin (1980) amended to allow for money entering the economy via the cash-in-advance constraints.

For purposes of discussing international asset-market linkages in the presence of uncertainty, suppose that the benchmark model is extended along the lines of Lucas (1982).[14] In his setup, uncertainty arises because of the stochastic nature of national endowments and random elements surrounding the future course of monetary policies. In the present context, fiscal policies can also be viewed as another source of uncertainty. The timing of transactions is the same as in the benchmark model, and uncertainty regarding the current-period state variables is resolved at the start of the period. Future states, however, remain uncertain although they follow a known stochastic process conditional on the current state.

As was the case before, in this framework the cash-in-advance constraints (3.1a) and (3.1b) will hold with equality in all periods. The period-t budget constraint facing the home consumer can thus be written as

$$\begin{aligned} P_{Tt}c_{Tt} + P_{Nt}c_{Nt} = {} & P_{Tt-1}y_{Tt-1} + P_{Nt-1}y_{Nt-1} \\ & + P_{Tt}(\mu_t - \tau_t) + (1 + i_{t-1})B_{t-1} \\ & + (1 + i^*_{t-1})e_tB^*_{t-1} + (e_t - f_{t-1})A_{t-1} \\ & - B_t - e_tB^*_{t-1} \end{aligned}$$

where the menu of available assets has been assumed to include bonds denominated in the home and foreign currencies, B_t and B^*_t, and contracts to buy or sell foreign exchange in the forward market, A_t. Home consumers are interested in maximizing the expected value of (3.3a) and the solution to this problem is given by the value function

$$V(s_t) = \max_{c_{Tt}, c_{Nt}, B_t, B^*_t, A_t} \{U(c_{Tt}, c_{Nt}) + \beta E_t[V(s_{t+1})]\}$$

subject to the preceding budget constraint, where E_tx_{t+1} denotes the expectation of x_{t+1} based on the information available at time t (i.e., on the current state) and s_t is the period-t state vector, which includes among its elements the consumer's initial holdings of financial assets: B_{t-1}, B^*_{t-1}, and A_{t-1}.

The first-order conditions relating to the home consumer's period-t

portfolio choices can be shown to be given by

$$\frac{U_T(\cdot t)}{P_{Tt}} = (1+i_t)\beta E_t\left[\frac{U_T(\cdot t+1)}{P_{Tt+1}}\right] \qquad t = 1, 2, \ldots \qquad (3.26)$$

$$\frac{U_T(\cdot t)}{P^*_{Tt}} = (1+i^*_t)\beta E_t\left[\frac{U_T(\cdot t+1)}{P^*_{Tt+1}}\right] \qquad t = 1, 2, \ldots \qquad (3.27)$$

$$E_t\left[\frac{U_T(\cdot t+1)}{P_{Tt+1}}(e_{t+1} - f_t)\right] = 0 \qquad t = 1, 2, \ldots \qquad (3.28)$$

where $U_T(\cdot t) \equiv \partial U(c_{Tt}, c_{Nt})/\partial c_{Tt}$.

The first-order conditions (3.26)–(3.28) can be manipulated to yield the covered-interest-parity condition, (3.25). Thus, at the theoretical level covered interest parity survives the extension of the benchmark model to incorporate uncertainty. At the empirical level, covered interest parity has also held up well as a description of observed movements in nominal interest rates. This has been documented in a pair of studies by Frenkel and Levich (1975, 1977). They argue that in actual asset-market trading, two types of transactions costs, those in foreign-exchange markets (both spot and forward) and in bond markets (both domestic and foreign), create a "neutral band" around the covered-interest-parity condition (3.25). Within this band no unexploited profit opportunities exist, while outside of the band profitable arbitrage opportunities present themselves to market participants. If covered interest parity holds, most of the observed interest-rates and exchange-rates pairs should fall within the neutral band.

To see how transactions costs create such a band about the covered-interest-parity condition, let T_e denote the cost of transacting in the spot market for foreign exchange, T_f the cost of transacting in the forward market for foreign exchange, and T and T^* the costs of transacting in domestic and foreign bond markets, where, for simplicity, transactions costs are assumed to be constant over time. Under these circumstances, it can be shown that holders of domestic bonds will find it unprofitable to switch into foreign bonds when

$$1 + i_t \geq \frac{f_t}{e_t}\Omega(1 + i^*_t)$$

while holders of foreign bonds will find a switch in the opposite direction unprofitable when

$$\Omega(1 + i_t) \leq \frac{f_t}{e_t}(1 + i^*_t)$$

where $\Omega \equiv (1-T)(1-T^*)(1-T_e)(1-T_f)$. [Note that these conditions reduce to (3.25) when there are no transactions costs.] By manipulating these two conditions, it can be seen that, for no unexploited profit opportunities to exist, the forward premium, $(f_t - s_t)/s_t$, must satisfy

$$\frac{\Omega(1+i_t)-(1+i_t^*)}{1+i_t^*} \leq \frac{f_t - e_t}{e_t} \leq \frac{(1+i_t)-\Omega(1+i_t^*)}{\Omega(1+i_t^*)} \tag{3.29}$$

The upper and lower bounds in (3.29) are the limits of the neutral band around the covered-interest-parity relationship, which implies that

$$\frac{i_t - i_t^*}{1+i_t^*} = \frac{f_t - e_t}{e_t}$$

should hold in the absence of transactions costs. The tests conducted by Frenkel and Levich (1975, 1977) consist of examining whether or not observed nominal interest rates and exchange rates tend to satisfy (3.29). The evidence they present strongly suggests this to be the case, and thus supports the view that covered interest parity is a valid characterization of the international relationship between nominal interest rates.

Forward Rates and Expected Future Spot Rates

In the presence of uncertainty the uncovered-interest-parity condition, (3.23), becomes

$$1+i_t = \frac{E_t e_{t+1}}{e_t}(1+i_t^*)$$

From this and (3.25), it is immediately obvious that, for covered interest parity and uncovered interest parity to hold simultaneously when the economic environment is characterized by uncertainty, the forward rate must equal the expected future spot rate. That is, covered and uncovered interest parity will both hold only if $f_t = E_t e_{t+1}$. Accordingly, much recent theoretical and empirical research has been devoted to studying the relationship between forward and spot exchange rates.[15]

Theoretical work by Stockman (1978), Frenkel and Razin (1980), and others has derived intertemporal asset-pricing equations for forward contracts that are similar in spirit to (3.28), which can be solved to show that the equilibrium forward exchange rate at time t is given by

$$f_t = \frac{E_t\{[U_T(\cdot t+1)/P_{Tt+1}]e_{t+1}\}}{E_t[U_T(\cdot t+1)/P_{Tt+1}]} \qquad t = 1, 2, \ldots \tag{3.30}$$

Following Frenkel and Razin (1980) and exploiting the fact that the covariance between two variables x and y satisfies $\text{cov}(x,y) = Exy - ExEy$, (3.30) can be manipulated to yield

$$f_t = E_t e_{t+1} + \frac{\text{cov}_t[U_T(\cdot t+1)/P_{Tt+1}, e_{t+1}]}{E_t[U_T(\cdot t+1)/P_{Tt+1}]} \qquad t = 1, 2, \ldots \qquad (3.31)$$

where $\text{cov}_t(\cdot)$ denotes that the covariance is conditioned on the information available to consumers at time t. However, the consumer's optimality condition for traded-goods consumption at time $t+1$ implies that $U_T(\cdot t+1)/P_{Tt+1} = \lambda_{t+1}$, where λ_{t+1} is the marginal utility of income at time $t+1$. Using this in (3.31), it follows that

$$f_t = E_t e_{t+1} + \frac{\text{cov}_t(\lambda_{t+1}, e_{t+1})}{E_t \lambda_{t+1}} \qquad t = 1, 2, \ldots \qquad (3.32)$$

is the equilibrium asset-pricing equation for forward contracts in the foreign-exchange market.

As (3.32) indicates, equality between the forward rate and the expected future spot rate requires that the conditional covariance between the marginal utility of income and the spot exchange rate be zero. This will be the case, for example, if either the spot exchange rate does not change over time, as would be the case with a credible and sustainable fixed-exchange-rate regime, or if the marginal utility of income is constant.[16]

Further insight into the risk-premium term appearing in (3.32) can be gained by assuming, for example, that $\text{cov}_t(\lambda_{t+1}, e_{t+1}) > 0$. Under these circumstances, when the spot exchange rate is unusually high, and thus the return on a net open position in foreign currency is unusually high, is also when additional income is most highly valued (i.e., λ_{t+1} is high). As a result, risk-averse consumers will be willing to sacrifice expected return for the insurance provided by taking a net open position in foreign currency. This is exactly what (3.32) implies, as $E_t e_{t+1} - f_t = -\text{cov}_t(\lambda_{t+1}, e_{t+1})/E_t \lambda_{t+1}$, the expected return on forward-market speculation, is negative in this case.

In studying the empirical relationship between spot and forward exchange rates, numerous investigations have been undertaken to determine whether or not the expected return on speculation in the forward market for foreign exchange is zero. One common test of this hypothesis (see, for example, Frenkel and Razin 1980, and Frenkel 1981b), is to run a regression of the form

$$\ln e_{t+1} = b_0 + b_1 \ln f_t + u_{t+1} \qquad (3.33)$$

Zero expected returns to speculation in the forward market for foreign exchange cannot be rejected if the residuals in this regression are uncorrelated and if the joint hypothesis that $b_0=0$ and $b_1=1$ cannot be rejected. In his empirical work, Frenkel (1981b) cannot reject the null hypothesis that the expected returns to speculative activity in the forward market are zero. Frenkel and Razin (1980) attempt to test the economic validity of the asset-pricing equation (3.32) and the economic significance of the risk-premium term by running the regression given in (3.33) both with and without the slope coefficient, b_1, restricted to equal one. The rationale behind this test follows from noting that if $b_1=1$, the constant term, b_0, is a measure of the risk premium. Frenkel and Razin (1980, p. 170) find that the estimated value of b_0 is statistically insignificant in all of their regressions, and thus are led to conclude that the economic factors underlying the covariance term in (3.32) do "not seem to be of great quantitiative importance."

Hansen and Hodrick (1980) also test to see if the expected rate of return to speculation in the forward market for foreign exchange is zero. Their methodology entails running regressions of the form

$$\ln e_{t+1} - \ln f_t = b_0 + \sum_{j=1}^{k} b_i(\ln e_{t+1-j} - \ln f_{t-j}) + u_{t+1}$$

and testing for the joint significance of $b_0, b_1, \ldots, b_k$. The idea is that if expected returns to forward-market speculation are zero, then realized returns should be uncorrelated with any information available at the time forward contracts are entered into. Since past realized returns are a subset of the relevant information set, a test of the null hypothesis $b_0=b_1=\ldots=b_k=0$ is a test of the null hypothesis of zero expected returns. In implementing their tests, Hansen and Hodrick use sophisticated new econometric techniques that significantly increase the power of their tests. Their results reject the null hypothesis that $b_0=b_1=\ldots=b_k=0$ and thus imply that expected returns to speculation in the forward market for foreign exchange are not zero. This is an indication that the risk-premium term appearing in (3.32) is not zero and that the time-series properties of risk premia in the forward market for foreign exchange should be thoroughly investigated. Other studies yielding results pointing in the same direction have been undertaken by Geweke and Feige (1979) and Hakkio (1981), among others. According to Hansen and Hodrick (1983, p. 114), "the contribution of this literature is to show that while the deviations between forward rates and expected future spot rates may be small relative to the movement of spot rates, it is possible to devise and implement econometric procedures that are powerful enough to reject the notion that these deviations are zero."

Building on their earlier results and methodology, Hansen and Hodrick

(1983) use the intertemporal asset-pricing model to develop and test linear time-series models of the risk premia in forward markets for foreign exchange. The conclusions emerging from this work are (a) risk premia in the forward market are not appropriately treated as a constant, as in the earlier work of Frenkel and Razin (1980), but vary over time; (b) the time variation in risk premia are not adequately summarized by movements in nominal interest rates; and (c) in some cases the risk premia in forward markets appear to be economically important. The key conclusion, of course, is the finding that risk premia in the forward market for foreign exchange are time varying. In terms of the asset-pricing equation (3.32), this reflects the evolution of the consumer's information set over time and its impact on the conditional covariance and expectations terms that constitute the risk premium. Fama (1984) also provides evidence that time-varying risk premia are economically significant. As in much of Hansen and Hodrick's (1983) work, his results are based on an investigation of the properties of $\ln e_{t+1} - \ln f_t$.

In a related study, Mark (1985b) tests the first-order condition (3.28) directly. His results are based on a one-good, representative-consumer model.[17] The utility function he uses for his empirical tests is of the constant-relative-risk-aversion variety and his methodology is quite similar to that of Hansen and Singleton (1983). Mark obtains unusually large but, for the most part, statistically insignificant point estimates for the coefficient of relative risk aversion. He also finds weak evidence against the model underlying (3.28) in the sense that its overidentifying restrictions are rejected in some cases.

Besides tests based on the intertemporal asset-pricing model, there have also been studies aimed at uncovering the properties of risk premia in the forward market based on the portfolio-balance approach. The theory underlying this approach for the case where investors optimize over the mean and variance of returns is sketched by Hodrick (1981) and Frankel (1982). These models predict that the return to speculating in the forward market for foreign exchange should be related to investors' attitudes toward risk and the outstanding supplies of assets denominated in different currencies. Frankel constructs an empirical test relating to this theory and cannot reject the null hypothesis of risk neutrality (which in his setup is equivalent to there being no risk premium in the forward market). However, he is careful to point out that the power of his tests is not high and that some of the assumptions he makes in order to implement his tests may not be econometrically valid.

One last study of the properties of expected returns to speculation in the forward market for foreign exchange that is worth discussing in some detail is that of Engel (1984). He argues that by focusing on the nominal returns to forward-market speculation, several of the studies cited earlier, as well as others, implicitly assume money illusion on the part of market participants. An appropriate test of zero expected returns to speculation in the forward market for foreign exchange, which from the perspective of the intertemporal asset-pricing model is a joint test of market efficiency, rational expectations, and risk neutrality, requires that expected real returns be zero. That is, the appropriate hypothesis to test is that

$$E_t\left(\frac{f_t - e_{t+1}}{P_{t+1}}\right) = 0 \qquad t = 1, 2, \ldots \tag{3.34}$$

This hypothesis places no restrictions on the stochastic properties of nominal returns to forward market speculation; but such returns are irrelevant because consumers have preferences over goods, not currencies.

Engel derives (3.34) and shows the role of risk neutrality using a one-good setup. That (3.34) is the appropriate test in this case can be seen directly from (3.28). However, to see the appropriateness of the test in the two-good case being used here, suppose that the home-consumer's within-period utility function takes the Cobb-Douglas form $U(c_{Tt}, c_{Nt}) = c_{Tt}^{1-\theta} c_{Nt}^{\theta}$. In this case, the lifetime utility function (3.3) exhibits risk neutrality with respect to real consumption, $c_t = (P_{Tt}c_{Tt} + P_{Nt}c_{Nt})/P_t$, where the true consumer price index is again given by (3.19). Under these conditions, it can be shown that

$$U_T(\cdot t + 1)/P_{t+1} = \lambda_{t+1} = (1 - \theta)^{1-\theta}\theta^{\theta}(1/P_{t+1})$$

Using this in (3.28) yields the condition tested by Engel (1984) as given in (3.34).

In order to test the condition (3.34), Engel runs the regressions

$$\frac{f_t^j - e_{t+1}^j}{P_{t+1}} = b_0 + \sum_{k=1}^{3} b_k\left(\frac{f_{t-k}^j - e_{t+1-k}^j}{P_{t+1-k}}\right) + u_{t+1}^j$$

and

$$\frac{f_t^j - e_{t+1}^j}{\mathrm{P}_{t+1}} = b_0 + \sum_{k=1}^{5} b_k\left(\frac{f_{t-1}^k - e_t^k}{P_t}\right) + u_{t+1}^j$$

and tests for the joint significance of the b's, where the superscript j denotes an exchange rate of the U.S. dollar against currency j and P_t is the U.S. consumer price index or a world weighted-average price index. In no case is Engel able to reject the null hypothesis that $b_0 = b_1 = \ldots = 0$. That is, Engel is unable to reject the notion that expected real returns from speculation in the forward market for foreign exchange are zero. In this regard, it should be pointed out that since one element of this joint hypothesis is the assumption of risk neutrality on the part of market participants, the findings of Frankel (1982) and Mark (1985b) appear to be broadly consistent with Engel's (1984) results.

In summary, the evidence on forward and spot exchange rates seems to indicate that there are time-varying risk premia (Hansen and Hodrick 1983 and Fama 1984). However, the economic significance of these risk premia appears possibly to be an open question in light of their magnitude and the failure, so far, to relate them to underlying economic variables predicted to be important by modern portfolio-balance theories (Frankel 1982). Further, Engel (1984) provides evidence that the null hypothesis of risk neutrality, market efficiency, and rational expectations cannot be rejected. Support for not rejecting risk neutrality also comes from the results of Frankel (1982) and Mark (1985b). In conjunction with the result that risk premia in the forward market appear to be time varying, these findings and the theory underlying (3.32) suggest that risk premia in the forward market can usefully be viewed as being given by $\text{cov}_t(1/P_t, e_{t+1})/E_t(1/P_{t+1})$. This suggests two observations. First, it is interesting that Frenkel and Razin (1980), assuming constant risk premia, find their estimated values, the b_0's in regressions like (3.33), to be very close to the term $\text{cov}(1/P_{t+1}, e_{t+1})/E(1/P_{t+1})$ as calculated from the sample data. Further tests of this condition allowing for the time-varying nature of agents information sets, perhaps using Engle's (1982) ARCH estimation technique, would be illuminating. Second, it is straightforward to show that if absolute purchasing power parity holds,

$$\frac{\text{cov}_t(1/P_{t+1}, e_{t+1})}{E_t(1/P_{t+1})} = \frac{E_t(1/P^*_{t+1})}{E_t(1/P_{t+1})} - E_t\left(\frac{1/P^*_{t+1}}{1/P_{t+1}}\right) \tag{3.35}$$

However, the term on the right-hand side of (3.35) is simply a Jensen's inequality term (see Mood, Graybill, and Boes 1974), which McCulloch (1975) has shown to be quite small quantitatively. Therefore, in a world where purchasing power parity holds, the risk-premium term $\text{cov}_t(1/P_{t+1}, e_{t+1})/E_t(1/P_{t+1})$ should not be economically significant. This is one view of the results on the time-series properties of risk premia in the forward market for foreign exchange. Another view is that risk premia in the forward market are economically significant and, since there is independent evidence that this would not be the case if purchasing power parity held as indicated by (3.35), the empirical finding of important time-varying risk premia in the forward foreign-exchange market can be viewed as evidence symptomatic of the failure of purchasing power parity. The available evidence thus seems to suggest a strong connection between the purchasing-power-parity relationship, on the one hand, and the link between forward and spot exchange rates, on the other.

Real Interest-Rate Linkages

As was just demonstrated, the empirical evidence points to the possibility that the purchasing-power-parity relationship may play an important role in explaining risk premia in the forward market for foreign exchange and the connection between forward and spot exchange rates. It also turns out that the purchasing-power-parity relationship is central to understanding and interpreting the third, and final, key international asset-market linkage: that between real interest rates. The international linkage of real interest rates is crucial from the standpoint of monetary- and fiscal-policy effectiveness. To see this, note that if real interest rates were equalized across countries, stabilization policies enacted by small open economies would be rendered substantially ineffective. The reason for this is that one channel through which such policies influence real activity is by altering real interest rates, and in a world where real interest rates are equalized across countries this channel will be inoperative for a small open economy unless impediments to free trade in goods and assets are introduced. This, of course, means sacrificing some of the gains from trade in order to carve out an effective scope for stabilization policy. Even if real interest rates are not completely equalized across countries, it is important to understand the sign and the magnitude of comovements in real interest rates since they are a key channel through which disturbances are internationally transmitted.

Several recent studies have tested for the equality of real interest rates across countries. The general methodology used in a number of these studies is similar to that of Mishkin (1984b), which shall be outlined here. The ex post, or realized, real interest rates on assets denominated in different currencies are given by

$$1 + \tilde{r}_t \equiv \frac{P_t}{P_{t+1}}(1 + i_t)$$

and

$$1 + \tilde{r}_t^* \equiv \frac{P_t^*}{P_{t+1}^*}(1 + i_t^*)$$

The international difference in realized real rates of return is thus given by

$$\tilde{r}_t - \tilde{r}_t^* \equiv \frac{P_t}{P_{t+1}}(1+i_t) - \frac{P_t^*}{P_{t+1}^*}(1+i_t^*) \tag{3.36}$$

However, it is expected real interest rates that are crucial for determining intertemporal resource-allocation decisions, such as the consumption-saving choice, and thus it is the equality of expected real interest rates that is of interest. A test for the equality of expected real interest rates can be conducted by regressing the realized real-return differential $\tilde{r}_t - \tilde{r}_t^*$, as given by (3.36), on elements of the period-t informtion set as indicated by

$$\tilde{r}_t - \tilde{r}_t^* = \sum_{j=1}^{k} b_j x_j + u_{t+1} \tag{3.37}$$

where the x_j are elements of the period-t information set. The equality of expected real interest rates cannot be rejected if the null hypothesis $b_1 = b_2 = \cdots = b_k = 0$ is supported by the data.[18] If this condition holds, $E_t(\tilde{r}_t - \tilde{r}_t^*) = E_t u_{t+1} = 0$, since under rational expectations the discrepancy between realized and expected real interest rates is unforecastable on the basis of current information.

Using real rates on Eurocurrency deposits in order to avoid issues relating to international differences in default risk and capital controls, Mishkin (1984b) obtains strong rejections of the equality of expected real rates across countries. Support for this finding comes from Cumby and Obstfeld (1984) and Mark (1985a). Using somewhat different empirical techniques than those employed by Mishkin, Cumby and Obstfeld reject the equality of expected real rates for both Eurocurrency deposit rates and domestic money-market rates. Mark uses essentially the same empirical methodology as Mishkin and he also strongly rejects the equality of real interest rates for both pretax and net-of-tax real rates. Mishkin concludes that the evidence

> . . . is not supportive of the equality of real rates across countries. However, this result does not imply the existence of irrationality or unexploited profit opportunities in international financial markets. In a world of risk-averse economic agents, real rates can differ across countries because risk premiums in the forward exchange market and for securities denominated in different currencies should exist, differ across countries, and undergo variation over time. Furthermore, transactions costs and non-substitutability of different countries' goods can imply the violation of purchasing power parity even when there are no unexploited profit opportunities. (Mishkin 1984b, pp. 1355–1356)

Mishkin thus points to the possible breakdown of purchasing power parity as one potential source of the failure of real interest rates to be equalized across countries. To understand this point, which has been demonstrated by Dornbusch (1983) and others, return to the benchmark model outlined earlier. In this setup,

$$1+\tilde{r}_t \equiv \frac{P_t}{P_{t+1}}(1+i_t) \equiv \frac{P_t}{P_{t+1}}\frac{P_{Tt+1}}{P_{Tt}}(1+r_t)$$

where r_t is the real interest rate in terms of tradeables, which is equalized across countries because world capital markets are fully integrated. If preferences are such that the appropriate domestic consumer price level is given by (3.19), it follows immediately that

$$1+\tilde{r}_t = \left(\frac{p_t}{p_{t+1}}\right)^{\theta}(1+r_t) \tag{3.38a}$$

In a similar manner, it can be demonstrated that

$$1+\tilde{r}_t^* = \left(\frac{p_t^*}{p_{t+1}^*}\right)^{\theta^*}(1+r_t) \tag{3.38b}$$

Expressions (3.38a) and (3.38b) indicate that when a country is experiencing a rising relative price of nontraded goods over time, its real interest rate in terms of its consumption bundle, $\tilde{r}_t$ or $\tilde{r}_t^*$, will be less than the world real interest rate in terms of traded goods, r_t.

The international link between real interest rates follows immediately upon combining (3.38a) and (3.38b) to obtain

$$1+\tilde{r}_t = \frac{(p_{t+1}^*/p_t^*)^{\theta^*}}{(p_{t+1}/p_t)^{\theta}}\cdot(1+\tilde{r}_t^*) \qquad t=1,2,\ldots$$

As this expression indicates, real interest rates will not typically be equalized across countries. For example, if tastes are identical, so that $\theta=\theta^*$, then the country experiencing the relatively greater rate of increase over time in its relative price of nontraded goods will have the lower real interest rate (in terms of its consumption bundle).

The benchmark model thus allows for a time-varying wedge between real interest rates even though world capital markets are fully integrated. This wedge depends on changes in the relative price of nontraded goods which, as shown earlier, are an important potential source of deviations from purchasing power parity. The link between deviations from purchasing power parity and international real-interest-rate differentials can be seen by using (3.21) in the preceding expression to obtain

$$1+\tilde{r}_t = \left[\frac{(1+\varepsilon_t)(1+\pi_t^*)}{1+\pi_t}\right](1+\tilde{r}_t^*) \qquad t=1,2,\ldots \tag{3.39}$$

The term in brackets in (3.39) is unity if the relative version of purchasing power parity holds, and in such a case real interest rates will be equalized across countries. However, when relative purchasing power parity fails to hold, and $(1+\varepsilon_t)(1+\pi_t^*)/(1+\pi_t) \neq 1$, important international differences in real interest rates will typically arise.

The characterization of international real-interest-rate differentials provided by (3.39) seems broadly consistent with the time series for realized real-interest-rate differentials and realized deviations from purchasing power parity (or real exchange rates) plotted in Cumby and Obstfeld (1984). However, a more formal empirical test of the link between real-interest-rate differentials and deviations from purchasing power parity clearly seems warranted. Before proceeding to sketch the outlines of such a test, it should be noted that the important point being made here is that persistent real-interest-rate differentials need not be symptomatic of the existence of impediments or barriers to free international capital flows.

Returning to the version of the benchmark model amended to allow for uncertainty, it is fairly straightforward to develop a test that is potentially able to assess the importance of deviations from purchasing power parity and other factors in causing real interest rates to differ across countries. The idea behind such a test is as follows: Mishkin (1984b) and others test for equality of real interest rates, reject this condition, and note that possible explanations include the existence of risk premia in forward markets and the failure of purchasing power parity. In light of this, it would seem to be of interest to adjust international real-interest-rate differentials for these two factors and test whether or not they account for observed international differences in real interest rates. Such a test can be devised by noting from the definitions of realized real returns that the international difference in expected real interest rates is

$$E_t(\tilde{r}_t - \tilde{r}_t^*) \equiv (1+i_t)E_t\left(\frac{P_t}{P_{t+1}}\right) - (1+i_t^*)E_t\left(\frac{P_t^*}{P_{t+1}^*}\right)$$

Using the covered-interest-parity condition (3.25), which has been shown to hold empirically (see, e.g., Frenkel and Levich 1975, 1977), this can be rewritten as the equilibrium condition

$$E_t(\tilde{r}_t - \tilde{r}_t^*) = (1+i_t^*)E_t\left(\frac{P_t}{P_{t+1}}\frac{f_t}{e_t} - \frac{P_t^*}{P_{t+1}^*}\right)$$

Adding and subtracting $(1+i_t^*)E_t(e_{t+1}P_t/e_tP_{t+1})$ from the right-hand side of the above and rearranging yields

$$E_t(\tilde{r}_t - \tilde{r}_t^* - z_t) = 0 \qquad t = 1, 2, \ldots \tag{3.40}$$

where

$$z_t \equiv (1 + i_t^*)\left\{\frac{P_t}{e_t}\left(\frac{f_t - e_{t+1}}{P_{t+1}}\right) + \frac{1}{1 + \pi_t^*}\left[\frac{(1 + \varepsilon_t)(1 + \pi_t^*)}{1 + \pi_t} - 1\right]\right\}$$

is the required adjustment to the real-interest-rate differential. This adjustment reflects both the profitability of forward-market speculation and deviations from relative puchasing power parity. If these two factors account for observed real-interest-rate differentials, then (3.40) should hold. This can be checked by running the regression

$$\tilde{r}_t - \tilde{r}_t^* - z_t = \sum_{j=1}^{k} b_j x_j + u_{t+1} \tag{3.41}$$

and testing for $b_1 = b_2 = \cdots = b_k = 0$.

Since (3.41) can essentially be viewed as a test of covered interest parity, and since the evidence strongly suggests this condition holds (see Frenkel and Levich 1975, 1977), it is very likely that it will not reject the condition stated in (3.40). However, in light of Engel's (1984) results indicating that (3.34) cannot be rejected, a somewhat stronger test can be formulated by testing the condition

$$E_t(\tilde{r}_t - \tilde{r}_t^* - d_t) = 0 \qquad t = 1, 2, \ldots$$

where

$$d_t \equiv \frac{1 + i_t^*}{1 + \pi_t^*}\left[\frac{(1 + \varepsilon_t)(1 + \pi_t^*)}{1 + \pi_t} - 1\right]$$

This condition, which ascribes all of the difference in real interest rates to the breakdown of purchasing power parity, can be tested by running a regression similar to (3.41) but with d_t replacing z_t. These sorts of tests should help to shed some light on the underlying causes of the international differences in real interest rates that have been documented to exist.

In light of the fact that real interest rates seem to differ across countries, another important question to ask concerns the sign and magnitude of international comovements in real interest rates. Building on the methodology and results of Mishkin (1984a), Cumby and Mishkin (1986) test not only for the equality of real rates across countries but also for these international linkages. Like others, they reject the equality of real interest rates. However, they also find that expected European real interest rates respond positively, but less than one-to-one, to movements in expected U.S. real interest rates. This is an important finding, as it suggests that even though real interest rates are not equalized across countries, capital markets are nonetheless an important channel through which disturbances are transmitted internationally. Furthermore, even if tests of the condition (3.41) indicate that real-interest-rate differentials can be attributed to deviations from purchasing power parity, it would still remain to explain the stylized facts concerning international real-interest-rate linkages emerging from Cumby and Mishkin (1986).

Alternative Exchange-Rate Regimes

The question of the proper role of exchange-rate and monetary policies in serving a nation's economic objectives has received considerable attention through the years. Classic contributions to the debate include the arguments of Friedman (1953) and Johnson (1969) for flexible exchange rates, the case for fixed exchange rates outlined by Kindleberger (1970), and the discussion of the optimum currency area presented by Mundell (1961). A topic of related interest that has also received considerable attention concerns the behavior of exchange rates and the balance of payments under alternative international monetary arrangements (see, e.g., the survey paper by Frenkel and Mussa 1985). In addition to discussing the welfare properties and functioning of fixed and flexible exchange-rate systems, recent research has begun to focus on the characteristics of alternative systems such as dual echange rates and foreign-exchange controls. Choice-theoretic macroeconomic models of the open economy, like those being surveyed here, have made a substantial contribution to the debate about exchange-rate policy in a fairly short time. A number of these contributions will be sketched in this section. The welfare properties and the functioning of fixed- and flexible-exchange-rate regimes in the context of the benchmark model presented at the beginning of the chapter will be taken up first; then the implications of closely related alternative models for these questions will be highlighted; and, finally, issues relating to capital controls, dual exchange rates, and foreign-exchange controls will be examined.

Properties of Fixed and Flexible Exchange-Rate Systems

Several key features of fixed and flexible exchange-rate systems in the benchmark model follow immediately from a careful consideration of the budget constraints facing consumers, the first-order conditions arising from utility maximization, and the budget constraints confonting the monetary and fiscal branches of government. Consider first the budget constraints facing home-country agents. By using the appropriate discount factors, the sequence of private-sector budget constraints in (3.2a) can be collapsed into a single lifetime budget constraint. The money terms appearing in the lifetime budget constraint can be eliminated by using the fact that, with positive nominal interest rates, the cash-in-advance constraints appearing in (3.1a) will hold with equality. This, in conjunction with the goods-market arbitrage condition (3.11), yields the lifetime budget constraint of the representative home consumer as

$$\sum_{t=1}^{\infty} d_t(c_{Tt} + p_t c_{Nt}) = \sum_{t=1}^{\infty} d_t\left[\left(\frac{P_{Tt-1}}{P_{Tt}}\right)(y_{Tt-1} + p_{t-1} y_{Nt-1}) + \mu_t - \tau_t\right] \tag{3.42a}$$

where

$$d_t \equiv \prod_{j=1}^{t-1} (1 + r_j)^{-1}$$

and $d_1 \equiv 1$. Similarly, it can be shown that the foreign-consumer's lifetime budget constraint is

$$\sum_{t=1}^{\infty} d_t(c^*_{Tt} + p^*_t c^*_{Nt}) = \sum_{t=1}^{\infty} d_t\left[\left(\frac{P^*_{Tt-1}}{P^*_{Tt}}\right)(y^*_{Tt-1} + p^*_t y^*_{Nt-1}) + \mu^*_t - \tau^*_t\right] \tag{3.42b}$$

The problem confronting domestic consumers is to choose $\{c_{Tt}, c_{Nt}\}_{t=1}^{\infty}$ so as to maximize lifetime utility as given by (3.3a) subject to (3.42a), while the analogous problem for the foreign consumer is to choose $\{c^*_{Tt}, c^*_{Nt}\}_{t=1}^{\infty}$ so as to maximize (3.3b) subject to (3.42b). The optimal consumption streams must be supported by the appropriate portfolios of bonds and money and, given equilibrium prices, these can be uncovered from (3.1a), (3.2a), (3.1b), and (3.2b).

As discussed by Helpman (1981), one fundamental property of both fixed and flexible exchange rates in the benchmark model is that all equilibrium allocations are Pareto efficient. To see this, note that the marginal conditions for the home-consumer's problem are

$$\frac{U_N(\cdot t)}{U_T(\cdot t)} = p_t \quad \text{and} \quad \frac{\beta^{t-1} U_T(\cdot t)}{U_T(\cdot 1)} = d_t \qquad t = 1, 2, \ldots \tag{3.43a}$$

and those for the foreign-consumer's problem are

$$\frac{U^*_N(\cdot t)}{U^*_T(\cdot t)} = p^*_t \quad \text{and} \quad \frac{(\beta^*)^{t-1} U^*_T(\cdot t)}{U^*_T(\cdot 1)} = d_t \qquad t = 1, 2, \ldots \tag{3.43b}$$

The intertemporal conditions in (3.43a) and (3.43b) imply that in equilibrium

$$\frac{\beta^{t-1}U_T(c_{Tt}, y_{Nt} - g_{Nt})}{U_T(c_{T1}, y_{N1} - g_{N1})} = \frac{(\beta^*)^{t-1}U_T^*(c_{Tt}^*, y_{Nt}^* - g_{Nt}^*)}{U_T^*(c_{T1}^*, y_{N1}^* - g_{N1}^*)} \qquad t = 1, 2, \ldots$$

Since it was not necessary to specify the exchange-rate regime to derive this result, the implication is that all equilibrium allocations are Pareto efficient under both fixed and flexible exchange rates.

Using the monetary and fiscal authorities' budget constraints and the fiscal authorities' cash-in-advance constraints (3.4a)–(3.6a) and (3.4b)–(3.6b) along with the money-market equilibrium conditions (3.22a) and (3.22b), the tax and transfer terms can be eliminated from (3.42a) and (3.42b). The resulting expressions are the overall resource constraints for the home and foreign economies and are given by[19]

$$\sum_{t=1}^{\infty} d_t(c_{Tt} + p_t c_{Nt}) = \sum_{t=1}^{\infty} d_t[y_{Tt} - g_{Tt} + p_t(y_{Nt} - g_{Nt})] \qquad (3.44a)$$

and

$$\sum_{t=1}^{\infty} d_t(c_{Tt}^* + p_t^* c_{Nt}^*) = \sum_{t=1}^{\infty} d_t[y_{Tt}^* - g_{Tt}^* + p_t^*(y_{Nt}^* - g_{Nt}^*)] \qquad (3.44b)$$

The resource constraints (3.44a) and (3.44b) have important implications for the roles and effectiveness of exchange-rate and monetary policies under fixed and flexible exchange rates. However, before sketching these implications, it is important to note that the government budget constraints were used in deriving (3.44a) and (3.44b). This means that the resource constraints incorporate the fact that the private sector fully capitalizes the interest earnings of the monetary authorities on their holdings of interest-bearing international reserves, b_{Rt} and b_{Rt}^*, and interest obligations implicit in the public debt, $-b_{gt}$ and $-b_{gt}^*$. This aspect of the benchmark model is essential for the policy implications arising from the domestic resource constraint (3.44a) and its foreign counterpart (3.44b).

Perhaps the most important implication of the resource constraints (3.44a) and (3.44b) is that real allocations, and hence welfare, in the benchmark model are independent of monetary and exchange-rate policies. That is, as demonstrated by Helpman (1981), Lucas (1982), and Persson (1984), monetary policies conducted at home and abroad, as characterized by shifts in monetary transfers or domestic credit, μ_t and μ_t^*, are neutral, and the choice between fixed and flexible exchange-rate regimes is of no consequence for national consumption streams and lifetime utilities.[20] This can be seen formally by noting that the real equilibrium of the world economy is determined by the marginal conditions (3.43a) and (3.43b), the resource constraints (3.44a) and (3.44b), and the market-clearing conditions (3.8a), (3.8b) and (3.12). Since these conditions do not involve the exchange rate, monetary-policy variables, or nominal magnitudes, monetary and exchange-rate policies are irrelevant for the real equilibrium.

The intuition underlying this result is that, with outputs given by the exogenous endowment streams $\{y_{Tt}, y_{Nt}\}_{t=1}^{\infty}$ and $\{y_{Tt}^*, y_{Nt}^*\}_{t=1}^{\infty}$, possibly because of inelastic factor supplies, the only channel through which monetary and exchange-rate policies can exert real effects is by altering wealth.[21] However, as (3.44a) and (3.44b) indicate, in the benchmark model these policies cannot alter wealth levels at home or abroad and thus are impotent with respect to influencing the world-economy's real equilibrium. The reason monetary and exchange-rate policies are powerless to affect wealth is that, while they alter the distribution of assets, money and bonds, between the private and public sectors, they do not alter the present value of the private-sector's tax liabilities which, ultimately, must equal the present value of the government's purchase stream, $\{g_{Tt}, g_{Nt}\}_{t=1}^{\infty}$ or $\{g_{Tt}^*, g_{Nt}^*\}_{t=1}^{\infty}$. Given that the private sector fully capitalizes all government income streams, only the present value and time profile of government purchases is relevant for private-sector wealth and consumption streams; the distribution of assets vis-à-vis the government and the private sector is irrelevant.

The role of factor-supply elasticities in assuring the neutrality of monetary policy and the irrelevance of the exchange-rate regime will be highlighted later in this section. However, as Persson (1984) points out, another important element underlying these results is the assumption that the monetary authorities at home and abroad hold interest-bearing international reserves.[22] To illustrate the importance of this feature of the benchmark model, suppose that the exchange rate is fixed at unity [that is, $e_t = 1$ for all t, so that $p_{Tt} = p_{Tt}^*$ and $i_t = i_t^*$ for all t, from (3.11) and (3.23)] and that the domestic monetary authorities have decided to hold non-interest-bearing international reserves in the form of foreign currency. In this case it can be shown that the resource constraints become

$$\sum_{t=1}^{\infty} d_t(c_{Tt} + p_t c_{Nt}) = \sum_{t=1}^{\infty} d_t\left[y_{Tt} - g_{Tt} + p_t(y_{Nt} - g_{Nt}) - \frac{i_t}{1+i_t} b_{Rt}\right]$$

and

$$\sum_{t=1}^{\infty} d_t(c_{Tt}^* + p_t^* c_{Nt}^*) = \sum_{t=1}^{\infty} d_t\left[y_{Tt}^* - g_{Tt}^* + p_t^*(y_{Nt}^* - g_{Nt}^*) + \frac{i_t}{1+i_t} b_{Rt}\right]$$

where b_{Rt} should now be interpreted as the real value in period t of the foreign currency held by the domestic central bank. Note that there is a real transfer from one nation to the other involved here and that this transfer reflects the inflation tax introduced into the system by the home monetary authority's decision to hold non-interest-bearing reserves. As is apparent, monetary policies now matter for the real equilibrium of the world economy since they can alter wealth at home and abroad by influencing the time path of nominal interest rates, nominal prices, and international reserves, which are the ingredients of the real transfer $(i_t/1+i_t)b_{Rt}$. In view of the fact that when non-interest-bearing international reserves are held monetary policies attain real effects through influencing the real transfer between nations, the real effects of monetary policy can, at least in part, be determined along the lines of the transfer problem of the pure theory of international trade.

Besides the irrelevance of monetary policies and the exchange-rate regime for the real equilibrium of the world economy, other important policy implications also follow from the resource constraints (3.44a) and (3.44b) that characterize the benchmark model in which countries hold interest-bearing international reserves. As has already been discussed, the domestic credit operations of the home and foreign monetary authorities have no real effects. However, while this is true under both fixed and flexible exchange-rate regimes, domestic credit operations take on added significance under fixed rates because, while the time path of domestic credit is irrelevant, it turns out that the present value of a country's domestic credit operations is important in the sense that for any given present value of monetary transfers there is a unique fixed exchange rate that will be sustainable.

This result, due to Helpman (1981), can be illustrated by viewing the home and foreign governments as determining the nominal monetary transfer streams $\{N_t \equiv P_{Tt}\mu_t\}_{t=1}^{\infty}$ and $\{N_t^* \equiv P_{Tt}^*\mu_t^*\}_{t=1}^{\infty}$. Assuming the exchange rate to be rigidly fixed so that $e_t = \bar{e}$ for all t, it can be shown using (3.6a), (3.11), (3.22a), and (3.23) that the intertemporal budget constraint facing the domestic monetary authorities is

$$\sum_{t=1}^{\infty} d_t\left(\frac{1}{P_{Tt}^*}\right)N_t = \bar{e}\left[\sum_{t=1}^{\infty} d_t\left(\frac{i_t^*}{1+i_t^*}\right)(y_{Tt}+p_t y_{Nt})\right] \tag{3.45}$$

Equation (3.45) simply states that the central-bank's monetary transfers must be financed via the inflation tax. The result linking the present value of domestic credit and the exchange rate is most easily seen by considering the home country to be small, although Helpman's (1981) proof shows that this is not essential. Under the small-country assumption, the term in brackets on the right-hand side of (3.45) is exogenous, as are the first two terms inside the summation sign on the left-hand side of (3.45). Therefore, for any fixed exchange rate $\bar{e}$, there is a unique present value of monetary transfers or domestic credit, N_t, that satisfies the central-bank's budget constraint. Put another way, given the domestic credit policies adopted by the monetary authorities, there is a unique fixed exchange rate that is credible in the sense that it is consistent with the central bank's budget constraint—that is, it satisfies (3.45).[23]

The benchmark model also can be used to study the behavior of the balance of payments under fixed exchange rates and the exchange rate under flexible exchange rates. The time path of the balance of payments under a fixed exchange-rate system can be seen by noting that the central-bank's budget constraint, (3.6a), can be rewritten as

$$b_{Rt} = (1 + r_{t-1})b_{Rt-1} + \frac{M_t - M_{t-1} - N_t}{P_{Tt}} \qquad t = 1, 2, \ldots$$

Since the money supply is demand-determined when the exchange rate is fixed, it follows directly from (3.22a) and the preceding expression that the dynamic behavior of a country's international reserves is described by

$$b_{Rt} = (1 + r_{t-1})b_{Rt-1} + \left[y_{Tt} + p_t y_{Nt} - \frac{P_{Tt-1}}{P_{Tt}}(y_{Tt-1} + p_{t-1}y_{Nt-1}) - \frac{N_t}{P_{Tt}}\right]$$
$$t = 1, 2, \ldots \qquad (3.46)$$

The change in reserve holdings from one period to the next thus reflects interest earnings on international reserves and the inflow of new reserves via the balance of payments as captured by the term in brackets. The balance of payments thus depends on the excess flow demand for money, a result which is standard in monetary-approach models of the balance of payments. As can be seen, the dynamic behavior of the balance of payments depends on the time paths of output, prices, and domestic credit.

Turning to the behavior of the exchange rate under a flexible exchange-rate system, recall that the goods-market arbitrage condition (3.11) implies that

$$e_t = \frac{P_{Tt}}{P^*_{Tt}} \qquad t = 1, 2, \ldots$$

Using the money-market equilibrium conditions (3.22a) and (3.22b) to solve for equilibrium traded-goods prices in terms of home and foreign currencies, it follows that, as shown by Helpman and Razin (1982),

$$e_t = \frac{M_t}{M^*_t} \cdot \frac{y^*_{Tt} + p^*_t y^*_{Nt}}{y_{Tt} + p_t y_{Nt}} \qquad t = 1, 2, \ldots \qquad (3.47)$$

where

$$M_t = \sum_{j=1}^{t} N_t \quad \text{and} \quad M_t^* = \sum_{j=1}^{t} N_t^*$$

As (3.47) highlights, the equilibrium exchange rate in the benchmark model depends on the behavior of national money supplies, outputs at home and abroad, and relative prices.[24] Equation (3.47) is a fairly standard-looking exchange-rate-pricing equation, although, unlike many recent asset-approach-type models, it does not have the typical forward-looking character (see, e.g., Frenkel and Mussa 1985 and Mussa 1976, 1979). The reason for this is that, in the cash-in-advance setup of the benchmark model, the velocity of money is constant and therefore money demands are independent of interest rates. It is through the sensitivity of money demands to interest rates that the exchange-rate equations of the asset approach gain their forward-looking character, and this channel is not operational in the benchmark model.

Departures from the Benchmark Model

One of the most striking policy implications of the benchmark model is the irrelevance of the choice between fixed and flexible exchange-rate regimes for real allocations and welfare in the world economy. As has already been discussed, this result breaks down when countries hold non-interest-bearing international reserves. However, since most nations in fact hold their international reserves in interest-bearing form, this theoretical rationale for the possible importance of the exchange-rate regime is not likely to be important in practice. A much more plausible explanation for a practical concern about the choice between alternative exchange-rate regimes centers on the role of factor-supply elasticities. In the benchmark model, national output streams, $\{y_{Tt}, y_{Nt}\}_{t=1}^{\infty}$ and $\{y_{Tt}^*, y_{Nt}^*\}_{t=1}^{\infty}$, are assumed to be exogenous. This can be viewed as arising because the factors entering the production processes for traded and nontraded goods are inelastically supplied both at home and abroad. As has already been noted, this means that monetary and exchange-rate policies can influence the world economy's real equilibrium only through wealth effects. Since monetary and exchange-rate policies do not generate wealth effects in the benchmark model, they turn out to be irrelevant for real allocations and welfare. Once allowance is made for nonzero factor-supply elasticities, however, monetary and exchange-rate policies can give rise to substitution effects and hence may generate important real effects.

In order to illustrate this result, consider modifying the benchmark model along the lines of Aschauer and Greenwood (1983). They modify Helpman's (1981) one-good version of the benchmark model by assuming that labor is employed in the production process and entering a labor-leisure choice into the representative-consumer's optimization problem. Modifications in this spirit can be incorporated into the benchmark model at the beginning of the chapter in the following manner. First, let the outputs of traded and nontraded goods at home and abroad depend on labor inputs. Focusing on the home country and taking it to be small in order to simplify the discussion, the relevant production technology for $t = 1, 2, \ldots$ is given by

$$y_{Tt} = f(L_{Tt}) \quad \text{and} \quad y_{Nt} = h(L_{Nt}) \tag{3.48}$$

where L_{Tt} and L_{Nt} are the amounts of labor employed in the traded and nontraded goods sectors and both production functions exhibit a positive and diminishing marginal product of labor.[25] Second, assume that the representative domestic consumer is endowed, in each period, with one unit of time that must be allocated between the traded and nontraded sectors and leisure. The individual's time constraint for $t = 1, 2, \ldots$ is thus

$$L_{Tt} + L_{Nt} + l_t = 1 \tag{3.49}$$

where l_t is period-t leisure. The choice between labor, $L_{Tt} + L_{Nt}$, and leisure is given economic content by allowing leisure to appear as an argument in the consumer's utility function so that his goal in life is to maximize

$$\bar{U} = \sum_{t=1}^{\infty} \beta^{t-1} U(c_{Tt}, c_{Nt}, l_t) \tag{3.50}$$

where $U(\cdot t)$ is strictly increasing in leisure.

With these modifications, the importance of factor-supply elasticities for the question of exchange-rate-regime choice can easily be highlighted by considering the consumer's optimization problem and the determination of the economy's real equilibrium. Using (3.48) and (3.49) in (3.2a), and recalling that in equilibrium with positive nominal interest rates the cash-in-advance constraints (3.1a) hold with equality, it can be shown that the consumer's budget constraints for $t = 1, 2, \ldots$ are given by

$$c_{Tt} + p_t c_{Nt} + b_t = \frac{P_{Tt-1}}{P_{Tt}}[f(1 - L_{Nt} - l_t) + p_{t-1} h(L_{Nt})] + (1 + r_{t-1}) b_{t-1} + \mu_t - \tau_t \tag{3.51}$$

With the home consumer interested in maximizing lifetime utility as given by (3.50), the solution to his optimization problem can be characterized by the value function

$$V(a_t,p_t) = \max_{c_{Tt},c_{Nt},b_t,l_t,L_{Nt}} \{U(c_{Tt},c_{Nt},l_t) + \beta V(a_{t+1}, p_{t+1})\}$$

subject to (3.51), where the consumer's period-t asset position, a_t, is defined by the right-hand side of (3.51).

In addition to the sequence of budget constraints in (3.51), the first-order conditions for the consumer's problem are

$$U_T(\cdot t) = \lambda_t \qquad t = 1, 2, \ldots \tag{3.52}$$

$$U_N(\cdot t) = \lambda_t p_t \qquad t = 1, 2, \ldots \tag{3.53}$$

$$\lambda_t = \beta(1 + r_t)V_a(\cdot t + 1) \qquad t = 1, 2, \ldots \tag{3.54}$$

$$U_l(\cdot t) = \beta \frac{P_{Tt}}{P_{Tt+1}} f_L(\cdot t)V_a(\cdot t + 1) \qquad t = 1, 2, \ldots \tag{3.55}$$

$$f_L(\cdot t) = p_t h_L(\cdot t) \qquad t = 1, 2, \ldots \tag{3.56}$$

where λ_t is the Lagrange multiplier associated with the consumer's period-t budget constraint.

The real equilibrium for this economy is determined by the consumer's first-order conditions and the economy's overall resource constraint, which, with appropriate modifications to (3.44a), is given by

$$\sum_{t=1}^{\infty} d_t(c_{Tt} + p_t c_{Nt}) = \sum_{t=1}^{\infty} d_t\{f(1 - L_{Nt} - l_t) - g_{Tt} + p_t[h(L_{Nt}) - g_{Nt}]\} \tag{3.57}$$

Combining (3.52)–(3.55), using the Fisher relation $1 + i_t - (P_{Tt+1}/P_{Tt})(1 + r_t)$, and applying the fact that $V_a(\cdot t + 1) = \lambda_{t+1}$ as implied by the envelope theorem (see Silberberg 1978), the first-order conditions for the consumer's problem can be rewritten in terms of the following conditions on the consumer's marginal rates of substitution for $t = 1, 2, \ldots$

$$\frac{U_N(\cdot t)}{U_T(\cdot t)} = p_t \tag{3.58}$$

$$\frac{\beta U_T(\cdot t + 1)}{U_T(\cdot t)} = \frac{d_{t+1}}{d_t} \tag{3.59}$$

$$\frac{U_l(\cdot t)}{U_T(\cdot t)} = \frac{f_L(\cdot t)}{1 + i_t} \tag{3.60}$$

The home-economy's real equilibrium, $\{c_{Tt},c_{Nt},l_t,L_{Nt},p_t\}_{t=1}^{\infty}$, is determined by (3.56)–(3.60) and welfare can then be calculated from (3.50). As

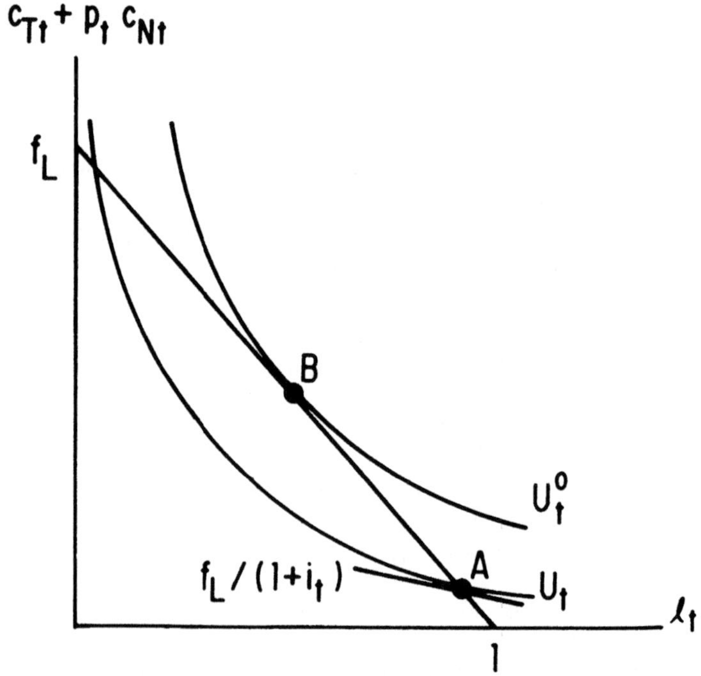

Figure 3–1. Welfare Implications of Wedge Between Marginal Rate of Substitution Between Consumption and Leisure Introduced by the Inflation Tax

can be seen from the first-order condition (3.60), which characterizes the consumer's labor-leisure choice, monetary and exchange-rate policies do influence the real equilibrium and associated level of welfare through their impact on the time path of nominal interest rates. Higher rates of inflation raise nominal interest rates, effectively taxing labor effort, and generating negative substitution effects on the consumer's labor supply. That is, monetary and exchange-rate policies have a real impact on the economy via an inflation-tax channel. This effect arises because the monetary mechanism of exchange requires that the consumer work during period t in return for cash paid at the end of the period and available for consumption purposes only in period $t+1$.

The foregone real return, $1 + r_t$, and the erosion of purchasing power through the inflation factor, P_{Tt+1}/P_{Tt}, which comprise the nominal-interest-rate factor, $1 + i_t$, thus introduce a wedge between the marginal rate of substitution between consumption and leisure, $U_l(\cdot t)/U_T(\cdot t)$, and the marginal product of labor, $f_L(\cdot t)$. The welfare implications of this wedge are illustrated in figure 3–1 which is, for simplicity, based on the assumptions that in equilibrium the home country chooses not to borrow or lend in the world capital market and that the production technology is linear so that the relative price of nontraded goods does not fluctuate over time (and hence the composite-good theorem applies). The economy's real equilibrium is at point A in the diagram, the wedge between the production-possibilities frontier and the consumer's indifference curve representing the impact of the inflation tax. As can be seen, if the distortion introduced by the inflation tax could be removed, the economy's real equilibrium would shift from A to B and in each period the consumer's utility would rise from U_t to U_t^0. This obviously desirable result can be achieved by following Friedman's (1969) optimum-quantity-of-money rule, which requires policy makers to choose the time path for monetary transfers, $\{N_t\}_{t=1}^{\infty}$, so as to generate an inflation rate that yields a nominal interest rate of zero in all periods. This requires the country to adopt a flexible-exchange-rate system [or to choose the time path of its exchange rate in accord with a condition analogous to (3.45) so that $e_{t+1}/e_t = 1/(P^*_{Tt+1}/P^*_{Tt})(1 + r_t)$, which follows from (3.11) and the Fisher relation with $i_t = 0$ for all t]. Therefore, with an operative labor-leisure choice giving rise to a less than perfectly inelastic supply of labor, monetary and exchange-rate policies matter for the economy's real equilibrium and welfare. Flexible exchange rates dominate fixed exchange rates in terms of consumer welfare, because they allow a country to pick its inflation rate in accord with the optimum-quantity-of-money rule.

The superiority of flexible exchange rates that emerges when a labor-leisure choice is incorporated into the benchmark model may be thought to rest in part on the assumption that lump-sum taxes are available to the government, since the welfare argument for the optimum-quantity-of-money rule can break down when distorting taxes must be enacted to raise revenue (see, e.g., Phelps 1973). To deal with this issue, suppose for the moment that only distorting taxes are available. In such a case, the Ramsey rules for optimal taxation—which entail setting taxes so as to maximize private-sector welfare subject to the government's revenue requirements[26]—call for taxing consumption in order to raise revenue. However, as the preceding discussion and figure 3–1 indicate, this can be acheived by taxing consumption directly or by taxing consumption indirectly via the inflation tax. From the welfare perspective, the choice is a matter of indifference. If consumption is taxed directly, then the country would want to adopt a flexible exchange-rate system and follow the optimum-quantity-of-money rule so as to avoid levying an additional inflation tax on consumption. Alternatively, if the government taxes consumption indirectly via the inflation tax, the Ramsey rules for optimal taxation imply a unique time path for the inflation rate that must be adopted. Since this requires the country to choose its own inflation rate, the optimal policy once again entails adopting a flexible exchange-rate system and setting the time path of monetary injections so as to yield the appropriate time path for inflation. The need to levy distorting taxes to raise revenue thus does not alter the inflation-tax-based case for flexible exchange rates.[27]

To gain further insight into these results, and to see the importance of labor-leisure choice (and hence factor-supply elasticities) as opposed to sectoral resource-allocation decisions, suppose that the home-consumer's utility function is given by (3.3a) rather than by (3.50). In this case, since the consumer attaches no value to leisure, $l_t = 0$ for all t and the economy's real equilibrium is determined by (3.56)–(3.59). As is readily apparent, monetary and exchange-rate policies are irrelevant for the economy's real equilibrium and hence its welfare level in this instance. Sectoral resource-allocation decisions alone are thus not sufficient to give rise to an important choice between fixed and flexible exchange-rate regimes; something like a labor-leisure choice or other modifications giving rise to elastic factor supplies is necessary.

In addition to Aschauer and Greenwood (1983), several other recent papers sharing the same monetary mechanism as the benchmark model have also demonstrated that, in the presence of elastic factor supplies, monetary and exchange-rate policies can influence the world economy's real equilibrium. Stockman (1985) considers a framework similar to the one sketched above but with two modifications. First, he allows for two internationally trade goods. This enables him to investigate the impact of inflation on the pattern of international trade. Second, he allows capital to enter the production process and assumes that cash is required to finance both consumption and investment expenditures. Using this setup, Stockman demonstrates that changes in the rate of inflation can produce real effects by altering the supplies of both labor and capital. Inflation-induced changes in factor supplies are shown to alter both production and consumption patterns and to have a potentially dramatic effect on a nation's pattern of international trade. Helpman and Razin (1984) consider a world economy in which outputs depend on the existing capital stock and firms choose optimal investment strategies so as to maximize their net value. Given the timing of transactions in their model, Helpman and Razin show that efficient capital accumulation in the world economy requires that monetary and exchange-rate policies be set so as to generate constant nominal interest rates at home and abroad. Other policies lead to inefficiencies in the investment process. Helpman and Razin show that this result holds in the benchmark case where the seller's currency is used for transactions purposes as well as in the case where the buyer's currency is used. Last, Svensson (1985) considers a cash-in-advance setup similar to the benchmark model but with uncertainty at the time consumers choose their cash holdings giving rise to a variable velocity of money. He demonstrates that in this setup monetary policy can produce important real effects.

The potential real effects of monetary and exchange-rate policies, and the welfare implications of alternative exchange-rate regimes, have also been analyzed in settings that depart more significantly from the benchmark model than those just outlined. Broadly speaking, these other models can be grouped into two categories, the categories reflecting recent developments in business-cycle theory. First, several authors stress the role of various nominal rigidities in giving rise to a meaningful choice between alternative exchange-rate regimes. Examples of this literature include Flood and Marion (1982), who use a framework with wage contracting to consider optimal wage indexing under alternative exchange-rate regimes; Bhandari (1982), who compares exchange-rate policies given the wage-setting structure; and Turnovsky (1983) and Aizenman and Frenkel (1985), who study the interaction between the optimal exchange-rate system and the optimal degree of wage indexing. The second class of models dealing with the issue of exchange-rate-regime choice outside the general framework of the benchmark model are the equilibrium business-cycle models of Weber (1981), Kimbrough (1983, 1984a, 1984b), and others. This literature tends to stress the importance of incomplete information and to highlight the role of the exchange rate as a source of information. Such reasoning draws attention to the fact that fixed-exchange-rate systems can prevent the price system from conveying useful information to agents.

Currently then, the literature seems to have focused on three channels through which the question of exchange-rate-regime choice can be given economic significance. These channels have been illustrated by models emphasizing the impact of the inflation tax on factor supplies, models highlighting the role of nominal rigidities and indexation schemes, and models stressing informational issues and the role of the exchange rate as a source of valuable information.

Dual Exchange Rates and Capital Controls

In addition to the traditional fixed- and flexible-exchange-rate regimes that have already been examined, the benchmark model also serves as a useful backdrop for discussing other exchange-rate systems, such as dual exchange rates and foreign-exchange controls. As documented by Greenwood and Kimbrough (1986), these nontraditional types of exchange-rate systems are quite popular in the sense that in recent years a substantial fraction of IMF member countries have had international monetary arrangements characterized by one of these two systems. This part of the chapter deals with dual-exchange-rate systems and the closely related topic of capital controls, while the following part of the chapter takes up the issue of foreign-exchange controls. As will be seen, systems of foreign-exchange controls and dual exchange rates both share the property that, while being implemented via financial-market interventions, they have all the characteristics of commercial policies.

Dual-exchange-rate systems have recently been examined within the context of optimizing models of macroeconomic behavior by Adams and Greenwood (1985), Obstfeld (1986b), and, in a cash-in-advance setup, by Frenkel and Razin (1986c).[28] The key feature of dual-exchange-rate systems is that different exchange rates are used for commercial transactions and financial transactions. Typically, all commercial- or goods-market transactions under dual exchange rates are conducted using the commercial exchange rate, e_t, the path of which is pegged by the monetary authorities. Financial-market transactions, on the other hand, are carried out using the financial exchange rate, s_t. As highlighted by Frenkel and Razin (1986c), there are two alternative mechanisms by which the financial exchange rate may be determined. First, the government may peg the path of the financial exchange rate and allow domestic residents to conduct any volume of capital-market transactions they desire at this rate. Alternatively, the government may impose a binding quota on the volume of private-sector capital-market transactions and allow the financial exchange rate to adjust so that the market clears at the regulated volume of transactions. Both types of dual-rate systems will be considered here. To simplify the analysis, the home country will be taken to be a small country.[29]

In order to analyze private-sector behavior under dual exchange rates, the only necessary modification to the benchmark model that is required is to adjust the private-sector's sequence of budget constraints in equation (3.2a) to reflect the fact that financial-market transactions are carried out using the financial exchange rate, s_t, rather than the commercial exchange rate, e_t. This can be accomplished by replacing the term $(1 + r_{t-1})P_{Tt}b_{t-1} - P_{Tt}b_t$ appearing on the right-hand side of (3.2a) with the term $(1 + r_{t-1})s_tP^*_{Tt}b_{t-1} - s_tP^*_{Tt}b_t$.[30] Having done this, and following the steps leading up to (3.42a), yields the consumer's lifetime budget constraint as

$$\sum_{t=1}^{\infty} \frac{e_t}{e_1} \frac{s_1}{s_t} d_t(c_{Tt} + p_t c_{Nt}) = \sum_{t=1}^{\infty} \frac{e_t}{e_1} \frac{s_1}{s_t} \left[\left(\frac{P_{Tt-1}}{P_{Tt}} \right) (y_{Tt-1} + p_{t-1} y_{Nt-1}) + \mu_t - \tau_t \right] \tag{3.61}$$

The marginal conditions for the consumer's optimization problem, which entails choosing $\{c_{Tt}, c_{Nt}\}_{t=1}^{\infty}$ to maximize (3.3a) subject to (3.61), are easily shown to be given by

$$\frac{U_N(\cdot t)}{U_T(\cdot t)} = p_t \qquad t = 1, 2, \ldots \tag{3.62}$$

$$\frac{\beta^{t-1} U_T(\cdot 1)}{U_T(\cdot 1)} = \frac{e_t}{e_1} \frac{s_1}{s_t} d_t \qquad t = 1, 2, \ldots \tag{3.63}$$

Given the nature of the dual-rate system, that is, whether the path of the financial exchange rate is pegged or a binding quota on private-sector capital-market transactions is established, the first-order conditions (3.62) and (3.63) along with the economy's overall resource constraint (3.44a) determine the real equilibrium.

The first-order conditions (3.62) and (3.63) underscore the essential economic ramifications of dual-exchange-rate systems. The key feature of dual-exchange-rate systems is apparent from (3.63). As can be seen, the financial policies supporting a system of dual exchange rates drive a wedge between the domestic real interest rate, embodied in the domestic discount factor $(e_t/e_1)(s_1/s_t)d_t$, and the world real interest rate, embodied in the world discount factor d_t. The force of the wedge depends on whether the commercial exchange rate or the financial exchange rate is depreciating more rapidly. To further understand this result, note that (3.63) implies that in equilibrium the marginal rate of substitution across any two adjacent periods satisfies the condition

$$\frac{U_T(\cdot t)}{\beta U_T(\cdot t+1)} = \frac{e_t}{e_{t+1}} \frac{s_{t+1}}{s_t} (1 + r_t) \qquad t = 1, 2, \ldots \tag{3.64}$$

Therefore, when the financial exchange rate is depreciating more rapidly than the commercial exchange rate, the domestic real interest rate will exceed the world real interest rate; while the situation is reversed when the commercial exchange rate is depreciating more rapidly than the financial exchange rate.

The characteristics of the wedge between domestic and world real interest rates, and the functioning of the dual-exchange-rate system, depend on the financial policies that are implemented to support the regime. When the government pegs the path of the financial exchange rate, the wedge between domestic and world real interest rates, $(e_t/e_{t+1})(s_{t+1}/s_t)$, is fixed by government policy. In this case a system of dual exchange rates is analogous to a set of taxes on international borrowing at the rate $(e_t/e_{t+1})(s_{t+1}/s_t) - 1$ for $t = 1, 2, \ldots$. In the alternative case, where a binding quota on private-sector capital-market transactions is enacted, the wedge between the domestic and world real interest rates is endogenously determined as the financial exchange rate adjusts to clear the market. In this case a system of dual exchange rates is equivalent to capital controls.

Recent work by Greenwood and Kimbrough (1985a) has sketched the very different implications for the international transmission process of taxes on international borrowing and capital controls. They show that when international borrowing is subject to a tax, world real-interest-rate shocks will be transmitted positively to the domestic real interest rate; but that when capital controls are in place, the possibility of negative international transmission arises. To see the intuition behind these results, consider an economy with capital controls that limit the amount of borrowing the private sector may undertake. Under these circumstances, a rise in the world real interest rate represents a deterioration in the home-country's (intertemporal) terms of trade. The negative-wealth effect that is associated with the rise in the world real interest rate thus reduces the home-country's demand to borrow on world capital markets, since the demand for current consumption declines. Given that capital controls are placing a binding quota on international borrowing, the price of current consumption—the domestic real interest rate—must fall to clear the market. In the case where capital controls are effectively in place as a result of a dual-exchange-rate system with a binding quota on private-sector capital-market transactions, it can be seen from (3.64) that these events would manifest themselves in a decline in the rate of depreciation of the financial exchange rate, s_{t+1}/s_t, and an observed negative comovement in domestic and world real interest rates. In the alternative case where international borrowing is being taxed, possibly as a result of the government imposing a dual-exchange-rate system and pegging the path of the financial exchange rate, the wedge between domestic and foreign real interest rates is fixed by policy and thus changes in world real interest rates will be transmitted positively to the domestic real interest rate. In light of the fact that dual-exchange-rate systems can have such markedly different implications depending on their supporting financial policies, it follows that they can also have strikingly different ramifications for the observed international comovements in macroeconomic aggregates such as consumption, output, and employment. This follows because of the central role real-interest-rate movements play in determining the direction and magnitude of the intertemporal substitution effects and wealth effects that govern the optimal time path of macroeconomic aggregates.[31]

Several other important features of dual-exchange-rate systems have also attracted attention in the literature. First, because dual-exchange-rate systems drive a wedge between the real interest rates facing the private sector and the government when borrowing on international markets, Ricardian equivalence breaks down in the sense that changes in the government's portfolio of interest-bearing assets now have real effects. In particular, as Obstfeld (1986b) demonstrates, devaluations have real effects under dual exchange rates, because they alter the central bank's holdings of international reserves (and thus effectively relax the restrictions dual exchange rates place on private-sector international borrowing). Second, as emphasized by Frenkel and Razin (1986c), the viability of dual-exchange-rate regimes is limited because of the severe constraints the solvency requirements of the government and the private sector place on the set of policies that is consistent with a permanently sustainable system of dual exchange rates. Finally, since the benchmark model highlights the fact that dual-exchange-rate systems are similar to other forms of commercial policies that interfere with free trade, it follows that, for a distortion-free small open economy, dual exchange rates are dominated in welfare terms by both fixed and flexible exchange rates.[32]

Foreign-Exchange Controls

Another mechanism for regulating international payments that is in widespread use in today's world economy is foreign-exchange controls. Typically, foreign-exchange controls place a limit on the amount of foreign exchange that consumers can acquire during a given period. These quantitative restrictions can relate to consumers' overall acquisition and use of foreign exchange or to the acquisition and use of foreign exchange for particular classes of purchases. Foreign-exchange controls are most often implemented in conjunction with a fixed-exchange-rate system, although in principle they can also be adopted along with a system of flexible exchange rates.

Systems of foreign-exchange controls have recently been analyzed in a cash-in-advance setting by Greenwood and Kimbrough (1986).[33] Only a few modifications of the benchmark model are needed in order to highlight the basic flavor of their results. First, assume that there are two traded goods and that traded-good one is produced and consumed at home while traded-good two is not produced domestically and thus has to be imported from abroad for consumption purposes.[34] Second, in order to pin down the circulation of money in the economy, assume that domestic residents buy all of traded-good one that they consume from domestic firms, with any additional output being exported. With these modifications, the sequence of cash-in-advance constraints facing the home consumer becomes

$$P_{T1t}c_{T1t} + P_{Nt}c_{Nt} \leq M_{Ht}, \quad P^*_{T2t}c_{T2t} \leq M_{Ft} \tag{3.65}$$

where the new notation is readily apparent by analogy with that used earlier. In addition, the sequence of budget constraints for $t = 1, 2, \ldots$ that face the consumer are given by

$$\begin{aligned} M_{Ht} + e_t M_{Ft} = {} & P_{T1t-1}y_{T1t-1} + P_{Nt-1}y_{Nt-1} \\ & + (M_{Ht-1} - P_{T1t-1}c_{T1t-1} - P_{Nt-1}c_{Nt-1}) \\ & + e_t(M_{Ft-1} - P^*_{T2t-1}c_{T2t-1}) + (1 + r_{t-1})P_{T1t}b_{t-1} \\ & - P_{T1t}b_t + P_{T1t}(\mu_t - \tau_t) \end{aligned} \tag{3.66}$$

The consumer's problem is to maximize his lifetime utility,

$$\bar{U} = \sum_{t=1}^{\infty} \beta^{t-1} U(c_{T1t}, c_{T2t}, c_{Nt})$$

subject to (3.65), (3.66), and the foreign-exchange controls imposed by the government. These controls can be modeled by assuming that the government puts a ceiling, $\bar{M}_{Ft}$, on the amount of foreign exchange the consumer can acquire. Thus, in addition to the constraints (3.65) and (3.66), the consumer also faces the constraints[35]

$$M_{Ft} \leq \bar{M}_{Ft} \qquad t = 1, 2, \ldots \tag{3.67}$$

Besides the constraints (3.65)–(3.67), the first-order conditions for the consumer's optimization problem are given by

$$\frac{\beta^{t-1}U_{T1}(\cdot t)}{U_{T1}(\cdot 1)} = d_t \qquad t = 1, 2, \ldots \tag{3.68}$$

$$\frac{U_N(\cdot t)}{U_{T1}(\cdot t)} = \frac{P_{Nt}}{P_{T1t}} \qquad t = 1, 2, \ldots \tag{3.69}$$

$$\frac{U_{T2}(\cdot t)}{U_{T1}(\cdot t)} = \left(1 + \frac{\alpha_t}{\lambda_t}\right)\frac{P^*_{T2t}}{P^*_{T1t}} \qquad t = 1, 2, \ldots \tag{3.70}$$

where λ_t is the Lagrange multiplier associated with the consumer's period-t budget constraint and α_t is the Lagrange multiplier associated with the foreign-exchange constraint imposed upon the consumer by the government.

Along with the economy's overall resource constraint, which is a straightforward modification of (3.44a), the first-order conditions (3.68)–(3.70) fully characterize the economy's real equilibrium. Conditions (3.68) and (3.69) are the familiar intertemporal efficiency and nontraded-goods-market equilibrium conditions from the earlier analysis. It is condition (3.70) which captures the key feature of foreign-exchange controls. As can be seen, foreign-exchange controls drive a tariff-like wedge between the domestic relative price of importables, which equals $U_{T2}(\cdot t)/U_{T1}(\cdot t)$ in equilibrium, and the world relative price, P^*_{T2t}/P^*_{T1t}. However, the wedge between domestic and world relative prices is endogenously determined, as underlying economic conditions alter the shadow value, α_t, that domestic residents attach to foreign exchange. Thus, in terms of their effect on the economy, foreign-exchange controls are closely related to import quotas.[36]

The commercial-policy flavor of foreign-exchange controls has a number of important policy implications. First, unlike dual exchange rates, foreign-exchange controls do not drive a wedge between the international borrowing rates facing the government and the private sector. Therefore, contrary to widespread belief (see, e.g., Krueger 1983), foreign-exchange controls are not sufficient to give rise to real effects associated with devaluations. Devaluations and other domestic monetary policies remain neutral in the presence of foreign-exchange controls. Second, when foreign-exchange controls are in place, monetary disturbances abroad will typically have real repercussions in the home country. This can easily be seen by combining (3.65) and (3.67) to obtain

$$c_{T2t} \leq \frac{\bar{M}_{Ft}}{P^*_{T2t}} \qquad t = 1, 2, \ldots$$

which is the effective constraint foreign-exchange controls place on imports. As can be seen, purely monetary disturbances abroad, which alter P^*_{T2t} while leaving P^*_{T2t}/P^*_{T1t} unchanged, will have a real impact on the home country when foreign-exchange controls are in place, because they are equivalent to adjusting the import quota associated with the controls. Third, just as world real-interest-rate disturbances can be negatively transmitted to the home country under capital controls, terms-of-trade shocks can be negatively transmitted to domestic relative prices under foreign-exchange controls. Finally, since systems of foreign-exchange controls interfere with free trade, standard arguments imply that in terms of welfare both fixed and flexible exchange rates dominate foreign-exchange controls for a distortion-free small open economy.

Fiscal Policies and International Transmission

The preceding section presented an overview of the effects of monetary and exchange-rate policies on the world-economy's real equilibrium from the perspective of the benchmark model. Much recent attention on the part of both economists and policymakers, however, has focused on the ramifications of changes in fiscal policy. The role of government spending and the method of financing have both been matters of concern. This section of the chapter deals with the international transmission of fiscal policies in the world economy. Much of the recent work that has been done on the effects of fiscal policy has ignored monetary considerations but can easily be recast into a monetary setting using the cash-in-advance setup of the benchmark model. A useful feature of the benchmark model is that, with its lump-sum taxes and transfers, Ricardian equivalence holds, meaning that government financing decisions are irrelevant for the world-economy's real equilibrium. The benchmark model is thus well suited for highlighting the impact of changes in government spending. Accordingly, this will be the first topic taken up in this section. Next, the role of budget deficits and government financing decisions will be highlighted using the finite-horizon framework of Blanchard (1985). Finally, the case where financing decisions matter because of the need to levy distorting taxes to raise revenue will be taken up.

The Influence of Government Purchases

In order to examine the role of government purchases succinctly and in a self-contained fashion, the infinite-horizon version of the benchmark model will now be replaced with a two-period framework. None of the qualitative results that follow depend in any important way on this modification. The two-period model may be taken literally or, perhaps more usefully, viewed as arising from aggregating across periods so as to collapse time into the present and the future. Time aggregation of this sort in the context of fiscal policies in the open economy is discussed by Frenkel and Razin (1986b). For purposes of working with the two-period version of the benchmark model, it is sufficient to note that all of its key building blocks—equations (3.1a), (3.1b), (3.2a), (3.2b), (3.4a)–(3.9a), (3.4b)–(3.9b), and (3.10)—continue to hold for $t = 1$, 2. The lifetime utility functions (3.3a) and (3.3b), however, need to be replaced with

$$\bar{U} = \sum_{t=1}^{2} \beta^{t-1} U(c_{Tt}, c_{Nt})$$

and

$$\bar{U}^* = \sum_{t=1}^{2} (\beta^*)^{t-1} U^*(c_{Tt}^*, c_{Nt}^*)$$

in order to facilitate the transition to a two-period description of the world economy. Finally, it should be noted that all of the results sketched in the preceding three sections continue to hold in the two-period setup (summations are, of course, over periods $t = 1, 2$, rather than over $t = 1, 2, \ldots$).

Closed-form solutions for the world-economy's real equilibrium are readily obtained once specific within-period utility functions are imposed, the optimization problems facing home and foreign consumers are solved, the government budget constraints (3.4a)–(3.6a) and (3.4b)–(3.6b) are accounted for, and the market-clearing conditions (3.7a)–(3.9a), (3.7b)–(3.9b), and (3.10) are utilized. The specifications of the within-period utility functions given by (3.18a) and (3.18b) are easy to work with and thus are adopted here.[37] The discussion of fiscal policies that follows is closest in spirit to and draws heavily on the work of Frenkel and Razin (1985), although similar results have been derived elsewhere by Greenwood (1983, 1984) Greenwood and Kimbrough (1985a), Kimbrough (1985a), and Ahmed (1986).

Following the procedures mentioned in the preceding paragraph, a full solution for the world-economy's real equilibrium can easily be derived. However, for present purposes the solutions for the following real variables are all that is needed (similar expressions hold abroad):

$$p_1 = \frac{\theta}{1+\beta} \frac{W}{y_{N1} - g_{N1}}, \quad p_2 = \frac{\theta\beta}{1+\beta} \frac{(1+r)W}{y_{N2} - g_{N2}} \tag{3.71}$$

$$W = \frac{1}{1-\theta}\left(y_{T1} - g_{T1} + \frac{y_{T2} - g_{T2}}{1+r}\right) \tag{3.72}$$

$$1 + r = \frac{\frac{1}{1+\beta}(y_{T2} - g_{T2}) + \frac{1}{1+\beta^*}(y_{T2}^* - g_{T2}^*)}{\frac{\beta}{1+\beta}(y_{T1} - g_{T1}) + \frac{\beta^*}{1+\beta^*}(y_{T1}^* - g_{T1}^*)} \tag{3.73}$$

The expressions in (3.71) give the equilibrium relative price of nontraded goods in periods $t = 1, 2$. Given the specification of the utility function, these relative prices depend on the ratio of nontraded-goods demand and nontraded-goods supply (net of government purchases). For example, the equilibrium relative price of nontraded goods in period one depends on demand, $[\theta/(1+\beta)]W$, relative to supply, $y_{N1} - g_{N1}$, where

$$W \equiv \sum_{t=1}^{2} d_t[y_{Tt} - g_{Tt} + p_t(y_{Nt} - g_{Nt})]$$

is domestic wealth. $1/(1+\beta)$ is the marginal propensity to spend out of wealth on current-period goods and θ is the fraction of this spending that falls on nontraded goods.

Using (3.71) in the definition of wealth gives (3.72) as the equilibrium level of wealth in the home country. Notice that the equilibrium value of wealth rises more than one-for-one with changes in the present value of net tradeables output, $y_{T1} - g_{T1} + (y_{T2} - g_{T2})/(1+r)$, because increases in the availability of traded goods in either period increase wealth, thereby raising the market-clearing relative price of nontraded goods in both periods.

The equilibrium real interest rate is given by (3.73) (the time subscript has been dropped since there is only one real interest rate in the two-period model). Note that the greater the relative supply of current goods (that is, the greater $y_{T1} - g_{T1}$ and $y^*_{T1} - g^*_{T1}$ relative to $y_{T2} - g_{T2}$ and $y^*_{T2} - g^*_{T2}$), the lower the relative price of current goods. Also, the greater the domestic and foreign marginal propensities to spend on current goods—that is, the larger $1/(1+\beta)$ and $1/(1+\beta^*)$, the higher the relative price of current goods. It should be noted that since the markets for traded goods provide the only direct real linkage between countries, an implication of (3.73) is that nontraded-goods-market shocks at home and abroad, as captured by movements in $y_{Nt} - g_{Nt}$ and $y^*_{Nt} - g^*_{Nt}$ for $t = 1, 2$, are not internationally transmitted. This arises because, with the specification of the utility function being used here, uncompensated price elasticities are unity. The upshot is that the value of the net output of nontraded goods in either period, $p_t(y_{Nt} - g_{Nt})$, and hence wealth as (3.72) illustrates, is not affected by changes in the supply of nontraded goods. This result highlights the important role played by price elasticities in determining the extent to which nontraded-goods-market supply shocks are internationally transmitted.

In light of these features of the current framework, the following analysis will focus exclusively on the effects of shifts in government purchases of traded goods. Before examining these effects, two further implications of the utility functions being used here should be recalled from the earlier discussion. First, deviations from purchasing power parity, or fluctuations in the real exchange rate, are given by (3.20). Second, real interest rates in terms of home and foreign consumption baskets are given by (3.38a) and (3.38b).

Consider, first, the impact of a temporary rise in government purchases of traded goods occurring during the current period. As can be seen from

(3.73), the world relative price of current (traded) goods in terms of future (traded) goods increases by

$$\frac{d(1+r)}{dg_{T1}} = (1+r) \cdot \frac{\frac{\beta}{1+\beta}}{\frac{\beta}{1+\beta}(y_{T1} - g_{T1}) + \frac{\beta^*}{1+\beta^*}(y^*_{T1} - g^*_{T1})} > 0 \quad (3.74)$$

reflecting the increased scarcity of current goods relative to future goods as a result of the temporarily high level of government purchases.

Using (3.72) and (3.74), it is easy to show that home-country wealth drops by

$$\frac{dW}{dg_{T1}} = \frac{-1}{1-\theta}\left(1 + \frac{\frac{\beta}{1+\beta}y_{T2}}{\frac{1}{1+\beta}(y_{T2} - g_{T2}) + \frac{1}{1+\beta^*}(y^*_{T2} - g^*_{T2})}\right) < 0 \quad (3.75)$$

as a result of the increased level of government spending on traded goods. Since it follows from the consumer's optimization problem that

$$c_{T1} = \frac{1-\theta}{1+\beta}W \quad (3.76)$$

it can be seen that current-period domestic consumption of traded goods declines. Similarly, the rise in the real-interest-rate factor $1+r$ can be shown to reduce foreign wealth and foreign consumption of traded goods during the current period. The change in government purchases thus crowds out both home and foreign consumption of traded goods and results in positive international transmission in the sense that positive comovements in consumption arise in response to temporary changes in government purchases.[38] Were employment and output endogenously determined, they too would exhibit positive international comovements (see Greenwood and Kimbrough 1985a).

As a consequence of the fact that home and foreign wealth move in the same direction in response to a temporary rise in government purchases, the relative price of nontraded goods falls in both countries. That is, there is positive international transmission of relative price movements as well as of macroeconomic aggregates like consumption. However, as is apparent from (3.20), when international comovements in the relative price of non-traded goods arise, movements in the real exchange rate are not clear-cut at the theoretical level. Additionally, using (3.71) and its foreign counterpart in (3.38a) and (3.38b), it can be shown that

$$1+\tilde{r}=\left[\frac{y_{N2}-g_{N2}}{\beta(y_{N1}-g_{N1})}\right]^{\theta}(1+r)^{1-\theta} \tag{3.77a}$$

and

$$1+\tilde{r}^{*}=\left[\frac{y^{*}_{N2}-g^{*}_{N2}}{\beta^{*}(y^{*}_{N1}-g^{*}_{N1})}\right]^{\theta^{*}}(1+r)^{1-\theta^{*}} \tag{3.77b}$$

which implies that movements in consumption-based real interest rates will also be positively related across countries.

In conjunction with (3.75) and (3.76), the definition of the current-period trade balance,

$$tb_1=y_{T1}-g_{T1}-c_{T1} \tag{3.78}$$

can be used to demonstrate that a temporary increase in government spending on traded goods leads to a deterioration of the trade balance by

$$\frac{dtb_1}{dg_{T1}}=\frac{-\beta}{1+\beta}\left[\frac{\frac{1}{1+\beta^{*}}(y^{*}_{T2}-g^{*}_{T2})}{\frac{1}{1+\beta}(y_{T2}-g_{T2})+\frac{1}{1+\beta}(y^{*}_{T2}-g^{*}_{T2})}\right]<0 \tag{3.79}$$

This result, which reflects the permanent-income-hypothesis flavor of the benchmark model, has been derived by numerous authors, including Greenwood (1983, 1984), Frenkel and Razin (1985), and Kimbrough (1985a). Intuitively, all else equal, a temporary increase in government purchases reduces the private-sector's disposable income, and consumers wish to borrow against their future income so as to cushion the fall in their current consumption by spreading the effects of the disturbance out more evenly over their lifetimes. This increased borrowing manifests itself in a worsening of the current trade balance. As can be seen from (3.78), the magnitude of the impact of temporary changes in government purchases on the trade balance depends crucially on effective country size—as measured by the term in braces in (3.78)—with smaller countries tending to exhibit a stronger trade-balance response to temporary changes in government purchases.

Intertemporal optimizing models, such as the benchmark model, have been used to stress the influence not only of current policy shifts on the current-period equilibrium but also of anticipated future policy shifts. Accordingly, as a second comparative-statics exercise, consider the repercussions of an anticipated future increase in government purchases of traded goods. The key comparative-statics results needed in order to examine the international comovement of prices and quantities in response to such a disturbance are

$$\frac{d(1+r)}{dg_{T2}} = \frac{\frac{-1}{1+\beta}}{\frac{\beta}{1+\beta}(y_{T1} - g_{T1}) + \frac{\beta^*}{1+\beta^*}(y^*_{T1} - g^*_{T1})} < 0 \tag{3.80}$$

$$\frac{dW}{dg_{T2}} = \frac{-1}{1-\theta}\frac{1}{1+r}\left[\frac{\frac{1}{1+\beta^*}(y^*_{T2} - g^*_{T2})}{\frac{1}{1+\beta}(y_{T2} - g_{T2}) + \frac{1}{1+\beta^*}(y^*_{T2} - g^*_{T2})}\right] < 0 \tag{3.81}$$

As can be seen from (3.80), the anticipated future rise in government purchases means that current goods are now relatively more abundant, and hence their price in terms of future goods drops. The fall in the world real interest rate increases foreign wealth and thus causes foreign consumption to rise in anticipation of the home-country's higher future level of government spending on traded goods. However, home-country wealth falls as indicated by (3.81), although the direct effect of the fall in future disposable income, $y_{T2} - g_{T2}$, is mitigated somewhat by the decline in the real interest rate. As a result of the fall in home-country wealth, domestic consumption declines, as is apparent from (3.76). The decline in current-period consumption in response to the anticipated future increase in government purchases leads to an improvement of the current-period trade balance, as can be seen from (3.78). The rationale behind this result is that in order to smooth consumption, domestic consumers must now save more for the future, since their future disposable income has been reduced by the shift in fiscal policy. In addition, (3.71) and its foreign counterpart imply that the current-period relative price of nontraded goods falls at home and rises abroad as a consequence of the divergent movements in wealth at home and abroad. It is also clear from (3.20) that the real exchange rate, $e_1 P^*_1/P_1$, depreciates.

Therefore, macroeconomic aggregates, like consumption, and relative prices of nontraded goods exhibit negative international comovements in response to anticipated future changes in government purchases. This negative international transmission of anticipated future changes in government purchases is in direct contrast to the positive international transmission of current shifts in government purchases. However, note that (3.77a) and (3.77b) continue to hold for the case of anticipated future disturbances to government purchases, and hence consumption-based real interest rates continue to be characterized by positive international transmission. This feature of the model reflects the fact that world capital markets are fully integrated. As shown by Greenwood and Kimbrough (1985a), negative international comovements of real interest rates in response to changes in government purchases tend to arise when capital controls or other quantitative restrictions on international capital market transactions (such as dual exchange rates) are in place.

Finally, the results for temporary and anticipated future increases in government spending on traded goods can be combined to highlight the impact of a permanent increase in government purchases (for which $dg_{T1} = dg_{T2} = dg_T > 0$). It is straightforward to show using (3.74) and (3.80) that in response to a permanent increase in government purchases of traded goods

$$\frac{d(1+r)}{dg_T} = [(1+r)\beta - 1]\left[\frac{\frac{1}{1+\beta}}{\frac{\beta}{1+\beta}(y_{T1} - g_{T1}) + \frac{\beta^*}{1+\beta^*}(y^*_{T1} - g^*_{T1})}\right] \gtrless 0 \quad (3.82)$$

As indicated by (3.82), a permanent increase in government purchases will raise or lower real interest rates according to whether the initial real interest rate is greater or less than the rate of time preference of consumers in the country from which the fiscal shock emanates.

To better understand this result, note that after substituting (3.72) and (3.76) into (3.78), it can be shown that at the initial real interest rate the desired change in the home country's current trade balance is

$$\left.\frac{dtb_1}{dg_T}\right|_r = \frac{-[(1+r)\beta - 1]}{(1+\beta)(1+r)}$$

In response to a permanent rise in government spending, the home country thus desires to dissave or to save according to whether the initial real interest rate is greater than or less than the home country's rate of time preference. The intuition behind this can be seen by noting, for example, that when the initial real interest rate exceeds the home country's rate of time preference, domestic residents will desire to save in response to a permanent increase in income and dissave in response to a permanent decline in income. Since a permanent increase in government purchases represents a permanent decline in the private sector's disposable income, the trade balance will tend to worsen at the initial real interest rate. The incipient excess demand for current goods that thus arises must be eliminated by a rise in real interest rates, as shown by (3.82), in order to restore equilibrium. Alternatively, when the initial real interest rate is less than the rate of time preference, the real interest rate mut fall to clear the market.

This result has important implications for the international transmission of permanent shifts in government purchases. To see this, note that home-country wealth unambiguously falls, since home-country wealth falls in response to both current and anticipated future increases in government purchases. As a consequence, home-country consumption falls and the current-period relative price of nontraded goods drops, when government purchases are permanently increased. However, foreign wealth, consumption, and relative prices of nontraded goods all fall or rise according as $(1+r)\beta - 1 \gtrless 0$; since this datum determines the sign of the shift in real interest rates, which is crucial for the international transmission of fiscal shocks. Therefore, permanent changes in government purchases will generate positive or negative international comovements in macroeconomic aggregates and relative prices of nontraded goods according as the initial real interest rate is greater than or less than the rate of time preference of consumers in the country where the fiscal shock originates.

One additional result of interest concerns the trade-balance effects of permanent changes in government purchases. It can be shown that

$$\frac{dtb_1}{dg_T} = \frac{-[(1+r)\beta - 1]}{(1+\beta)(1+r)} \left[\frac{\dfrac{1}{1+\beta^*}(y^*_{T2} - g^*_{T2})}{\dfrac{1}{1+\beta}(y_{T2} - g_{T2}) + \dfrac{1}{1+\beta^*}(y^*_{T2} - g^*_{T2})} \right]$$

so that, in general, the trade-balance response is ambiguous. However, it is easily seen that the trade balance cannot worsen more in response to a permanent increase in government purchases than in response to a temporary increase. This follows from the fact that

$$\frac{dtb_1}{dg_T} = \frac{dtb_1}{dg_{T1}} + \frac{dtb_1}{dg_{T2}}$$

Since the first term of the right-hand side of this expression is negative and the second term positive, the trade balance cannot worsen more in response to a permanent increase in government purchases than in response to a temporary increase. That is, the model implies that, in addition to the condition $0 \geqslant dtb_1/dg_{T1} \geqslant -1$ implied by (3.79),

$$\frac{dtb_1}{dg_T} \geqslant \frac{dtb_1}{dg_{T1}} \tag{3.83}$$

should hold.

Two recent empirical studies deal directly with the predictions of the benchmark model for the effects of shifts in the time profile of government purchases.[39] Azam (1984) and Ahmed (1986) both focus on the distinction between permanent and temporary changes in government purchases. Both authors conduct their empirical investigations under the assumption that the country they are studying is a small open economy, and hence they focus their attention on the trade-balance effects of changes in the government purchase stream. The Canadian experience of 1962–1980 is studied by Azam. He tests the qualitative predictions of the benchmark model given by (3.79) and (3.83), and cannot reject either of these null hypotheses. Azam also finds that the Canadian trade balance was not influenced by changes in the government's budget deficit over the same period, a result that is also consistent with the benchmark model. Ahmed (1986) studies the behavior of the trade balance in the United Kingdom for 1908–1980 using a model which, unlike the benchmark model, allows government purchases to yield consumption and production benefits. His model, however, generates predictions concerning the trade-balance effects of permanent and temporary changes in government purchases that are qualitatively the same as those of the benchmark model. Ahmed is unable to reject the null hypotheses implied by (3.79) and (3.83).

In addition to formal statistical testing of a model's implications, economists are also generally swayed by the ability of models to generate predictions that are capable of explaining stylized facts arising from the raw data or from time-series studies describing the relationships between various prices and quantities. Two such opportunities present themselves for examining the benchmark model's usefulness. First, Frenkel and Razin (1986a) have recently presented evidence indicating that over the past few years U.S. consumption has risen relative to foreign consumption, the real U.S. dollar exchange rate has appreciated, real interest rates have risen, and the U.S. trade balance has deteriorated substantially. They explain these stylized facts as a response to the large U.S. government budget deficits over the period. However, in the benchmark model, financing decisions do not have real effects. An alternative explanation of these stylized facts based on the benchmark model is that they reflect an anticipated rise in future disposable income in the U.S. as a consequence of an expected rise in future output, y_{T2}, or an anticipated future cut in government spending, g_{T2} (as one might anticipate if one expected the U.S. government budget to be balanced without a tax hike).

Another stylized fact that one might attempt to explain using the benchmark model concerns the results presented by Cumby and Mishkin (1986) concerning U.S.-European real-interest-rate linkages. They regress

European real interest rates on a constant and the U.S. real interest rate and, as noted earlier, find that European real interest rates respond positively to movements in U.S. real interest rates but that the response is less than one-to-one. As already noted, with fully integrated capital markets, or even with taxes on international capital flows, the consumption-based real interest rates, $\tilde{r}_t$ and $\tilde{r}_t^*$, studied by Cumby and Mishkin should be positively related. This is apparent from (3.77a) and (3.77b), provided that simultaneous nontraded-goods-market shocks do not disrupt the positive international transmission arising from international asset-market linkages. Such would be the case if technological innovation in the nontraded sector proceeded slowly, as is frequently suggested (see, e.g., Balassa 1964). The puzzle then is why European real interest rates, $\tilde{r}_t^*$, respond less than one-to-one to movements in U.S. real interest rates, $\tilde{r}_t$. The benchmark model is capable of providing a potential explanation of this result. This can be seen by solving (3.77a) for $1+r$, substituting the result in (3.77b), and taking logarithms of the resulting expression to obtain the following condition linking U.S. and European real interest rates:

$$\tilde{r}^* \approx \alpha + \left(\frac{1-\theta^*}{1-\theta}\right)\tilde{r} \tag{3.84}$$

where

$$\alpha = \ln\left\{\left[\frac{y_{N2}^* - g_{N2}^*}{\beta^*(y_{N1}^* - g_{N1}^*)}\right]^{\theta^*}\left[\frac{y_{n2} - g_{N2}}{\beta(y_{N1} - g_{N1})}\right]^{-\theta(1-\theta^*)/(1-\theta)}\right\}$$

The benchmark model thus predicts a positive link between U.S. and European real interest rates, and a less than one-to-one response of European real interest rates to movements in U.S. real interest rates provided that the share of nontraded goods in European expenditure is greater than the share of nontraded goods in U.S. expenditure (and assuming that negative movements in α are not the predominant source of the apparent international linkage of real interest rates). These predictions of the benchmark model are consistent with the stylized facts uncovered by Cumby and Mishkin (1986).[40]

Finite Lives and Government Financing Decisions

The focus so far has been on the international transmission of changes in government purchases, because in the benchmark model with its lump-sum taxes and infinitely lived individuals, Ricardian equivalence holds and hence government financing decisions have no real effects. However, for many purposes, for instance explaining the potential real effects of current and prospective U.S. government budget deficits, it is useful to explore models that allow government financing decisions to influence the world-economy's real equilibrium. One way to introduce such considerations into the benchmark model is along the lines of Helpman and Razin (1985b) and Frenkel and Razin (1986b) who, following Blanchard (1985), replace the assumption of infinitely lived consumers with an overlapping-generations setup in which a cohort of size one is born each period in both countries and the probability of a consumer living from one period to the next is γ. In this framework the age distribution of each country's population will be constant over time with γ^a individuals of age a alive in each period. Each country's population will thus remain constant at $1/(1-\gamma)$.

Being immortal, both governments can borrow at the risk-free real interest rate r_t. However, loans to consumers must carry a risk premium to cover the probability that they will not live to repay their loans. As a consequence, the real interest rate facing consumers will be $[(1+r_t)/\gamma]-1$, since by charging this rate financial institutions assure themselves of a real return on their portfolio equal to the risk-free rate (see Blanchard 1985). The one-period discount factor used by the private sector to evaluate future income streams is thus $(1+r_t)/\gamma$.

Embedding this demographic and financial-market structure in the cash-in-advance framework, it can be shown that the budget constraint facing a home-country consumer who is age a at time t is

$$\begin{aligned} c_{Ta,t}+p_t c_{Na,t} = {} & \frac{P_{Tt-1}}{P_{Tt}}(y_{Tt-1}+p_{t-1}y_{Nt-1}) \\ & + \frac{1+r_{t-1}}{\gamma}P_{Tt}b_{a-1,t-1} \\ & - b_{a,t}+P_{Tt}(\mu_t-\tau_t) \end{aligned}$$

where $c_{Ta,t}$ is consumption of traded goods by a consumer of age a at time t and other variables relating to this individual are correspondingly subscripted.[41]

Using the government budget constraints (3.4a)–(3.6a) in the above expression yields the lifetime budget constraint for this consumer as

$$\sum_{k=t}^{\infty}\gamma^{k-t}\frac{d_k}{d_t}(c_{Ta+k-t,k}+p_k c_{Na+k-t,k}) = W_{a,t} \tag{3.85}$$

where $W_{a,t}$ is the wealth of a consumer who is age a at time t and is given by

$$W_{a,t} = \sum_{k=t}^{\infty} \gamma^{k-t} \frac{d_k}{d_t} [y_{Tk} - g_{Tk} + p_k(y_{Nk} - g_{Nk}) - (1-\gamma)(b_{gk} + b_{Rk})]$$

$$+ \frac{1+r_{t-1}}{\gamma} b_{a-1,t-1} + (1 + r_{t-1})(b_{gt-1} + b_{Rt-1}) \tag{3.86}$$

In these expressions $\gamma^{k-t}(d_k/d_t)$ is the discount factor used by consumers for discounting income accruing at time $k \geq t$ back to period t. Expressions similar to (3.85) and (3.86) can be derived for the foreign country; but they are not presented here, as (3.85) and (3.86) are sufficient for illustrating the main implications of the finite-horizon setup. Before discussing these implications, it should be noted that per capita consumption of traded and nontraded goods is given by $(1-\gamma)\sum_{a=0}^{\infty}\gamma^a c_{Xa,t}$, $X = T,N$, so that inferences made from (3.85) and (3.86) concerning aggregate behavior are qualitatively valid.

Several implications concerning the impact of fiscal policies on the world-economy's real equilibrium with finite horizons are apparent from (3.85) and (3.86) in conjunction with the fact that the consumer's optimization problem implies that current consumption depends on wealth. First, as underscored by Frenkel and Razin (1986b), balanced-budget changes in government purchases affect the world-economy's real equilibrium in essentially the same manner as in the infinite-horizon framework. The reason for this is that in both cases changes in government purchases generate wealth effects that influence the private-sector consumption pattern.

Second, Ricardian equivalence does not hold so long as $\gamma < 1$. That is, government financing decisions matter. This feature of the finite-horizon economy is reflected by the appearance of the fiscal-authority's bond holdings, b_{gk}, in (3.86). To see this, consider a one-unit tax cut at time t. This raises the consumer's disposable income by 1 unit at time t. However, inherent in the debt the government issues in order to finance its given purchase stream is an additional future tax liability of $1 + r_t$ of which the consumer is fully cognizant. The change in the consumer's wealth is thus

$$1 - \frac{\gamma}{1+r_t}(1 + r_t) = 1 - \gamma$$

Therefore, a switch from tax to debt financing increases private-sector wealth and raises private-sector consumption at the initial real interest rate. These effects will be transmitted to the rest of the world via an increase in the real interest rate and a worsening of the home-country's trade balance. The effect is proportional to $1 - \gamma$, which is the probability that the consumer will not live to share in the future tax burden implied by the increased reliance on deficit financing.

Finally, consider the implications of the finite-horizon framework for monetary and exchange-rate policies. Under flexible exchange rates the exchange rate adjusts to clear the money market in response to shifts in domestic credit, and hence no international-reserve movements are required in response to such policies. As a consequence, the world-economy's real equilibrium under flexible exchange rates is independent of monetary policy, as in the infinite-horizon version of the benchmark model, since monetary policy exerts no wealth effects. However, under fixed exchange rates monetary policy does exert real effects, because changes in domestic credit bring about changes in a country's stock of international reserves, which alter wealth as shown by (3.86). As is apparent, this result is related to the failure of Ricardian equivalence. These effects of monetary policies in the finite-horizon economy are explored in detail by Helpman and Razin (1985b).

Distorting Taxes and Government Financing Decisions

The finite-horizon, overlapping-generations modification of the benchmark model introduces a role for government financing decisions and budget deficits by focusing on the potential wealth effects that such policies may have. An alternative route to introducing the effects of budget deficits into the benchmark framework is to assume the government cannot rely on lump-sum taxes in order to raise revenue but must instead levy distorting taxes in order to finance its expenditures. This approach essentially leaves Ricardian equivalence intact—in the sense that there are no direct wealth effects associated with changes in the method of financing—and thus does not rely on wealth effects in order to produce a meaningful discussion of the effects of budget deficits. Instead, models with distorting taxes stress the substitution effects that are generated when the time profile of taxes is altered in order to accomodate a switch in the fiscal-authority's debt policy while maintaining solvency (i.e., an intertemporally balanced budget). As it turns out, the effects of shifts in the budget deficit on the world-economy real equilibrium depend crucially on the relationship between the initial tax structure and the optimal tax structure (in the Ramsey sense).

To illustrate the types of results that are possible, return to the two-period version of the benchmark model outlined in the first part of this section and imagine extending that model to include two traded goods as in the earlier discussion of foreign-exchange controls. Suppose further that the home country has decided not to undertake any government purchases currently or in the future and that the only tax instruments available are tariffs on imports. If the home country is taken to be small, it is well known that the optimal tax structure calls for a policy of free trade. Suppose that, starting from a free-trade equilibrium, the government decides to implement a small increase in its current-period budget deficit (which is initially zero). This policy can be implemented, and solvency maintained, by subsidizing current imports and imposing a tariff on future imports. As the work of Razin and Svensson (1983a) indicates, this policy will worsen the trade balance for the following reasons. The subsidy to current imports and the tariff on future imports lower the relative price of current consumption in terms of future consumption. The substitution effects arising from the policy thus operate to shift consumption away from the future and toward the present. These substitution effects worsen the current-period trade balance. Since the initial equilibrium was the free-trade optimum, there are no welfare changes associated with the shift to deficit financing and hence no additional trade-balance effects of the policy. In this setting, then, an increased reliance on deficit financing leads to a deterioration of the trade balance just as in the finite-horizon framework. However, the mechanism is entirely different. In the finite-horizon framework, wealth effects were the driving force behind the impact of budget deficits on the trade balance. Here, such wealth effects are absent and the link between budget deficits and the trade balance rests entirely on substitution effects.

The importance of the initial tax structure relative to the optimal tax structure for the effects of government financing decisions can be highlighted by assuming the policy change outlined above is initiated from an initially distorted situation. First, consider the case where in the initial equilibrium the budget is already in deficit and hence current imports are being subsidized and future imports subjected to a tariff. An increased reliance on budget deficits will result in an increased current import subsidy and an increased future tariff. These additional distortions drive the economy further away from the free-trade optimum in both periods and thus generate negative wealth effects. As a result, the wealth effects associated with the increased budget deficit discourage current consumption and act to improve the trade balance. Since the substitution effects outlined earlier continue to work to worsen the trade balance, the net effect of the policy on the trade balance can go in either direction. On the other hand, if the initial situation had been one of a budget surplus (i.e., a current tariff on imports coupled with a future subsidy), the move toward a budget deficit would generate wealth effects that reinforce the substitution effects, so that the trade balance would unambiguously worsen.

In view of the fact that the trade balance and other effects of shifts in government financing decisions depend on the relation between the initial and optimal tax structures, the analysis of the relationship between budget deficits and the trade balance has recently been conducted in a public-finance setting in which distorting taxes are set optimally. The relationship between the budget deficit and the trade balance is thus viewed as arising from the optimal response of both to changes in some third variable (or set of variables). This is the approach that has been adopted by Razin and Svensson (1983b). They consider a setup similar to that of Aschauer and Greenwood (1983) that was discussed earlier and take the government to be maximizing consumer welfare subject to the constraint that a given stream of government purchases must be financed by distorting taxes on labor income. Given this framework, Razin and Svensson demonstrate that there is a tendency for the optimal response to a temporary decline in the marginal product of labor to be a worsening of the trade balance and an increased reliance on deficit financing. These responses serve to cushion the decline in current consumption that is associated with the temporary decline in productivity. This is accomplished by borrowing against future income, which is not directly influenced by the shock. On the other hand, the optimal response to a permanent fall in productivity tends not to involve any intertemporal shifting, such as a worsening of the trade balance, as there is no opportunity to shift resources from an unscathed future to the present (or vice versa).

When the government-purchase stream is exogenously given, as in Razin and Svensson (1983b), it can be shown that when optimal financing is pursued, the trade balance and other effects of permanent and temporary changes in government purchases will be qualitatively the same as those outlined in the first part of this section. This considerably enhances the general appeal of those results, which were based on lump-sum taxes being available, as a guide to the effects of changes in government spending. However, treating the government spending stream as exogenous does not seem entirely consistent with a government that chooses its tax structure so as optimally to finance its expenditures. It seems more appropriate to view the government's purchase stream and time profile of taxes as being jointly optimally determined. This is the approach adopted by Kimbrough (1986a), who studies the optimal response of government purchases and labor tax rates to changes in a country's foreign-aid receipts in a setting in which government purchases yield consumption and production benefits. It is shown that the optimal response of the fiscal-policy variables, and hence the trade balance, depends crucially on whether the foreign-aid flows accrue to the private sector or the government. For example, when an increased inflow of foreign aid accrues to the government, it is as if the government has lump-sum tax revenue suddenly available to it. The additional foreign aid can thus be used to cut tax rates and increase government purchases. On the other hand, when additional foreign aid is received by the private sector, the optimal response is shown to be a tax hike coupled with a cut in government purchases.

The question of optimal policies is an interesting and important one; but, as is by now well known, when governments are free to exercise discretion such policies are not generally time consistent. Governments have an incentive to announce a certain set of policies and then, after the desired private-sector response is induced, renege and change course. The problem is that if the private sector anticipates this, optimal outcomes under discretion will be inferior in terms of welfare to those that might be obtained with commitment (that is, without discretion). The issue of whether or not mechanisms and institutions can be designed to move the discretionary equilibrium closer toward the optimum that would be obtained with commitment thus has important implications for a broad range of topics in international macroeconomics, including, for example, the optimal exchange-rate regime and the possible timing of collapses of such regimes. Work on the time consistency of optimal fiscal policies in open economies has recently been provided by Persson and Svensson (1986), but much remains to be done on the topic of the time consistency of optimal policies in an explicit monetary general-equilibrium open-economy setting.

In the work on optimal policies of Razin and Svensson (1983b), Kimbrough (1986a), and Persson and Svensson (1986), the public-finance perspective which views monetary and fiscal policies as the solution to a Ramsey tax problem is taken. This is fine given the assumption of identical individuals, which implies that solution would also be produced by well-known models that treat government policies as emerging from a political equilibrium (such as the median-voter model). However, once heterogeneity is introduced, say by assuming individuals differ in their endowments of the factors of production, the Ramsey solution will not generally be the outcome generated by a political equilibrium (see, e.g., Mayer's 1984 work on trade policy using the median-voter model). It may, therefore, be fruitful from the standpoint of positive economics to treat observed monetary and fiscal policies as the manifestations of an underlying political equilibrium, and to study how these policies as well as macroeconomic aggregates respond to changes in the political and economic environment.

Notes

1. The outputs of traded and nontraded goods, as well as the corresponding prices and related quantities that will be introduced shortly, can be thought of as vectors without significantly altering any key results.

2. In the benchmark model without uncertainty, there is no need to deal explicitly with trade in firm shares since, given the existence of bonds, shares add no new trading opportunities.

3. For a survey of and some new empirical evidence on international goods- and asset-market linkages, see Cumby and Obstfeld (1984).

4. It has been assumed here that the foreign government does not purchase the entire foreign endowment of traded goods. If $g^*_{Tt} = y^*_{Tt}$, then the foreign-currency price of traded goods would be irrelevant for private-sector behavior.

5. See Aizenman (1986b) for a discussion of how transport costs and preset prices can combine to introduce bias into tests of goods-market arbitrage.

6. The same type of evidence is also presented by Dornbusch (1984) and others.

7. Although it does not fall directly out of the modified benchmark model being used here, it is noteworthy that modern theories of exchange-rate determination—see, for example, Frenkel (1976) and Mussa (1976)—predict $\text{cov}(1+\varepsilon_t, e_t) > 0$ and hence $b_1 > 0$ if differential changes in money-growth rates across countries are dominating exchange-rate movements. The reason for this is that an increase in, say, home money growth relative to that abroad would raise domestic inflation relative to that abroad and thus raise the rate of depreciation of the home currency, thereby causing the current exchange rate, e_t, to rise as individuals move out of home currency and into foreign currency. This could explain the predominance of positive b_1's found by Isard. A prediction like this might fall directly out of a modified version of Svensson (1985), where, although maintaining the cash-in-advance constraints, money demand is nonetheless sensitive to movements in inflation rates and nominal interest rates.

8. Bilson (1983) contains a recent effort at modeling the choice of an invoicing currency and a brief summary of some earlier work in the area.

9. This same point can be seen in a two-traded-good setting from Stockman (1980), and in a more ad hoc fashion from Kimbrough (1985b). The results of Dornbusch (1976a) are also broadly consistent with this view.

10. Mark (1986) also concludes that evidence for the 1970s points to the primary importance of real shocks.

11. To see this, take logarithms of (3.20) to obtain $\ln e_t = \ln(P_t/P^*_t) + u_t$, where $u_t \equiv -\theta \ln p_t + \theta^* \ln p^*_t$ is the period-t deviation from purchasing power parity. With permanent real shocks, current-period relative prices will be expected to prevail in future periods, and deviations from purchasing power parity will follow the stochastic process $u_t = u_{t-1} + v_t$ with $E_{t-1}v_t = 0$. In light of this, it follows that $E_t(\Delta \ln e_t) = E_t[\Delta \ln(P_t/P^*_t)]$, since $E_t \Delta u_t = E_t v_{t+1} = 0$. This view is consistent with the evidence presented by Frenkel and Hakkio.

12. For detailed surveys of these and related issues concerning the functioning of international asset markets, see Levich (1979, 1985).

13. However, as pointed out by Helpman and Razin (1984), when the buyer's currency is used for transactions purposes, the model is not generally consistent with the interest-parity conditions and equality of real interest rates in terms of traded goods. While the interest-parity conditions will hold in such a world because the foreign-exchange and bond markets are open at the same time, real interest rates in terms of traded goods will not be equalized unless the rate of change of the exchange rate is constant over time so that $e_{t+1}/e_t = e_{t+2}/e_{t+1} = \ldots$.

In addition to the factors outlined under *Real Interest-Rate Linkages* below, the use of the buyer's currency for transactions purposes thus provides another potential channel through which real interest rates in terms of national consumption bundles might fail to be equalized even if international capital markets are fully integrated and asset markets are efficient.

14. However, the complete market structure used by Lucas is not necessary for the results derived here. In the discussion that follows, the minimal asset-market structure compatible with the basic asset-pricing relationships is employed.

15. Kimbrough (1984b) highlights the implication of this work for the appropriate role of monetary and exchange-rate policies in open economies.

16. Frenkel and Razin (1980) stress the roles of the marginal utility of consumption and the time-series properties of prices in determining the stochastic behavior of the marginal utility of income.

17. However, his tests are identical to those that fall out of the current model when the within-period utility function takes the form $(c_{Tt}^{1-\theta}c_{Nt}^{\theta})^{1-\gamma}/1-\gamma$, where γ is the coefficient of relative risk aversion.

18. Mishkin (1984b) conducts his test for the international equality of real interest rates by running (3.37) for several countries vis-à-vis the U.S. and testing simultaneously for $b_1 = b_2 = \cdots = b_k = 0$ in all regressions.

19. In light of the market-clearing conditions for nontraded goods, (3.8a) and (3.8b), these constraints indicate that in equilibrium trade must balance intertemporally. Solvency conditions for the home and foreign monetary and fiscal authorities, which require an intertemporally balanced budget, have also been used in deriving (3.44a) and (3.44b).

20. This means, for instance, that policies such as devaluations and sterilization operations, which occur frequently under fixed exchange rates, have no real effects. For discussion of these results using a money-in-the-utility-function approach, see Obstfeld (1981a, 1982) and Stockman (1983).

21. It should be clear from this remark that the results currently being highlighted carry over to more-elaborate production structures than the endowment economy being studied here, so long as factors of production are inelastically supplied. For example, the results would also characterize a world economy where production patterns were dictated by the standard two-sector model or the specific-capital model.

22. A similar point is also made in Obstfeld (1982).

23. Obstfeld (1986a) is suggestive of the features that might characterize an economy that is currently committed to an exchange rate that is not credible and must ultimately come under speculative attack.

24. Dornbusch (1976a) also stresses the role of relative prices in the exchange-rate-determination process.

25. The assumption that the technology is time independent is not essential for any of the results that follow.

26. See Sandmo (1976) for a survey of this literature.

27. This result is especially true in setups such as Kimbrough (1985c), where, as a result of the monetary mechanism underlying the demand for money, the optimum-quantity-of-money rule should be adhered to even when distorting taxes must be levied for revenue-raising purposes.

28. The properties of dual-exchange-rate systems have been studied in the context of nonoptimizing models by Flood (1978), Flood and Marion (1982), and Gardner (1985), among others.

29. As will become apparent shortly, the only loss of generality with this assumption is that issues relating to the optimum-tariff question are ruled out.

30. This formulation assumes that both principle and interest are repatriated at the financial exchange rate, while in practice interest income is often repatriated at the commercial exchange rate. This distinction is inconsequential for the general features of dual-rate regimes that are highlighted below.

31. The distinctions between taxes on international borrowing and capital controls for the international transmission of fiscal policies is taken up by Greenwood and Kimbrough (1985a). Other recent work on capital controls and taxes on international borrowing includes Kaminsky (1984), who integrates black markets into the analysis; Aizenman (1986a), and Persson and Svensson (1986), who study the roles of such policies in the optimal revenue-raising tax package; and Kimbough (1986b), who examines the role of capital controls and taxes on international borrowing in optimally attaining balance-of-payments-related objectives.

32. Adams and Greenwood (1985) show that flexible exchange rates coupled with the optimum-quantity-of-money rule are superior to dual exchange rates when monetary policy has real effects along the lines of Aschauer and Greenwood (1983) that were sketched earlier in this section.

33. Quantitative restrictions such as foreign-exchange controls create incentives for black markets to develop in order to circumvent the controls. The implications of black markets for the functioning of foreign-exchange controls are outlined by Greenwood and Kimbrough (1985b). The basic result they demonstrate is that a foreign-exchange-controlled economy with a black market is a hybrid of a foreign-exchange-controlled economy without a black market and an unregulated, free-market economy. Other recent work on foreign-exchange controls includes Stockman and Hernandez D. (1985), who explore the implications of complete versus incomplete asset markets for the operation of foreign-exchange controls.

34. Domestic production of the imported good is easily allowed for without affecting any of the results that follow.

35. Greenwood and Kimbrough (1986) study this type of foreign-exchange control as well as regimes in which the controls are adjusted so as to restrict the real amount of foreign exchange held by domestic residents.

36. As discussed by Greenwood and Kimbrough (1986), certain types of multiple-exchange-rate systems take on similar characteristics. For example, it can be shown that if e_t is the exchange rate used for export-market transactions and s_t the exchange rate used for import purposes, the first-order condition (3.70) becomes

$$\frac{U_{T2}(\cdot t)}{U_{T1}(\cdot t)} = \left(1 + \frac{s_t - e_t}{e_t}\right) \frac{P^*_{T2t}}{P^*_{T1t}}$$

If both exchange rates are fixed, then the multiple-exchange-rate system is equivalent to levying a tariff; while if either exchange rate is floating, the system is more like an import quota.

37. It should be noted at the outset that in addition to restricting the price and income elasticities to unity, (3.18a) and (3.18b) also imply that $U_{TN}(\cdot t) = U^*_{TN}(\cdot t) = 0$ for $t = 1, 2$ and that government purchases are not valued by consumers. These considerations are taken up in the literature by Greenwood (1984), Djajić (1985), Greenwood and Kimbrough (1985a), Kimbrough (1985a), and Ahmed (1986). Several of these papers also consider the potential role of government purchases in the production process.

38. Note that this is true for aggregate consumption, $c_{T1} + p_1 c_{N1}$ and $c^*_{T1} + p^*_1 c^*_{N1}$, as well, since spending on nontraded goods is constant.

39. Of course, due to the fact that the benchmark model embodies the permanent-income hypothesis, the large literature on the permanent-income hypothesis can be viewed as an indirect test of the model's predictions for the effects of fiscal policies.

40. While (3.84) was derived from the two-period version of the benchmark model, it can be shown using the infinite-horizon version of the model with the within-period utility functions given by (3.18a) and (3.18b) that

$$\bar{r}_t^* \approx \alpha_t + \left(\frac{1-\theta^*}{1-\theta}\right)\bar{r}_t$$

where

$$\alpha_t = \ln\left\{\left[\frac{x_t^*(y_{Nt+1}^* - g_{Nt+1}^*)}{y_{Nt}^* - g_{Nt}^*}\right]^{\theta^*}\left[\frac{x_t(y_{Nt+1} - g_{Nt+1})}{y_{Nt} - g_{Nt}}\right]^{-\theta(1-\theta^*)/(1-\theta)}\right\}$$

$x_t = 1 - (tb_t/W_{t+1})$, and $x_t^* = 1 + (tb_t/W_{t+1}^*)$. Therefore, the general argument following (3.84) continues to hold even in the broader context of the infinite-horizon setup.

41. The endowment stream could be made to depend on the consumer's age without affecting any of the results that follow.

References

Adams, C., and J. Greenwood. 1985. "Dual Exchange Rate Systems and Capital Controls: An Investigation." *Journal of International Economics* 18 (February), pp. 43–63.

Adler, M., and B. Lehmann. 1983. "Deviations from Purchasing Power Parity in the Long Run." *Journal of Finance* 38 (December), pp. 1471–1487.

Ahmed, S. 1986. "Temporary and Permanent Government Spending in an Open Economy: Some Evidence for the United Kingdom." *Journal of Monetary Economics* 17 (March), pp. 197–224.

Aizenman, J. 1985. "Monopolistic Competition and Deviations from PPP." Unpublished manuscript, University of Chicago.

Aizenman, J. 1986a. "On the Complementarity of Commercial Policy, Capital Controls, and Inflation Tax." *Canadian Journal of Economics* 19 (February), pp. 114–133.

Aizenman, J. 1986b. "Testing Deviations from Purchasing Power Parity." *Journal of International Money and Finance* 5 (March), pp. 25–35.

Aizenman, J., and J. A. Frenkel. 1985. "Optimal Wage Indexation, Foreign Exchange Intervention, and Monetary Policy." *American Economic Review* 75 (June), pp. 402–423.

Aschauer, D., and J. Greenwood. 1983. "A Further Exploration in the Theory of Exchange Rate Regimes." *Journal of Political Economy* 91 (October), pp. 868–875.

Azam, A. H. M. G. 1984. "Current Account Analysis: An Empirical Investigation." Unpublished Ph.D. dissertation, Duke University, 1984.

Balassa, Bela. 1964. "The Purchasing Power Parity Doctrine: A Reappraisal." *Journal of Political Economy* 72 (December), pp. 584–596.

Benninga, S., and A. Protopapadakis. 1984. "The Equilibrium Pricing of Exchange Rates and Assets When Trade Takes Time." Federal Reserve Bank of Philadelphia Working Paper No. 84–5.

Bhandari, J. S. 1982. "Staggered Wage Setting and Exchange Rate Policy in an Economy with Capital Assets." *Journal of International Money and Finance* 1 (December), pp. 275–292.

Bilson, J. F. O. 1983. "The Choice of an Invoice Currency in International Transactions." In J. S. Bhandari and B. H. Putnam, eds., *Economic Interdependence and Flexible Exchange Rates*, pp. 384–401. Cambridge: MIT Press, 1983.

Blanchard, O. J. 1985. "Debt, Deficits, and Finite Horizons." *Journal of Political Economy* 93 (April), pp. 223–247.

Branson, W. H., and D. W. Henderson. 1985. "The Specification and Influence of Asset Markets." In R. W. Jones and P. B. Kenen, eds., *Handbook of International Economics*, vol. 2, pp. 749–805. Amsterdam: North-Holland, 1985.

Cantor, R., and N. C. Mark. 1985. "The International Transmission of Real Business Cycles." Unpublished manuscript, Ohio State University.

Cassel, G. 1916. "The Present Situation of the Foreign Exchanges." *Economic Journal* 26 (March), pp. 62–65.

Cumby, R. E., and F. S. Mishkin. 1986. "The International Linkage of Real Interest Rates: The European-U.S. Connection." *Journal of International Money and Finance* 5 (March), pp. 5–23.

Cumby, R. E., and M. Obstfeld. 1984. "International Interest Rate and Price Level Linkages Under Flexible Exchange Rates: A Review of Recent Evidence." In J. F. O. Bilson and R. C. Marston, eds., *Exchange Rate Theory and Practice*, pp. 121–151. Chicago: University of Chicago Press, 1984.

Djajić, S. 1985. "Current Account Effects of a Temporary Change in Government Expenditure." Unpublished manuscript, Queen's University.

Dornbusch, R. 1976a. "The Theory of Flexible Exchange Rate Regimes and Macroeconomic Policy." *Scandinavian Journal of Economics* 78 (May), pp. 255–275.

Dornbusch, R. 1976b. "Expectations and Exchange Rate Dynamics." *Journal of Political Economy* 84 (December), pp. 1161–1176.

Dornbusch, R. 1983. "Real Interest Rates, Home Goods, and Optimal External Borrowing." *Journal of Political Economy* 91 (February), pp. 141–153.

Dornbusch, R. 1984. "Exchange Rates and Prices." Unpublished manuscript, M.I.T.

Dornbusch, R. 1985. "Purchasing Power Parity." NBER Working Paper No. 1591.

Engel, C. M. 1984. "Testing for the Absence of Expected Real Profits from Forward Market Speculation." *Journal of International Economics* 17 (November), pp. 299–308.

Engle, R. F. 1982. "Autoregressive Conditional Heteroscedasticity with Estimates of the Variance of United Kingdom Inflation." *Econometrica* 50 (July), pp. 987–1007.

Fama, E. F. 1984. "Forward and Spot Exchange Rates." *Journal of Monetary Economics* 14 (November), pp. 319–338.

Flood, R. P. 1978. "Exchange Rate Expectations in Dual Exchange Markets." *Journal of International Economics* 8 (February), pp. 65–78.

Flood, R. P., and N. P. Marion. 1982. "The Transmission of Disturbances under Alternative Exchange Rate Regimes with Optimal Indexing." *Quarterly Journal of Economics* 97 (February), pp. 43–66.

Frenkel, J. A. 1976. "A Monetary Approach to the Exchange Rate: Doctrinal Aspects and Empirical Evidence." *Scandinavian Journal of Economics* 78 (May), pp. 200–224.

Frenkel, J. A. 1978. "Purchasing Power Parity: Doctrinal Perspective and Evidence from the 1920's." *Journal of International Economics* 8 (May), pp. 169–191.

Frenkel, J. A. 1981a. "The Collapse of Purchasing Power Parity During the 1970's." *European Economic Review* 16 (May), pp. 145–165.

Frenkel, J. A. 1981b. "Flexible Exchange Rates, Prices, and the Role of 'News': Lessons from the 1970's." *Journal of Political Economy* 89 (August), pp. 665–705.

Frankel, J. A. 1982. "In Search of the Exchange Risk Premium: A Six-Currency Test Assuming Mean-Variance Optimization." *Journal of International Money and Finance* 1 (December), pp. 255–274.

Frenkel, J. A., and H. G. Johnson, eds. 1976. *The Monetary Approach to the Balance of Payments*. Toronto: University of Toronto Press.

Frenkel, J. A., and H. G. Johnson, eds. 1978. *The Economics of Flexible Exchange Rates: Selected Studies*. Reading, MA: Addison-Wesley.

Frenkel, J. A., and R. M. Levich. 1975. "Covered Interest Arbitrage: Unexploited Profits?" *Journal of Political Economy* 83 (April), pp. 325–338.

Frenkel, J. A., and R. M. Levich. 1977. "Transactions Costs and Interest Arbitrage: Tranquil versus Turbulent Periods." *Journal of Political Economy* 85 (December), pp. 1209–1226.

Frenkel, J. A., and M. L. Mussa. 1985. "Asset Markets, Exchange Rates, and the Balance of Payments." In R. W. Jones and P. B. Kenen, eds., *Handbook of International Economics*, vol. 2, pp. 679–747. Amsterdam: North-Holland, 1985.

Frenkel, J. A., and A. Razin. 1980. "Stochastic Prices and Tests of Efficiency of Foreign Exchange Markets." *Economics Letters* 6, pp. 165–170.

Frenkel, J. A., and A. Razin. 1985. "Government Spending, Debt, and International Economic Interdependence." *Economic Journal* 95 (September), pp. 619–636.

Frenkel, J. A., and A. Razin. 1986a. "The International Transmission and Effects of Fiscal Policies." *American Economic Review* 76 (May), pp. 330–335.

Frenkel, J. A., and A. Razin. 1986b. "Fiscal Policies in the World Economy." *Journal of Political Economy* 94 (June), pp. 564–594.

Frenkel, J. A., and A. Razin, 1986c. "The Limited Viability of Dual Exchange-Rate Regimes." NBER Working Paper No. 1902.

Friedman, M. 1953. "The Case for Flexible Exchange Rates." In his *Essays in*

Positive Economics, pp. 157–203. Chicago: University of Chicago Press, 1953.
Friedman, M. 1969. "The Optimum Quantity of Money." In his *The Optimum Quantity of Money and Other Essays*, pp. 1–50. Chicago: Aldine, 1969.
Gardner, G. W. 1985. "Money, Prices, and the Current Account in a Dual Exchange Rate Regime." *Journal of International Economics* 18 (May), pp. 321–338.
Geweke, J., and E. Feige. 1979. "Some Joint Tests of the Efficiency of Markets for Forward Foreign Exchange." *Review of Economics and Statistics* 61 (August), pp. 334–341.
Giovannini, A. 1985. "Exchange Rates and Traded Goods Prices." Unpublished manuscript, Columbia University.
Grassman, S. 1973. "A Fundamental Symmetry in International Payments Patterns." *Journal of International Economics* 3 (May), pp. 105–116.
Greenwood, J. 1983. "Expectations, the Exchange Rate, and the Current Account." *Journal of Monetary Economics* 12 (November), pp. 543–569.
Greenwood, J. 1984. "Non-traded Goods, the Trade Balance, and the Balance of Payments." *Canadian Journal of Economics* 17 (November), pp. 806–823.
Greenwood, J., and K. P. Kimbrough. 1985a. "Capital Controls and Fiscal Policy in the World Economy." *Canadian Journal of Economics* 18 (November), pp. 743–765.
Greenwood, J., and K. P. Kimbrough. 1985b. "Foreign Exchange Controls in a Black Market Economy." Centre for the Study of International Economic Relations. University of Western Ontario. Working Paper No. 8501C. Forthcoming, *Journal of Development Economics*.
Greenwood, J., and K. P. Kimbrough. 1986. "An Investigation in the Theory of Foreign Exchange Controls." Duke University Working Paper No. 86–13. Forthcoming, *Canadian Journal of Economics*.
Hakkio, C. S. 1981. "The Term Structure of the Forward Premium." *Journal of Monetary Economics* 8 (July), pp. 41–58.
Hakkio, C. S. 1984. "A Re-Examination of Purchasing Power Parity: A Multi-Country and Multi-Period Study." *Journal of International Economics* 17 (November), pp. 265–277.
Hansen, L. P., and R. J. Hodrick. 1980. "Forward Exchange Rates as Optimal Predictors of Future Spot Rates: An Econometric Analysis." *Journal of Political Economy* 88 (October), pp. 829–853.
Hansen, L. P., and R. J. Hodrick. 1983. "Risk Averse Speculation in the Forward Foreign Exchange Market: An Econometric Analysis of Linear Models." In J. A. Frenkel, ed., *Exchange Rates and International Macroeconomics*, pp. 113–142. Chicago: University of Chicago Press, 1983.
Hansen, L. P., and K. J. Singleton. 1983. "Stochastic Consumption, Risk Aversion, and the Temporal Behavior of Asset Returns." *Journal of Political Economy* 91 (April), pp. 249–265.
Helpman, E. 1981. "An Exploration in the Theory of Exchange-Rate Regimes." *Journal of Political Economy* 89 (October), pp. 865–890.
Helpman, E., and A. Razin. 1982. "Dynamics of a Floating Exchange Rate Regime." *Journal of Political Economy* 90 (August), pp. 728–754.

Helpman, E., and A. Razin. 1984. "The Role of Saving and Investment in Exchange Rate Determination Under Alternative Monetary Mechanisms." *Journal of Monetary Economics* 13 (May), pp. 307–325.

Helpman, E., and A. Razin. 1985a. "Floating Exchange Rates with Liquidity Constraints in Financial Markets." *Journal of International Economics* 19 (August), pp. 99–117.

Helpman, E., and A. Razin. 1985b. "Exchange Rate Management: Intertemporal Tradeoffs." NBER Working Paper No. 1590.

Hodrick, R. J. 1981. "International Asset Pricing with Time Varying Risk Premia." *Journal of International Economics* 11 (November), pp. 573–587.

Isard, P. 1977. "How Far Can We Push the 'Law of One Price'?" *American Economic Review* 67 (December), pp. 942–948.

Johnson, H. G. 1969. "The Case for Flexible Exchange Rates, 1969." *Federal Reserve Bank of St. Louis Review* 51 (June), pp. 12–24.

Kaminsky, G. 1984. "The Black Market and its Effects on Welfare and on the Current Account." Unpublished manuscript, University of California at San Diego. Forthcoming, *International Economic Review*.

Kimbrough, K. P. 1983. "The Information Content of the Exchange Rate and the Stability of Real Output under Alternative Exchange Rate Regimes." *Journal of International Money and Finance* 2 (April), pp. 27–38.

Kimbrough, K. P. 1984a. "Aggregate Information and the Role of Monetary Policy in an Open Economy." *Journal of Political Economy* 92 (April), pp. 268–285.

Kimbrough, K. P. 1984b. "The Forward Rate as a Predictor of the Future Spot Rate, the Role of Policy, and Exchange Rate Regime Choice." *International Economic Review* 25 (October), pp. 527–543.

Kimbrough, K. P. 1985a. "An Examination of the Effects of Government Purchases in an Open Economy." *Journal of International Money and Finance* 4 (March), pp. 113–133.

Kimbrough, K. P. 1985b. "Rational Expectations, Market Shocks, and the Exchange Rate." *Journal of Macroeconomics* 7 (Summer), pp. 297–312.

Kimbrough, K. P. 1985c. "The Optimum Quantity of Money Rule in the Theory of Public Finance." Duke University Working Paper No. 86–16. Forthcoming, *Journal of Monetary Economics*.

Kimbrough, K. P. 1986a. "Foreign Aid and Optimal Fiscal Policy." *Canadian Journal of Economics* 17 (February), pp. 35–61.

Kimbrough, K. P. 1986b. "Optimal Tax Policy for Balance of Payments Objectives." In J. A. Frenkel, ed., *International Aspects of Fiscal Policies*. Chicago: University of Chicago Press, 1986.

Kindleberger, C. P. 1970. "The Case for Fixed Exchange Rates, 1969." In *The International Adjustment Mechanism*, pp. 93–108. Federal Reserve Bank of Boston, 1970.

Kravis, I. B., and R. E. Lipsey. 1978. "Price Behavior in the Light of Balance of Payments Theories." *Journal of International Economics* 8 (May), pp. 193–246.

Krueger, A. O. 1983. *Exchange Rate Determination*. Cambridge: Cambridge University Press.

Kydland, F. E., and E. C. Prescott. 1982. "Time to Build and Aggregate Fluctuations." *Econometrica* 50 (November), pp. 1345–1370.

Levich, R. M. 1979. "On the Efficiency of Markets for Foreign Exchange." In R. Dornbusch and J. A. Frenkel, eds., *International Economic Policy: Theory and Evidence*, pp. 246–267. Baltimore: Johns Hopkins, 1979

Levich, R. M. 1985. "Empirical Studies of Exchange Rates: Price Behavior, Rate Determination and Market Efficiency." In R. W. Jones and P. B. Kenen, eds., *Handbook of International Economics*, vol. 2, pp. 979–1040. Amsterdam: North-Holland, 1985.

Lucas, R. E., Jr. 1982. "Interest Rates and Currency Prices in a Two-Country World." *Journal of Monetary Economics* 10 (November), pp. 335–360.

McCulloch, J. H. 1975. "Operational Aspects of the Siegel Paradox." *Quarterly Journal of Economics* 89 (February), pp. 170–172.

Mark, N. C. 1985a. "Some Evidence on the International Inequality of Real Interest Rates." *Journal of International Money and Finance* 4 (June), pp. 189–208.

Mark, N. C. 1985b. "On Time Varying Risk Premia in the Foreign Exchange Market: An Econometric Analysis." *Journal of Monetary Economics* 16 (July), pp. 3–18.

Mark, N. C. 1986. "Real and Nominal Exchange Rates in the Short Run and in the Long Run: An Empirical Investigation." Unpublished manuscript, Ohio State University.

Mayer, W. 1984. "Endogenous Tariff Formation." *American Economic Review* 74 (December), pp. 970–985.

Mishkin, F. S. 1984a. "The Real Interest Rate: A Multi-Country Empirical Study." *Canadian Journal of Economics* 17 (May), pp. 283–311.

Mishkin, F. S. 1984b. "Are Real Interest Rates Equal Across Countries? An Empirical Investigation of International Parity Conditions." *Journal of Finance* 39 (December), pp. 1345–1357.

Mood, A. M., F. A. Graybill, and D. C. Boes. 1974. *Introduction to the Theory of Statistics*. New York: McGraw-Hill.

Mundell, R. A. 1961. "A Theory of Optimum Currency Areas." *American Economic Review* 51 (November), pp. 509–517.

Mussa, M. 1976. "The Exchange Rate, the Balance of Payments and Monetary and Fiscal Policy Under a Regime of Controlled Floating." *Scandinavian Journal of Economics* 78 (May), pp. 229–248.

Mussa, M. 1979. "Empirical Regularities in the Behavior of Exchange Rates and Theories of the Foreign Exchange Market." In *Policies for Employment, Prices, and Exchange Rates*, vol. 11 of the Carnegie-Rochester Conference Series on Public Policy, 1979, pp. 9–57.

Obstfeld, M. 1981a. "Capital Mobility and Devaluation in an Optimizing Model with Rational Expectations." *American Economic Review* 71 (May), pp. 217–221.

Obstfeld, M. 1981b. "Macroeconomic Policy, Exchange Rate Dynamics, and

Optimal Asset Accumulation." *Journal of Political Economy* 89 (December), pp. 1142–1161.

Obstfeld, M. 1982. "The Capitalization of Income Streams and the Effects of Open-Market Policy under Fixed Exchange Rates." *Journal of Monetary Economics* 9 (January), pp. 87–98.

Obstfeld, M. 1986a. "Speculative Attack and the External Constraint in a Maximizing Model of the Balance of Payments." *Canadian Journal of Economics* 19 (February), pp. 1–22.

Obstfeld, M. 1986b. "Capital Controls, the Dual Exchange Rate, and Devaluation." *Journal of International Economics* 20 (February), pp. 1–20.

Officer, L. H. 1976. "The Purchasing Power Parity Theory of Exchange Rates: A Review Article." IMF *Staff Papers* 23 (March), pp. 1–61.

Persson, T. 1984. "Real Transfers in Fixed Exchange Rate Systems and the International Adjustment Mechanism." *Journal of Monetary Economics* 13 (May), pp. 349–369.

Persson, T., and L. E. O. Svensson. 1986. "International Borrowing and Time Consistent Fiscal Policy." *Scandinavian Journal of Economics* 88(1), pp. 273–295.

Phelps, E. S. 1973. "Inflation in the Theory of Public Finance." *Swedish Journal of Economics* 75 (March), pp. 67–82.

Razin, A., and L. E. O. Svensson. 1983a. "Trade Taxes and the Current Account." *Economics Letters* 13, pp. 55–57.

Razin, A., and L. E. O. Svensson. 1983b. "The Current Account and the Optimal Government Debt." *Journal of International Money and Finance* 2 (August), pp. 215–224.

Sachs, J. D. 1981. "The Current Account and Macroeconomic Adjustment in the 1970's." *Brookings Papers on Economic Activity* (1, 1981), pp. 201–268.

Sandmo, A. 1976. "Optimal Taxation: An Introduction to the Literature." *Journal of Public Economics* 6 (July–August), pp. 37–54.

Silberberg, E. 1978. *The Structure of Economics: A Mathematical Analysis*. New York: McGraw-Hill.

Stockman, A. C. 1978. "Risk, Information and Forward Exchange Rates." In J. A. Frenkel and H. G. Johnson, eds., *The Economics of Flexible Exchange Rates: Selected Studies*, pp. 159–178. Reading, MA: Addison-Wesley, 1978.

Stockman, A. C. 1980. "A Theory of Exchange Rate Determination." *Journal of Political Economy* 88 (August), pp. 673–698.

Stockman, A. C. 1983. "Real Exchange Rates under Alternative Nominal Exchange-Rate Systems." *Journal of International Money and Finance* 2 (August), pp. 147–166.

Stockman, A. C. 1985. "Effects of Inflation on the Pattern of International Trade." *Canadian Journal of Economics* 18 (August), pp. 587–601.

Stockman, A. C., and D. A. Hernandez. 1985. "Exchange Controls, Capital Controls, and International Financial Markets." Rochester Center for Economic Research, Working Paper No. 25.

Svensson, L. E. O. 1985. "Currency Prices, Terms of Trade, and Interest Rates: A General Equilibrium Asset-Pricing Cash-in-Advance Approach." *Journal of International Economics* 18 (February), pp. 17–41.

Turnovsky, S. J. 1983. "Wage Indexation and Exchange Market Intervention in a Small Open Economy." *Canadian Journal of Economics* 16 (November), pp. 574–592.

Weber, W. E. 1981. "Output Variability under Monetary Policy and Exchange Rate Rules." *Journal of Political Economy* 89 (August), pp. 733–751.

Comment

Marianne Baxter

Kent Kimbrough has done an outstanding job of surveying important recent contributions to the field of international macroeconomics and highlighting their common methodological starting point: an explicit optimizing model. Kimbrough's contribution to this volume is a complete, very clearly written survey of some of the most promising current research in international trade and finance. In the process of synthesizing the material, Kimbrough has provided a sharply focused picture of what has been done in each subject area, and has provided his readers with a bonus: in the concluding paragraphs of each section, he includes some very interesting suggestions for further research.

Because Kimbrough has done such a complete job of surveying and summarizing the literature, I shall devote most of my discussion to some methodological issues and to forecasts of the directions in which substantial further progress is likely to occur. The focal point of Kimbrough's chapter is that optimizing frameworks are important to advances in our understanding of issues in international finance because, after confrontation with the data, the theory can be refined to better fit the data on the next iteration. Yet Kimbrough does not put the point clearly enough or forcefully enough. Throughout the 1960s and 1970s, "theories" in the form of estimated decision rules for firms and consumers were continually revised in order to better fit the data. But now, ten years after the publication of Lucas's (1976) critique of policy evaluation, it is well understood that such theories cannot help us to predict the outcomes of future changes in policy, no matter how well they fit past data. Our only hope is to study models in which the optimization problem is described explicitly. Then, if the model is rejected by the data, the researcher may contemplate changes in the technological or institutional structure of the model.

A desirable element of this research strategy is the starkness with which key assumptions are laid out, and the discipline thereby imposed. For instance, if "fitting the data" meant that the researcher had to assume an intertemporal elasticity of substitution that was wildly inconsistent with other empirical estimates of this parameter, this would constitute grounds for doubting the validity of the theoretical model, regardless of the tightness with which it fit the data. Thus, the use of explicit optimizing frameworks provides an added dimension of discipline on researchers—the requirement of cross-investigation consistency in preferences, technologies, and institutional structures.

Toward a Unified Explanation of Some Puzzles

In the second and third sections of the chapter, Kimbrough surveys the current state of theory and empirical evidence on three important concepts in international finance—puchasing power parity (PPP), interest-rate parity (IRP), and the international equality of real interest rates. He summarizes evidence documenting the resounding failure of PPP in any of its forms, the existence of risk premia in foreign exchange, and the lack of international equality of real interest rates. He suggests that these deviations from the predictions of theory are not independent events, noting (for example) Mishkin's (1984) comments that deviations from purchasing power parity are consistent with nonequality of real rates across countries. However, Kimbrough makes a conceptual error in stating that the breakdown of PPP is a "potential source" of the nonequalization of international real rates, or of the existence of risk premia. This view comes dangerously close to the research strategy Kimbrough is arguing we should avoid—viewing reduced-form relationships (such as PPP) as important theoretical constructs in and of themselves. Rather, Kimbrough's point is better made in the following way. We observe in the data various refutations of our simple theory, as described above. Since our theoretical model begins at the level of tastes and technology, we can trace out the effects of variations in our assumptions about tastes and technologies on predictions about PPP, risk premia, and international interest-rate equalization. In general, variation in any component of the model will result in variations in the models' predictions about these issues of interest. What we require of an acceptable theory is that it simultaneously be able to account for observed patterns of relative prices (PPP), relative international real interest rates, and risk premia in foreign exchange. What is *not* acceptable is to construct a different model for each relationship of interest. To reiterate: an important and highly desirable feature of the optimizing approach is the cross-study discipline it imposes on the researcher.

Advantages and Limitations of the Cash-in-Advance Model

In order to make his text accessible to readers not already familiar with the literature, Kimbrough has very commendably discussed all the surveyed papers within the context of a basic, "benchmark" model, variations of which are used by virtually all of the papers surveyed. This benchmark model is a two-country version of an infinitely-lived-agent model. A central feature of the model is the exogenously imposed requirement that goods be purchased with currency accumulated in advance (usually, the home currency of the seller). Without this requirement, there is no place in the model for money—the barter equilibrium is optimal and money is typically a dominated asset. The effect of this cash-in-advance (CIA) constraint is therefore to provide a determinate demand for a government's non-interest-bearing debt.

Kimbrough argues that the CIA model, being an optimizing model (given the exogenous assumptions about acceptable payments mechanisms), is a major improvement over earlier models, which simply postulated agents' decision rules for choice variables such as money demand and desired portfolio composition. And, while there are difficulties with the CIA setup, it has the great virtue of being very clear about what is happening in the economy under study. We can observe the timing of information arrival, study agents making asset/portfolio decisions, and watch as they choose time paths for goods and money to maximize their lifetime utility. We can also see very clearly the sense in which money has been introduced in an ad hoc way—people are not allowed to purchase a particular good using any medium other than a particular national currency.

While the CIA assumption may capture important aspects of current institutional arrangements, it is dangerous to assume that this institutional feature would remain fixed under all the variations in policy or disturbances to the environment that the researcher may want to study. For instance, and as Kimbrough himself notes, the invoicing currency should itself be viewed as an endogenous object of choice. To continue this line of thought, the extent of credit markets, interest-paying demand deposits, and other institutional means of avoiding the inflation tax are endogenous responses to variations in monetary policy. They will not remain fixed if monetary policy changes, as assumed by the CIA models used by the authors surveyed by Kimbrough.

To take a specific example, consider the analysis of Aschauer and Greenwood (1983), surveyed by Kimbrough. In their analysis, Greenwood and Aschauer find that, in an economy where individuals value consumption and leisure, and where workers must carry cash balances overnight and so are possible targets for an inflation tax, monetary policy can have real effects by altering the marginal rate of substitution between consumption (which is hit by the inflation tax) and leisure (which is not).

But if inflation is substantial, we expect to observe changes in the institutional framework: for example, workers will have their wages paid directly to checking accounts which pay interest at market rates. This will tend to destroy the real effects of money and inflation. Such changes in payments mechanisms are exactly what we observe in high-inflation countries; but the CIA model is not equipped to study such effects. Further, I am unaware of any empirical evidence that expected inflation reduces hours worked in the way predicted. That we can see so clearly the defects of the current model, and that we immediately perceive some obvious extensions in the direction of greater realism and theoretical integrity are the result of the model's chief virtue—its starkness and simplicity.

Kimbrough neglects to mention that international trade and exchange-rate dynamics have been examined in frameworks other than versions of his benchmark CIA model. In particular, the overlapping-generations (OLG) paradigm is the CIA model's chief competitor as a model of a monetary economy. Kareken and Wallace (1981) use an OLG framework to demonstrate that, if currencies are perfect substitutes in exchange and as assets, then exchange rates (and thus price levels) are indeterminate. This contrasts markedly with the predictions of the CIA models surveyed by Kimbrough, where the cash-in-advance constraint guarantees that the quantity theory of money holds for each national currency. No such condition holds in the Kareken/Wallace economy. Neither does it hold in analogues of the Kareken/Wallace analysis which have infinitely-lived agents and a requirement that cash be used for transactions purposes, but in which agents are free to choose the currency they will use for transactions purposes.[1] Further, the CIA model of the type used by the papers in Kimbrough's survey predicts that exchange rates should move in predictable ways that depend on the movements of national outputs and money supplies, so that exchange rate variability is limited by the variability of these other variables—in obvious contradition with reality. But the models outlined above, which allow choice in currency holdings, can display a large class of equilibrium processes for exchange rates, processes that can involve an arbitrary degree of exchange-rate variability.

The preceding discussion is not intended to say that there is nothing useful to be learned from the CIA models surveyed by Kimbrough. Rather, it is intended to press the following two points. First, whenever an institutional feature is exogenously imposed on a model, we must be cautious in interpreting the results of comparative statics or policy intervention within the model. The reason is that exogenously imposed institutional or behavioral features of the model will not be invariant to all contemplated changes in policy or in the economic environment.

Second, it is necessary that models developed to explain observed phenomena in international trade and finance be confronted with the data. While the literature on interest-rate parity, purchasing power parity, and risk premia in foreign exchange consists principally of empirical papers, the literature employing CIA models consists mainly of theoretical papers whose purpose is to produce a theoretical justification for a particular covariance observed in economic data. While this is a desirable first step, it remains to be seen whether versions of the CIA models can ever fit actual data or produce artificial, simulated time series that mimic actual time series.

It seems clear that substantial progress can be made in the field of international trade and finance through application of the methods and standards of evaluation employed in the best current work in macroeconomics, all of which demands that a good theory be directly confronted with actual time series and its usefulness evaluated in that light. For example, Kydland and Prescott (1982) have shown that small-scale dynamic general-equilibrium models can explain a large portion of business-cycle comovements of economic aggregates, yielding summary statistics that mimic to a surprising degree those of actual U.S. time series. Application of their methods to the study of open-economy macroeconomics is a promising area for further research.

Notes

1. See a recent paper by King, Wallace, and Weber (1986) for an analysis of this type of economy.

References

Aschauer, D., and J. Greenwood. 1983. "A Further Exploration in the Theory of Exchange Rate Regimes." *Journal of Political Economy* 91 (October), pp. 402–423.

Kareken, J., and N. Wallace. 1981. "On the Indeterminacy of Equilibrium Exchange Rates." *Quarterly Journal of Economics* 96 (May), pp. 207–222.

King, R., N. Wallace, and W. Weber. 1986. "Nonfundamental Uncertainty and Exchange Rates." *Federal Reserve Bank of Minneapolis Working Paper* #307, July.

Kydland, F., and E. Prescott. 1982. "Time to Build and Aggregate Fluctuations." *Econometrica* 50 (November), pp. 1345–1370.

Lucas, R. E., Jr. 1976. "Econometric Policy Evaluation: A Critique. In *The Phillips Curve and Labor Markets*, Carnegie-Rochester Conferences on Public Policy, vol. 1, pp. 19–46. Reprinted in his *Studies in Business-Cycle Theory*, pp. 104–130. Cambridge, MA: MIT Press, 1981.

Mishkin, F. 1984. "The Real Interest Rate: A Multi-Country Empirical Study." *Canadian Journal of Economics* 17 (May), pp. 283–311.

4 NATIONAL POLICIES AND THE INTERNATIONAL MONETARY SYSTEM

J. Carter Murphy

While it is not uncommon to characterize the international monetary experience from the mid-1960s to the mid-1980s as that of a system undergoing shocks which have had to be accommodated, the experience comes into better perspective when it is seen as a continuum involving a slippage by many countries into high inflation in the 1970s with a painful aftermath in the 1980s. In an earlier work (Murphy 1979, p. 136), I referred to inflation as the almost inescapable product of Keynesian ideas when they are fed into the forge of pressure-group politics, and this mixture was present in many countries in the late 1960s and the 1970s. Then, beginning about 1978 and carrying into the 1980s, profound political changes brought disinflation to many (but not all) countries. In a number of countries the reaction to inflation was a sociopolitical response that included a rebirth of respect for competitive markets and for decentralized decision making. These extensive economic and political changes have dominated the experiences of the recent past, and they set the stage for opportunities ahead.

---

* The author wishes to thank, without otherwise implicating, the editor of this volume and Sir Joseph Gold for their helpful comments on an initial version of the chapter.

A surge of inflation like that of 1964–1980 leaves a long and turbulent wake, and in the wake are a host of problems which constrain policymakers' choices and confound their advisors. As of this writing, it is not yet certain that contemporary political institutions have the flexibility and durability to accommodate sustained disinflation. In many less-industrialized countries inflation has slowed little or not at all. In the industrialized countries, political authorities take risks of inflation's return with their monetary and fiscal policies in order to deal with the perceived needs of groups distressed by inflation's unexpected end.

Meanwhile, economic policies have had to be devised and implemented in unfamiliar settings. As a result of inflation's force having disrupted the environment of traditional regulatory arrangements, "deregulation" of a multitude of markets, especially financial markets, has gained acceptance. The new market structures are still strangers to policymakers and their economists, and new systemic responses are not well predicted by familiar statistical relationships.

Debt burdens, internal and international, that were borne lightly during the escalating inflation became problematic in the postinflation world, and a degree of financial intermediation by the world's banks that would not have been excessive had inflation been sustained has become, in a less-inflationary environment, a threat to continued growth in debtor areas and a threat to viability for the international financial system.

Gross saving and investment behavior that was distorted during the inflationary part of the period has not returned to historical norms in the aftermath. While inflation was accelerating, the world's public and private investment was financed in signficant degree out of "forced saving"—the real-income loss, largely to consumers, as a result of price increases that were in turn financed by money and government debt creation. More recently, with real-interest incentives restored in the disinflationary conditions of the 1980s, private voluntary saving has to some extent been rebuilt. Public dissaving, nonetheless, has grown. As a result, the post-1982 recovery of private investment in industrialized countries was accompanied by extraordinarily high real interest rates worldwide.

Differences in this legacy of distortions across countries have created inducements for international capital flows and generated exchange-rate distortions that have caught official policymakers and economic modelers off guard. In the early stages of the inflationary floodtide, uneveness in the demand-management policies of different nations swept away the fragile international monetary system that was based on parity exchange rates conforming to the original IMF charter. After 1973 the world's currencies floated; in time they gathered hesitantly into currency blocs which have since slid, sometimes gently, sometimes violently, past each other. Between the end of 1973 and 1979 the dollar depreciated 36 percent against the deutchemark; then, between 1979 and 1984, it appreciated 81 percent. These giant swings in the value of the North American and continental European nucleus currencies, along with an uneven variation of the rates around the trends, have played havoc with some traditional production, consumption, and international-trade relationships and have given rise to political demands for protection for producers where currencies were appreciated or appreciating excessively.

Perhaps, above all, inflation has left in its trail people who are unusually uncertain, bringing new volatility to all asset markets. In the 1980s, individuals and firms were more active wealth managers than they had been in the past. They demonstrated increased willingness to shift the form in which their wealth was held in response to changing, albeit always fragmentary, information, and new institutions emerged to facilitate the exchange and to provide new avenues for risk management.

The shift to more disinflationary monetary policies in the world has been part of a political shift to the right that has affected socialist and nonsocialist countries alike. In the words of Sir Jeremy Morse:

> The spread of the free-market gospel around the world has been remarkable. It has always been strong in much of the Far East and steady in Germany. In 1979–80 it gained two powerful new prophets in Mrs. Thatcher and President Reagan; and when President Mitterand tried to break out on his own he was fairly soon compelled to rejoin the pack. Then we began to see in Europe and Australasia a number of incoming socialist administrations which, whatever the rest of their programme, deliberately adopted orthodox financial and economic policies from the outset. And now the three giants, China, India, and the U.S.S.R., are all in their different ways trying to inject more private enterprise into their ponderous economics. (Morse 1985, p. 12)

Regrettably, policymakers in the major industrialized countries seem less able than they were forty years ago to deal with the necessity of cooperation in an interdependent world system, and they either do not understand, or feel they cannot build a political consensus on, the forms that such cooperation must take in a regime of flexible exchange rates. At the close of World War II, in the euphoria of peace, political leaders could embrace the United Nations, the IMF, and the World Bank—but not the ITO—because their constituents understood and accepted responsibility toward an international order. More recently, regional wars, East-West and North-South hostilities, inflation, an international energy crisis, and post-inflation debt burdens and distortions have eroded those foundations and led to a resurgence of political and economic nationalism.

Robert Solomon (1977, p. 336) has emphasized that the case for international cooperation is one of externalities—one government's policy choices have significance for the outcomes of other government's choices. Ralph Bryant is more precise in characterizing international cooperation as a public good:

> As with other public goods, . . . the supply of international cooperation is likely to fall short of what would be mutually beneficial; many nations in the world have strong incentives to behave as "free riders," with the result that the world as a whole fails to further its common interests. Yet each nation has an interest in preventing unsatisfactory outcomes for the global economy resulting from untrammeled noncooperative behavior. (Bryant 1980, p. 500)

As the largest national economy in the world and the reserve-center country of the international financial system, the United States has special responsibilities to the rest of the world; yet this country continues to make its policy decisions with little attention to the external implications of "internal" policies. Inflationary U.S. monetary and fiscal policies during the latter half of the 1960s fatally undermined the fixed-exchange-rate arrangements that had evolved under terms of the original charter of the International Monetary Fund. Similarly, in the 1980s, the unbalanced mix of U.S. monetary and fiscal policies contributed to the problems of floating currencies—the regime that emerged from the disorder of the 1970s.

Either a fixed or a floating exchange-rate regime can serve the international community well if governments make policies that are appropriate to the regime in existence. In a system with exchange rates fixed on the dollar, for example, peripheral countries must harmonize their demand-management policies with those of the Unites States, and the United States, as the center country, must maintain a degree of economic stability that is acceptable to the rest. In a system of floating rates, governments have some freedom to follow demand-management policies of their choice, but they must avoid policy *mixes* that induce international capital flows that, in turn, distort trading relationships through inappropriate exchange-rate adjustments. The truth that apparently is still to be learned is that there is no escaping interdependence, and there is no way of reaping the benefits of international cooperation without the sacrifice of some policy autonomy.

Inflation and the Postinflation World

Inflation

The IMF's weighted index of national inflation rates in industrialized countries averaged 8.0 percent for the decade of the 1970s with peaks of 13.3 percent in 1974 and then 11.9 percent in 1980 accompanying the sharp increases in world oil prices in those years. The inflation was driven by expansive monetary and fiscal policies undertaken simultaneously in many countries with, in the closing years, a part also played by increasing velocity of money circulation. Monetary growth in the industrialized countries (for narrowly defined money supplies) averaged 9.8 percent per annum in 1970–1979, as compared to only 6.3 percent in the 1960s. Money plus quasi-money increased more than three times in the industrialized countries during 1970–1980, and more than four times in the world as a whole.[1] While the velocity of spending this money on newly produced goods and services slowed in the early 1970s with the initial onslaught of the money-supply growth, velocity in industrialized countries then accelerated to the end of the decade.

Central-government budget deficits contributed to the inflation in that the financing of the deficits contributed to the net financial holdings of the private sector of the world economy.[2] The U.S. federal-government deficit increased from 1.67 percent of the gross domestic product in 1972 to 4.64 percent in 1976, and that in the United Kingdom increased from 2.73 in 1972 to 7.34 percent in 1975. In the world as a whole, such deficits grew from an average 1.86 percent of GDP in 1972 to 4.28 percent in 1975.[3]

Cost increases, especially as a result of the petroleum price increases in 1973–74 and 1979–80, of course also contributed to the inflationary process. Still, an argument can be made that much of the petroleum-cartel's success in raising prices in the 1970s was due to the inflationary environment in which the cartel operated. Oil-consuming countries provided ample financial assets to purchase oil at ever-rising prices.

The Turn to Disinflation

Inflation broke in all industrialized countries (except Luxembourg) in 1981–82, although in the less-developed countries of the world it continued to accelerate, partly as a result of the turmoil accompanying worldwide recession and international debt crises. The rebellion of the middle classes that brought conservative governments to power in the United

Kingdom, the United States, and the Federal Republic of Germany, confirmed the end of rapid monetary growth and induced, especially in the United Kingdom, a rapid decline in the income velocity of the broadly defined money supply. The inflation rate (the IMF's weighted average of consumer price increases) in all industrial countries fell from 11.9 percent, in 1980, to 4.8 percent in 1984 and 3.8 percent in September 1985. In the less-developed part of the world, however, inflation accelerated from an average 28.2 percent in 1980 to 48.1 percent in 1984 and 56.5 percent in July 1985.

The Debt Burden

One of the most conspicuous leftovers from the period of high inflation in industrialized countries is the burden of excessive debt. While the international component of this debt has caught the world's attention, the domestic components are hardly less troublesome. Domestic loans for agriculture, urban real estate, and oil drilling in the United States comprised a larger part of bank-loan losses than did international credits in the early 1980s. This is no doubt partly due to the fact that the size (and relative homogeneity in the eyes of supervisory authorities) of the international loans caused banks to reschedule and postpone loss recognition on their international loans, more than they did on their domestic ones.

Total external debts of developing countries increased from about $75 billion in 1972 to $660 billion in 1981 and to $865 billion in 1985. While the ratios of external debt to export values and to GDP for these countries did not increase much in the latter 1970s, they increased sharply with the decline in primary commodity prices and export earnings of the debtor countries when the industrialized countries reversed the course of inflation. By 1985, the combined external debts of indebted developing countries were about 1.5 times their combined exports and more than a third of their combined gross domestic products.[4] Of course, the debt is not evenly distributed among developing countries. Perhaps fortunately, now, it is borne more by the more advanced of the developing countries and less by the very poorest countries—a result of the fact that the more-advanced developing countries gained access to the international credit markets in the 1970s whereas the poorest were still deemed to be inadequate credit risks by institutional lenders.

High Interest Rates

Servicing the debt totals that became bloated during the 1970s' inflation has been made more difficult by the high real interest rates that have characterized the period of disinflation in industrialized countries. Nominal short-term interest rates in the United States—important because a large proportion of the international debt is denominated in dollars and was originally of short- to intermediate-term maturity—soared from an average 5.3 percent in 1977 to an annual average peak of 14.0 percent in 1981; and nominal long-term dollar rates rose from 7.4 to 13.9 percent. Inflation-adjusted long-term rates, a proxy for real expected rates, rose above 10 percent in 1982 and again in 1984 before declining to less than 8 percent in 1985.[5]

Causes of the high rates are, at least on hindsight, not difficult to fathom. Disinflation in all industrialized countries, and especially in the United States, was accomplished more by monetary restraint than by fiscal restraint, and high spending propensities by consumers provided too little private-sector savings to finance the postinflation private investment and public-sector credit demands at real interest rates near historical norms.

The decline in monetary growth rates in major industrialized countries in the later 1970s was sharp. Growth of money plus quasi-money peaked in the United States, Germany, and Japan in 1976; and the money-expansion rates were cut to roughly one-half to one-third their earlier levels by 1980.[6] Fiscal policy, on the other hand, contributed less to demand restraint. The annual growth rate in U.S. federal-government expenditures accelerated from 8.6 percent in 1976 to 18.4 percent in 1980; and, perhaps more important, annual growth in federal-government debt decelerated in the United States only from 15.8 percent to 12.1 percent between the same years. In Germany, central-government expenditures accelerated from a 5.1 percent annual growth rate to 18.4 percent, between 1976 and 1980; but the growth rate for central-government debt did fall by almost half, from 24.7 percent to 13.5 percent, as a result of increases in government revenues. In Japan, expenditure growth changed from a decline of 6.1 percent in 1976 to a positive growth of 9.2 percent in 1979, the last year reported in IMF data; the growth rate for Japanese domestically held government debt declined about a third, from 37.8 percent to 25.6 percent, during 1976–1979.[7] Altogether, fiscal *deficits* of seven major countries held near 3.5 percent of GNP between 1977 and 1980 but swelled to 6.4 percent of GNP in the less inflation-pressured and slower-growing world economy of 1984.[8]

Private saving rates, in industrialized countries, have shown some response to the high real interest rates, but public-sector dissaving has resisted reduction. While gross saving, as a percentage of GDP for the seven largest OECD countries, had recovered somewhat at the end of the 1970s from earlier, mid-1970s, depressed levels, it had fallen again to only 15.2 percent (against a norm of 19.8 percent for the last half of the 1960s) by 1983.[9] This measure includes government dissaving as well as private saving, and since government deficits have been a rising share of GDP, while private gross savings has in the 1980s been steady at historical norms, the data indicate the important role that net government dissaving has played in keeping interest rates high. In the United States, government dissaving grew to an average annual 4.8 percent of GNP, 1982–1985, against an average of 1.5 percent in the preceding four years, while private gross saving held steady at 17.8 percent of GNP in both periods.[10]

The persistence of inflationary expectations is suggested by the unusual premium of long-term over short-term interest rates that was maintained virtually to the end of 1985. Throughout 1982, 1983, and 1984, long-term dollar borrowing rates remained approximately a full 3.5 percentage points above short-term rates,[11] although a remarkable rally in the bond market reduced the differential to only about 1.6 percentage points at the beginning of March 1986, after world oil prices had tumbled. The inflationary-expectations hypothesis is confounded somewhat by the decline in the velocity of money's turnover in the United States, the United Kingdom, Canada, and Germany after 1980; but long-term inflationary expectations and growth in liquidity preference are not inconsistent changes in attitudes when short-term developments are thought to be fraught with increased uncertainty. It appears that people in this period accepted more liquidity in order to meet short-term uncertainty needs while they remained unwilling to hold claims against money in a distant future without being paid a significant premium for bearing a long-term inflation risk.

Oil and Other Commodity Prices

The reduction of inflation in industrialized countries coincided, not accidentally, with the stripping of market power from the oil-exporting countries. As a result of a number of years of accelerated energy conservation measures, production increases in non-OPEC areas, and then the slowing of aggregate spending, world petroleum prices dropped from their lofty peaks. From an average price of $39.83 in 1981, Libyan Es-Sidra-grade oil was off to $30.15 per barrel in July 1985, and continued declining. Mexican oil was on offer at $26 per barrel at the close of the year and fell below $15 early in 1986.

Other commodity prices in the first half of the 1980s were also off their inflationary peaks. The IMF index of wholesale commodity prices, which was up from 33.1 in 1971, to 100 in 1980, was off to 69 by September 1985; and some prices had, of course, fallen much more than the average. Nonoil commodity prices showed some recovery during 1983 in response to the restoration of economic growth, especially in the United States, but they sagged again in 1984 and 1985 in the face of increased supplies and diminished hopes for rapid economic recovery in a number of industrialized countries.

These dramatic shifts in oil and other commodity prices had, of course, broad implications for the pattern of international balances of payments and for the fortunes of primary-commodity producers and consumers. The value of Saudi Arabia's exports—wholly petroleum—fell, for example, by more than two-thirds, from 377 billion ryals in 1981 to an estimated 111 billion in 1985, while U.S. annual savings on oil imports amounted to nearly $30 billion in 1985 compared to 1982.[12] Producers and consumers of coffee, rubber, copper, tin, rice, and other commodities experienced similar exchanges of income, although, in general, the exchanges only partly redressed the inflation-induced shifts of the previous decade. Whereas the terms of trade of industrialized countries deteriorated by 23 percent, 1970–1980, they had recovered only by 2 percent, 1980–1985. Developing countries, on the other hand, had enjoyed a terms-of-trade improvement of 92 percent in the 1970s and had lost only 5 percent of that gain by 1984.

Unemployment and Economic Growth

Disinflation in the industrialized countries unavoidably retarded economic growth and exacerbated unemployment, not only in the industrialized countries but in all those countries dependent upon the industrialized-country markets. The setbacks were uneven, and the recoveries to 1985 even more uneven. Growth in real output in all industrialized countries fell from 4.1 percent in 1978 to 1.3 percent in 1980 and then to −0.2 percent in 1982 before recovering to 4.9 percent in 1984. The recession in North America was sharper than in any country of Western Europe, except the United Kingdom, and the rebound was equally more vigorous. Canada and the United States suffered reductions in total real output of 4.4 and 2.1 percent, respectively, in 1982, but both had recovered to strong positive growth rates (5.0 and 6.8 percent) by 1984. The four largest Western European countries, on the other hand, barely saw a negative growth rate in 1982 but then correspondingly saw only a hesitant recovery to a 2.4 percent growth by 1984 and 1985.

Developing countries were hit by the "second round" oil-price increase in 1979–80 and then were battered by the effects of demand-restraint policies in their overseas market areas in 1981–82. With their domestic policies dictated in many cases by their burden of external debt, growth rates in developing countries taken as a whole were down from 5.8 percent in 1977 to a low of 1.5 percent in 1983; they then recovered to 4.0 percent in 1985.[13]

Generally, recovery in North America proceeded under the shelter of an appreciating exchange value of the U.S. dollar, which limited the risk of an immediate resumption of inflation. In Europe, where the exchange value of currencies depreciated, growth was export-led but raised the specter of renewed inflation if the export growth were to be supplemented by domestic-demand expansion. Differentials in the patterns of recovery among less-developed countries often reflected the wisdom with which austerity measures were early applied and production and consumption adjustments encouraged. Countries that postponed adjustment to the loss of markets abroad and to the reversal of the terms-of-trade improvement of the 1970s generally faced more critical setbacks when the inevitable "end of the rope" came than did countries which early eased back growth in investment and consumption and avoided measures to protect the incomes of those in overextended sectors of the economy.

Exchange Rates, Trade, and Capital Flows

The strains experienced by the world economy as a result of the uneven transition from high inflation to greater price stability were reflected in exchange-rate pressures and balance-of-payments distortions. After 1979 the U.S. dollar began an appreciation which raised its effective value by roughly 60 percent by early 1985. Against the yen, the appreciation was only 24 percent, 1980 to first quarter 1985; but against the deutschemark, the appreciation was 79 percent.

The causes of extraordinary dollar appreciation have been widely discussed and are certainly multiple in number. Since the current account of the U.S. international balance of payments was steadily deteriorating during the period of dollar appreciation, it is clear that the appreciation was driven by net international capital movements toward the dollar. Nominal interest rates in the United States exceeded those in both Europe and Japan by several percentage points; and, for the foreign investor, so long as the dollar was not expected to depreciate, the nominal interest-rate differences amounted to "real" differences. In addition, there was capital flight toward the dollar from a number of Latin American and African countries where political instability threatened or where critical balance-of-payments conditions seemed to foreshadow tightening of exchange controls. Perhaps most important as a force changing the net international capital flows was the fact that at the same time that money- and capital-market conditions were directing a flow of funds toward the dollar, difficulties emerged with the maintenance of the debt service on obligations of major developing country borrowers, bringing to a rather abrupt halt the dollar-denominated capital exports by European and North American banks to those areas. The dollar also seemed to be favored as a result of some financial-market-deregulation measures outside the United States. The measures in Japan that freed institutional funds to hold foreign as well as Japanese securities in their portfolios, for example, seems to have released a large portfolio-rebalancing flow of funds away from Japanese yen and toward dollar-denominated government securities. It is notable that the sustained dollar appreciation *could not* be attributed to substitution of the dollar in official-reserve holdings. While non-U.S. official holdings of dollars increased, from SDR 170 to SDR 197 billion, 1981–1984, the *share* of worldwide official reserves in dollar-denominated assets fell from 69.8 percent to 65.1 percent; reserves of industrialized countries tended to be shifted toward deutschemarks and yen during this period—partly, of course, reflecting official-intervention activities aimed at limiting the dollar's exchange-value gain.[14] Growth in the reserves of fuel-exporting countries, which had resulted in a significant flow of funds toward dollar assets in the mid-1970s and in 1979–81, also largely came to an end in 1983–84.

In a fundamental sense, the capital flow into dollar claims reflected differences in the gross saving and investment ratios in the United States and the rest of the world. Low saving, relative to investment opportunities, in the United States, as compared with other countries, especially Japan, created an interest differential in favor of the U.S. dollar that helped induce large private international capital flows. Of considerable importance in this matter was the difference among countries in fiscal policies; U.S. federal fiscal deficits absorbed saving in massive amounts, whereas greater foreign fiscal prudence avoided absorption in anything like the same degree. Different time structures in the interest-rate patterns, reflecting differing asset-holder time preferences in real terms along with different inflation fears across countries, also played a role in the shift of capital flows that changed the United States from the world's largest international creditor nation to a net debtor in the span of a few years.

Whatever the complete picture of the capital flows may turn out to be, the flows financed and helped sustain mirror-image net movements of goods and services together with unilateral transfers. The U.S. balance of payments on current account shifted from a \$6.6 billion surplus in 1980 to a \$93.4 billion deficit in 1984, while the German and Japanese balances improved from deficits of \$8.3 and \$9.5 billion, respectively, to surpluses of \$13.1 and \$36.4 billion. Largely as a result of the rather precipitate shutdown of net capital flows from the United States and the United Kingdom to the developing-country debtors of the world, "market borrower" debtor countries reduced their overall current-account deficits from \$72.2 billion in 1981 to only \$8.4 billion in 1984.[15]

Of all these very significant changes in the international economy which have accompanied the shift from an inflationary to a disinflationary environment, no doubt the one that has raised most apprehension about the continuing viability of the international monetary system has been the inability of a large number of major international-debtor countries to maintain service on their external debts. We turn now to some of the issues in this area.

The International Debt of Developing Countries

The 1982 suspension of service on its external debt by Poland, while not the first such suspension resulting from the disinflationary environment, was the first suspension by a large-scale, sovereign debtor, and was a forerunner of the string of suspensions, reschedulings, and restructurings of international debts that would necessarily continue through the 1980s. In view of the fact that the international loans were often short- to intermediate-term so that sovereign and nonsovereign borrowers alike typically faced the maturation of a number of individual loan contracts each year—with the creditor groups (governments, international agencies, or banks) differing across loans—the rescheduling and restructuring negotiations were exceedingly complex. Had it not been for the preexistence of institutionalized arrangements for official debt renegotiation, such as the Paris Club, and the active role undertaken by the IMF (as "honest broker"), the rescheduling efforts might have broken down. An IMF study has described the typical process for restructuring bank debt:

> An advisory group or steering committee of bankers has been established to assist liaison with all bank creditors, to discuss the coverage and terms of the restructuring and, where required, to coordinate the maintenance of short-term bank exposure and the provision of new financing. There have also generally been close links between the debtor country's negotiation of a restructuring

> through the advisory committee and its discussion of a Fund-supported adjustment program. In this context, the Fund, at the request of the interested parties, has participated in meetings with bank creditor groups. (Dillon, Watson, Kincaid, and Puckahtikom 1985, p. 13)

As it was, 32 countries rescheduled $168 billion of their debt to banks and official agencies during 1983 and 1984 alone in 62 separate agreements. The IMF has estimated that the volume of *bank* debt formally rescheduled, excluding short-term debt rolled over, was $35 billion in 1983 and $117 billion in 1984, or "about 6 percent and 21 percent of the total stock of bank debt of developing countries in 1983 and 1984, respectively."[16] In some cases, loan restructuring has involved additional lending commitments by creditors. Such additional lending, in 1983 and 1984, constituted 40 percent or more of total bank new lending to developing countries.[17]

Origins and Growth of the Debt

The explanation of the dramatic increase in bank lending to developing countries in the 1970s is found in a number of developments, all related to the pervasive inflationary milieu of the period. The emergence of the Euro-money and Euro-capital markets in the 1960s and 1970s provided a part of the institutional support necessary for the supply of the financial flows, and these relatively new institutional arrangements were, of course, encouraged in the 1960s and early 1970s by the national restraints (especially in the United States and the United Kingdom) on interest rates and bank lending imposed during a period when there was excessive central-bank credit creation, inflation, and high and rising nominal world-market interest rates.[18] Developing-country loan demand expanded in the 1970s in connection with the achievement of international creditworthiness by a number of countries. The new creditworthiness was a manifestation of the success of prior growth and development policies in those countries, and it was exaggerated when inflation dramatically improved developing-country terms of trade. From the point of view of the world's financial-center banks, both the demand for and the supply of internationally loanable funds were increased when the rise in world petroleum prices placed the banks in the role of intermediary between the earnings of the petroleum-exporting countries and the balance-of-payments needs of the petroleum-importing countriess. Profoundly causal in the whole process of excessive financial intermediation in the 1970s, were the monetary-expansion policies of the world's central banks and international organizations—especially the expansive policies of the Federal Reserve System in the United States.

Growth in U.S. bank reserves made possible the ballooning of credit by U.S. banks that in turn supported sympathetic expansion of dollar lending by banks in many parts of the world.

The growth in developing-country debt was dramatic. As a point of reference, the total international loans of banks in eleven industrial countries, including the United States, were $61 billion in 1970; these grew to $261 billion by 1975. By 1977, the first year for which official data on external debt of indebted developing countries exists, developing-country debt had reached $332.4 billion, and, by 1981, it had doubled to $660.5 billion. Bankers' interest in additional lending to developing countries melted away in the spring and summer of 1982 and helped precipitate the initial Polish and then the Mexican debt crises. Developing-country debt subsequently grew primarily as a result of accumulations of unpaid interest and principal, as a result of some further bank lending intended to maintain the viability of borrowers, and as a result of the lending activities of official agencies. There was, however, some renewal of "voluntary" bank lending in Asia in 1985. By the spring of 1985, total developing-country debt was approximately $865.3 billion, of which 41 percent was the debt of Western Hemisphere areas and 27 percent was due from Asia, with the remainder distributed among Africa, nonoil Middle Eastern countries, and Europe. About 43 percent of the debt was the responsibility of seven major borrowing countries, although not all of those had experienced debt-servicing problems.[19] Some $503.2 billion of the total of $865.3 billion of developing-country debt in 1985, nonetheless, was due from countries experiencing debt-servicing difficulties; and, of this total of troubled debt, $214.8 billion was due to private financial institutions and $156.2 was due to official creditors. Governments in the indebted nations were inescapably involved in the debt-settlement negotiations in that three-quarters of the total developing-country debt bore, as of 1985, some form of guarantee by a government agency in the borrowing country.[20]

Implications of the Debt

Difficulties in servicing the debt without the inflationary environment in which it was contracted have potentially profound implications for debtor and creditor countries alike. The debt-service payments of all indebted developing countries amounted to approximately 23.1 percent of those countries' exports in 1985, and for Western Hemisphere debtors the debt service ratio was 40 percent. Governments of countries that are typically dependent on imports for significant supplies of manufactured goods and sophisticated services find themselves in serious political difficulties when they attempt to suppress domestic consumption drastically in order to save foreign-exchange earnings for foreign-debt service. In 1985, Peru unilaterally declared that it would permit no more than 10 percent of export earnings to be made available for debt service; and, at the beginning of 1986, Nigeria proclaimed a similar ceiling at 30 percent of exports.[21] The Cartagena Group of Latin American debtor countries, meeting in Montevideo in December 1985, restated a popular demand for a linkage between each country's debt-service payments and its minimum economic-growth targets.[22]

Officials in debtor countries naturally have carefully considered the costs and benefits of default. Nondefault, of course, implies national economic austerity with unemployment and economic distress and a compulsion for officials to play the humiliating role of beggar in international financial circles. Default, on the other hand, also implies austerity since it would bring to an end the vital bank-trade credits on which the flow of imports depends as well as impair growth for a decade or more by temporarily destroying a defaulter's credit standing in the sensitive international capital markets. Political leaders in indebted countries have had to weigh carefully the costs to their countries as well as to the future of their political parties of the sustained austerity necessary to maintain service on external debts, on the one hand, against the austerity and hardship that would result from default, on the other. Fortunately, the weight of judgment at the time of this writing has favored a middle course that has consisted of renegotiating, but maintaining, external interest payments while stretching out the time schedule for principal repayments. Cries from the political far left, including Field Castro's proposal for collective action that would involve complete or partial debt repudiation, have attracted little support. Instead, political leaders in most indebted countries have performed a balancing act worthy of a veteran circus performer's acclaim; they have asserted nationalist sentiments and threats to default to creditors, while playing on creditor-country guilts and fears when they could; and then they have turned to home audiences to condemn incipient radicalism and to enjoin their constituents to accept greater austerity.

Creditor countries, too, are at risk. Not only is a substantial part of such nations' capital involved, but their political relations with the indebted nations and with each other are at stake if the negotiations to restructure the debt fail. More dramatic is the threat that default on the international bank credits poses for the stability of the vital international banking network. It is clear that default by more than one debtor country would make insolvent some of the world's major money-center banks. Interbank dependency would quickly spread a crisis at one or more major banks to many others, and across international borders, both because of the extensive network of interbank claims and because of the dependence of all banks in the system on continued access to the interbank market.[23] Federal Reserve data showed short-term liabilities of large, weekly-reporting banks in the United States to other U.S. banks to be about $106 billion in November 1985. IMF data show the *cross-border* interbank assets and liabilities for banks of all countries, in the second quarter, 1985, to be approximately $2 trillion. Threats to one link in this network are quickly transmitted to banks that are believed to hold claims in the threatened bank and from those banks to still others. Bank failure sets threads unraveling in many directions in the market tapestry that is woven of interbank cash and longer-term claims.

Safeguards to the Financial Structure

Central banks have moved swiftly to repair lesions in the banking fabric. In the United States, Federal Reserve and FDIC rescue of the Continental Illinois National Bank in Chicago, in 1984, provided the most dramatic bank rescue of recent years, although the bank's problems were primarily related to domestic, rather than international, loans. In the United Kingdom, Bank of England support for Johnson and Matthey Bankers was a controversial rescue operation that was rationalized by the importance of that firm's role in the international market for gold bullion. Smaller banks have complained that the authorities provide them less assurance of viability than is provided for the major banks, and critical observers of the scene point out that large banks are relieved of some "moral hazard" because of the unlikelihood that they will be allowed to fail. Banks have, however, moved to strengthen their capital-to-asset ratios; in the United States, for example, that ratio rose for the 17 largest bank-holding companies from 4.4 percent at the end of 1981 to 5.6 percent in June 1984.[24] Both in Germany and the United States, regulators have, on one occasion each, extended the coverage of deposit insurance from those normally covered deposits to all depositors of an institution in order to calm public apprehensions about the institution's creditworthiness and to contain a possible crisis. Some financial reporters in the United States worry that the Federal Reserve System has substantially extended its traditional authority in the name of "crisis management."[25]

Loopholes still exist in the safety network that central banks can spread over the international banking system, because of limitations on the ability of each central bank to provide liquidity to its domestic banks in currency denominations other than its own. The Bank of England, for example, can provide sterling to U.K. banks without limit, but it can monetize the banks' dollar assets only in the degree that the Bank of England can obtain dollars through the inter-central-bank-swap credit lines or other means.[26] Central bankers have issued reassuring statements to the international banking community to the effect that they are prepared to assure the liquidity needs of well-run banks and the banking community at large. Whether or not central banks will consistently bail out large banks that are judged to be in difficulties because of the *credit* risks the banks have taken is not clear. It is clear that the guarantees to the international financial network are informal, judgmental, and not public, and that in an international financial crisis even the best-intentioned central-bank leaders could be overwhelmed by events in which there were misunderstandings or in which nationalist sentiments inspired political leaders to delay critical central-bank responses.

In the meanwhile, a facade of strength and profitability is maintained for the banks as a result of the positions taken by the bank supervisory authorities in the creditor countries. While U.S. and British banks have set aside loan-loss reserves agaist some of their claims on foreign debtors, it appears that the bulk of such assets are carried on the lenders' books at undiscounted values, in spite of failure of the debtors to meet original debt-amortization schedules.[27] U.S. regulations that require banks to classify a loan as "nonperforming" when interest is 90 days in arears on the loan have been one of the constraints shaping international loan negotiations. Lending institutions have had to insist that interest payments be sustained, even when they have had to commit to new loans in order to fund such payments. Payments due on principal have typically been simply rescheduled. Supervisory authorities in all major financial-center countries have overlooked the loss in liquidity and value of their banks' portfolios in order to prevent the possible precipitation of systemic financial-market problems. By contributing to the facade of strength in the financial institutions they supervise, they have helped to gain time for possible resolution of the international debt crisis.

There is no doubt that an extensive market for troubled bank assets would have provided a useful means for individual banks to rearrange their portfolios so as to balance out risks and returns; it would have enabled some banks to restore their creditworthiness to near-impeccable standards by recognizing losses while enabling others, previously unencumberd with significant amounts of international debt, to assume some belated risk for an adequate return. A market that would have placed objective values on individual debt instruments, however, would have made it impossible for the supervisory facade recognizing ficticious values for bank assets to continue. Such a market, therefore, was not in the interest of banks holding troubled debt, and it was of course not supported by central banks. While a very limited market materialized, it played no significant role in the redistribution of debt exposure.

The 1985 U.S. Initiative

In October 1985, U.S. Secretary of the Treasury James Baker announced at the annual meetings of the IMF and World Bank a plan for the Treasury to assume a larger role in the international debt negotiations. He called on developing-country debtor nations to sit down with their bankers, and with representatives of the IMF, the World Bank, and regional international-development banks, to work out their problems. He urged on the debtors more market-oriented policies, and, in return for their cooperation, he offered his influence toward obtaining $20 billion of additional funding from the commerical banks and $9 billion from the multilateral development banks.

The Baker initiative was a useful if limited undertaking. Constrained by the already excessive U.S. fiscal deficit, the Secretary was in no position to offer additional U.S. government funding for either borrowers or lenders in the debt negotiations. And while borrowers and lenders publicly praised his stated intention to assume a more-active role in the process, his presence alone would not change the appraisals of self-interest which determined the positions that other negotiators would take. The government of Brazil, appraising domestic conditions and international opportunities, announced in September, for example, that it was unwilling to accept IMF conditions for further aid, and soon thereafter Peru announced its unwillingness to allocate more than 10 percent of its earnings in any year to debt service. The risk associated with the Baker initiative was that, in more directly involving the U.S. government officially in the negotiations, it could convert talks between borrowers and their bankers into intergovernmental talks that could then more easily be politicized in debtor or creditor countries or both.

The U.S. Secretary's announcement at the October IMF-World Bank meetings had been preceded, on September 22, by a meeting with other members of the "Group of Five" (the United Kingdom, France, Germany, and Japan) at which agreements were reached to seek more-rapid depreciation of the dollar on the exchanges by adjustments in national monetary and fiscal policies and by exchange-market intervention. Ironically, there was a small inconsistency in the U.S. initiatives on the debt, on the one hand, and on the exchange value of the dollar, on the other, since any arrangement that raised additional dollars for dollar-denominated international debt service would tend to *raise* the exchange value of the dollar. This would be true whether the debt arrangement involved additional World Bank dollar borrowing (which would raise dollar interest rates), additional U.S. bank lending, or World Bank or IMF borrowing abroad with exchanges of those funds for dollars. The simple fact was that improving the servicing of loans denominated in dollars would serve to strengthen the exchange value of the dollar and perpetuate an already excessive strength.

Reducing the International Debt Burden

While the exchange-rate and debt-policy initiatives did not seem to have made a great impact by 1986, the average dollar price of foreign currencies did rise approximately 30 percent, February 1985 to February 1986, from more-fundamental market causes. One cause was that U.S.-dollar long-term interest rates declined dramatically. Both the decline in interest rates and the decline in value of the dollar were causally entangled with the rapid decline in world petroleum prices and with sustained U.S. easy-money policies. The developments had implications for the international debt problem.

The decline in petroleum prices had adverse consequences for oil-exporting developing countries, including Mexico, which was a large debtor outside of OPEC. But most heavily indebted developing countries were oil-importing countries, and the petroleum price slide had highly salutary consequences for those countries' balances of payments and their ability to service debt.

Similarly, the slide in U.S. interest rates was a boon to countries with dollar-denominated external debt. With much of the interest on such debts tied, as a result of reschedulings, to the London Interbank Offer Rate (Libor), it did not take long for a decline in market rates to affect interest obligations on the loans. The Libor rate on one-year dollar deposits declined from 11.82 percent in 1984 to 8.22 percent in December 1985, with the decline continuing into 1986.

Dollar depreciation had both a bright and a dark side. On the one hand, cheaper dollars were less burdensome for debtors to buy in terms of their own currencies and in terms of non-dollar foreign-exchange earnings.[28]

Cheaper dollars would, on the other hand, be more difficult to earn. U.S. purchases abroad could be expected to be curtailed with dollar depreciation, and U.S. exporters would be more in evidence as competitors on world markets.[29] Nonetheless, the interest and exchange-rate developments of 1985 seemed, on balance, to be a helpful development in the resolution of the international debt problems. Even more important than their role in easing debt-service payment burdens, the changes would help ensure continued economic expansion in the industrialized countries of the world and ensure markets for the exports of all developing countries.

In 1985, a World Bank economist (Krueger 1985) estimated that 8 percent would be a minimum rate of growth for debtor-countries' exports in order for those countries to finance 5-percent real-interest payments on debt. She went on to say that 3.5-percent real-GNP growth rates in OECD countries, could, based on past experience, generate as much as 7-percent growth in OECD imports.[30] With, then, only limited steps toward trade liberalization, the markets for 8-percent export growth by developing countries might be obtained. When real interest rates fell to not more than 3 percent in 1986, the growth requirements clearly became less demanding. By parallel reasoning, 3-percent growth in OECD countries could, if there were no political surrender to illiberal trading practices, provide growth in developing-country exports of 6 percent, enough to cover interest payments, some amortization of principal, and a slim margin of growth in developing-countries' domestic supplies. What is essential to successful servicing of the international debts is sustained real growth in industrial-country markets, declining real interest rates, and the maintenance of trading conditions that are, at the least, no more restrictive of trade than conditions have been in the recent past.[31] For their part, governments of indebted nations must encourage domestic savings, restrain inflation, woo back flight capital, encourage inward investment, and limit their own protectionism.[32] A means of significantly altering indebtedness exists for many of the major debtors, should they choose to use it. That means is to sell off nationalized enterprises to foreign investors, converting an international debt to an equity obligation. Both Brazil and Argentina did denationalize a number of properties in 1985 with no bar on foreign participation in the acquisition of shares. In the longer term, savings must be found in the more-developed countries to finance development at home without inflation and to help finance development abroad—perhaps using the facilities of the World Bank and other multilateral international lending agencies to place the funds—if the international debts are to be serviced without threats to political stability in the indebted countries. Inauguration, in 1985, of the Multilateral Investment Guarantee Fund

(MIGA) by the World Bank was a step in the right direction of reasserting the importance of direct-investment flows from developed to developing countries in a period when debt financing has been overdone.[33]

The enormous balance-of-payments deficits on current account of the United States in 1985–86 transformed this country quickly from one of the world's great creditor countries to one of the world's great debtors. The U.S. foreign debt, however, was of a different character from that of the developing countries. To begin with, the debt, while large in dollar terms, remained small in terms of the U.S. gross national product, and its service was only a few percent of annual exports.[34] In addition, the fact that the debt was denominated in dollars meant that the burden of servicing it was not directly influenced by changes in exchange rates. Finally, and most important, the 30-percent 1985 depreciation of the dollar from its lofty height at the beginning of that year ensured that the net foreign borrowing would not continue unabated for long, since the exchange-rate change would reduce the deficits in the current account of the balance of payments and the net capital inflows.

The International Money and Capital Markets

Perhaps the most significant change in the structure of the international monetary system since the collapse of the regime of fixed exchange rates in 1971–1973 has been the continued rapid integration of the international money and capital markets. While that process, resulting in improved international capital mobility, has been evolutionary for centuries, it accelerated to unusually rapid change in the 1960s and 1970s with the extensive development of Eurocurrency banking, and again in the 1980s with a broad move toward financial-market reform and deregulation in the world's major financial centers. Fundamental forces directing the change have included high, variable, and uncertain inflation and interest rates, changing government regulations, and the rapid progress in information technology.

Eurocurrency banking, sometimes attributed to the inventiveness of George Bolton, was more fundamentally the result of political forces, exchange-rate misalignments, incentives to avoid the burden of capital-export and other banking regulations, and other aspects of the market environment. Following World War II, the preeminence of the dollar as the currency for denomination of international trade and investment was well established. For a time this created a marketing advantage for American financial institutions, which enjoyed a near-monopoly in the ability to provide trade financing, risk-management resources, and underwriting facilities denominated in dollars. It is said that the Soviet Union became the first Eurocurrency depositor when, fearing for the safety of its U.S. dollar deposits as a result of U.S. anticommunist hysteria, it approached British banks with the proposal to establish working deposits denominated in U.S. dollars. In the British banking community, traditionally bound to banking in sterling, the idea was novel but not without appeal in view of the enormous world-market opportunity for placing dollar funds. The appeal of dollar deposits became all the greater when the U.K. government, in an effort to alleviate balance-of-payments pressures, tightened its restrictions on the access of foreigners to the sterling capital market. The capital-export restrictions did not extend to nonsterling loans, creating an incentive for British lending institutions to improve their access to dollar funding. Continental banks, inspired by the profitable opportunities opened to their British competitors, quickly emulated the British practice of seeking deposits in external currencies.

American banks were then catapulted into the burgeoning Eurocurrency market in the 1960s by a number of forces. Overvaluation of the dollar was driving American corporations abroad as a means of controlling costs and maintaining market shares. That same overvaluation cheapened the costs to banks of establishing a presence abroad, especially in London, where subsidiary banks could escape the deposit reserve requirements of the Federal Reserve System, insurance premiums on deposits, and other U.S. regulations. When, in 1967, a desire to protect the U.S. balance of payments led the U.S. government to impose restraints on capital exports, the die was cast that would result in the shift of a substantial share of U.S. banking business overseas. In cities around the world, U.S. banks subsequently undertook not only to service the needs of U.S. corporations but also to seek good borrowers and to fund loans that were originated anywhere in the banks' worldwide network. With the onset of the petroleum crisis in 1973–1974, banks of all countries that were prepared to do business in dollars, became the important financial intermediaries between oil importers and oil exporters.

Eurocurrency banking profoundly influenced the character and emphasis of domestic and international banking. From emphasis on deposit collection in local or national markets and more-or-less-durable lender relationships with familiar-client individuals and firms, money-center banks shifted emphasis toward a role of being "wholesalers" of funds and syndicators of loans in a worldwide market to governments, public agencies, international corporations, and other large borrowers.[35] Client relations in this market are determined by competitive bidding for the job.

Recently, as the markets for bank CDs, treasury bills, commercial paper, and longer-maturity securities with variable interest rates have enlarged, and markets for financial futures and interest-rate and currency options have appeared, the money-center banks have moved still further away from their traditional functions, now emphasizing fee income for expert services in arranging to fill the financial needs of large customers. The business sought by the money-center banks in London has encroached steadily on the business at one time reserved to the British investment banks, and, in the United States, banks have found themselves increasingly in competition with the investment houses—the traditional underwriters and marketers of long-term U.S. securities.

These changes have been accompanied by a battle for funds at the retail level, a battle enhanced by the disintermediation induced by interest-rate regulation in the traditional institutions while market interest rates were soaring. Savings institutions (savings and loan associations, credit unions, and savings banks in the United States and, in the United Kingdom, building societies) sought to offer new services (commonly check-writing privileges) as a means of holding deposits they could not hold with regulated interest rates in high-interest-rate markets. Banks sought to pay limited interest on checkable deposits to maintain the dwindling demand for this low-cost source of funds. As a consequence, the lines of demarcation between banks and the thrift institutions blurred.

The breakdown of traditionally separate functions among institutions in some major international financial centers, together with the appearance of new competitors (such as mutual funds in the United States and similar unit trusts and trust companies in the United Kingdom and Canada) to offer small depositors an alternative to the low regulated interest rates payable by traditional deposit takers, created inescapable pressures for market reorganization and reform.

It is a plausible hypothesis that, had the banks of the United States and the United Kingdom not been able to participate with special privileges each in the market of the other, and had not the internationalization of the collection and placement of funds been by then so extensively developed, the market-restructuring movements of the late 1970s and early 1980s might have taken the form of revised but tighter regulations to protect the traditional market fiefdoms of established institutions instead of taking the direction of "deregulation" as it did. But in the sequence of events that developed, and in the presence of market-oriented, conservative governments in both the United States and the United Kingdom, solution of the problems by increased regulation was preempted.

Deregulation in the United States

In the United States, banks were encouraged to repatriate some of their off-shore activities by a 1981 amendment to Federal Reserve Regulations D and Q to provide for International Banking Facilities. The changes exempted specially chartered domestic institutions (IBFs) from most regulatory requirements if their sources and placements of funds were predominantly outside the country.

The U.S. Deregulation and Monetary Control Act of 1980 authorized the progressive relaxation of ceilings on interest rates payable on deposits subject to check and brought all financial institutions offering such "transactions deposits" under the umbrella of the Federal Reserve System—requiring reporting and the maintenance of reserves against deposits and, in turn, providing access to Federal Reserve discount facilities.

The historic ban on interstate banking in the United States was assailed by events which ensure its demise. Failures of bank and thrift institutions, as the cost of funds soared above income earnable on older investments in some of these institutions' portfolios, led to selected takeovers that crossed state lines and crossed also previously regulated separations of function for thrift institutions and banks. At the same time, foreign banks, unencumbered by regulations limiting their activity to one state alone, acquired banks and opened offices in numerous metropolitan centers. Avoiding the Federal Reserve's rules on interstate banking, "nonbanks," which either do not accept deposits or do not make loans, proliferated under the aegis of national financial institutions. In consequence, the pressures for abandonment of official restraints on interstate banking and on the different privileges accorded thrifts, banks, foreign banks, and nonbanks mounted, even as large banks and some institutions seeking to create "financial supermarkets" sought repeal of the Glass-Steagall Act, which prevents banks in the United States from participating in new securities underwriting. It is clear that disassembly of much of the core of regulations that had framed U.S. financial markets for a half century passed the point of no return in the early 1980s.

The economies of scale inherent in providing a wide range of financial services to customers inspired a movement toward "financial supermarkets." The services that are demanded by many individuals and firms, both in the United States and abroad, have increasingly included access to foreign as well as domestic investment and borrowing opportunities. The perception of the existence of an enormous market for fast and virtually continuous worldwide financial opportunities, together with the new technological capabilities of providing such services, has motivated U.S. firms to seek greater access to financial markets abroad and similarly motivated European and Japanese firms to establish beachheads in the United States. It is the success that financial institutions have had in obtaining that access that gives the movement toward financial-market deregulation special importance for the present and future functioning of the international monetary system. International capital mobility, already very substantial, will become increasingly high in the years immediately ahead. We shall see below that this has important consequences for the possibilities of independent national monetary policies and for the functioning of the international monetary system.

Deregulation in the United Kingdom

Reform of the U.K. markets came later than that in the United States but was in some ways more dramatic. Until the mid-1980s there was a kind of dichotomy in London's City between the outward looking, innovative, and highly competitive Eurobanking, international investing, and insurance activities on the one hand and the traditional, functionally distinct activities of (a) jobbers and brokers in the stock exchange, (b) discount houses in the money markets, and (c) investment banks in the capital markets on the other. The blurring of the lines between the activities of the clearing banks and the investment banks has been mentioned above, along with the increasing competition of the clearing banks with the building societies for U.K. domestic deposits and small loans.

Change was brought to the stock and bond markets with the opening, in 1979, of a government investigation of fixed commissions on stock-exchange transactions. The investigation ended in a compromise in which the Stock Exchange agreed to an end to the fixed-commission system in 1986. Since fixed broker commissions, in the past, had covered fixed markups paid by brokers to jobbers on the exchange and had sustained a "single capacity" system in which brokers bought and sold on the exchange only through the jobbers, who made markets in selected stocks and bonds, termination of the fixed broker fee threatened also the fixed jobber fee and the division of broker and jobber functions. In 1986, the year that came to be called that of the "big bang," the system of fixed commissions ended and, with it, the separation of broker and jobber capacities. The new system called for exchange member firms to have larger capital and greater securities-marketing capacity and led to elimination of the barriers that had kept foreigners and domestic clearing and merchant banks from exchange membership. In an unprecedented series of mergers and acquisitions, three of the big four U.K. clearing banks, eight British merchant banks, 14 foreign banks, and several large international securities firms acquired interests in the existing London broker and jobber firms. And in the gilt-edged (government-bond) market, after the Bank of England decided to broaden its dealings to include more than the 3 firms it had dealt with traditionally, 29 firms became involved in that system, including 11 U.S. firms (Wyles 1986).

Regulation in the new, much more-open securities markets is carried out through an official Securities and Investment Board and a number of "self-regulatory organizations" (SROs) organized by participants in subsectors of the investment market.

Intended to ensure London's very important role as a securities market, the liberalization of access to the share and gilt-edged markets was almost too late. Quarrels over the rules to be administered by the SROs and the maintenance of high Stock-Exchange commissions during the transition period led to threats to establish in London a competitor to the venerable Stock Exchange and other veiled threats to the effect that in an electronically linked international market a London exchange was no longer necessary. Shares of 200 London listed firms were traded in New York in 1985 in the form of American Depositary Receipts, and off-market trading, in both London and New York, of these and other shares and receipts proliferated in 1985–86. International trade in a wide variety of securities and money-market instruments, at low transactions costs, had come of age in both the United States and United Kingdom.

Continental Europe

On the continent of Europe, changes in the structure of financial markets was slower than in the United States and the United Kingdom. This may be partly because inflation in the 1970s in countries like Germany and Switzerland was slower and less destructive of existing regulatory patterns. In other countries, such as Greece, and in less degree Italy and France, the scope of regulation was sufficiently pervasive effectively to suppress change.[36] In France, for example, only the rapid development of the bond market provided bank depositors an alternative to the low, regulated interest rates payable on bank deposits in the early 1980s. By sponsoring and offering to their customers mutual funds that would invest in variable-rate, short-maturity bonds, French banks found a means of attracting funds outside the burden of regulated deposit interest rates. But much of the French regulatory apparatus remained resistant to change.

Japan

While still restricted in important ways, Japanese financial markets underwent more profound change than the markets in any other financial center outside the United States and the United Kingdom.[37] In the early 1970s the Japanese markets were tightly controlled and segmented. Bank deposit rates had ceilings, and bank lending rates were tied to the discount rate of the Bank of Japan. Bond markets were poorly developed because government deficits were small and because business firms depended on their banking relationships for funds. Syndicates of banks and securities houses were required to assume new government debt and to hold it for a specified time before reselling it in the secondary market. Exchange controls limited international transactions, and domestic residents were banned from depositing in or borrowing from Japanese banks in a foreign currency. Pension and certain other funds were required to invest in domestic securities, and foreign brokerage firms were denied access to a number of Japanese markets, including that for stocks and newly issued bonds.

The disruptive forces of inflation, large Japanese-government deficits, and growing Japanese involvement in the world economy outside Asia have broken down many of these restrictions. While the U.S. government has carried on talks with the Japanese government aimed at opening Japanese financial markets to further foreign involvement and with a view to internationalizing the yen, the transformation of the Japanese markets has probably been much more due to market and political forces in Japan than to U.S. "pressures."[38] While not eliminated, Japanese ceilings on bank-deposit interest rates have been mitigated by the creation of negotiable certificates of deposits and money-market certificates by banks, by the creation of medium-term government-bond funds (*chugoku* funds) by the securities houses, and by an enormous expansion of the bond markets in conjunction with large government deficits and declining dependence of corporations on bank financing.

Most Japanese foreign-exchange restrictions were swept away by the foreign-exchange law of 1980; but, because the government remained reluctant to see the rapid development of a Euroyen market, domestic residents were denied for a time the right to hold foreign-currency deposits in Japan, they were denied access to the forward-exchange markets in order to limit arbitraging between domestic and external yen markets, and foreigners were restricted in the uses they could make of their yen deposits in Japan. By 1984 the restrictions on resident foreign-exchange transactions were removed, and the restrictions on foreigners were eased. Earlier, the Japanese institutional investors had been permitted to diversify into foreign securities and thereby escape Japan's low interest yields. Both Japanese and foreign banks and securities houses continued in the 1980s to press for further development of the external market in yen, which requires opportunities to invest and arbitrage in the domestic yen market. In 1985 Japanese authorities permitted several foreign firms access to the Tokyo stock exchange and permission to deal in other short- and long-term securities. They also opened to domestic banks and insurance companies, singly, jointly, or in association with foreign institutions, access to the lucrative market of investment-advising for the immense Japanese pension funds. In anticipation of the opportunity to manage such funds in a fiduciary relationship, Japanese competitors for this business reached out to strengthen further their ties to financial markets in the United States and the United Kingdom.

Some Implications

But even as some U.S., European, and Japanese financial firms were offering round-the-clock and round-the-world cash management, borrowing, and lending services, some of their corporate and government-agency clients found themselves less dependent on their bankers. Increasingly well-developed markets for short-term securities provided the borrowers an alternative to the lending services of the financial specialists. Morse (1985, p. 8) noted that the "corporate treasurers have grown in self-confidence and expertise" in the use of the securities market, while the banks themselves, to assure their own liquidity, have had to keep their loans "marketable" in that same arena. Among the new services banks have found profitable in these circumstances are note issuance facilities (NIFs) and revolving underwriting facilities (RUFs). Both of these facilities, in which banks provide a credit-guarantee service, generate fee income for the banks without on-balance-sheet liabilities. Consequently, the business does not mandate new capital requirements, although central bankers in 1986 were looking carefully at the additional risks assumed by banks in these operations. RUFs, in general, provided prime borrowers access to a source of funds which was lower in cost than bank credit.

The "securitization" of the international capital markets is no doubt here to stay. McRae (1985, pp. 4–5) has noted some reasons:

a. Securities-market instruments spread the risk of credits among a much wider body of creditors.
b. They have an active secondary market which enables new credits to be realistically valued.

c. They do not bear on balance sheets of financial institutions in the sense that a default is a charge against capital.
d. The supply of funds is likely to grow rapidly as the pension and life-assurance funds of the industrial world grow in response to an ageing population's demand for better pension provision.
e. Securities are more suitable than bank deposits as assets for the main institutional investors. In the case of bonds, their long maturity is more readily matched against the long-lasting liability of a pension or life policy; in the case of equities, they offer a share in economic growth.

Other new practices have improved opportunities for investment and risk-management in the national and international markets. Stock and interest-rate futures and currency options have made possible the wider sharing of financial risks. The "modern swap" makes arbitrage possible between the interest rate paid by a borrower who prefers to borrow at a fixed interest rate and that paid by a borrower who prefers a variable rate. And agreements between the London Stock Exchange and the U.S. National Association of Securities Dealers to share price quotations on stocks traded in both countries opens the way to extended-hour international trade in listed securities.

What are the implications of this spurt in the rate of institutional change? Integration of the leading financial markets reduces the independence with which financial authorities in those countries can pursue financial policies, whether moneys remain linked only with flexible exchange rates or whether the nations move toward targeted exchange rates or other constrained exchange-rate arrangements. If the exchange rates become more fixed, efforts by any country to move away from credit conditions extant on world markets will result in capital flows through many avenues —perhaps too many any longer to be controlled by legal restraints. Efforts to tighten credit conditions will be thwarted by capital inflows and by money-supply growth resulting from international-reserve money accumulation. Efforts to ease credit conditions, on the other hand, will be thwarted by capital outflows and reserve-money losses. If exchange rates are flexible, similar capital flows will appreciate the currency of a country where credit is tightened—making little tightening necessary to achieve a given target of disinflation—and capital flows will depreciate the currency of a country where credit is eased. Whatever the regime, small policy impacts on domestic credit conditions will have large effects, making it necessary for the industrialized nations generally to avoid actions that create divergences in international-credit-market conditions.

Whether the world is ready for this increased coordination of official economic policies or not, and whether or not it is efficient, in view of changes in labor-market conditions that may occur unevenly across countries, remains to be seen. What is clear is that we move into an era in which greater fixity in the exchange rates is possible, and probably desirable, *if but only if* governments do back away from their commitment to use domestic financial instruments to influence domestic economic conditions in response to domestic political pressures. Since fiscal and monetary policies may affect international capital flows differently depending on the *mix* of those policies at home and abroad, coordination of the mix of those policies among nations becomes of great importance. Whether a given nation finds capital inflows desirable or not in its efforts to achieve given short-run macroeconomic objectives can depend on the exchange-rate regime, since capital inflows affect the supply of money in a fixed-exchange-rate regime but the exchange rate in a flexible-rate regime. Above all, it is no longer immaterial whether financial expansion in a country is obtained by fiscal ease, on the one hand, or monetary ease, on the other. The choice depends on the capital flows desired and the circumstances to be encountered abroad. International policy coordination must take place on two levels: (a) an intergovernmental determination of policy measures to obtain global macroeconomic policy goals, and then (b) determination of the pattern of national policies that will optimize national objectives within the constraint of global needs. That degree of coordination seems unattainable at present but represents the challenge for the near future. Before assessing it further, we turn to recent experience in the markets for foreign exchange, recent developments in the use of national and supranational currencies for international settlements, and recent changes in the goals for and practices of international financial organizations.

The Foreign-Exchange Markets

At the heart of any international monetary "system" is the exchange-rate regime, consisting of the rules and practices that establish the relationships among the various national moneys. Prior to 1971 the accepted rules were those codified in the amended charter of the International Monetary Fund, calling for all member governments to "adopt appropriate measures" in their national markets to keep their respective exchange rates on the U.S. dollar within close and defined margins on the dollar. The U.S., in turn, met its obligations by converting into gold at $35/ounce the official dollar holdings of other IMF members. The result was a global pattern of fixed exchange rates with the dollar as the common numeraire. After abrogation by the United States in August 1971, of its commitment to keep the dollar convertible into gold, the world moved toward managed floating of the rates, and the Second Amendment to the IMF charter, in 1978, allowed countries to choose their own exchange-rate regimes—pegging against another currency or group of currencies, pegging against a preselected index of currencies or the IMF's own Special Drawing Right (SDR), or floating more or less freely against all currencies.

As of January 1986, 31 countries pegged their currencies to the U.S. dollar, 14 pegged to the French franc, 5 pegged to some other national currency, 11 pegged to the SDR, and 22 pegged to an individually selected composite of currencies. A few countries regularly adjusted their exchange rates following preselected internal and/or external indicators, 8 countries of Western Europe linked their exchange rates under terms of the European Monetary System (EMS), and 42 countries floated more freely (although 8 limited rate flexibility in some degree toward a single foreign currency).[39]

This regime of managed floating, characterized by shifting participation in the large currency blocs, has seen the world through rampant and uneven inflation and (in some countries) sharp disinflation, massive reorientation of trading patterns in connection with the petroleum crisis and its aftermath, a substantial increase in the size and volatility of international capital flows, vigorous adjustments in some countries to a dangerous overhang of international debt, numerous turnovers of governments, and, with them, national economic policies. The regime has accommodated the end of the 1970s inflationary swing in the industrialized countries while high inflation rates continue in many of the world's developing countries.

Yet the regime is only a means for resolving and distributing stress, not a mechanism for eliminating it. In response to massive real and financial economic disturbances, exchange rates have exhibited wide swings and high volatility.[40] In the process, the concept of managed floating has come, mostly mistakenly, under continued attack.

The dollar's "effective" (weighted-average) value against other currencies fell by 22 percent, 1970–1979, and then climbed by 60 percent to the first quarter, 1985, before depreciating by 30 percent again by early 1986. Its swing against some currencies was, of course, greater than this. Volatility in the daily and weekly movement of the rates, and widening spreads between buying and selling rates, also occurred, especially in periods of rapid change in economic conditions. The increased volatility and widened spreads to some extent reflected unwillingness by those who normally take positions in the market—for short-run profit or to accommodate customers—to take those positions at near-market rates, and, consequently, reflected increased uncertainty (or increased risk aversion) in periods of rapidly changing events.[41] The volatility no doubt also reflected responses by market participants to changing information, or "news."[42]

The failure of the exchange markets to provide steady guidance as to what exchange rates would be, together with the wide swings that the rates experienced, gave rise to steady criticism of the floating-rate idea.[43] Ardent supply-side economists in the United States advocated a return to the rigid exchange rates that would be enforced by an international gold standard. Others, while rejecting a return to rigidly controlled rates, called for a system of internationally agreed targeted rates to be maintained by governmental exchange-market interventions and macroeconomic policy adaptations.[44]

The idea of a return to less-variable exchange rates found ready political support among those directly involved in international trade and investment, on whom flexible rates had thrust a greater share of the risk burden inherent in international markets. In the United States, legislation in 1981 mandated reconsideration of the merits of a return to a national or international gold standard. The report of the commission appointed for this review, however, failed to support the gold-standard idea. In November 1985, a conference on exchange-rate stability, convened in Washington by a group of congressmen, was a media event to protest an overvalued dollar but little more. In the international arena, a competent Working Group on Exchange Market Intervention was convened following the 1982 Versailles Economic Summit meeting but concluded in its report in January 1983 that there was no reason to retreat from the system of floating exchange rates and that government interventions in the exchange markets were of limited value unless accompanied by more fundamental changes in macroeconomic policies.[45] Again, in 1985, this time under a mandate from the finance ministers of the Group of Ten countries, the Deputies to the ministers reported on "The Functioning of the International Monetary System" and endorsed the exchange-rate-policy conclusions of the Jurgensen Report. Among members of the Group of Five (United States, United Kingdom, France, Germany, Japan), France was the most steadfast advocate of a return to officially stabilized exchange rates.[46] Developing countries, through their Group of Twenty-four and in other gatherings, also pressed for stabilized rates.[47] In January 1986, the President of the United States, in his State of the Union Address, called on the Secretary of the Treasury "to determine if the nations of the world should convene to discuss the role and relationship of our currencies." The Interim Committee of the IMF's Board of Governors, in its communique of April 10, 1986, asked the IMF's Executive Board "to consider further whether there are any modifications in the exchange rate system which could contribute to enhancing exchange rate stability and the mutual consistency of economic policies without sacrificing the essential flexibility of the system."

Following an agreement by Finance Ministers of the Group of Five countries on September 22, 1985, there was some coordinated intervention in the exchange markets by governments with the objective of driving the value of the dollar down. By the end of October, according to the Federal Reserve Bank of New York, the group had sold $10.2 billion, with the United States having provided $3.2 billion of the total. By January 1986, the value of the dollar was off, in effective value, about 9.3 percent from September and 23.4 percent from the preceding February. In view of the decline in interest rates in the United States relative to those abroad through 1985 and the depreciating course of the dollar well before September, it is difficult to assess the effects of the interventions. Probably they had some effect in confirming expectations; beyond that, the dollar's decline may have been due more to changes in fundamental market forces.

Exchange-Market-Intervention Issues

Much of the will to return to a regime in which governments take responsibilities for keeping exchange rates within bounds stems from a nostalgia for the good times under the Bretton Woods rules. It must be remembered, however, that the original IMF charter, or "Bretton Woods rules," did not always work well. From the end of World War II to the mid-1950s, the U.S. dollar was chronically overvalued, and international trade and investment were burdened with import and payments restrictions. From the mid-1950s to the mid 1960s, a period when North American and European currencies were near equilibrium values as the dollar moved from overvaluation toward a subsequent period of undervaluation, the regime of fixed exchange rates accommodated a broad movement toward trade and payments liberalization. In the subsequent period from the mid-1960s to the demise of the Bretton Woods rules in 1971, however, international commerce, with an undervalued dollar and an undervalued pound, became again burdened with new protectionism and capital-export controls, this time on the part of the United States along with the United Kingdom. Financial markets were characterized by ever-more frequent balance-of-payments "crises" until the official-exchange-rate pledges were abandoned by a number of leading countries in the 1970s.[48]

Critical to an argument favoring official intervention in the exchange markets is the matter of defining the equilibrium exchange rate. Without doubt, much of the sense that the dollar was overvalued in the period

1981–1985 was based on the notion that the rate should have maintained purchasing power parity among currencies. Countless studies have tracked the "real" exchange rates of the period and noted their inconstancy. Quite apart from the conceptual and statistical problems of measuring this parity, there is the matter that equilibration of the current account of a nation's balance of payments is not the only task that the exchange rate performs and should perform.[49] Accommodation of long-term capital transfers, when such transfers are induced by differences in private investment and savings flows across countries, for example, would generally be accepted as a proper role for the exchange rate, although cross-country differences in saving and investment that are attributable to government policies, rather than private voluntary decisions, might be questionable.[50] On a parallel argument, there seems no reason why the exchange rate should not also accommodate *short*-term capital movements which respond to changes in excess demands and supplies for liquidity across countries and to changes in the perception, by capital's owners, of the safety or earnings-stability of their claims. Competitively determined prices are generally applauded for reflecting expectations about the future and thereby consolidating information for market participants about needs to prepare for forthcoming events; one should probably expect no less from a competitively determined exchange rate. Rates that perform these multiple tasks, however, will not always equate currencies' purchasing powers across national markets. They may, nonetheless, meaningfully be "equilibrium rates."[51]

Critics of recent experience under floating exchange rates contend that the rates "overshoot" their intermediate- to long-term equilibrium values in their initial adjustments to disturbances, taking on values and a degree of volatility that serve no social purpose. Numerous theoretic models have demonstrated this possibility by imposing lags on the speed of adjustment of some (usually "real") variables relative to the speed of adjustment of the exchange rate.[52] Frenkel and Rodriguez (1982) have demonstrated that, with proper assumptions, exchange rates can equally well "undershoot." More interesting than whether or not exchange rates do overshoot is the question of whether or not they should. Alfred Marshall (1890), in his famous distinction between the "short run" and the "long run," noted that prices in competitive markets typically move beyond long-run equilibria as a matter of short-run response to changes in demand, thereby restraining demand while hastening the slower supply responses to the demand change. Marshall saw such price adjustments as means of absorbing the shock of unexpected changes while the slower behavioral adjustments took place. Frenkel accepts the same role for the exchange rate:

> First, . . . differences [in the characteristics of exchange rates and the prices of

national outputs] which result from the much stronger dependence of exchange rates (and other asset prices) on expectations, suggest that the fact that exchange rates have moved more than the price level is not sufficient evidence that exchange rate volatility has been excessive.

Second, ... when commodity prices are slow to adjust to current and expected economic conditions, it may be desirable to allow for "excessive" adjustment in some other prices.

Third, there are continuous changes in real economic conditions that require adjustment in the equilibrium relative prices of different national outputs. Under these circumstances what seem to be divergences from purchasing power parities may really reflect equilibrating changes.

Fourth, if there is short-run stickiness of prices of domestic goods in terms of national monies, then rapid exchange rate adjustments which are capable of changing the relative prices of different national outputs are a desirable response to changing real economic conditions. (Frenkel 1983, p. 51)

In a simulation model designed to track a country's exchange rate under a managed float, Shelburn (1984, p. 47) concluded that "intervention that smooths nominal exchange-rate change in the aftermath of a disturbance consistently increases the volatility of the real variables reported.... The policymaker thus has a clear choice between adjustment via change in the nominal exchange rate and adjustment via change in real variables."

Risk is typically an issue in discussions of proposals to limit exchange-rate movements. While traders and investors complained, after 1973, of the increased burden of risk of exchange-rate changes they were required to bear, it seems clear that the change in exchange-rate regime did not increase risk so much as it redistributed it. Risks that there will be unexpected disturbances to markets exist regardless of whether the exchange rate is fixed or flexible, unless a regime itself constitutes some form of unique discipline that reduces disturbances. Given that the market responses to disturbances are, at least in the short run, somewhat different under fixed, as opposed to flexible, exchange rates, different groups encounter different adjustment risks under the two regimes. It is not clear in equity who *should* bear the risks inherent in international economic relations, but it is probably true as a matter of efficiency that professional international traders and investors, who make it their business to gather information concerning the nature, duration, and likelihood of such disturbances, manage the risks better than can the alternative bearers of it.[53]

Other issues in the controversy over exchange-rate policy revolve around the ability of governments to manage the exchange markets. One problem here arises from the sheer size of the daily volume of trading in recent years. A survey by the Group of Thirty yielded estimates that the daily volume of trading in U.S. dollars in eight leading market centers has grown from $75 billion in 1979 to $150 billion in 1984.[54] In view of the fact that the latter figure is approximately equal to the combined nongold monetary reserves of the seven industrial countries with the largest reserves in 1984, it is clear that official reserves are no longer large relative to the market, although countries' reserve holdings admittedly do not reflect the size of their potential official credit lines and hence their potential capacities for intervention.

Another matter impairing governments' ability to manage the markets by the purchase and sale of foreign currencies is the fact that unless the authorities forgo "sterilizing" the domestic monetary consequences of their exchange-market interventions and let the interventions influence the course of domestic monetary policy, they are unlikely to gain by their actions more than transitory effects on the exchange markets. Sterilized interventions (those not permitted to influence on-going monetary policies) tend, with a lag, to generate capital flows which undo the governments' actions. To illustrate, consider a completely sterilized sale of dollars by a central bank. The total operation has the net effect of placing additional dollar-denominated securities in the hands of U.S. residents and of removing foreign-currency securities from the hands of foreigners, because the central banks reverse, by domestic-securities-markets transactions, the money-supply changes in their own markets. After it has made a sterilized purchase of foreign exchange, the Federal Reserve Bank of New York has added foreign currencies to its assets while having reduced its holdings of U.S. government securities. If sterilization is complete, the foreign central bank involved has purchased securities in its own market to replace in circulation the amount of money acquired by the New York bank. The net changes in the securities required to be held in the private market, however, affect interest rates raising them in the United States and lowering them abroad, and consequently inducing a capital reflow toward the United States. In "perfect" capital markets this reflow, in time, exactly offsets the exchange-rate effect of a central bank's exchange-market intervention, requiring renewed interventions to maintain any given displacement of the exchange rate.[55]

Insofar as private speculation is available in exchange markets where governments have not specified any official intervention points, government purchases and sales to influence the exchange rate displace, at least in some degree, private speculation; official views of where the exchange rate is going are substituted for private market-participants' views. The official intervention uses public funds, expecting to reconstitute them to their original currency denomination through a subsequent reversal of the original intervention. The reconstitution, of course, is at a gain or a loss depending upon whether the currency the authorities hold depreciates or appreciates in the interim. Some of the issues in this connection concern (a) whether or not public officials are better predictors of where future equilibrium exchange rates lie than are private speculators who commit their own funds, and (b) whether or not it is in the social interest for governments to risk funds that were not volunteered by the providers when voluntary speculative funds are available. These issues amount to the question of whether or not there is a case for socializing the function of exchange-market speculation.

The case of a government pledge to stabilize the course of the exchange rate is sometimes defended as a means of disciplining the financial policies of political leaders. Drafts on official reserves to support the exchange rate will eventually halt profligate policies of politicians, it is argued. Yet experience does not give this argument good marks. In the 25 years under Bretton Woods, from 1947 to 1971, governments again and again abandoned their existing exchange-rate commitments when these commitments conflicted with the expansive domestic financial policies espoused by political leaders. Ironically, it was in the 1980s, under a floating-exchange-rate regime, that most governments of the industrialized countries turned to disinflation, and then the decisions were not made on balance-of-payments grounds and were probably little influenced by exchange rates.

Limited government exchange-market interventions can probably be justified to add depth to markets in periods of high uncertainty, to slow or halt purely bandwagon runs in exchange rates when these can be identified, and to give order to markets when officials are privy to information (for example, concerning forthcoming policy changes at home or abroad) that nonofficials do not have. Unduly large or sustained interventions, however, suggest government efforts to defend an exchange rate that the market thinks indefensible and are usually unwise.

Macroeconomic Policies, the Exchange Rates, Trade, and Investment

The theory of the international balance of payments and the exchange rate his, since the 1960s, increasingly been incorporated into macroeconomic models of open economies, emphasizing the global character of the financial markets and the necessity of considering international interactions in the making of national economic policies. In view of the overwhelming evidence of the swiftness and volume with which the markets in capital claims—asset markets—respond to market stimuli and new information, as compared to the slower speed and more ponderous adjustment of the markets for goods and services, exchange-rate movements have increasingly been thought to be dominated by asset-market considerations. The impacts of government monetary and fiscal policies, as a result, have come to be viewed in terms of the effects of combined policies on domestic credit conditions, relative to those abroad, and consequently on the inducement the policies give to international capital flows and the exchange rates, which, in turn, strongly influence the total effectiveness of the policy package. In fact, the total policy stance, including domestic regulations and external commercial policies, must be considered as part of the policy package.[56] The recent approach corresponds, of course, to the "theory of economic policy" pioneered by Tinbergen (1952) and others in the 1950s, but its relevance was dramatically demonstrated by the experience of the United States in the early 1980s, when very expansive fiscal policies were matched by high relative interest rates, a strong dollar, and international-trade deficits equal in size to the fiscal deficits, with the consequence that the United States experienced an unbalanced and not very buoyant recovery from the recession of 1981–82.[57]

The strong dollar and unprecedentedly large trade deficit of the United States in 1984 and 1985, indeed, came conventionally to be explained in terms of international differences in saving and investment rates. Discussing the U.S. current-account deficits, Corden wrote:

> Thers is a budget deficit and something of an investment boom. Domestic savings are inadequate to finance both the deficit and private investment. If capital could not flow in from abroad, the interest rate would rise until private investment were sufficiently "crowded out" and savings increased sufficiently for a private sector surplus to finance the public sector borrowing requirement. But with capital mobility and a floating exchange rate, the exchange rate appreciates and a current account deficit emerges, matched by a foreign capital inflow equal to the domestic financial gap. (Corden 1985, p. 18)

In particular, the low value of the Japanese yen, with implications for the competitiveness of Japanese goods on world markets, was explained by a large excess of Japanese private saving, at world interest rates, relative to Japanese domestic investment and public-sector consumption. The placement of the excess-savings flows abroad depreciated the yen against all currencies, helped to appreciate the dollar against all currencies, and induced enormous Japanese surpluses on international current account.

While a number of observers have pointed out that the relation between U.S. government deficits and the dollar's exchange value is not invariant—in particular, they have noted that government deficits in the 1970s were associated with a weak dollar—they err in concluding that government deficits in the first half of the 1980s were not an important cause of the strong dollar and balance-of-payments problems in that period.[58] What is important is the *mix* of policies in one country relative to others and not the size of the government deficit or surplus alone. The effect of a government deficit on the balance of payments depends, among other things, on whether the deficit is due to discretionary policy changes or tax and expenditure changes induced by changes in economic activity caused by other disturbances. The effect also depends on the extent to which the deficit arises from tax reductions or expenditure increases and on the sectors of the economy to which the tax and expenditure changes are directed. Probably most important, however, is the way deficits are financed and their association with monetary policy. Prior to the 1980s, for example, the U.S. Federal Reserve authorities focused monetary policy on interest-rate stabilization, implying a matching of monetary policy to fiscal policy and central-bank financing of the deficits to prevent the deficit from raising domestic interest rates. After 1980, this policy was abandoned in favor or more attention to limiting growth in the monetary aggregates even while the fiscal deficits continued to grow. The U.S. monetary and fiscal policy mix, therefore, was significantly different in the 1980s from that of the 1970s. Furthermore, shifts in monetary policy in Europe at the end of the 1970s were similar to those in the Uinted States—that is, there was a shift of emphasis from interest rates to money supplies in the determination of monetary policy—while fiscal deficits were much better controlled in both Europe and Japan. These developments significantly changed the international *pattern* of the policy mixes. The policy changes lifted real interest rates in the United States relative to those in the other leading industrialized countries and contributed to the capital flows toward the United States during the period, the strong dollar, and the large U.S. current-account trading deficits.

Dollar appreciation on the exchange markets played a role in suppressing inflation in the United States in 1982–1984 but only by exporting U.S. inflationary forces to other countries. Jeffrey Sachs (1985) estimated that the 1984 dollar appreciation reduced the U.S. inflation rate by 1.9–2.8 percent in that year. The reverse of the experience, of course, was to come when the dollar's appreciation was reversed, and in that period the deterioration in the U.S. net-creditor position with respect to the rest of the world would necessarily exacerbate the dollar's loss of value.

An enormously important corollary of the thesis that it is the policy *mix* across countries that counts is the proposition that monetarism, either in its national-economy variant or in its global variant, provides an inadequate guide to monetary policy. Monetary policy must be designed in conjunction with fiscal and other policies and in coordination with policy mixes adopted in all countries if it is to achieve many of its possible objectives of stabilizing real output, prices, interest rates, or exchange rates. We return to this topic in the final section of the chapter.

Finally, in this discussion of macroeconomic relationships and foreign-exchange rates, a word might be said about the new "disequilibrium" economics, which considers markets as dynamic systems in which the actors are characterized by more or less uncertainty about the properties of the system and the timing and nature of disturbances. Some analysis is possible, and the continuing work promises at least a minor revolution in macroeconomic theory.[59]

Barter and Countertrade

Surprisingly, events of the 1980s stimulated, in a degree unknown since the 1930s, a return to trade without the use of money. Popularly called *countertrade*, it received new publicity when some large trading organizations, including Sears Roebuck in the United States, organized countertrading subsidiaries to ride the wave of goods available for exchange against other goods in world markets. A GATT estimate put the extent of such trade at 8 percent of world trade in the early 1980s, although some estimates put the share as high as 30 percent.[60]

In view of the fact that among the services money provides is a reduction in the transactions costs associated with barter, one must look to market imperfections for an explanation of the rise in countertrade activity. Among the imperfections that seem to have been at work are the following:

1. The presence of exchange controls and other quantitative trade restrictions in some areas made money prices inside and outside these countries different and blocked a money-mediated private opportunity for arbitrage; to mitigate the inefficiencies of the systems, governments themselves became active proponents of countertrade, using it as a means of handling particular circumstances in particular ways.
2. The efforts of members of the OPEC oil cartel to increase their respective market shares without overtly selling oil at below-cartel-agreed prices was a prime mover in the creation of some countertrade agreements.
3. Some governments found countertrade an easier means of implementing monopoly or monopsony power against individual trade partners

than other commerical-policy instruments would have been. Loss of externally provided trade credit by some countries, due to nonperformance on existing loans, drove the countries toward countertrade.

The future of countertrade is not clear. Some large and many small transactions will no doubt continue to occur; still, some firms established to do primarily a countertrade business had ceased operations by 1986. If OPEC's grip on world oil prices has ended, and if continuing adjustment to the needs of international debt servicing allows the elimination of some exchange and payments restrictions, the unusual stimulus that countertrade enjoyed in the late 1970s and early 1980s will fade.

Currency Blocs

The world of floating exchange rates coalesced in the 1970s and 1980s, as the theory of optimum currency areas suggested it would, into a number of blocs within which exchange-rate movements were more or less suppressed. The outlines of the broad blocs were sketched earlier in this section in terms of the linkages of various exchange rates to common numeraires—such as the dollar, the SDR, and the French franc. The result is that a part of world trade takes place between countries whose currency exchange rates are fixed against each other (because they are fixed to a common denominator), and another part takes place between currencies where the exchange rates are quite flexible. The author's own estimates in 1979 (Murphy 1979, p. 22) suggested that about one-seventh of world trade in 1975 moved in channels that implied fixed exchange rates, according to the exchange-rate practices of 1978, while six-sevenths moved in paths that implied exchange-rate flexibility. The G-10 Deputies, in their 1985 study of "The Functioning of the International Monetary System," put the shares at one-fourth and three-fourths, respectively.

Besides the blocs implicitly formed by the acceptance by various countries of the same standard for exchange-rate stabilization, other blocs have been formed with additional reciprocal commitments. Two of them deserve mention.

The European Monetary System (EMS) was launched on March 13, 1979, with the objectives of creating in Europe a zone of monetary stability and greater convergence of economic policies. Behind the facade of stated objectives and long-run hopes lay an immediate need to maintain the carefully negotiated agricultural price-support structure of the European Economic Community (EEC) and a widespread European desire to be hedged against "irresponsible" financial policies in the United States. A grid of central exchange rates with accompanying prescribed official-intervention levels establishes a pattern of exchange rates at which the central banks must intervene to restrain movements of the market rates. Intervention when the rates are within the margins is permissible. A composite European Currency Unit (ECU), with a value equal to a weighted average of EEC member currencies, is both the numeraire for inter-central-bank claims and the medium of 45-day settlement of excessive central-bank balances that are cleared through the European Monetary Cooperation Fund.[61] All but the newest members of the EEC are members of the EMS, and all but the United Kingdom, which does not maintain fixed exchange-rate margins against other countries' currencies at all, and Italy, which maintains margins of plus or minus 6 percent, maintain exchange-rate-intervention margins of plus or minus 2.25 percent around their bilateral parity rates.

Appraisals of the experience of the EMS vary. To some, the fact that it has survived the years since 1979 is evidence of success. To others, the fact that it had to go through its ninth realignment of the central exchange rates in 1986, that Italy still retains its wider intervention margins, that exchange controls and one dual-exchange market (Belgium) still exist, and that the United Kingdom has not chosen to join the exchange-rate grid are all evidences of failure of the arrangement to achieve its hoped-for goals. Furthermore, efforts in Europe to maintain the pattern of stabilized exchange rates in the face of divergent macroeconomic policies in the several countries have given rise to balance-of-payments and exchange-rate crises within the group that have been absent among countries where exchange rates are flexible. It is probably, but not certainly, true that there is a stronger feeling of common destiny in Europe in the 1980s, as compared to 1958 when the Common Market was born, as evidenced by a greater willingness by European individuals to sacrifice for European, as opposed to national goals. But the path to the harmonization of economic policies when national markets experience divergent economic disturbances is in any case a long one that ultimately involves achieving such a degree of resource mobility among nations that labor markets are "tight" or "loose" in most countries simultaneously. Integration of Europe's capital markets, while still impaired by some exchange restrictions and variations in market instrumentalities, has had the effect of making policy coordination among governments more necessary and in some cases easier.[62] It may now ensure the continuance of the EMS as a base from which still further policy coordination can be achieved.

A rare example of a circumstance in which governments actually pool their international monetary reserves comes from West, Equatorial, and

Central Africa. Both the West African Monetary Union and the Equatorial, and Central African Monetary Union use the Communaute Financiere Africaine franc as currency, pegged since 1948 to the French franc at CFAF 50 = FF 1. France guarantees convertibility of the CFA franc into French francs and provides overdraft facilities.

Bhatia (1985) has surveyed 24 years of experience in the West African Monetary Union (WAMU). The six countries that were members of the union, 1962–1983 (Benin, Burkina Faso, Ivory Coast, Niger, Senegal, and Togo), and a seventh (Mali) which rejoined in 1984 after having left the union in 1961, share a central bank, the Banque Central des Etats de l'Afrique de l'Ouest (BCEAO). The bank's authority over rediscount facilities, reserve requirements, and requirements that commercial banks obtain prior authorization for credit beyond a limit to any single enterprise, enable it to create a common rate of growth of the monetary base for the union, although not necessarily common rates of growth of member-countries' money supplies. Fiscal coordination among union members, nevertheless, was not strong throughout the 1970s, partly because of the opportunities that this period provided for individual member governments to finance their public deficits by borrowing outside the union. In view of the fact that the members have little trade with, and factor movements between, each other, their divergent financial policies did not create intraunion payments imbalances so much as disparate balance-of-payments imbalances with the rest of the world. In this case, IMF stabilization programs, initiated in Senegal, Ivory Coast, and Togo, became a chief factor limiting disparities in member financial policies. Probably only because France assured external currency convertibility for the group did the union survive what otherwise would have materialized as an intraunion conflict over scarce external means of payment. Consequently, the survival of that union through a turbulent period cannot be used as very credible evidence that other currency unions involving developing countries can prosper and survive stress. The external financing that France provided the BCEAO was a critical source of support to the whole scheme in this case.

International Organizations

While the role of the International Monetary Fund in the monetary system was significantly changed by events in the early 1970s and by the Second Amendment to the Fund's charter in 1978, it was changed even more by the rapid expansion of international bank lending in the late 1970s and the subsequent crisis of international indebtedness. The revision of the Fund's charter took from it its role of financing temporary payments imbalances in order to defend a pattern of fixed-parity exchange rates and gave it instead a wider but less explicit assignment to exercise surveillance over "the exchange-rate policies of member countries" and "the international monetary system." The evolution of the international capital markets, discussed above, took from the Fund its role as a significant provider of the means of international settlement and then thrust it into the center of negotiations between debtors and creditors in order to save the monetary system. The future of the Fund becomes an interesting subject for conjecture.

The Fund's Role in Surveillance

The Fund's obligations to exercise surveillance have for the time being settled into two ongoing exercises—the regular Article IV mandated discussions with individual member countries concerning their economic policies and the preparation and discussion of the *World Economic Outlook* studies. The narrower Article IV discussions increasingly became in the 1970s not simply reviews of "the use a member had made of reserves or . . . its policies of intervention in exchange markets or even only . . . its domestic monetary and other macroeconomic policies" but reviews of a member's "entire economic situation" (de Vries 1985, p. 840) Work on the *World Economic Outlook* constituted the effort to assemble information relevant to surveillance of the entire international monetary system.

The Fund is, of course, not the only forum for discussion of international policy coordination. Bilateral contacts and the entire range of international organizations (including especially the OECD, the GATT, the BIS, the IBRD, the EEC, UNCTAD, and the various ministerial groups G-5, G-10, and G-24) are also important. But the Fund, in its amended charter, is given special responsibility.

One major problem with surveillance is not surveillance itself but sanction. In the original vision of the Fund, its sanction on errant members was its ability to deny those members access to the Fund's resources. With the decline in the significance of those resources to many countries, the Fund's persuasive power has similarly declined. Countries dependent on the Fund for its seal of approval of their creditworthiness, including most countries involved in debt restructuring and countries that have never gained access to the private-capital markets, complain of the severity of the conditions the Fund places on their policy choices but cannot disregard it. Countries whose access to bank- and securities-market funding is clear, however, listen politely to Fund counsel and then do as they please. Continuing developments in the capital markets and resolution of the 1980s overhang of international debt will exacerbate the weakness of Fund sanctions.

The Deputies of the Group of 10, in their 1985 report, offer some suggestions. These include a "confidential exchange of views" between the Managing Director of the Fund and the Finance Minister of the country involved at the close of each regular Article IV consultation, a follow-up report to be submitted by the member country indicating measures introduced or considered to deal with the problems identified by the IMF, and the release of Article IV consultation documents at the request of the member country. Acknowledging that breach of the confidentiality of the information exchanged and the discussions would probably create more problems that it would solve, the Deputies did not reject the idea of a public statement by the Managing Director, on his own authority and without involving the Fund's Executive Directors, at the end of the consultation process.

In its communique of April 10, 1986, paragraph 6, the Interim Committee of the IMF called on the Fund's Executive Board "to consider ways in which its regular reviews of the world economic situation could be further adapted to improve the scope for discussing external imbalances, exchange rate developments and policy interactions among members." It also said "an approach worth exploring further was the formulation of a set of objective indicators."

Satisfactory coordination of the economic policies of the countries that have a large impact on the world economy will not come until the electorates of those countries recognize both the extent and some of the forms of international interdependence. Only then will politicians' constituents demand policies that take account of the international economic environment. The challenge to economic education, always great, has moved into the spotlight.

The Fund and Debt Negotiations

There was no provision in the IMF's charter for the role it assumed in the early 1980s of "honest broker" between sovereign debtors and their international banks. The role materialized because there was no other actor on the stage to play it and because the Fund's Managing Director and staff saw the need and stepped forward. The Fund itself was, of course, a major creditor of the countries whose debts came into difficulties, and its ongoing discussions with them about their balance-of-payments problems put it in the right place at the right time. Still, its staff was keenly aware that the Fund had no provisions for providing instantaneous liquidity to either borrowers or lenders, should a market liquidity crisis occur, and it had no guidelines for lending for the direct or indirect maintenance of debt service. The Managing Director, in conjunction with heads of leading central banks and finance ministries, had to proceed in uncharted territory.

The outcome of the Fund's efforts had not been decided in early 1986 when possibilities for collapse of debt talks and outright default could still not be ruled out. Still, by 1986, half a decade of time had been gained, economic recovery from the 1980–81 recession was well under way in the United States and was accelerating in Europe and Japan, a large proportion of the short-term debt had been restructured into longer maturities, market interest rates were plunging, banks had strengthened their capital positions, and the mood of crisis had abated. Oil-importing indebted countries were getting balance-of-payments support as oil prices collapsed, even as the oil exporters, such as Mexico and Venezuela, were staring at rapidly deteriorating international terms of trade. Some countries, such as Argentina, had made considerable progress toward circumstances in which contractual debt service could be resumed; others, such as Brazil and Peru, were unable to act decisively and teetered on the brink of international insolvency.

The Managing Director of the Fund had publicly, as well as privately, put great pressure on the banks to sustain their flow of loans to their problem-loan countries even as he equally pressured governments of the borrowing nations to institute adjustment policies appropriate to the new international economic circumstances. In both cases his leverage on the situation was (a) the funding the IMF could provide and (b) his indispensibility as honest broker if catastrophe were to be avoided.

A problem bedevilling the negotiations from the beginning was paucity of information. The extent of debt, the terms of debt-service obligations, and the implications of those obligations for policy management had not been recorded and analyzed in the haste of borrowing to meet financial needs in the later 1970s. An early task was the accumulation and organization of information, and some debtors and creditors were less than enthusiastic cooperators in the task when they thought that revelation would impair their own respective bargaining positions. Only slowly have the IMF, the World Bank, the BIS, the intergovernmental Development Advisory Committee, central banks, and others systematized the compilation and updating of the relevant information.

It must be assumed that debt management will continue to be a part of the subject matter of Fund Article IV consultations with members and of its analysis of the problems and performance of the monetary system. More controversial are questions relating to the part the Fund and Bank should play in providing information and country-credit appraisals for the capital markets of the future. There are those who see the Fund assuming a credit-rating-agency task for other lenders on global markets. Such a role is assymetrical among countries, however, serving more the needs of lender than borrower countries, and would not augur well for the Fund's future as an even-handed agency of world government. The Fund has, however, agreed to engage in "enhanced surveillance" of members, in selected circumstances, permitting a member to release to creditors the Fund's appraisal of the member's progress toward macroeconomic goals in connection with a multiyear refunding agreement. Furthermore, the credit-rating function can be executed by private agencies, using published and other information, and, indeed was appearing in the form of economic- and political-risk analyses purchasable by subscription in the late 1970s.

Fund Financing

Use of the Fund's resources more than quadrupled, 1980–1985, from $8 billion to $35 billion, as the Fund stepped into the gap left by the pullback of banks from international lending and as many countries dependent on the export of primary products experienced balance-of-payments problems. Much of the activity after 1981 was made possible by "enlarged access" drawings which permitted countries to draw on the Fund to the extent of multiples of their quotas, unrestricted by normal drawing-right ceilings. To fund itself, the IMF used its privilege of borrowing, but limited such borrowing to arrangements with members, their central banks, and other official institutions. During its financial year 1984–85, the Fund borrowed 34.2 percent of the funds that it, in turn, sold to members that were utilizing drawing rights. Its debt and unused lines of credit at that time amounted to 37 percent of the total of member quotas in the Fund.

The Fund's "gearing ratio," the ratio of its total assets to its subscriptions, in 1986 did not exceed a range of 1.5 to 1.6, as a result of agreements with member countries concerning Fund borrowings, but even this made the Fund a quite different institution than had been envisaged at its outset when it was expected to make available to members only its own funds.

Should the Fund become a financial intermediary between public and private savers (and central banks as base-money creators), on the one hand, and sovereign borrowers who meet Fund conditionality requirements, on the other? While the Fund since its beginning has had the authority to borrow, the G-10 Committee of Deputies rejected any regular intermediary role for the Fund in its report, calling on a return to normal-access policies for its members as soon as possible and recourse by the Fund to borrowing to supplement its own resources "only in exceptional circumstances."

The counsel seems wise. There can be little doubt now of the private-markets' ability to provide ample intermediation when circumstances are propitious for it, and permanent assumption of a role in that drama by the Fund would expose it to the same solvency and liquidity hazards that from time to time jeopardize the private intermediaries. While, if the Fund's own subscribed capital is not adequately expanded, there may be occasions when borrowing from the private sector is appropriate in order to avoid over-rapid swings in the availability of balance-of-payments financing, IMF recourse to this process should generally be limited and infrequent.

Has, then, the Fund any future as a financing organization at all? Does the Fund need any funds? Experience of the early 1980s did show that there is a useful role for the IMF to play in compensating for sudden shifts in international capital flows. Furthermore, in such cases the Fund's authority to impose conditionality on the users of its resources is still of great importance. While the Fund's role as a compensator for sudden changes in the flows of capital between countries will no doubt continue to include a role as a reopener of doors for members to private sources of financing, the Fund's ability to open such doors may often depend on its own ability to assume a part of the financing, and, consequently, part of the risk, in any arrangement. Furthermore, there are the countries, many of which are near the bottom of the world's per-capita income scale, that do not yet have creditworthiness in the world's capital markets but do, from time to time, require temporary balance-of-payments financing. There is, then, still some role for the Fund to play that is close to the original vision of its work.

It is worth noting, however, that the recognition of a role for the Fund in stabilizing international capital flows implies that the role should operate both in times when there is a paucity of such financing and in times when the financing is excessively abundant. The Fund's eagerness to help finance petroleum-related balance-of-payments deficits in the 1970s probably added to the inflationary forces of that period and the prolongation of the power of the oil-exporters' cartel.[63] That error should not be repeated.

Terms of Conditionality

Countries in external-payments difficulties have inevitably complained of excessive harshness in the conditions IMF teams have demanded of applicants' policy choices in return for approval of their IMF drawings. Since most Fund drawings in the early 1980s were made by less-developed countries, it was easy for the developing countries as a group to contend that the Fund was making demands on them it did not make on the more-developed Fund members and that it was not evenhanded in its relationships. In making that contention, however, they confused the IMF's Article IV consultations and surveillance responsibilities with the Fund's conditionality terms in connection with its provision of resources.[64]

Among questions that deal with the design of appropriate conditions on members' drawings on the Fund are these: (a) should the performance criteria applied go beyond performance specifications in terms of the broad macroeconomic variables such as government deficits, money-supply growth, inflation rates, and balances of payments, and into microeconomic variables such as factor prices, selected industry performances, and the like; and (b) should the criteria invade questions of just how—by what specific policy measures—the performance requirements are to be achieved?[65] In view of increasing awareness that growth, political stability, and the balance of payments are not simply matters of managing effective aggregate demand and that, without specification of means, governments may sacrifice longer-run goals to political expediency and short-run need, some Fund critics seek to make a case for extension of conditionality in both of these directions. Doing so, however, would put the IMF staff in the impossible position of assuming infallibility and of making political decisions without political responsibility. While there is every reason for candor by the staff in its various dealings with member countries, ensuring that all policy options are considered and openly appraised, there is nothing to be said for making of the IMF a national and international planning agency.

The Fund and the International Development Banks

The events of the 1970s and 1980s went far toward dissolving the traditional division of labor between the IMF and the World Bank. In original concept, of course, the Bank was expected to be an intermediary that provided developing countries access to the world's long-term capital markets on favorable terms, Its capital and guarantees, provided by member countries, constituted a security for its borrowings that made it a "prime" borrower. Its low interest costs as a borrower were passed on to developing countries whose credit was less impeccable. Its loans were project oriented. The IMF, on the other hand, provided its members temporary financing for short-term balance-of-payments needs. Its mission was to bridge transitory international-payments imbalances that arose in the fixed-exchange-rate regime, enabling countries to carry the imbalances while undertaking adjustment measures consistent with high levels of employment and liberal trade and payments policies. The Fund's resources consisted of member-country subscriptions.

But to countries seeking financial assistance, money was money, and the World Bank was pressured toward the provision of program financing, which included the indirect balance-of-payments consequences of domestic development programs, while the IMF was pressured toward extended-term financing and, especially in the 1980s, commitments to support countries' creditworthiness for project loans.

Do grounds exist for a continued sharp distinction between the missions of the IMF and the IBRD (World Bank) and regional-development banks? In an earlier study, (Murphy 1979, ch.7), this author argued that the distinction is important because balance-of-payments financing should be kept limited while developmental financing for the world's poorer countries deserves to be accelerated. Too-easy access to balance-of-payments financing encourages governments to postpone the correction of policies that are not sustainable, and, in a worldwide environment of incipient inflation, it allows countries engaging in inflationary financial policies to export the deleterious effects of their policies to others. Early exchange-rate adjustments, on the other hand, when errant policymakers do not make recourse to other changes, help to contain the consequences of inflationary policies to the areas where they have originated and where political pressures can build for a change of policy.

In the meanwhile, developmental capital should be directed to projects that stand the scrutiny of economic analysis, and should proceed at a pace that is as much as possible independent of the short-run state of the borrowing country's balance of payments.

While American opinion has not been kind to the World Bank for its reluctance to rush into the balance-of-payments problems of heavily indebted countries, the Bank's inaction was fundamentally correct. The World Bank, and similarly the regional-development banks, did not have clear charter authority to lend for balance-of-payments needs not related to approved development programs, and their own borrowing ability on world credit markets could well have been impaired had they undertaken such lending on a significant scale. The immediate debt issues were partly political and partly related to the functioning of the international monetary system. Clearly, a pause in growth programs in the excessively indebted countries was necessary. While the Bank properly had concern for its own investments and for the long-run prospects for growth in its members' countries, it could be patient for the transition adjustments to be made. Other avenues for resolving the debt crisis were always at hand; what was difficult was sorting out who would absorb the losses of loans made on poor projections.

The American proposals at the Fund/Bank annual meetings in 1985, which called on the developmental banks to provide $20 billion in new financing over three years, did not breach the World Bank's responsibilities. The new funding called for, while conditional upon adjustment policies being undertaken in the borrowing areas, will presumably be based upon traditional Bank lending criteria. The intent is for the international organizations to step into the gap in essentially developmental finance that has been vacated as a result of the world's commerical-bank pullback. It is appropriate that the roles of the several actors in the capital markets—that were confused in the recent past—now again be carefully considered.

The Fund as Incipient Global Central Bank

Those who see the salvation of the world in a nuclear age as depending on not-too-gradual abandonment of aspects of national sovereignty and on the emergence of supranational institutions of government have typically mentioned the IMF as the seed from which a global central bank can grow. Especially at the time of the IMF charter's First Amendment—when the Fund was given precedent-breaking authority to allocate SDRs, a non-national "money"—this idea that the IMF would one day function as the supranational manager of an SDR that was usable as money worldwide achieved considerable popularity.[66]

One must hope that the dream is not dead, although one's vision of the evolutionary path through which the goal is attained must necessarily be revised from time to time. Inflationary finance in national currencies—dollars, sterling, French francs, and the rest—have reaffirmed for now Gresham's law that "bad money drives out good." Use of the SDR for private-sector financial intermediation has not gotten off the ground, and even use of the SDR as a private-sector unit of account has waned. No allocation of SDRs was made between 1981 and 1986, because the desire to contain inflationary forces precluded the creation of any additional liquidity from an international organization.

IMF resources, as a share of world trade, and as a share of the total of international reserve media, are smaller than they were a decade ago, when they were smaller than the decade before that.

Where is the path now toward a larger role for the Fund? IMF contacts with the private-banking sector have been greatly expanded as a result of the debt-restructuring negotiations, and, in the debt crisis, the IMF has been able to serve where the leading central banks could not. Can something useful be built on these foundations? Some bankers have suggested that the Fund could improve its record of stabilizing the flow of balance-of-payments financing to heavily indebted countries in the 1980s by borrowing from the commerical banks, securing the borrowings with marketable securities, and then onlending the funds to the debtor countries during the period when prudence for many banks requires them to slow their international lending.[67] While a significant role for the Fund as such a financial intermediary has been rejected above, a limited role to supplement the intermediation normally provided by the banks might be acceptale.

Under its responsibilities for surveillance of the exchange-rate policies of members, the Fund might undertake, and be given by member governments, a stronger voice in decisions concerning when and how exchange-market interventions take place, granting such interventions should be limited.

Expansion of private use of the SDR, while in short-term decline, is certainly not dead. The supply of bank intermediation of SDR deposits, of course, waits on demand for that service, but a world of flexible exchange rates is a conducive environment for private SDR use. One cannot help but wonder what would have happened if oil-exporting nations in the 1970s had taken the decision—often considered—to price oil in SDR terms. They might then have sought to bank and otherwise invest their earnings in SDR terms. Borrowers would have required SDR loans, and the banks would have recycled SDRs. The reputation of the SDR as a medium of exchange and store of value would, by now, have been very different had those things transpired. Some time in the future, such a major step forward for the SDR will probably occur.

Most important to the future of the Fund is the task of influencing member governments to take into account the international implications of the policies that the governments adopt to satisfy domestic political needs. This is the bastion of national sovereignty that, in the end, must be assailed. Fortunately, time and events now work on the Fund's side in this matter, as increasing interdependence in all nations makes neglect of the international side of policy results more and more hazardous to the neglectors. Without alienating the governments on whom its own support depends, the Fund must seek every possible means of reaching a wide public with its analyses of world economic developments and the way national policies are interacting. If its analyses are wise, it will in due time attract its own constituency.

International Liquidity, SDRs and Reserve Currencies

Between the introduction of generalized floating of exchange rates in 1973 and the end of 1985, total international-monetary-reserve holdings of members of the International Monetary Fund grew by 2.8 times, from SDR 154 billion to SDR 431 billion, a bit faster than the growth during the preceding twelve-year period, which was 2.5 times. In both cases, of course, the largest component of the growth in absolute terms was foreign exchange (which grew from SDR 103 billion to SDR 341 billion, 1973–1985), although members' reserve positions in the Fund were a larger relative part of the growth in the later than in the earlier period. Total member holdings of SDRs grew from SDR 8.7 billion in 1973 to SDR 18.2 billion in 1985, and physical stocks of monetary gold were essentially unchanged.

It is acknowledged, however, that official holdings of monetary reserves no longer represent the constraint on countries' foreign-exchange policies it once was thought to be, because of the continuing opportunity that at least the more-advanced countries have to tap the international capital markets. Indeed, the reserve balances of countries are now, more than ever, endogenous, rather than exogenous, variables in the world economic system, determined by the demand and market supply conditions characterizing each government's choices. In fact, reserve balances have grown roughly in proportion to international trade, remaining within 20 to 50 percent of total trade throughout the period 1974–1984.

The currency composition of the foreign-exchange component of reserves has also shown less instability than some observers feared it would. The share of such reserves held in U.S.-dollar-denominated assets drifted downward, 1977–1984—from 78.0 percent to 65.1 percent—as holdings in sterling, deutschmarks, and yen crept upward—from a total of 13.3 percent to 20.1 percent of the total—and holdings in unspecified currencies increased from 4.4 to 11.0 percent.[68] The increased holdings of unspecified currencies was entirely reflected in the holdings of developing countries.

What is clear is that the currencies of choice in official holdings trended away from the dollar over the period, but they did not change drastically from year to year. The mean *annual* change in quantity of dollar holdings (excluding changes due to variations in the SDR valuation of the dollar) was SDR 7.1 billion, 1979–1984, and no doubt represented largely official interventions in the exchange markets toward supporting the value of currencies other than the strong dollar.[69] These shifts could have had no more than a very small long-run influence on exchange rates, since the annual average changes are tiny in relation to the SDR 20—30 trillion of total *annual* foreign-exchange-market transactions. It seems likely that each government's choice in the matter of reserve composition was dictated more by its choice of an exchange-rate peg, if any, and a corresponding currency for exchange-market intervention than by expected returns (through interest or exchange-rate adjustment) on the reserve holdings. The fear of some observers that there would be significant amounts of currency substitution by official-reserve holders, aggravating instability of the foreign-exchange rates, did not materialize.

The share of international reserves in the form of SDRs declined from 5.7 percent in 1973 to 4.2 percent in 1985, in spite of the SDR 12.1-billion allocation in the 1978–1981 base period for such allocations. The experience is counter to the intent stated in Article VIII, Section 7, and Article XXII of the amended IMF charter that the SDR is to become the principal reserve asset in the international monetary system. No doubt, the statement of intent in the character is largely a vestige of earlier discussions in which a different monetary system was envisaged than that which actually developed.[70] Still, the statement of intent has been an encouragement to those who earnestly desire to promote the SDR's use.

In present circumstances, the growth in importance of the SDR does not seem to lie in its increased use as a component of official reserves but rather in its increased use as a private means of payment, unit of account, and store of value. As suggested above, there is reason to hope that such increased use may develop as the value of international transactions continues to grow in an environment of changing values for national currencies.

While the SDR is described in IMF documents as a "supplemental reserve asset," it was viewed at one time also as a possible means of constraining total reserve growth and hence as a possible instrument for managing global money supplies. The IMF's Managing Director once proposed for consideration a scheme to require members' reserves to be held, say, 25 percent in SDRs. Limiting SDR allocations could then limit reserve creation and presumably, in the context of fixed exchange rates, limit worldwide monetary expansion and inflation.[71] In such a scheme now, one would want to be clear that the SDR component of reserves would have to be held in the IMF, since it is desirable that private SDR's come into use for nongovernment holders through banking claims denominated in SDRs, and one does not want to foreclose IMF SDR dealings with the private markets. The scheme would still be workable if the world, through stable and well-designed national macroeconomic policies, approached a degree of exchange-rate stability that made an official fixing of the rates again desirable. Analysis reveals, however, that the mandate for a minimum SDR share in reserves would have to be applied to *net* reserve holdings of countries, rather than *gross* holdings, if the mandate were to constitute the desired constraint on the monetary policies of members.[72] One must also take note of the fact that national monetary changes have not in the past been closely tied to national reserve holdings.[73]

Meanwhile, with highly developed capital markets increasingly available to governments throughout the world and with economic nationalism showing little signs of waning, the time for the SDR to assume a role as "principal reserve asset in the international monetary system" awaits an uncertain future.

Further Visions of the International Monetary System

Stabilizing World Money Supply

Ronald McKinnon (1982, 1984) has attributed much of the instability in the foreign-exchange markets and in the real performance of national economies in the 1970s and 1980s to the problem of private-sector currency substitution in connection with nationally independent monetary rules. This leads him to advocate international monetary cooperation to achieve steady growth in the *world* money supply rather than in the money supplies of individual nations.

According to McKinnon, the monetarist rule of steady money growth for an individual nation depends on stable demand for money in that nation—a condition that was more often met before the 1970s than after. Integration of the money markets of the world has made the assumption of stable demand for national moneys obsolete, since people have in recent years shifted their assets among currencies in response to small disturbances or expected disturbances. McKinnon feels that stabilizing the supplies (or growth) of national moneys has created excess demands or excess supplies of those currencies as demand for the currencies rose or fell due to currency substitution, and that national monetary policies have consequently exacerbated variations in spending on real goods and services and on foreign exchange. McKinnon proposes to stabilize a world measure of the money stock; he supports fixed exchange rates with nonsterilized intervention to maintain those rates. Under these rules, a shift of demand away from a currency would give rise to an appropriate decline in supply of that currency, and a shift of demand toward a currency would give rise to an appropriate increase in supply.

McKinnon's rule does not provide hope for a well-ordered world monetary system. Franco Spinelli (1983) has summarized the arguments against the McKinnon proposal by denying each of what he asserts are key assumptions. The assumptions are: (a) monetary interdependence is caused *mainly* by currency substitution, (b) the world demand for money is stable, and (c) world money is all that matters. Spinelli cites data indicating that the world demand for money is not stable. But more important is his awareness that monetary disequilibrium is often but a reflection of real disturbances and his acceptance of the doctrine that money is not all that matters. In fact, divergent fiscal policies and changing regulatory policies among nations also have an impact on real sectors, financial sectors, and international balances of payments and exchange rates. What is required in terms of international policy coordination is more than a coordination of monetary targets: what is required is coordination of whole policy mixes, especially with regard to the implications for international capital flows.

With flexible exchange rates, governments can follow overall financial policies that are expansive or contractive to domestic aggregate spending without inducing international capital flows if their policies are balanced. What is essential is that changes in debt-financed government spending, say, and changes in the domestic money supply are parallel and that they keep domestic real interest rates in line with those abroad. In the absence of policy-induced capital flows, exchange rates can vary so as to keep international balances of payments on current account in line with private-sector-induced international capital flows. Adherence by governments to this policy guideline would at least reduce the disturbances that public policy imposes on the financial markets, and the system of relative prices would be freed to accommodate disturbances arising in the private sectors of national economies.

Separating the Unit of Account from the Medium of Exchange

Some work going to the foundations of monetary theory has appeared in recent years suggesting that, especially in an age in which electronic accounting makes physical money all but unnecessary, there is no reason to continue the linkage between units of a medium of exchange and the standard unit in which value is measured. While Greenfield and Yeager (1983) and Yeager (1985) credit Fischer Black, Eugene Fama, and Robert Hall for pioneering ideas on the matter and, indeed, refer to the reform proposal as the BFH system to recall the initials of the pioneers, the clearest statements of a specific proposal appear in the referenced Greenfield and Yeager and Yeager papers. The proposal concerns radical reform of a national monetary system to achieve price-level stability in conjunction with total financial-market deregulation. So far, the international dimensions of the proposal do not seem to have been explored.

The essence of the BFH system is for the government to provide a legal definition of a unit of value (say, a "dollar") in terms of an extensive collection of goods, and possibly services, significant to a typical person's cost of living. The government then leaves all further financial arrangements to private contracting. The expectation is that institutions will arise to offer a variety of financial services, including perhaps the issue of notes, but especially including claims by the public on a variety of securities, or income and capital gain from those securities, much as mutual funds and money-market deposit accounts offer now. Some of these claims will be transferable, and the financial institutions will provide collection and clearing services. Equality between a dollar accounting claim and a legally defined dollar will be assured by "indirect redeemability" of the accounting claim into the bundle of goods defining the dollar. Indirect redeemability will not involve storage of the commodities constituting the bundle or even anyone's taking possession of them; it suffices for redeemability if the accounting unit is redeemed in terms of any member of the bundle (for example, an easily exchangeable commodity such as gold) in the amount required to purchase one unit of the bundle on the specified day. Arbitrage between that commodity and the other components of the bundle would then keep the units of account at parity with the whole of the bundle comprising the value unit. Competition among institutions for the deposit of claims would presumably lead to the redeemability pledge. Financial institutions would effect settlement among themselves in a unit such as that used for indirect redemption, further ensuring the parity of the accounting claims with the legally defined unit of value.

The advantages that might be expected from such a radical reform would include stability through time of the purchasing power of a unit of account and continuous market matchings of the demand for means of payment with the supply. Monetary disturbances to the real economy would therefore be avoided.[74]

Having in mind the linkages of any nation's economy with the rest of the world's economy, how would such a radical reform as the BFH system be expected to function in an international setting?

If one assumes perfect substitutability of foreign for domestic goods and foreign for domestic securities (with labor immobile between countries), and if the value standards in one country, say the United Kingdom, and in another, say the United States, consisted of the same bundle of goods, then the regime is one of fixed exchange rates between the pound and the dollar, because the value units represent identical goods bundles in integrated markets. If, on the other hand, substitutability of goods and claims across countries is "high but imperfect," or the value standards significantly differ in content, then the pound standard in such a system will vary in value against the dollar standard, the variance depending on the degrees of imperfection and difference in value-unit definition.

In the case incorporating imperfections and differences, an increase in, say, U.S. preference for claims vs. goods would cause U.S. residents to reduce purchase of U.K. as well as U.S. goods and to increase buying of U.K. as well as U.S. claims. The value of the U.K. unit of account would rise in the degree that the U.K. and U.S. claims were closer substitutes than were U.K. and U.S. goods. An increase in U.S. preference for *goods* relative to claims, of course, would lead to pound appreciation in the degree that goods were internationally better substitutes than claims.

Unemployment would not be eliminated in the system if factor prices were rigid and labor were immobile across industries, for relative-price adjustments would still be required. Still, the Keynesian problem of "mass unemployment" would be avoided.

Government monetary policies would, of course, be eliminated as sources of national and international disturbance, because governments would not offer money supplies. Fiscal policies would also be less disturbing simply because governments, without the power to print money, would have to balance their budgets over time. The Ricardian equivalence theorem would at last come into its own.

In all, it is clear that government policies would be greatly reduced as sources of disturbance. Private sectors, too, should be more stable against macroeconomic disturbances, because flights from goods to financial claims and vice versa would not change the national value of any national accounting unit, and such changes could therefore not induce the expectational changes that typically induce velocity-of-turnover changes of the accounting money units.

The proposal deserves further exploration in both its national and international contexts.

Progress Through Formation of Blocs

Robert Triffin, among others, has become associated with the idea that progress toward greater international financial stability and more global integration is best to be secured through the formation of currency and trading blocs such as the EMS and the EEC.[75] The issue, in its financial dimensions, is analogous to that in the trade dimension, where the historical dynamics of preferential-trading blocs vs. GATT-type multilateralism have long been debated.

In fact, in both the trade and the monetary fields, the contributions of the regional approach remain undecided. In monetary terms, to the extent that dominant currencies in different blocs become better substitutes for each other by virtue of being more nearly equal in economic importance, the formation of blocs could exacerbate the currency-substitution problem and become a source of monetary instability. On the other hand, to the extent that monetary federations among countries reduce the scope for divergent government policies within the groups, the federations may also reduce variations in government policies between the groups.

If preferential-trade liberalization accompanies financial-market integration within blocs, there will be the gains in productivity from trade creation and losses from trade diversion that is predicted by customs-union theory. In the degree that greater exchange-rate stability within the group as compared with the outside world fosters intragroup trade (through the social subsidy to risk-bearing that exchange stabilization provides to international traders and investors), group-wide exchange-rate pegging will have positive and negative effects of the same sort as any preferential-trading arrangement.

Proponents of currency unions have argued that a union can spare some social investment by the group in foreign-exchange reserves in the degree that the covariation of balance-of-payments deficits and surpluses of members of the group with the rest of the world is negative. While this is true, the proposition biases against the formation of currency groupings on a geographically regional basis, since countries in a given geographical region tend to be exporters and importers of similar goods to the outside world and consequently tend to experience positive covariation in their balances of payments.

The route to world market integration through initial integration into blocs, therefore, has both pluses and minuses. One cannot deny, however, that politically it may be the easier course to follow.

Additional Implications of International Capital Mobility

We are witnessing an era in which money and capital markets are being more efficiently organized on a global scale while national labor markets become perhaps even more tightly closed. Economic nationalism is strong.

It must be acknowledged that, in such a world, capital flows will be attracted to areas where government is successful in stimulating economic growth, providing protection to property, and maintaining the value of the currency. Capital flows and successful policies will be self-reinforcing. Countries that succeed on all counts will succeed magnificently. Countries that fail will fail miserably. It must be expected, therefore, that increased international capital mobility will aggravate differences between countries' performances. The distinction, however, need not be one between rich countries and poor. The Koreas, Hong-Kongs, and Taiwans will succeed, while the Indias and Pakistans fail unless there is a change in the approaches that these countries take to their growth goals.

There will be pressures for governments to be less concerned about internal equity goals and more concerned about growth and efficiency goals. Success toward the latter goals, of course, can make success toward the former less important if the fruits of growth are well distributed.

Change in the international monetary system in the remainder of the twentieth century will both reflect and contribute to change in world society.

Notes

1. IMF, *International Financial Statistics*, Yearbook, 1985, p. 87. Indexes of money plus equasi-money based on 1980.

2. While the "Ricardo Equivalence Theorem" espoused by some economists denies that central-government deficits create any net increase in the private-sector's perception of its wealth (see, e.g., Barro 1981, pp. 227–242), the argument that government borrowing in one period implies a perceived tax liability for future periods is unacceptable. At the very least, public debt created today can be retired by money creation, rather than taxes, tomorrow; and, in view of experience, market participants must regard this as a strong possibility. For two of many critical discussions of the "Ricardo equivalence" position, see Haberler (1985, pp. 125–127) and Cox (1985).

3. IMF, *Government Finance Statistics*, Yearbook, 1984, p. 64.

4. IMF, *World Economic Outlook*, April 1985, Table 48, p. 266.

5. Real rates quoted here are from *IMF Annual Report, 1985*, p. 4.

6. The U.S. rate fell from 13.0 percent in 1976 to 6.0 in 1980; in Germany the decline was from 10.6 to 3.5; and in Japan the decline was 15.2 to 7.9 percent—IMF, *International Financial Statistics*, Yearbook, 1985, p. 85.

7. Growth rates for central-government expenditures and central-government debt are calculated from data in country tables, IMF. *International Financial Statistics*, Yearbook, 1985. Germany's expenditures are "expenditures plus lending minus repayments." Japan's debt is yen-dominated debt.

8. The countries are the United States, Canada, Japan, France, Federal Republic of Germany, Italy, and the United Kingdom. Data are from IMF, *World Economic Outlook*, April 1985, Appendix Table 15, p. 220. While most writers assess the significance of government budget deficits across countries and through time by scaling the deficits to GNP size, this practice can be seriously misleading. In particular, it can be used to suggest that a deficit that does not grow as a share of GNP is not a source of disturbance, whereas in fact the

deficit may be a significant casual factor in driving the GNP change. This error has no doubt supported inflationary fiscal policies from time to time.

9. OECD, *Economic Outlook*, June 1985, Table R3, p. 158.

10. *Economic Report of the President*, 1986, p. 51.

11. The yield on U.S. Treasury long-term bonds in April 1985, for example, was 11.69 percent as compared to a 3–month bill rate of 8.00 percent.

12. U.S. oil import costs were off from $80 billion in 1982 to approximately $50 billion in 1985.

13. Growth data are from IMF, *World Economic Outlook*, April 1985 and October 1985.

14. The distribution of world reserve holdings into currencies of denomination are reported annually in IMF *Annual Reports*. Data in the text are from the *Annual Report, 1985*.

15. The term "market borrower" is that of the IMF, which distinguishes the countries that had access to large-scale borrowing in the private capital markets during the 1970s from those that had access only to borrowing from governmental and intergovernmental agencies. The former group included 34 developing countries. For a listing, see IMF, *Annual Report, 1985*, Appendix IX, pp. 179–183.

16. IMF, *Annual Report, 1985*, p. 60.

17. While there was very little net new lending by U.S. banks to developing countries in 1983–1984 and with deduction of "nonspontaneous" lending to Brazil, Mexico, and other Latin American countries, there was an absolute decline, the estimates based on outstanding claims underestimate the lending. Loan charge-offs, sales of claims to nonbank investors, the exercise of official guarantees, and the translation effects of exchange-rate changes hide some $3.5 billion of net new lending from the outstanding-claims totals. See Terrell and Mills (1985).

18. For elaboration of this and subsequent discussion in the paragraph, see Murphy (1979, ch. 7).

19. The seven countries were Argentina, Brazil, Indonesia, Korea, Mexico, Philippines, and Venezuela. Korea's successful adjustment and reduction of its debt-to-export ratio is chronicled in Aghevli and Marquez-Ruarte (1985).

20. Data on the 1985 debt are from IMF, *World Economic Outlook*, April 1985, Appendix Tables 45 and 46, pp. 262–263.

21. *Wall Street Journal*, January 3, 1986, p. 17.

22. *Wall Street Journal*, December 23, 1985, p. 19.

23. Guttentag and Herring (1985) discuss the interbank-funding risk. Some of their earlier work on international bank interdependency is reported in Guttentag and Herring (1983).

24. World Bank, *Coping With External Debt in the 1980s* (Washington: 1985), p. xxi.

25. *Wall Street Journal*, December 10, 1985, p. 64.

26. See Murphy (1979, ch. 7).

27. In October 1985, Peru joined Poland, Sudan, Zaire, Nicaragua, and Bolivia as a country whose debt had to be "reserved" by U.S. banks under order of the U.S. Inter-agency Country Exposure Review Committee. The regulatory body is made up of representatives of the Board of Governors of the Federal Reserve System, the Comptroller of the Currency, and the Federal Deposit Insurance Corporation. Peru, whose international debt totaled $14 billion ($2.5 billion to U.S. banks), was, as consequence, further deprived of trade credit. *Wall Street Journal*, October 29, 1985, p. 33.

28. Since some debtor countries tied the exchange value of their currencies to that of the dollar, they consequently saw no gain on the former account.

29. Dornbusch (1985) has pointed out that developing-country exports stimulated by an

expensive dollar helped debt financing but were not necessarily helpful to developing-countries' welfare since the net exports were themselves valuable.

30. The general approach follows that of Cline (1983, 1985) in focusing on the ratio of debt to developing-country exports as an indicator of debt serviceability. Concentrating on welfare losses of debt service, Dornbusch (1985) was less sanguine that the debt problems were headed for resolution and less certain that they should be solved by attempts to get full restitution of loans.

31. In one study, Kirmani, Molajoni, and Mayer (1984) estimated that complete liberalization of trade by the United States, the EEC, Japan, and Canada would increase the real annual exports of ten major developing-country exporters by approximately 9 percent while increasing the import-penetration ratio by the developing countries in the industrialized-country markets by only 2 percent.

32. This list parallels that of Morse (1985).

33. A number of other fruitful suggestions concerning vehicles for longer-term capital transfers to developing countries are made in Lenard and Williamson (1985) and *Report of the Technical Committee of the Global Economic Action Institute* (1985).

34. Admittedly, if the foreign borrowing were continued unabated for a decade, these ratios would rapidly change.

35. See Morse (1981).

36. See Goodhart (1984).

37. For discussion of changes in the Japanese markets, see Germany and Morton (1985), Sakakibara (1984), McRae (1985), and Yoshitomi (1985).

38. See Patrick (1984).

39. IMF, *International Financial Statistics*, March 1986, p. 18.

40. De Grauwe, Janssens, and Leliaert (1985), however, have recently shown that the monthly movements of exchange rates of 1973–82 were less turbulent, while subject to wider swings, than the exchange rates of the first half of the 1920s. Willett (1985) has argued that while the volatility of exchange rates "has not been trivial," it has not been as damaging to the ratios of international trade to GNP as it might have been, because the volatility has reflected underlying instabilities which have affected domestic and international economic activities alike.

41. McKinnon (1976) argued that some exchange-rate volatility in 1973–74 was due to too little speculation rather than too much. Keynes (1923, p. 136) had earlier mentioned the same possibility in connection with the early 1920s.

42. See Frenkel (1981).

43. A number of the arguments are summarized in Dunn (1983) and Williamson (1983).

44. See, for example, Williamson (1983) and Bergsten (1985).

45. See *Report of the Working Group on Exchange Market Intervention* (1983), chaired by P. Jurgensen.

46. The French position is discussed in Atali (1986).

47. See, for example, the summary of the report of the G-24 in *IMF Survey*, August 25, 1985, pp. 257 ff.

48. This image of the implications of a thirty-year decline in the dollar's equilibrium value is due to Gray (1974).

49. For a discussion of the measurement problems, see Officer (1976) and Katseli-Papaefstratiou (1979).

50. Williamson (1983, p. 14), in arguing for exchange-rate targeting, defines a "fundamental equilibrium exchange rate" to be one that is "expected to generate a current account surplus or deficit equal to the underlying capital flow over the cycle, given that the country is

pursuing 'internal balance' as best it can and not restricting trade for balance of payments reasons."

51. Solomon (1984) provides a useful discussion of some of these issues.

52. Some of these studies are discussed in Dunn (1983) and Williamson (1983).

53. See Murphy (1979, ch 3; 1985).

54. See Group of Thirty (1985, p. 5).

55. The ineffectiveness of sterilized interventions was accepted in the official study commissioned at the Versailles Economic Summit meeting in June 1982. See *Report of the Working Group on Exchange Market Intervention* (1983).

56. Numerous writers have emphasized the close relationship between the macroeconomic policies that influence the exchange rate and external commerical policy—which sometimes goes in a new guise as "industrial policy." See, for example, Richardson (1984) and Corden (1980, 1985).

57. Bryant (1980) is an eloquent statement of the necessity of policy coordination within and among countries if policies are to be successful.

58. Extensive bibliographies of the literature can be found in Somensatto (1985, pp. 223–279) and Laney (1985).

59. An example of such analysis is the effort at synthesis by Hey (1981).

60. See Salacuse (1985) and sources cited therein.

61. A clear technical description of the ECU and the intra-EMS settlement procedures is given in Gold (1984, pp. 227–235).

62. On the impairments to integration, see Dudler (1984, pp. 227–261).

63. See Murphy (1979, ch. 7).

64. George von Furstenberg, at one time Chief of the Financial Studies Division in the Research Department of the IMF, has made an interesting attempt at modelling the decisions of the Fund in circumstances in which members are drawing and the Fund is setting conditions on their policies. See Fusrstenberg (1985).

65. See Nowzad (1983). A careful discussion of the issues and the Fund's position is in Gold (1979, pp. 31–34).

66. Some of the technical problems of operating an SDR world money are considered in Fischer (1983). See also Murphy (1979, ch. 6).

67. See Amex Bank Review (1982).

68. International Monetary Fund, *Annual Report, 1985*, p. 54.

69. Data are from International Monetary Fund, *Annual Report, 1985*, p. 55.

70. Gold (1984, p. 203) points out that the phraseology was taken over from the *Outline of Reform* drafted by the Committee of Twenty early in the IMF reform discussions. The elements of the *Outline* that would have given operational meaning to the phrase were mostly omitted from the actual Second Amendment.

71. See address of Johannes Witteveen to the Conference Board in Frankfurt, Germany, *IMF Survey*, October 28, 1975, pp. 313–316.

72. For problems with the scheme when applied to gross reserve holdings, see Murphy (1979, pp. 182–199).

73. See De Grauwe (1983).

74. McCallum (1985) provides a bibliography and critique of the early literature.

75. See for example, Triffin (1984).

References

Aghevli, B., and J. Marquez-Ruarte. 1985. *A Case of Successful Adjustment: Korea's Experience During 1980–84.* Occasional Paper No. 39. Washington, D.C.: International Monetary Fund, August.

Amex Bank Review. 1982. *The International Monetary Fund and the Private Banks: The Expanding Relationship.* Special Papers, no. 6. London: American Express International Banking Corporation, August.

Atali, Jacques. 1986. "A French Proposal on Monetary Reform." *Europe* (March), pp. 18 ff.

Barro, R. 1981. *Money, Expectations, and Business Cycles.* New York: Academic Press.

Bergsten, C. F. 1985. "Effects on Trade of Exchange Rates and Policies." In J. J. Norton, ed., *World Trade and Trade Finance.* pp. 1-1–1-17. New York: Matthew Bender, 1985.

Bhatia, R. J. 1985. *The West African Monetary Union: An Analytical Review.* Occasional Paper No. 35. Washington, DC: International Monetary Fund.

Bryant, R. C. 1980. *Money and Monetary Policy in Interdependent Nations.* Washington, DC: The Brookings Institution.

Cline, W. C. 1983. *International Debt: Systemic Risk and Policy Response.* Washington, DC: Institute for International Economics.

Cline, W. C. 1985. "International Debt: From Crisis to Recovery?" American Economic Review 75 (May), pp. 185–190.

Corden, W. M. 1980. "Relationship Between Macroeconomic and Industrial Policies." *The World Economy* 3 (September), pp. 167–184.

Corden, W. M. 1985. "Protection, the Exchange Rate, and Macroeconomic Policy." *Finance and Development* 22 (June), pp. 17–19.

Cox, M. 1985. "Inflation and Permanent Government Debt." Federal Reserve Bank of Dallas *Economic Review* (May), pp. 13–26.

De Grauwe, P. 1983. "What Are the Scope and Limits of Fruitful International Monetary Cooperation in the 1980s?" In G. M. von Furstenberg, ed., *International Money and Credit: The Policy Roles*, pp. 375–408. Washington, DC: International Monetary Fund, 1983.

De Grauwe, P., M. Janssens, and H. Leliaert. 1985. *Real-Exchange-Rate Variability from 1920 to 1926 and 1973 to 1982.* Princeton Studies in International Finance, no. 56, September 1985. Princeton, NJ: International Finance Section, Princeton University.

de Vries, M. G. 1985. *The International Monetary Fund 1972–1978: Cooperation on Trial.* vol. II. Washington DC: International Monetary Fund.

Dillon, K. B., C. M. Watson, G. R. Kincaid, and C. Puckahtikom. 1985. *Recent Developments in External Debt Restructuring.* Occasional Paper 40. Washington, DC: International Monetary Fund.

Dornbusch, R. 1985. "Policy and Performance Links Between LDC Debtors and Industrial Nations." *Brookings Papers on Economic Activity* (2), pp. 303–368.

Dudler, H. -J. 1984. "Domestic Monetary Control in EC Countries Under Different Exchange Rate Regimes: National Concerns and Community Options." In R. S. Masera and R. Triffin, eds., *Europe's Money: Problems of European Monetary Co-ordination and Integration*, pp. 227–261. Oxford: Clarendon Press, 1984.

Dunn, R. M., Jr. 1983. *The Many Disappointments of Flexible Exchange Rates*. Essays in International Finances, no. 154, December 1983. Princeton, NJ: International Finance Section, Princeton University.

Fischer, Stanley. 1983. "The SDR and the IMF: Toward a World Central Bank." In G. M. von Furstenberg, ed., *International Money and Credit: The Policy Roles*, pp. 179–199. Washington, DC: International Monetary Fund, 1983.

Frenkel, J. 1981. "Flexible Exchange Rates, Prices, and the Role of 'News': Lessons from the 1970s." *Journal of Political Economy* 89 (August), pp. 665–705.

Frenkel, J. 1983. "Monetary Policy: Domestic Targets and International Constraints." *American Economic Reivew* 73 (May), pp. 48–53.

Frenkel, J., and C. A. Rodriguez. 1982. "Exchange Rate Dynamics and the Overshooting Hypothesis." International Monetary Fund *Staff Papers* 29 (March), pp. 1–30.

Furstenberg, G. M. von. 1985. "Adjustment with Fund Lending." *Journal of International Money and Finance* 4 (June), pp. 209–222.

Germany, J. D., and J. E. Morton. 1985. "Financial Innovation and Deregulation in Foreign Industrial Countries." *Federal Reserve Bulletin* 71 (October), pp. 743–753.

Gold, Sir J. 1979. *Conditionality*. IMF Pamphlet Series, no. 31. Washington, DC: International Monetary Fund.

Gold, Sir J. 1984. *Legal and Institutional Aspects of the International Monetary System: Selected Essays*. vol. II. Washington, DC: International Monetary Fund.

Gold, Sir J. 1986. "IMF, Some Effects on Private Parties and Private Transactions." Paper presented at the Fourth Institute on International Finance, at Southern Methodist University, April 1986.

Goodhart, C. 1984. "Structural Changes in the Banking System and the Determination of the Stock of Money." In R. S. Masera and R. Triffin, eds., *Europe's Money: Problems of European Monetary Co-ordination and Integration*, pp. 111–149. Oxford: Clarendon Press, 1984.

Gray, H. P. 1974. *An Aggregate Theory of International Payments Adjustment*. Lexington: Heath.

Greenfield, R. L., and L. B. Yeager. 1983. "A Laissez-Faire Approach to Monetary Stability." *Journal of Money, Credit and Banking* 15 (August), pp. 302–315.

Group of Thirty. 1985. *The Foreign Exchange Market in the 1980s*. New York.

Guttentag, J., and R. Herring. 1983. *The Lender-of-Last-Resort Function in an International Context*. Essays in International Finance, no. 151, May. Princeton, NJ: International Finance Section, Princeton University.

Guttentag, J., and R. Herring. 1985. "Funding Risk in the International Interbank

Market." In W. J. Ethier and R. C. Marston, eds., *International Financial Markets and Capital Movements*, pp. 19–32. Essays in International Finance, no. 157, September. Princeton, NJ: International Finance Section, Princeton University.

Haberler, G. 1985. "International Issues Raised by Criticism of the U.S. Budget Deficits." In P. Cagan, ed., *Essays in Contemporary Economic Problems, 1985: The Economy in Deficit*, pp. 121–146. Washington, DC: American Enterprise Institute, 1985.

Hey, J. D. 1981. *Economics in Disequilibrium*. Oxford: Martin Robertson.

Katseli-Papaefstratiou, T. 1979. *The Reemergence of the Purchasing Power Parity Doctrine in the 1970s*. Special Papers in International Economics, no. 13, December. Princeton, NJ: International Finance Section, Princeton University.

Keynes, J. M. 1923. *A Tract on Monetary Reform*. London: Macmillan.

Kirmani, N., L. Molajoni, and T. Mayer. 1984. "Effects of Increased Market Access on Exports of Developing Countries." International Monetary Fund *Staff Papers* 31 (December), pp. 661–684.

Krueger, A. O. 1985. "Developing Countries' Debt Problems and Growth Prospects." Paper presented at the Atlantic Economic Society Conference, Washington, DC, August 30, 1985.

Laney, L. 1985. "Twin Deficit Issues." Processed, Federal Reserve Bank of Dallas, 1985.

Lenard, D. R., and J. Williamson. 1985. *Financial Intermediation Beyond the Debt Crisis*. Washington, DC: Institute for International Economics.

Marshall, A. 1890. *Principles of Economics*. London: Macmillan.

McCallum, B. T. 1985. "Bank Deregulation, Accounting Systems of Exchange, and the Unit of Account: A Critical Review." In K. Brunner and A. H. Meltzer, eds., *The 'New Monetary Economics,' Fiscal Issues and Unemployment*, pp. 13–46. Carnegie-Rochester Conference Series on Public Policy, vol. 23, Autumn 1985.

McKinnon, R. I. 1982. "Currency Substitution and Instability in the World Dollar Standard." *American Economic Review* 72 (June), pp. 320–333.

McKinnon, R. I. 1976. "Floating Exchange Rates, 1973–74: The Emperor's New Clothes." In K. Brunner and A. H. Meltzer, eds., *Institutional Arrangements and the Inflation Problem*, pp. 79–114. Carnegie-Rochester Conference Series on Public Policy. vol. 3, 1976.

McKinnon, R. I. 1984. "A Program for International Monetary Stability." In T. Agmon, R. G. Hawkins, and R. M. Levich, eds., *The Future of the International Monetary System*, pp. 55–77. Lexington, MA: Heath, 1984.

McRae, H. 1985. *Japan's Role in the Emerging Securities Market*. New York: Group of Thirty.

Morse, Sir J. 1981. *How British Banking Has Changed*. Stamp Memorial Lecture, delivered at the University of London, November 30, 1981.

Morse, Sir J. 1985. *Do We Know Where We're Going?* Per Jacobsson Lecture, delivered at Seoul, Korea, October 6, 1985.

Murphy, J. C. 1979. *The International Monetary System: Beyond the First Stage of*

Reform. Washington, DC: American Enterprise Institute.

Murphy, J. C. 1985. "Reflections on the Exchange Rate System." *American Economic Review* 75 (May), pp. 68–73.

Nowzad, B. 1983. *The Extent of IMF Involvement in Economic Policy-Making*. Amex Bank Review, Special Papers, no. 7. London: Ameican Express International Banking Corporation, September.

Officer, L. H. 1976. "The Purchasing-Power-Parity Theory of Exchange Rates." International Monetary Fund *Staff Papers* 23 (March), pp. 1–60.

Patrick, H. 1984. "Comment." In T. Agmon, R. G. Hawkins, and R. M. Levich, eds., *The Future of the International Monetary System*, pp. 186–193. Lexington, MA: Heath, 1984.

Report of the Technical Committee of the Global Economic Action Institute. 1985. New York: Global Economic Action Institute.

Report of the Working Group on Exchange Market Intervention. 1983. March.

Richardson, J. D. 1984. "The New Nexus among Trade, Industrial, and Exchange-Rate Policies." In T. Agmon, R. G. Hawkins, and R. M. Levich, eds., *The Future of the International Monetary System*, pp. 253–279. Lexington, MA: Heath, 1984.

Sachs, J. D. 1985. "The Dollar and the Policy Mix: 1985." National Bureau of Economic Research Working Paper No. 1636.

Sakakibara, E. 1984. "The Japanese Financial System in Transition." In T. Agmon, R. G. Hawkins, and R. M. Levich, eds., *The Future of the International Monetary System*, pp. 157–185. Lexington, MA: Heath, 1984.

Salacuse, J. W. 1985. "Developments in Countertrade: Barter Isn't What It Used To Be." In J. J. Norton, ed., *World Trade and Trade Finance*, pp. 12-1–12-56. New York: Matthew Bender, 1985.

Shelburn, M. R. 1984. *Rules for Regulating Intervention under a Managed Float*. Princeton Studies in International Finance, No. 55, December, Princeton, NJ: International Finance Section, Princeton University.

Solomon, R. 1977. *The International Monetary System, 1945–1976: An Insider's View*. New York: Harper & Row.

Solomon, R. 1984. "The Consequences of Exchange-rate Variability." Brookings Discussion Papers in International Economic, no. 26. Washington, DC: The Brookings Institution.

Somensatto, E. 1985. "Budget Deficits, Exchange Rates, International Capital Flows, and Trade." In P. Cagan, ed., *Essays in Contemporary Economic Problems, 1985: The Economy in Deficit*, pp. 223–279. Washington, DC: American Enterprise Institute, 1985.

Spinelli, F. 1983. "Currency Substitution, Flexible Exchange Rates, and the Case for International Monetary Cooperation." International Monetary Fund *Staff Papers* 30 (December), pp. 755–783.

Terrell, H. S., and R. Mills. 1985. "U.S. Banks' Lending to Developing Countries: A Longer Term View." International Finance Discussion Papers. no. 255. Washington, DC: Federal Reserve Board.

Tinbergen, J. 1952. *On the Theory of Economic Policy*. Amsterdam: North-

Holland.

Triffin, R. 1984. "How to End the World 'Infession': Crisis Management or Fundamental Reform." In R. S. Masera and R. Triffin, eds., *Europe's Money: Problems of European Monetary Co-ordination and Integration*, pp. 13–70. Oxford: Clarendon Press, 1984.

Willett, T. D. 1985. "Exchange Rate Volatility, International Trade, and Resource Allocation: A Perspective on Recent Research.' Paper presented at the Arizona State Conference on International Risk. May 1985.

Williamson, J. 1983. *The Exchange Rate System*. Washington, DC: Institute for International Economics.

World Bank. 1985. *Coping with External Debt in the 1980s*. Washington, DC.

Wyles, J. 1986. "London to Rival New York, Tokyo as Financial Center." *Europe* (January-February), pp. 22–23.

Yeager, L. B. 1985. "Deregulation and Monetary Reform." *American Economic Review* 75 (May), pp. 103–107.

Yoshitomi, M. 1985. *Japan as a Capital Exporter and the World Economy*. New York: Group of Thirty.

COMMENT

Michael R. Darby*

Carter Murphy has provided a thorough and masterful survey of the evolution of the modern international financial system and his opinion of its implications for the international economy. I (1986) have essayed a similar, albeit more limited, task elsewhere and shall not attempt in these brief remarks to detail our broad areas of agreement and narrow points of difference. Instead I will propose a structure for pondering Murphy's historical survey. This structure organizes the competing hypotheses for recent movements in the real U.S. exchange rate. I do so because I believe that there is much yet to be learned before we can feel confident that we understand the influence of particular recent developments on the value of the dollar.

In this discussion, I focus on the determinants of capital flows as the root explanation of trends in the flow's *alter ego*, the current account, and in exchange rates. National-income accounting relates net imports or net capital inflows to the excess of investment over saving. The competing

* Any opinions expressed are those of the author alone and may not be shared by his employers, past, present, or future.

explanations generally explain the appreciation of the dollar—and subsequent rise in net imports[1]—by (a) a downward shift in U.S. saving, (b) an upward shift in U.S. investment, or (c) an increase in the equilibrium foreign less U.S. real-interest-rate differential (the risk premium).[2] These basic explanations come in variations and may well be operating in combination rather than only one being *the* cause of the 1980–1985 dollar appreciation.

The downward shift in U.S. saving was supposed to occur because of the increased federal-government deficit. Total government spending on real goods and services was little changed under President Reagan; so the deficit increase was due to a fall in "net taxes," resulting especially from increases in interest on the national debt. For national saving to fall as a result of such a shift, consumers must increase their spending. Ultrarationalists argue that they will not do so, because shifts between government borrowing and taxing do not alter the rate at which present goods can be transferred to the future. Fisherians argue that increases in government interest payments arising from higher *nominal* interest rates due to inflation will be saved (as we keep national-income accounts), so that the real value of government debt is maintained. While it is not clear that either argument is valid,[3] neither is there clear and convincing evidence that national saving is low on a cyclically adjusted basis or an explanation why real interest rates and the dollar began to rise in the third quarter of 1980.[4]

An upward shift in the U.S. investment function seems quite plausible to me. Certainly, the Republican electoral victory predictably signaled a more favorable business climate in terms not only of taxation but also of regulation. Empirically, an increase in real interest rates makes more sense as a result of an upward shift in investment demand than of a tax-induced shift in the consumption function. This is so because the long-run investment-demand curve, which is relevant for long-term changes in trend real interest rates, seems to be rather interest elastic.

A variant of this approach relates the upward shift in investment demand (as a function of the real interest rate) not to tax or regulatory changes but to the disinflation. The mechanism envisioned by proponents of this view—which is, perhaps, persistent expectational error—is not clear to me, but they do point to an impressive empirical regularity that ex post real interest rates rise dramatically during disinflationary periods in a variety of countries and time periods.[5]

In contrast to the domestic focus of these saving- and investment-shift hypotheses, the risk-premium view is profoundly international. The type of risk being contemplated in these arguments is primarily a type of default risk in which the economic fruits of an investment are not reaped by its owners because of expropriation or imposition of currency controls. Some observers view this in terms of the United States being a "safe haven" for capital flight from newly socialist France and other countries threatened by adverse political changes. Others emphasize the sudden aversion to investment in less-developed countries. This is consistent with the data, which indicate that increased U.S. net-capital inflows have been associated primarily with reduced outflows and not with increased inflows. Either version of the risk-premium view would suggest a fall in U.S. real interest rates rather than the rise which actually occurred. Therefore, proponents of this view must posit that some exogenous foreign factor was increasing foreign real interest rates by more than the increase in the risk premium.

From winter 1985 to June 1986, the dollar depreciated sharply. Unfortunately, this movement provides little evidence, since simultaneously (a) expectations of falling federal deficits have replaced a future of steady increases;[6] (b) a tax-reform initiative raising business taxes was proposed in early 1985; (c) the disinflation process was waning in the United States, while major foreign countries tightened money growth further; and (d) socialist governments became less so or were replaced by conservative governments, while fears of general collapse of LDCs attenuated with time. So the hypotheses for 1980–1985 cannot be distinguished among on the basis of the 1985–86 experience.

Elsewhere (1986) I have suggested that our understanding of the dollar appreciation of 1980–1985 should encompass the simultaneous increase in real interest rates *and* the equally dramatic fall in real interest rates and the dollar during the breakdown of the Bretton Woods system. I believe that quantifying the contribution of the different hypotheses will take a great deal of difficult empirical work by a number of talented researchers. I think that Carter Murphy has discussed factors that will prove significant but am perhaps skeptical that we yet know just which factors those are.

Notes

1. A rough rule of thumb lags the induced net-import effects of exchange-rate changes by 11/2 to 2 years, due to J-curve effects. The basic analytical framework implies that changes in basic determinants of capital flows have immediate effects primarily on the exchange rate, so that the actual capital-flow/net-import change is not significant until much later. (There are quantity changes in the short run, but they are offset by the import price change so that the net dollar amount is little changed.)

2. The foreign real interest rate less the U.S. real interest rate equals the sum of the expected real depreciation of the foreign currency and its risk premium. While I believe that there are some predictable short-run movements in the real exchange rate, these are

negligible in long-run equilibrium, so that only the risk premium remains. See Darby (1983) for an analytical discussion and empirical evidence.

3. The ultrarationalists are usually challenged on intergenerational linkage, and much of the increase in government interest represented an increase in the real interest rate (at least ex post).

4. While Reagan's election victory might have been anticipated at this time, I cannot believe that the subsequent federal deficits were.

5. Some proponents of the disinflation view seem to argue for a backward shift in the LM curve due to increases in money demand. This view does not make sense to me, because it appears to confuse shifts in money demand with movements along money demand as interest rates decline and because, over a five-year period, the IS curve should dominate the LM curve in determining interest rates.

6. However, over this period actual federal deficits continued to climb. Proponents of the government-deficit view have to appeal to expectations in any case, since the rise in real interest rates and the dollar preceded the dramatic increases in the federal deficit by almost two years.

References

Darby, M. R. 1983. "Movements in Purchasing Power Parity: The Short and Long Runs." In M. R. Darby, J. R. Lothian, et al., *The International Transmission of Inflation*, pp. 462–477. Chicago: The University of Chicago Press for NBER, 1983.

Darby, M. R. 1986. "The Internationalization of American Banking and Finance: Structure, Risk, and World Interest Rates." *Journal of International Money and Finance* 5 (December), pp. 403–428.

GPSR Compliance

The European Union's (EU) General Product Safety Regulation (GPSR) is a set of rules that requires consumer products to be safe and our obligations to ensure this.

If you have any concerns about our products, you can contact us on ProductSafety@springernature.com

In case Publisher is established outside the EU, the EU authorized representative is:

Springer Nature Customer Service Center GmbH
Europaplatz 3
69115 Heidelberg, Germany

Batch number: 10755292

Printed by Printforce, the Netherlands